Theory of Mind

Beyond the Preschool Years

Theory of Mind
Beyond the Preschool Years

TOURO COLLEGE LIBRARY
Kings Hwy

Scott A. Miller
University of Florida

Psychology Press
Taylor & Francis Group

New York   London

KH

Psychology Press
Taylor & Francis Group
711 Third Avenue
New York, NY 10017

Psychology Press
Taylor & Francis Group
27 Church Road
Hove, East Sussex BN3 2FA

© 2012 by Taylor & Francis Group, LLC
Psychology Press is an imprint of Taylor & Francis Group, an Informa business

Printed in the United States of America on acid-free paper
Version Date: 20120227

International Standard Book Number: 978-1-84872-927-8 (Hardback) 978-1-84872-928-5 (Paperback)

Library of Congress Cataloging-in-Publication Data

Miller, Scott A., 1944-
    Theory of mind : beyond the preschool years / Scott A. Miller.
        p. cm.
    Includes bibliographical references and index.
    ISBN 978-1-84872-927-8 (hardcover : alk. paper) -- ISBN 978-1-84872-928-5 (pbk. : alk. paper)
    1. Belief and doubt. 2. Childhood. I. Title.

BF773.M55 2012
153--dc23   2012005218

Visit the Taylor & Francis Web site at
http://www.taylorandfrancis.com

and the Psychology Press Web site at
http://www.psypress.com

5/1/13

To Sylvia, Brielle, and Tavio

Contents

Preface

Some titles are more informative than others. If you were one of the (not very many) moviegoers who sought out *Snakes on a Plane* or *Cowboys & Aliens*, you knew what you were in for.

My title is not as catchy as those, but it does let you know what you are in for. This book is about developments in theory of mind that occur from about age 5 and on. Much of Chapter 1 presents my reasons for writing such a book, but I can summarize the argument briefly here. Most books about theory of mind concentrate on the preschool period, for the good reason that most research on theory of mind has involved the preschool period. Theory-of-mind development is not complete at age 5, however, and several hundred (mostly quite recent) studies have told us a fair amount about what the further developments are. This recent research joins a larger and more longstanding research literature that addressed mentalistic understanding from a variety of perspectives prior to the advent of theory of mind—a literature that has not been fully integrated with that under the theory-of-mind heading (indeed, many theory-of-mind treatments ignore it entirely). My goal is to bring together new and old in a way that will make clear both what we know and what we still need to know about higher-order theory of mind.

This book has both an immediate and a more long-term predecessor. The immediate predecessor is a review article that I published in *Psychological Bulletin* in 2009 (Miller, 2009). The article dealt with the most often studied development under the higher-order heading: Second-order false belief. This book updates and expands that coverage and adds to it work on several dozen other post-preschool developments, some from the theory-of-mind literature and some from the work that predated theory of mind.

The more long-term predecessor is my immersion—as teacher, author, and researcher—in this earlier, pre–theory-of-mind work. This experience is not quite of the present-at-the-creation sort (for that, one would have had to be in Geneva in the 1920s). Still, it does provide a perspective on the study of social and mental understanding that many authors who write about theory of mind do not possess. And it contributes, I believe, to the two (as we will see, related) ways in which this book attempts to expand the usual age period for writings on theory of mind: in terms of the age of the child, and in terms of the age of the research literature.

Like most authors, I hope that my book will be of use to a wide range of different readers. Because of the breadth of the coverage, even veteran researchers may find things of interest of which they were previously unaware. But I have tried as well to make the presentation accessible to students just embarking on the study of theory of mind. Parts of the book might serve as a useful supplement in courses on cognitive development.

I am grateful to a number of colleagues for sharing unpublished or pre-publication materials with me. Janet Astington was especially helpful in this regard. I also thank Robin Banerjee, Daniel Bernstein, David Bjorklund, Julie Comay, Melanie Glenwright, Elizabeth Hayward, Nancie Im-Bolter, Ashley King, Jorie Koster-Hale, Lynn Liben, Lauren Myers, and Rebecca Saxe.

Several colleagues at the University of Florida helped in various ways. I am grateful to Shengying Zhang for translation of a key source from Chinese. Thanks also to Jackie Rollins and Jim Yousse for help with word processing issues, to Juliana Vassolo for drawing Figure 2.2, and to Connie Ordaz for drawing Figure 7.1.

It has been a pleasure to work with Debra Riegert, Andrea Zekus, Tara Nieuwesteeg, Jessica Lauffer, and other members of the Psychology Press team. Among their many good services was selection of an outstanding group of reviewers to whom I express my gratitude: Derek Montgomery (Bradley University), John D. Bonvillian (University of Virginia), Manuel Sprung (Harvard University), Martin Doherty (University of Stirling, Scotland), Janet Wilde Astington (University of Toronto), Eric Phillip Charles (The Pennsylvania State University, Altoona), and one anonymous reviewer. A special thanks to Derek, a long-time friend whose opinion I value highly.

Finally, my thanks to Sujata for so many things.

1

Theory of Mind

Juliet takes a sleeping potion that mimics death; Romeo, however, believes that she is actually dead and kills himself in his grief. Hamlet believes that Claudius is behind the curtain and lashes out with his sword; it is actually Polonius behind the curtain, however, and it is Polonius whom Hamlet kills. Othello believes that Desdemona has been unfaithful to him and strangles her in his rage, but Othello is mistaken, for Desdemona was actually the most faithful of wives.

Much of literature would be impossible without two fundamental assumptions shared by its creators and its audience. One is that beliefs are representations of reality and not reality itself and as such they may sometimes be wrong. The second is that it is what people believe that determines how they act. If the belief is false, then the action may be something quite different from what the actor really wishes to happen.

Of course, the fact that adults share these assumptions does not mean that children do. Children, after all, are not the target audience for Shakespeare. But as any parent knows, stories for children often hinge on the same basic assumptions about beliefs and their fallibility. Thus, it is actually the wolf that Red Riding Hood finds in Grandmother's bed, but Red Riding Hood believes (at least for a while) that it is her grandmother. Dorothy and her friends believe that the ruler of Oz is a benevolent wizard who can grant all their wishes; in reality, however, the "wizard" is simply a man behind a curtain. Or as a final example (an example I take from the philosopher Dennett, 1978), children at a Punch and Judy show laugh with glee as Punch prepares to throw a box containing Judy over the cliff; they laugh because they know that Judy has escaped, and they also know that Punch does not know this.

Several of these examples illustrate a further point as well, a further component in our commonsense beliefs about belief. False beliefs do not always simply happen; rather they may be deliberately *created*. Thus, Othello believes in Desdemona's faithlessness because Iago has worked assiduously and skillfully to implant this belief in him. Red Riding Hood believes that her grandmother is in her bed because the wolf has donned a costume with the intention of creating exactly this belief. Often, comprehension of a story—or comprehension of a real-life social situation—requires taking not just one but two mental states into account: A *intends* that B *believes*….

The proliferation of mental states does not stop here. Any extended act of deception requires that the deceiver anticipate and monitor various mental states in his or her target. Thus, the wolf believes that Red Riding Hood *wants* to see her grandmother, that she *thinks* that he is her grandmother, that she is *happy* that her grandmother is awaiting her, and that she will therefore act as he wishes—namely, come close enough to be grabbed and eaten. Similarly, the wizard believes that Dorothy and her friends *want* various things (e.g., a brain, a heart), that they *think* that he has the power to grant them, and that they will therefore act as *he* wishes, namely, rid Oz of the Wicked Witch of the West. Furthermore, just as the child listeners or readers of these stories know what Red Riding Hood or Dorothy thinks, so too do they (or at least the more advanced of them) know what the wolf or wizard thinks about what Red Riding Hood or Dorothy thinks.

Let me introduce a little terminology that will be important later. Someone's belief about something in the world (e.g., Romeo's belief about Juliet, Red Riding Hood's belief about the wolf) is referred to as a *first-order belief*. Someone's belief about someone else's belief (e.g., the wolf's belief about Red Riding Hood's belief, the wizard's belief about Dorothy's belief) is referred to as a *second-order belief*.

Both first-order and second-order beliefs, along with many other cognitions about the mental world, constitute what has long been known as *folk psychology* and what in more recent writings is often referred to as *theory of mind*. As the term folk psychology suggests, the assumption is that adults in all cultures share certain beliefs about the nature of the mental world, beliefs that govern the social interactions in which they engage. Although these beliefs may vary to some extent across people and across cultures, certain elements are assumed to be constant. These constant elements include the core belief that there *is* a mental world that is different from the physical world and that (as in false belief) mental and physical may not always agree. As the Shakespearean examples indicate, such a belief system about the human mind was in place long before the emergence of psychology as a science to study the mind. Indeed, one could go back thousands rather than hundreds of years to find examples in Greek literature (most famously, the false beliefs of Oedipus about his parentage).

What about children? As I noted, children eventually come to understand at least one core aspect of the folk psychology around them: the basic realization that beliefs can be false. But is this always the case? To anticipate conclusions that will be developed at greater length—no, it is not always the case. Prior to age 4 most children fail to understand that a belief can be false—thus fail to understand first-order false belief. Prior to age 6 most children fail to understand that a belief about a belief can be false—thus fail to understand second-order false belief.

A LITTLE HISTORY

Few topics in psychology have a definite starting point—some event that could be said to have initiated the field of study. Theory of mind does, however. In fact, it has two.

The first came in 1978 in a paper by Premack and Woodruff, who reported a series of experiments with a chimpanzee named Sarah. Sarah was not just any chimpanzee; rather, she was a highly acculturated chimpanzee who at the time of the report had already been the subject of a number of language learning experiments. Sarah's task in the research was not language learning but problem solving. Premack and Woodruff presented a series of problems, conveyed via videos, in which a human actor faced some dilemma that he needed to solve. In one instance, for example, the actor was shivering with cold; in another he was hungry, but the bananas he desired were out of reach. The final step in the procedure was presentation of two photographs, one of which showed a solution to the problem (e.g., lighting a heater to combat the cold, using a stick to reach the bananas) and the other of which presented the relevant objects but no solution. The question was whether Sarah could select the outcome that would solve the problem. The answer was yes; in fact, Sarah was close to perfect across a range of different problems. (Indeed, almost her only errors occurred when the actor shown in the photos was a handler whom she disliked!)

In interpreting their results, Premack and Woodruff (1978) argued that Sarah's performance was possible only if she took into account the relevant mental states of the actor. Thus, to solve the bananas problem, for example, she would have to realize that the actor *desired* the bananas and *believed* that the stick would allow him to reach them. She would have to possess what Premack and Woodruff called a "theory of mind." In their words:

> In saying that an individual has a theory of mind, we mean that an individual imputes mental states to himself and to others…. A system of inferences of this kind is properly viewed as a theory, first, because such states are not directly observable, and second, because the system can be used to make predictions, specifically about the behavior of other organisms. (p. 515)

The Premack and Woodruff (1978) article was followed by a number of commentaries by both psychologists and philosophers. Although all agreed that Sarah's problem-solving prowess was impressive, several suggested that the task set for her was in a sense too easy. On each of the problems Sarah could reach a solution by acting on her own knowledge of reality—her belief, for example, about how to reach out-of-reach bananas. It is possible that she attributed the same belief to the actor, but there was no way to be certain as long as her own belief was sufficient. More impressive, and more clearly indicative of a theory of mind, would be a demonstration that Sarah could recognize and act on a belief different from her own—in particular, another's *false* belief. It was in this context that Dennett (1978) presented his Punch and Judy example. Children can recognize false beliefs in others. Can chimpanzees?

Thirty years later the question of whether chimpanzees can impute false beliefs—and indeed, what chimpanzees understand more generally about mental phenomena—is still not resolved. For those who are interested, I will note that the two leading programs of research directed to chimpanzees' mentalizing abilities come from teams headed by Michael Tomasello (e.g., Call & Tomasello, 2008) and

Daniel Povinelli (e.g., Povinelli & Vonk, 2004). In general, the Tomasello group is toward the more positive end of the chimps'-abilities continuum and the Povinelli group is toward the more negative end. That disagreements and uncertainties still exist—and exist despite the efforts of some of the most talented researchers in the field—is a testament to how challenging the question is.

For children, however, the situation is a good deal clearer. Interestingly, it was not clear at the time that Dennett (1978) posed his example, for at that point no one had studied understanding of false belief in children. A basic finding *has* been clear since 1983, however, which is the other starting-point date for the field of theory of mind.

In 1983 Wimmer and Perner reported the first false belief study with children. They devised a procedure that has come to be known as the *unexpected location* or *unexpected transfer* task. Children heard a story in which a boy named Maxi brought home some chocolate, put it in the green cupboard, and went out to play. In Maxi's absence his mother removed the chocolate from the green cupboard, broke off a piece for cooking, and put the rest back in the blue cupboard. Maxi then came in from playing and wanted his chocolate. The question for the children was, "Where will Maxi look for his chocolate?" The correct answer, of course, is the green cupboard, since Maxi has no way to know that the chocolate has been moved in his absence. To give this answer, however, the child must be able to set aside his or her own knowledge of the reality and realize that Maxi would hold a false belief. Some 4-year-olds and most 5-year-olds were able to do so, but 3-year-olds and many 4-year-olds could not. There have been hundreds of false belief studies since, but they have not changed the basic descriptive picture provided by this first study: Young preschool children fail the standard false belief task, and for most children success emerges by age 4 or 5.

I will return to false belief and other first-order achievements in Chapter 2. First, though, I will introduce yet one more starting-point date, one that initiated the aspect of theory of mind on which I concentrate in this book.

In 1985 Perner and Wimmer published the first study of second-order false belief—that is, the first examination of whether children can appreciate one person's false belief about another person's belief. Their approach (which I describe more fully in Chapter 3) was similar to that devised for first-order false belief, that is, presentation of a scenario in which the central character would form a false belief, followed by questioning about the character's belief. In this case, however, the false belief at issue was a belief about someone else's belief: John believed that his friend Mary believed that the ice cream truck was in the park; in fact, however, Mary, unbeknownst to John, had learned of the true location at the church.

Judging John's false belief about Mary's belief turned out to be difficult. Children in the 5- and 6-year-old age groups—ages that are typically close to perfect on first-order belief—showed little success. It was only at age 7 or 8 that most children were able to attribute a second-order false belief.

As we will see, later research has modified this conclusion somewhat. When simpler assessment methods are used, success on the second-order task often comes earlier than Perner and Wimmer (1985) reported. Nevertheless, their basic conclusion remains valid: Mastery of second-order false belief is a post-preschool development, a development that requires abilities beyond those sufficient for first-order success.

GOALS OF THE BOOK

Premack and Woodruff (1978) and Wimmer and Perner (1983) initiated a revolution in the study of young children's cognitive abilities. Theory of mind has been the most popular topic in research on cognitive development for at least 20 years now. Thousands of journal articles have been devoted to the topic, and the pace shows no signs of slackening. Numerous books have taken on the task of summarizing at least some parts of all this research effort. These books include three early contributions by three of the pioneering researchers of the topic: Janet Astington's (1993) *The Child's Discovery of the Mind*, Josef Perner's (1991) *Understanding the Representational Mind*, and Henry Wellman's (1990) *The Child's Theory of Mind*. More recently other established researchers have added their own overviews (Carpendale & Lewis, 2006; Doherty, 2009; Hughes, 2011; Moore, 2006). In addition to such general treatments, other books have taken up more specialized aspects of the topic, for example, the role of language in theory-of-mind development (Astington & Baird, 2005) and individual differences in theory-of-mind abilities (Repacholi & Slaughter, 2003).

I list these sources partly because they are wonderful resources for the interested reader but also to raise the obvious question: Why yet another book about theory of mind? The answer lies in my title. All previous treatments of the topic have concentrated on young children. By an admittedly rough estimate, approximately 90% of the space in the books just cited is devoted to developments in the first 4 or 5 years of life. Such an emphasis is understandable: The early years have been the focus for most theory-of-mind research, and this research has revealed numerous striking and important developments that typically occur by age 5. But neither the research literature nor the developmental picture stops once children turn 6. There are now several hundred studies that explore various aspects of theory of mind in older children (and in some instances adults). The second-order false belief task sketched earlier is the most often used paradigm, but it is only one of a number of interesting and informative measures. Many of these studies, moreover, address not only the further developments in understanding that occur beyond age 5 but also the consequences of these developments—that is, what can children now do socially or cognitively that they could not do before? They thus speak to the two reasons for an interest in theory of mind: as an important aspect of cognitive development in itself and as a contributor to other developments.

Beyond simply summarizing an important literature, several further reasons can be advanced for a focus on advanced forms of theory of mind. I note three here and pick up others as we go.

One concerns the question of individual differences in theory of mind. Theory of mind has always been primarily a normative topic, in the sense that it concerns basic developments (such as mastery of false belief) that eventually almost all children demonstrate. The individual differences that have been addressed in the first-order literature are of two sorts. One is differences in rate of development. Although almost all children master false belief, some do so more quickly than others, and the same point applies to every other development under the theory-of-mind heading. The second way individual differences enter in comes in the study of atypical development. In some syndromes (autism is the clearest and most heavily researched example), *not* all children master false belief and other basic aspects of theory of mind, and such departures from the norm have proved informative in two ways. Most obviously, they help us to understand the clinical condition in question—why, for example, children with autism show such striking deficits in social interaction. But they also, as we will see, help us to understand theory of mind, for the study of atypical cases extends the evidential base for a number of important questions.

These two approaches to individual differences remain available, of course, when the focus shifts to older ages. In general, however, differences in rate of mastery become more marked, and therefore potentially more informative, with increased age. Deficits in clinical conditions also become more likely the more advanced the ability in question. Beyond simply differences in rate or in presence/absence, however, individual differences of a more gradated or qualitative sort become more likely as children develop and as more and more forms of knowledge enter the repertoire. The possible effects of these differences also multiply as related cognitive and social abilities develop. For these reasons, a consideration of advanced forms of theory of mind provides a much richer basis than does first-order study alone for determining what it means to have, or to fail to have, a "good theory of mind."

A second justification for a focus on later developments is the expanded scope with respect to what is arguably the most interesting—and certainly by far the most often studied—mental state: the epistemic state of belief. The preschool literature includes hundreds of studies directed to various aspects of young children's understanding of beliefs. With a handful of exceptions, however, the beliefs that have been examined are limited to arbitrary physical facts of two sorts: the location of an object and the identity of a concealed object. This is not, of course, because these are the only kinds of beliefs with which preschoolers deal, and I will consider some other forms in Chapter 2. Nevertheless, the first-order literature has been remarkably restricted in what has been meant operationally by *belief*. The range of beliefs available to children clearly expands as their cognitive abilities develop. Even more markedly, however, the research literature expands as well once we move to research with older children, encompassing beliefs of a wide range of different sorts. The result is a much fuller picture of what is meant by *understanding of belief* than is provided by the first-order literature alone.

As I discuss at various points, psychology's attempt to probe understanding of mental phenomena did not begin with the study of theory of mind in the 1980s; rather, research directed to such understanding had long existed under a variety of subject headings (e.g., perspective taking, social cognition, person perception, attribution). A third justification for a focus on advanced forms of theory of mind concerns the possibility of integrating theory-of-mind work with this earlier (and in part still ongoing) research literature. This issue has received limited attention in writings about first-order theory of mind for the good reason that there is limited overlap between the ages of concentration in the two research traditions: mostly preschool for theory of mind, mostly older children, adolescents, and adults for the older literature. Indeed, one reason that theory-of-mind research has proved so fruitful is that the earlier work had left so much to be learned about the mentalistic understanding of preschool children. Once the focus shifts to older ages, however, the possibility—indeed the necessity—for integration becomes much greater. I will acknowledge now and note again later that mine is not the first such attempt. But I hope to provide a fuller and more helpful bringing together of old and new than anyone has attempted previously.

ORGANIZATION OF THE BOOK

Despite the emphases just noted, I begin in Chapter 2 with a summary of the literature on first-order developments during the preschool period as well as a brief consideration of early forms or precursors of theory of mind in toddlerhood and infancy. Such a beginning provides a necessary backdrop for the consideration of more advanced developments, in that it permits an answer to the question "more advanced than what?" We will see in Chapter 2 that the typical 5-year-old has made impressive strides in understanding of the mind. We will see in subsequent chapters, however, that many other important developments still lie ahead.

Chapter 3 is devoted to the second-order false belief task. It was this task that initiated the explicit study of advanced forms of theory of mind, and it is this task that remains the most popular focus of study for the 5- to 10-year-old age period. It is not, however, the only task developed specifically to address higher-level forms of theory of mind, and Chapters 4 and 5 therefore review findings from a variety of other such measures.

As I noted earlier, theory of mind has been of interest to researchers for two reasons: as an important outcome of children's cognitive development and as a contributor to other outcomes in both the cognitive and the social realms. If anything, a focus on the consequences of theory-of-mind understanding is a more marked feature of the second-order than the first-order literature, in that a high proportion of studies have the goal of relating children's newfound theory-of-mind abilities to other aspects of their development. Chapter 6 summarizes what such studies have shown.

As I noted, one goal of the book is to place the work on advanced forms of theory of mind in the context of earlier approaches to the study of mentalistic understanding. Although some relations between the two bodies of literature are noted throughout the book, it is the last two chapters that address this question most fully. Chapter 7 reviews the work on understanding of the social and mental worlds that predated the emergence of theory of mind. Chapter 8 provides a comparative treatment of the two literatures, pointing out ways each complements or extends the others. The chapter also offers some general summing-up and pointing-ahead commentary.

One more point about the coverage should be noted. For the most part this book is confined to what we know about development in typical populations. Theory of mind, including higher-level forms of theory of mind, has also been examined in a wide variety of different clinical conditions and populations. I mentioned the work on autism earlier. A partial list of the other populations that have been studied includes schizophrenia, bipolar disorder, mental retardation, brain damage, learning disability, communicative disabilities, attention deficit/hyperactivity disorder (ADHD), William's syndrome, and normal aging.

It is beyond the scope of this book to consider most of these populations. I do, however, bring in work with two of the groups at various points. One is individuals with autism. The work on autism constitutes by far the largest of the various sub-literatures, and it also provides the most relevant data for the issues considered throughout the book. The second population considered is the elderly. As with autism, work with the elderly helps to illuminate some of the issues that are points of contention in the basic literature. In addition, a consideration of the last part of the lifespan will provide a rounding off of the developmental description begun with the childhood studies.

2

First-Order Developments

In Chapter 1 I introduced the concept of second-order false belief. Most of the remainder of the book will be devoted to the second-order task and to other higher-level, post-preschool developments. Making sense of these developments, however, requires knowing what has come before and thus what is new and important about the new achievements. The purpose of the present chapter is to provide this necessary background. Because the coverage is brief and selective, I will note further sources as we go.

FIRST-ORDER FALSE BELIEF

The false belief task has been by far the most popular measure in the theory-of-mind literature. Indeed, some commentators have expressed dismay at the proliferation of false belief studies to the relative exclusion of other interesting forms of understanding (an emphasis that Gopnik, Slaughter, & Meltzoff, 1994, dubbed "neurotic task fixation"). Nevertheless, most regard false belief as an important measure for the same reason that led to the original development of the task: namely, that it tells us something basic about understanding of beliefs as mental representations (for an exception, see Bloom & German, 2000).

False belief tasks come in many forms, but most are variants of two basic assessment procedures. One is the unexpected location or unexpected transfer procedure developed by Wimmer and Perner (1983). As the label suggests, with this task the belief in question concerns the location of an object, something that is known to the child participant but not to the story character whose belief the child must judge. Figure 2.1 presents one often used version of the location task, the Sally/Anne scenario.

The other commonly used procedure—a procedure introduced by Hogrefe, Wimmer, and Perner (1986)—is labeled *unexpected contents*. Again, the label denotes the target for the belief in question, which in this case concerns the contents of a container. A container that typically holds one sort of content (e.g., a crayon box, a candy box) is revealed to contain something quite different (candles, ribbons, coins—anything familiar will work). The child is shown the unexpected contents,

Figure 2.1   The Sally/Anne false belief task. (From Frith, U., *Autism: Explaining the Enigma*, Basil Blackwell, Oxford, 1989, p. 160. Copyright 1989 by Axel Scheffler. Reprinted with permission.)

and the test question is then what someone else, someone who has not seen inside the box, will think is in the box. So just as on the location task, children must set aside their own knowledge of reality to attribute a false belief to someone else who lacks their knowledge. Figure 2.2 shows a typical example of how the contents task works.

The contents task lends itself to another measure as well. In addition to asking about someone else's belief, we can pose the question in terms of the child's own initial belief—thus "what did you think was in the box before we opened it?" The question now is whether children can recapture their initial false belief—can realize that they themselves can hold beliefs that are false.

The answer is that children younger than 4 typically cannot do this. The own-belief question might seem easy to answer, given that the child has just said "crayons" (or whatever) seconds before. It turns out, however, that the question about their own belief is just as difficult for children as the question about someone else's belief (Wellman, Cross, & Watson, 2001). Furthermore, just as there are no self–other differences on the contents task, so also are there no general differences in difficulty between the contents procedure and the location procedure (Wellman et al.). In both instances most 3-year-olds fail, 4-year-olds show a mixture of successes and failures, and most 5-year-olds succeed. This does not mean that individual children necessarily respond consistently across the different measures, because often they do not. But there are no on-the-average differences across any of the standard ways of measuring understanding of false belief.

Task Modifications

For those of us who have been around for a while, there are some striking similarities between the research literature on false belief and the earlier literature on the Piagetian concept of conservation. In both cases the initial studies revealed some surprising and hitherto unsuspected deficits in children's understanding of some basic principles of how the world works. In both cases a natural reaction was to wonder whether children's understanding was really as limited as the original research suggested. Perhaps if the assessment could somehow be made simpler, more natural, more child-friendly, then children would do better. Hundreds of Piaget-inspired studies were directed to this question across the decades of the 1960s, 1970s, and 1980s. The last 20 years have seen the development of a comparable research literature directed to false belief.

Do the typical assessment procedures underestimate what young children understand about false belief? The answer is almost certainly yes, but opinions differ with respect to how serious the underestimation is. Some believe that it is quite serious and that a basic understanding of belief is present well before children begin to succeed on the standard tasks. Among the sources for such early-competence arguments are Chandler and Hala (1994), Roth and Leslie (1998), and Onishi and Baillargeon (2005). (I return to the last of these sources shortly.) My own assessment is more conservative and is in line with what is probably the majority view among researchers who write about the topic (which, of course, does not mean that it is the correct view—this is still an ongoing issue). It is clear from a variety

Figure 2.2 The unexpected contents false belief task.

TABLE 2.1   Variations Examined in Wellman, Cross, and Watson's (2001) Meta-Analysis of First-Order False Belief

Year of publication

Mean age and number of participants in a condition

Percentage of participants passing control questions and percentage dropped from the research

Country of participants

Type of task: locations, contents, identity

Nature of the protagonist: puppet or doll, pictured character, real person

Nature of the target object: real object, toy, pictured object, videotaped object

Real presence of the target object: object present or absent

Motive for the transformation: deceptive context or not

Participation in the transformation: child an active participant or not

Salience of the protagonist's mental state: degree of emphasis on the protagonist's belief

Type of question: wording of question in terms of think, know, say, do

Temporal marker: whether the question included an explicit temporal marker (e.g., "look first")

of forms of evidence that children do sometimes show more understanding of belief than is revealed with the standard procedures. The improvements that have been demonstrated are modest, however, and seem at best to demonstrate partial knowledge of the concept. Thus, it is still reasonable to conclude that before age 4 most children do not have a full mastery of false belief.

Much of the relevant research through the late 1990s was summarized in an influential meta-analysis by Wellman et al. (2001). I have already mentioned two of the conclusions from their review: that there are no differences in difficulty between the locations paradigm and the contents paradigm and no differences in difficulty between the self and other questions on the contents task. Wellman et al. also examined the effects of a variety of other factors that might influence performance. Table 2.1 lists and briefly describes the factors that were considered. As can be seen, these included a number of would-be facilitators, including the method of wording the test question, the salience of the reality information, and the presence of a deceptive context.

Many of these variations turned out to have no effect. A few of the would-be facilitators, however, did result in better on-the-average performance. For example, Wellman and colleagues concluded that children do better when a deceptive context is provided and that they do better when they are actively involved in the manipulation of the stimuli. The differences are small, however, and also inconsistent, appearing in some studies but not others. Furthermore, there was no instance in which a procedural manipulation was differentially helpful for 3-year-olds (as would be expected if the complexity of the standard tasks masks young children's competence) and no instance in which the performance of 3-year-olds rose above chance level. In the authors' words, the meta-analytic results suggest that "young children's difficulties reflect difficulties with the conceptual heart of the task, beyond any difficulties with particular task requirements" (Wellman & Cross, 2001, p. 704).

Other Response Measures

The modifications discussed so far primarily involve changes at the independent variable end, in the sense that they alter the situation that the child must judge. It is also possible to explore variations at the dependent variable end, that is, the sort of response that the child must make.

In the standard task the child must make an explicit judgment about the protagonist's belief, responding to a test question that either asks directly about belief (e.g., "What does Elmo think is in the box?") or asks about an action that follows from a belief (e.g., "Where will Maxi look for his chocolate?"). How else might children demonstrate some budding realization that beliefs can be false? Clements and Perner (1994) had the clever idea of examining looking behavior. Their young protagonists heard a story, acted out with props, in which a mouse named Sam left his cheese in a blue box and then went off to take a nap; while Sam was sleeping, his friend Katie moved the cheese to a red box. Sam then woke up and announced his intention to get his cheese. At this point the tester said, "I wonder where he's going to look," and then paused to give the child a chance to look toward one of the locations.

Few children between the ages of 2 years 5 months and 2 years 10 months looked at the location where Sam had left the cheese, an expectable finding in children well short of the usual age for false belief success. Of those between 2 years 11 months and 4 years 5 months, however, 90% looked at the original location and thus the site at which a character with a false belief would search. This is a considerably higher percentage than the usual success rate on false belief for this age group. And indeed, only 45% of the children were able to answer an explicit question about false belief correctly. What this and subsequent looking-behavior studies (Garnham & Perner, 2001; Garnham & Ruffman, 2001; Low, 2010; Ruffman, Garnham, Import, & Connolly, 2001) suggest is that young children have an implicit knowledge of false belief that emerges prior to their ability to access that knowledge to make explicit judgments about what someone thinks.

Another variation was introduced by Bartsch and Wellman (1989). In the standard task the child must predict the response of the protagonist—thus say what the protagonist will think or what the protagonist will do based upon what he or she thinks. Bartsch and Wellman wondered whether children might find it easier to explain a false belief than to predict one. They therefore constructed scenarios in which a character was depicted as acting on a false belief—for example, searching under the piano for a missing kitten when the kitten was actually under the bed. The child's task was then to explain the seemingly odd behavior. The interest, of course, was in whether children would be able to make an after-the-fact attribution of a false belief prior to being able to make an in-advance prediction of one. Many in fact could. Half of the 3- and 4-year-old participants either succeeded or failed on both measures. Of the remaining half, however, 11 were successful on explanation only, whereas only 1 was successful on prediction only.

The explanation versus prediction contrast has proved controversial. Some studies (e.g., Dunn, Brown, Slomkowski, Tesa, & Youngblade, 1991; Robinson & Mitchell, 1995) have confirmed Bartsch and Wellman's (1989) finding of better performance with an explanation measure, but others have failed to do so (e.g., Foote & Holmes-Lonergan, 2003; Hughes, 1998); indeed, in some studies performance has been better with prediction than with explanation (e.g., Flynn, 2006; Perner, Lang, & Kloo, 2002). In addition, defenders of the traditional approach have pointed out complications in the prediction–explanation comparison (Perner, Lang, et al., 2002; Wimmer & Mayringer, 1998). It is difficult, for example, to ensure that the chance base rates are the same for the two measures. Conclusions may also vary as a function of how explanations are elicited and the sort of explanation that is credited. Most impressive, but also relatively rare, is a spontaneous mention of a false belief accompanied by an explanation for the belief. A more easily met criterion is simply to state the belief in response to a "What does X think?" question. On my reading of this literature, some young children are indeed able to explain false beliefs before they can predict them, thus demonstrating some understanding of belief that is not elicited by the standard task. The difference, however, is neither large nor universal.

Perhaps the most radical departure from the standard experimental tasks is not to use an experimental task at all. All of us, including children, talk frequently about mental states—what we (or others) want, think, feel, and so forth. Perhaps some evidence of mentalistic understanding can be gleaned simply from listening to young children talk. Pioneering efforts to do so were reported in early studies by Bretherton and Beeghly (1982) and Shatz, Wellman, and Silber (1983). The fullest exploration, however, comes in a book by Bartsch and Wellman (1995) titled, appropriately, *Children Talk About the Mind*.

Bartsch and Wellman (1995) made use of the Child Language Data Exchange System, or CHILDES. CHILDES is a shared database that brings together transcripts of child speech from hundreds of studies of early child language for use by interested researchers (MacWhinney, 2000a, 2000b). It is both a wonderful resource for researchers of child language and a primary example of the value of shared data for research in psychology. As of this writing, it has been the basis for more than 3,000 publications.

Bartsch and Wellman's (1995) interest was not in language per se but rather in references to mental states. Their analysis focused on two states: desire (and thus words like *want*, *hope*, and *wish*) and belief (and thus words like *think*, *know*, and *believe*). In coding such utterances they were careful to distinguish between genuine mental state references and other, more ritualistic uses (e.g., repetitions of something the parent had just said, conventional phrases such as "you know what?"). Especially informative in this regard were contrastive statements—that is, statements in which the child drew an explicit contrast either between belief and reality or between one belief and another.

Table 2.2 presents some examples of utterances that were coded as expressions of false belief. It can be seen that none occurred in children younger than 3, a finding in keeping with conclusions from experimental studies of false belief. But it can also be seen that many were produced by 3-year-olds, an age group that typically shows little success on standard false belief tasks. These findings thus suggest that young children may have some knowledge of false belief that does not come through in their response to the typical experimental assessments. This, of course,

TABLE 2.2   Examples of Spontaneous References to False Belief From Bartsch and Wellman's (1995) Analysis of the CHILDES Data Set

Child	Age	Statement
Adam	3 years 3 months	It's a bus. I thought a taxi.
Ross	3 years 4 months	I thought you were at your home.
Abe	3 years 6 months	The people thought that Dracula was mean. But he was nice.
Adam	3 years 7 months	(after tasting glue) I don't like it. I thought that was good.
Abe	3 years 8 months	I think … I thought I could rip the paper off, 'cept it doesn't have any paper.
Mark	3 years 8 months	When we were going on our walk I thought we were lost. I thinked we were lost.
Abe	4 years 8 months	Did you see the clouds? (Adult explains that they saw smoke from fireworks.) But I thought they was clouds.
Sarah	5 years 1 month	Where's Paul? … I thought he was gonna leave him here.

Source: From Bartsch, K., & Wellman, H. M., *Children Talk About the Mind*, Oxford University Press, New York, 1995, pp. 46, 52, 53, 115. Copyright 1995 by Oxford University Press, Inc. Reprinted with permission.

was also the conclusion from studies reviewed earlier in this section. As Bartsch and Wellman (1995), note, however, it is also possible that the 10 children who contributed data for the analyses were unusually precocious and hence not representative of 3-year-olds in general. Indeed, later research provides some support for this possibility (Sabbagh & Callanan, 1998).

Other Forms of Belief

The naturalistic speech data just discussed expand the range of situations and child behaviors from which to infer an understanding of belief. But such work also expands the range of beliefs with which children deal. Naturally occurring false beliefs may occasionally involve the location of an object or the contents of a container, a la the Maxi or crayon box scenarios, but they encompass many other types of belief as well. Table 2.2 provides a few examples.

Potentially, beliefs of any sort could be the target of a false belief assessment. In fact, only a handful of false belief studies have asked about anything other than the location or identity of an object. I consider two examples of such research here: some work by John Flavell and colleagues and some work of my own.

The Flavell studies (Flavell, Flavell, Green, & Moses, 1990; Flavell, Mumme, Green, & Flavell, 1992) encompassed beliefs—in particular, false beliefs—of a variety of sorts. These included beliefs about morality (e.g., a belief that it is OK to kick people), beliefs about social conventions (e.g., a belief that it is OK to wear pajamas to school), and beliefs about values (e.g., a belief that it is fun to eat grass). Also included for purposes of comparison were beliefs about physical facts, both the sort usually included in false belief assessments and beliefs that reflected a more basic misunderstanding of reality (e.g., a belief that dogs can fly). The studies provided some evidence that young children find it easier to judge discrepant beliefs about values than those concerned with physical facts, a perhaps expectable finding, given that values have a less objective, right or wrong quality than do physical facts. For the most part, however, the new forms of belief showed the same developmental course as that found with the standard assessments: namely, failure by young preschoolers and success by older, with few differences between the new and the standard forms of belief.

The focus of a series of studies by my collaborators and me (Miller, Holmes, Gitten, & Danbury, 1997) was on false beliefs that stem from developmental misconceptions—that is, misunderstandings about some aspect of the world that are natural forms of thought at certain points in development. The specific misconceptions on which we focused were a failure to understand the appearance–reality distinction (a development discussed later in this chapter), a failure to understand a difference in perspective, a failure to understand line of sight, and a failure to understand certain biological principles of growth and inheritance. The question was whether the preschool participants, who themselves had mastered the concepts in question, would realize that someone else might hold a belief different from their own. The answer was yes, but only by about age 4½ or 5. Thus, false beliefs based on misconceptions proved similar to false beliefs about physical facts: little understanding by age 3, good understanding by age 5.

Neither the Flavell et al. (1990, 1992) nor the Miller et al. (1997) studies suggest a revision in the generally accepted timetable for mastery of false belief. Both, however, do broaden the bases for conclusions about children's ability. The fact that children realize that someone can be momentarily mistaken about the location of an object does not guarantee that they also realize that someone could fail to distinguish between appearance and reality or could believe that it is possible to see around corners. The available evidence (still rather limited) suggests that they do.

False Belief in Infancy?

The research discussed in the preceding sections does not threaten the traditional picture of false belief as a preschool accomplishment. It does suggest two related corrections to this picture. The first is that mastery of false belief is not a single, absent-to-present transition; rather, there are forms of partial knowledge prior to full mastery. The second is that at least some children do possess some understanding of false belief prior to being able to pass the standard tasks.

A more serious challenge to the traditional view comes from recent work claiming that infants as young as 13 months are able to recognize false beliefs in others. If valid, this claim would require a fundamental change in the descriptive picture of false belief development. It would also require a major reworking of just about every theory of theory-of-mind development.

A word first about methods: Babies cannot talk, nor can they understand what is said when other people talk. This means that perhaps 99% of the assessment methods that are typically used with children or adults, methods that involve talking to participants and eliciting verbal responses from them, cannot be used with babies. Research with infants presents many challenges, but undoubtedly the greatest challenge is that of response measures: coming up with something that babies *can* do from which we can infer what they are thinking or perceiving or feeling.

The most often used response measure in the study of infant cognitive development has been looking behavior. Babies look at stimuli in their visual environment from birth. Furthermore, from birth they look at least somewhat differentially—that is, they find some stimuli more interesting than others. Among the determinants of what babies find interesting is surprise: Babies look longer at events that in some way surprise them. An event is surprising if it violates an expectation—if it is different from what we thought was going to occur. By seeing what surprises babies, we can therefore glean evidence about what they expect, which in turn gives us evidence about what they believe. For example (to take the most often studied example), suppose that we engineer an apparent violation of object permanence—that is, make an object magically disappear—and the infant reacts with surprise. The baby's reaction suggests that she expected the object still to be there and thus possesses what Piaget labeled stage 4 knowledge of object permanence.

The violation-of-expectation method has been widely applied in recent years to the study of what infants know about the physical world, encompassing both Piagetian developments such as object permanence and understanding of physical laws (e.g., gravity, inertia) more generally. The most influential programs of research are those of Renee Baillargeon (e.g., Baillargeon, 2004; Baillargeon, Li, Ng, & Yuan, 2009) and Elizabeth Spelke (e.g., Spelke, Breinlinger, Macomber, & Jacobson, 1992; Spelke & Kinzler, 2007). It is probably fair to say that this work has transformed the field's view of infants' cognitive abilities. Infants clearly know more, and know it earlier in life, than was believed when the Piagetian approach dominated the field. Exactly *how* much more, however, remains a subject of debate—a point to which I will return.

It was the violation-of-expectation approach that Onishi and Baillargeon (2005) used in the initial study of false belief in infancy. The infants saw scenarios acted out in which an actor was shown forming either a true belief or a false belief about the location of an object. The actor then searched either in the location that was compatible with her belief or in the alternative location. Infants looked significantly longer when the search did not match what would be expected from the belief, suggesting that they were surprised by the discrepancy between belief and action. This could occur, however, only if they had accurately judged what the belief was, including the instances in which the actor's belief was false. In Onishi and Baillargeon's words:

> The present results suggest that 15-month-old infants expect an actor to search for a toy where she believes, rightly or wrongly, that it is hidden. Such an interpretation calls into question the notion that preschoolers undergo a fundamental change from a nonrepresentational to a representational theory of mind. (p. 257)

Since the Onishi and Baillargeon study there have been a number of further demonstrations of apparent false belief understanding in babies (e.g., Buttelmann, Carpenter, & Tomasello, 2009; Scott & Baillargeon, 2009; Song, Onishi,

& Baillargeon, 2008; Surian, Caldi, & Sperber, 2007; Trauble, Marinovi, & Vesna, 2010). These demonstrations, it is worth noting, have emerged from several different laboratories, something that is always reassuring when a new and surprising finding is at issue. The Surian et al. study pushed the age of success down to 13 months.

Such surprising claims have not gone unchallenged, however. A number of critical commentaries have proposed simpler, lower-level explanations for the success shown in these studies (Perner, 2009; Perner & Ruffman, 2005; Ruffman & Perner, 2005; Stack & Lewis, 2008). More generally, recent years have seen the emergence of several broad critiques of the recent infant research literature (all, interestingly, from veteran researchers of infancy) that have called into question how much can be inferred from looking-time data (Cohen, 2009; Haith, 1998; Kagan, 2008). Although the specifics vary, the general theme is the same: concerns about attributing not only basic forms of knowledge such as object permanence and false belief but also all sorts of mental processes (e.g., infants "reasoning," "calculating," "inferring") from the single dependent variable of fixation time.

Having noted these dissenting views, I should add that several of the demonstrations of apparent false belief understanding in babies used response measures other than fixation time and thus are not subject to the only-looking time criticism (e.g., Buttelmann et al., 2009; Southgate, Senju, & Csibra, 2007). In addition, the most thorough examination to date of this literature—an excellent review by Caron (2009) (himself a veteran researcher of infancy)—comes down on the early-competence side of the debate (though see Sodian, 2011, for a somewhat more cautious evaluation). This is not to say that the issue is resolved. Not only but does the precocious success shown in these studies require further probing, but also there is an obvious question that is as yet unanswered: If babies have some understanding of false belief as early as 13 months, why is it another 3 years or so before they can pass the standard tasks? The answer must be that the standard tasks require something more, but there is no consensus yet with respect to what this something more is (cf. Apperly & Butterfill, 2009; Scott & Baillargeon, 2009; Wellman, 2010).

Many of the topics discussed in this book are very much in the stay-tuned-for-further developments category. There is probably no topic, however, for which this designation applies more certainly than that of false belief in infancy.

OTHER EPISTEMIC MEASURES

Important though it is, the construct of false belief does not exhaust the things that children must come to understand about epistemic states—that is, mental states (thoughts, beliefs, percepts, memories) that are meant to represent the world accurately. In this section I consider several other developments.

One major developmental task for children is to learn the various ways evidence leads to belief. The false belief task taps one form of such knowledge. In the case of false belief, misleading evidence leads to an incorrect belief. In contrast, in the case of true belief or knowledge, adequate evidence leads to a correct belief. In the case of ignorance, an absence of evidence results in no belief. Finally, in the case of ambiguity, evidence compatible with two conclusions results in an uncertain belief.

Children understand simple forms of knowledge or ignorance by about the same time that they master false belief. Thus, by age 4 most children realize that if A looks in a box and B does not look, then A will know what is in the box and B will not know (Pratt & Bryant, 1990). Most 4-year-olds can also make use of some (although not yet all) of the semantic cues to knowledge—can distinguish between "know" and "think," for example, and between "is" and "may be" (Montgomery, 1992).

In the look-in-the-box example perception is the source of knowledge. But perception is not the only way we learn things. We also learn things by being told them (thus communication as a source of knowledge) and by figuring them out from available evidence (thus logical inference as a source of knowledge). Children come to understand communication and inference as sources of knowledge also, although mastery of these sources comes somewhat later than is the case for perception (Miller, Hardin, & Montgomery, 2003).

In addition to judging *whether* something is known, children also come to appreciate *how* it is known. Here, young children show some striking deficits in understanding prior to eventual mastery. For example, 4-year-olds may claim that they have always known a fact that the experimenter taught them just moments before (Taylor, Esbensen, & Bennett, 1994). Seconds after learning something, 3-year-olds may be unable to say whether sight, touch, or hearing was the source of the information (O'Neill & Chong, 2001; O'Neill & Gopnik, 1991).

Despite these initial difficulties, children understand many of the basics of knowledge formation by age 5. In contrast, an understanding of most forms of ambiguity is not evident until the grade-school years. Such understanding, in fact, is a central achievement in one of the few theories of theory of mind to focus on developments beyond the preschool years, that of Michael Chandler and colleagues (Chandler & Carpendale, 1998; Chandler & Sokol, 1999). We will therefore return to ambiguity in Chapter 5.

The Piagetian notion of perspective taking deals with children's ability to figure out other people's mental contents (e.g., what they see, think, feel) and thus falls clearly under what today would be labeled as theory of mind. Piaget's studies, however, focused on fairly complex forms of perspective taking (e.g., the famous Three Mountain problem) that typically were not mastered until middle childhood. More recent research has identified simpler forms that emerge much earlier. Level 1 perspective taking refers to the realization that one person may see an object while a second person does not. If, for example, I orient a picture book toward me and away from you, then I see the picture and you do not. Level 2 perspective taking is more advanced. It is the realization that two people may have different perceptual experiences of the same object. Thus, if I lay the picture book flat between us, then I see the picture right side up and you see it upside down. In short, Level 1 perspective taking has to do with *whether* something is seen, whereas Level 2 has to do with *how* it is seen (Flavell, Miller, & Miller, 2002). Children as young as 2½ demonstrate some understanding of Level 1 perspective taking. Mastery of Level 2 perspective taking typically comes at about age 4.

One more entry under the epistemic heading is the appearance–reality task. The appearance–reality task was introduced by John Flavell (e.g., Flavell, Flavell, & Green, 1983) in the early 1980s and thus prior to the advent of theory of mind as a distinct topic of study; it was later easily subsumed, however, under the theory-of-mind heading. As the name suggests, the task tests children's ability to distinguish between the appearance of something and its true nature. Of greatest interest, of course, is the ability to do so when appearance and true nature diverge. Suppose, for example, that we show the child a picture of a white butterfly and then place a colored red filter over the picture. We can ask two questions: "When you look at the butterfly, does it *look* red or does it *look* white?" "For *real*, is the butterfly *really and truly* red or *really and truly* white?" (I will add that such studies typically include a fair amount of verbal pretraining to ensure that the child understands the questions being asked.) Most 3-year-olds and some 4-year-olds respond "red" to both questions, thus showing an inability to distinguish appearance and reality. They get the appearance right but misjudge the true nature.

Another form of the task makes use of objects that have been deliberately contrived to look like something else. A commonly used stimulus is the sponge/rock: a foam rubber sponge that looks for all the world like a gray rock. Once children have had a chance to touch the sponge and to learn its true nature, they are asked the usual two questions: What does it look like, and what is it really and truly? Here, young children tend to get the reality right; they can report that the object really is a sponge. Remarkably, however, they get the appearance wrong, claiming that the rock-like object also looks like a sponge. The pattern of errors is thus opposite to what is found with the colored filters task.

Like false belief, the appearance–reality task tells us something basic about the child's understanding (and, for a while, lack of understanding) of representation: namely, that the immediate perceptual appearance of something is simply a representation that may differ from its true nature. Another similarity—not just with false belief but with Level 2 perspective taking—is that all three developments could be argued to be dependent on a capacity for dual representation, that is, the ability to represent something in two ways simultaneously. Thus, the butterfly looks red but is really white. I see the turtle right side up, but you see it upside down. I know there are candles in the box, but Ernie thinks there are crayons. Given this common core, it is not surprising that responses to the three measures are positively correlated (Flavell, Green, & Flavell, 1986; Gopnik & Astington, 1988). (I should note that the basic appearance–reality tasks, like the standard false belief tasks, have been subject to methodological revisions and disagreements with regard to interpretation—see, e.g., Hansen & Markman, 2005; Sapp, Lee, & Muir, 2000.)

OTHER MENTAL STATES

In a sense, the work discussed so far epitomizes the first decade or so of research on theory of mind: a focus on belief as the mental state of greatest interest and on the preschool years as the developmental time period of greatest interest. Given this initial concentration, a reasonable question—one that many researchers in the 1990s faced—is where do we go next?

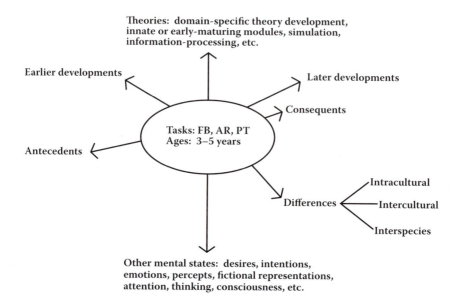

Figure 2.3   Research directions in the study of theory of mind. (From Flavell, J. H., *International Journal of Behavioral Development, 24,* 2000, p. 18. Copyright 2000 by SAGE Publications. Reprinted with permission of SAGE.)

Figure 2.3, taken from Flavell (2000), shows one way to think about the where-to-go-next question. One clear direction for expansion is chronological: Start earlier, go later. As the figure indicates, doing so will allow us to identify additional developmental achievements beyond those that emerge in the preschool years—simpler, more basic developments in the case of younger children, more advanced developments in the case of older children. The latter, of course, are the main topic of this book. The chronological expansion is also necessary to address two of the basic questions in theory of mind: what are the antecedents that make possible developments such as false belief and appearance–reality, and what in turn do these developments make possible in later childhood?

A second direction for expansion is topical rather than chronological. Important though beliefs and other epistemic states may be, they are not the only mental states that humans experience and thus not the only mental states that children must come to understand. Figure 2.3 lists some of the other targets for developmental acquisition (desires, intentions...), and as the "etc." indicates, the list is not complete. My discussion will be even less close to being complete, in that I will consider just two states: desire and emotion. Fuller presentations, of course, are available in the various books devoted to first-order achievements that were cited earlier.

Desire

Like beliefs, desires are "intentional" in the philosopher's sense, in that they are about something in the world. So just as we can think about an apple, a book, or a

TABLE 2.3   Examples of Spontaneous References to Desire From Bartsch and Wellman's (1995) Analysis of the CHILDES Data Set

Child	Age	Statement
Abe	2 years 5 months	I wanna cranberry muffin. I like them.
Adam	2 years 6 months	No, I don't want to sit seat.
Abe	2 years 8 months	I want you put hot chocolate on it.
Adam	2 years 8 months	Don't want book.
Naomi	2 years 11 months	I want push on this one.
Adam	3 years 5 months	I wish I could play with this.
Sarah	3 years 10 months	I want a turtle, but I can't have one.
Abe	4 years 2 months	I wish we had gotted some mail today.

Source: Bartsch, K., & Wellman, H. M., *Children Talk About the Mind*, Oxford University Press, New York, 1995, pp. 70, 71, 78. Copyright 1995 by Oxford University Press, Inc. Reprinted with permission.

friend, so may we desire an apple, a book, or a friend. The mind–world relation differs in the two cases, however. A belief is meant to reflect the world accurately and therefore is either true or false. A desire, however, does not have a truth status—it makes no sense to talk of true or false desires. Rather, a desire is either fulfilled or not.

Children begin to talk about desires very early in life. Table 2.3 shows some examples from Bartsch and Wellman's (1995) analysis of the CHILDES database. Most of the examples use the word *want*, and this is no accident—in Bartsch and Wellman's tally 97% of the desire references involved *want* (rather than *wish*, *hope*, *care*, *afraid*). It is also no accident that the examples come primarily from 2-year-olds, an age group not yet producing verbalizations about belief. One of Bartsch and Wellman's major conclusions was that children begin to talk about desires earlier in development than they talk about beliefs.

Do experimental measures also suggest an earlier understanding of desire than belief? There can be no single, across-the-board answer to this question, since it depends on which aspect of desire and which aspect of belief we focus on (a point that applies also to emotion, our next topic). Still, in many ways young children's understanding of desire does appear to be more advanced than their understanding of belief. Here are a few examples. By age 3 (and in some children even earlier) children realize that people act upon their desires—for example, that a boy who wants his pet rabbit will search for the rabbit. They also appreciate the consequences of either fulfilled or unfulfilled desires. They realize, for example, that if the boy finds his rabbit he will stop searching but if the initial search is unsuccessful he will continue to look. They appreciate as well the relation between desire fulfillment and emotion, judging that the boy will be happy if he finds the rabbit and sad if he does not (Wellman, 1990; Wellman & Woolley, 1990).

Perhaps the most impressively precocious achievement in the domain of desire comes not in 3-year-olds but in toddlers. Repacholi and Gopnik (1997) gave their 14- and 18-month-old participants a choice of two snacks: Goldfish crackers or broccoli. Not surprisingly, almost all preferred the crackers. Next, the children watched an adult experimenter sample both snacks and express a clear preference for the broccoli. The two snacks were then placed in front of the child, and the experimenter stretched out her hand, asking the child to give her one. Most of the 14-month-olds gave her the crackers, the snack that they themselves preferred. Most of the 18-month-olds, however, gave her the broccoli, thus demonstrating a realization that different people may have different desires. Understanding of discrepant desires thus seems to emerge long before understanding of discrepant beliefs (but see Doherty, 2009, for some cautions with respect to how to interpret this research).

Shortly I will discuss theories of theory of mind. The work reviewed in this section is one form of evidence for one of the most influential theories, that of Henry Wellman (1990). In Wellman's conceptualization young children initially form a *desire theory*, in which they explain behaviors in terms of desire but do not yet recognize the importance of belief. By age 4 this initial theory gives way to a *belief-desire psychology*, in which children realize that desires and beliefs work together to impel behavior.

Emotion

Emotion was not a topic in Bartsch and Wellman's (1995) analysis of the CHILDES database. It is clear, however, both from observations they cite and from other research (e.g., Bretherton & Beeghly, 1982), that children begin to talk about emotions very early in life. Here are a few examples, all taken from children who were just 2 years 4 months of age (Bretherton & Beeghly). "Santa will be happy if I pee in the potty." "Don't feel bad, Bob." "Daddy surprised me." "Bees everywhere. Scared me!" "Don't be mad, Mommy!"

Not only do children talk about emotions from early in life; they also hear much talk about emotions from those around them. Work by Judy Dunn and colleagues (Dunn, Bretherton, & Munn, 1987; Dunn, Brown, & Beardsall, 1991) suggests that such "family talk" about emotions contributes to children's understanding of emotion. Children who are frequently exposed to talk about emotions talk more about emotions themselves. They are also better at recognizing emotions in others.

Experimental studies make clear that mastery of different aspects of emotion is spread across several years. As we have seen, children appreciate the relation between desire satisfaction and subsequent emotion very early in development. Understanding of the belief-based emotions of surprise and curiosity develops a bit later, although there is some disagreement about how much later (Hadwin & Perner, 1991; Wellman & Banerjee, 1991).

In some situations the relation between available cues (such as facial expression) and underlying emotion is not straightforward. Such is the case with so-called display rules, in which a person may attempt to hide how he or she actually feels (e.g., smile after receiving a disappointing gift). Such is also likely to be the case with mixed emotions, in which a person may experience both positive and negative emotions about the same event. Although preschoolers show some success at judging simple versions of such scenarios, full understanding of concealed and mixed emotions develops gradually across childhood (Flavell et al., 2002).

Like desires, emotions cannot be true or false. They can, however, be at least temporarily inappropriate, in that we may sometimes feel one way because we are unaware of something that will soon make us feel very different. Such is the case with certain kinds of surprise. We may happily anticipate eating the last piece of cake when we arrive home, only to discover when we get there that someone else has beat us to it. In such situations there is a contrast between the immediate emotion (happy) and the eventual emotion (sad).

A number of studies (e.g., De Rosnay, Pons, Harris, & Morrell, 2004; Harris, Johnson, Hutton, Andrews, & Cooke, 1989; Wellman & Liu, 2004) have explored children's ability to reason about such situations. The procedure is similar to the unexpected contents form of false belief: a container that apparently holds one sort of content (say, something the protagonist very much wants) turns out to hold something quite different (something the protagonist does not want). The question, however, is directed to emotion rather than belief: How does the protagonist feel before opening the container? This question turns out to be difficult for preschoolers. Although exceptions exist, in most studies judging the temporarily "false" emotion has proved more difficult than judging the protagonist's false belief. Logically, this discrepancy makes sense, given that an accurate attribution of emotion would seem to depend on an at least implicit understanding of the protagonist's belief—in this case, a belief that he or she is about to get something good. What more is needed to make accurate attributions of emotion is not yet fully resolved (Bradmetz & Schneider, 2004; De Rosnay et al., 2004; Harris, 2009).

I will add that happy and sad are not the only emotions that pose challenges in this situation. Similar findings have been reported for surprise (Hadwin & Perner, 1991) and for fear (Bradmetz & Schneider, 1999). The latter study, as it happens, made use of one of my Chapter 1 examples: Red Riding Hood's response to her pseudo-grandmother. Children found it easier to judge Red Riding Hood's false belief (thinks it's her grandmother) than they did to judge her emotion (is happy, not scared).

A form of the belief–emotion contrast occurs in the second-order literature as well. As we will see, results in that case are somewhat more complicated.

DEVELOPMENTS IN INFANCY

Whether infants have any understanding of false belief is, as we have seen, an ongoing and controversial issue. There is no dispute, however, about the fact that theory-of-mind development in general gets its start in infancy. Infants distinguish in various ways between the social and nonsocial worlds from very early in life, and they eventually develop a number of competencies that are precursors to or early forms of later theory-of-mind developments. Here I discuss three such developments; fuller treatments of infant theory of mind can be found in Legerstee (2006); Poulin-Dubois, Brooker, and Chow (2009); and Reddy (2008). Of the general sources indentified earlier, Moore (2006) provides an especially thorough coverage.

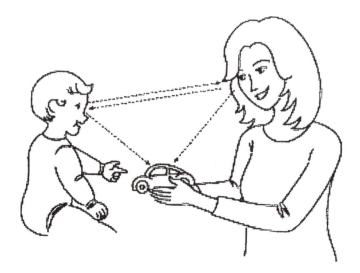

Figure 2.4   Example of a triadic interaction in infancy. (From Moore, C., *The Development of Commonsense Psychology*, Erlbaum, Mahwah, NJ, 2006, p. 94. Reproduced by permission of Taylor & Francis Group, LLC, a division of Informa plc. With permission.)

Before discussing specific developments, let us consider a general advance that is reflected in each of the more specific achievements. Figure 2.4, taken from Moore (2006), provides a pictorial depiction. During the early months of life, indeed from birth, infants are social creatures who engage in countless interactions with the important people in their lives. Initially, though, all such interactions are dyadic, in the sense that each partner's focus is on the other and any environmental element (a toy, a bottle, or whatever) is at best an incidental prop in the interpersonal back-and-forth. Infants do, of course, at times focus on toys and bottles and other parts of the inanimate environment; when they do, however, they do not maintain a simultaneous focus on an interactional partner. The interaction thus remains dyadic, either infant and social partner or infant and environmental object.

By sometime in the second half of the first year the situation changes. The change is gradual rather than abrupt, and there are disagreements among researchers with respect to exactly when it occurs. Eventually, however, the focus of interaction broadens to include not just two but three elements: infant, adult, and environment. Now the interaction between infant and adult is *about* something, and now the infant for the first time realizes that the adult has a psychological connection to something in the world—that the adult sees, likes, desires, or whatever the object on which both are focused. Such a realization marks a basic advance in theory of mind: the earliest understanding that other people have psychological states.

What sorts of psychological states must infants come to understand? Perhaps the most basic is attention: the realization that one's interactional partner is focused on and processing some aspect of the environment. Suppose, for example, that baby and mother are playing together and Mommy suddenly looks toward the corner of the room. Does the infant follow her gaze and look toward the same location? Young infants do not do so, but by the last third of the first year such gaze following has become a likely response. The establishment of a shared focus of attention in this way is referred to as *joint attention*, and it can be argued to reflect several basic realizations about the mind on the baby's part: Mommy is having an interesting visual experience; I am like Mommy; therefore I can also have an interesting visual experience if I look where she's looking.

Joint attention has been the most thoroughly studied aspect of theory of mind in infancy, and this brief description glosses over a number of complexities and disputes in its study. The probability and the ease of gaze following vary as a function of a number of factors—for example, does the partner turn her head or simply move her eyes, is there but one object or many that might be the target of the gaze, and is the gaze unimpeded or do obstacles intervene? In addition, eye movements are not the only clue to someone else's attentional focus; pointing also serves this function (more explicitly, in fact, than gaze), and infants must also learn to follow points. There is also the question of the infant as actor rather than recipient: When do infants themselves begin to use points to direct the attention of others? Mastery of these and other components of joint attention is not instantaneous but rather is typically spread across several months near the end of the first year and the beginning of the second year of life, and there is as yet no consensus with regard to their exact timing.

Finally, even if all the empirical facts could be agreed upon, marked differences of opinion remain with respect to how to interpret the facts. The interpretation of gaze following previously offered is an example of *rich interpretation*: inferring a good deal of underlying knowledge from the infant's overt behavior—specifically in this case, that the infant realizes that Mommy is having a perceptual experience, wants to share that experience, and believes that he can do so by following Mommy's gaze. Among the prominent researchers who generally subscribe to a rich interpretation of infant competencies are Simon Baron-Cohen (e.g., Baron-Cohen, 1995), Andrew Meltzoff (e.g., Meltzoff, 2007), and Michael Tomasello (e.g., Tomasello, 1999b). The alternative perspective is labeled *lean interpretation*. In this case the attempt is to explain the behavior in the simplest way possible, inferring only the minimum amount of knowledge that is necessary to account for what is seen. Researchers in this camp include Jeremy Carpendale and Charles Lewis (e.g., Carpendale & Lewis, 2010) and Chris Moore (e.g., Moore, 2006; Moore & Corkum, 1994).

The rich–lean issue is a general one in the study of infants' and young children's abilities. The terminology first arose in the study of language development in reference to the question of how much linguistic knowledge to infer on the basis of young children's primitive early utterances. It reemerged in the infant cognition literature with the disputes about how much to read into the looking-time data from the Baillargeon/Spelke line of research. As we saw, it is at present an unresolved issue in the study of infant false belief.

The same interpretive questions apply to a second major development under the heading of infant theory of mind, the construct of *social referencing*. Let us modify the earlier example a bit. Suppose now that the mother looks not to the corner of the room but to a door and that she does so because a stranger (i.e., someone unknown to the baby) has just appeared in the door. How does the baby respond? Again, a young infant is unlikely to respond at all to the mother's head turn. By sometime in the last third of the first year, however, the infant may not only follow the mother's gaze but do something more as well. Having seen the stranger, the infant now looks back at the mother's face, searching in her expression for cues that will help him make sense of this novel event. The search of the mother's face is an example of social referencing: using the emotional cues provided by others (via either facial expression or tone of voice) to guide one's own response in uncertain situations (Baldwin & Moses, 1996; Walker-Andrews, 1997). It implies (on a rich interpretation) the knowledge that other people have emotions and that these emotions can be guides to how one should feel and behave oneself.

So infants eventually (although again, there are disputes about when) understand at least something about what others are perceiving and what others are feeling. A third important achievement is to understand what others intend by their behavior. This achievement (and indeed, the ones already discussed) is actually twofold: first, realizing that other people *have* intentions, and then accurately judging what the intentions are in particular situations.

Let us modify the baby–mother example one more time. Suppose now that there are two toys in front of baby and mother and that the mother reaches toward one of the toys. Does the infant realize that she intends to obtain the toy? And how could we determine this? Research by Amanda Woodward (2005, 2009) makes use of the phenomenon of habituation: the decline in interest and attention when the same stimulus or event is encountered repeatedly. In one study, for example, the infant watched as an experimenter reached repeatedly toward one of two toys. The spatial position of the toys was then reversed, and the experimenter either reached for the same toy as before (thus changing the direction of the arm movement but maintaining the same goal) or reached for the other toy (thus maintaining the same arm movement but changing the goal). By 5 months of age infants looked longer when the reach was toward the other, previously ignored toy, suggesting that they had encoded the intention behind the reach and that they were surprised when the intention apparently changed.

Additional research by Woodward and others (e.g., Meltzoff, 2006; Tomasello, 1999a) demonstrates a number of further advances in infants' understanding of intention. Initially, infants understand goal-related action only when it results in a touch of the target object; eventually a point or a look is sufficient to infer the actor's intention. Infants also become capable of using the intentions of others to guide their own action. Having seen an adult reach for a particular toy, they are subsequently more likely to choose that toy themselves. The own–other relation goes in the other direction as well. Infants' understanding of acts such as reaching and pointing is correlated with their own ability to produce such behaviors, and further evidence suggests that the infant's own actions play a causal role with respect to understanding the actions of others. Finally, by 18 months infants can judge intentions even in the face of failed actions (Meltzoff, 1995). Having watched an adult try and fail to perform a task, they imitate selectively, reproducing only the behaviors that are compatible with fulfilling the goal.

The research discussed thus far has involved general relations between developments in infancy and later developments. A relatively recent line of research looks for specific, within-child links between early and later periods via longitudinal study of the same children from infancy through the preschool years (e.g., Aschersleben, Hofer, & Jovanovic, 2008; Colonnesi, Rieffe, Koops, & Perucchini, 2008; Wellman, Lopez-Duran, LaBounty, & Hamilton, 2008). A general conclusion from this research is that there *are* links: Infants who are relatively quick to master infant forms of theory of mind grow up to be children who are relatively quick to master later forms of theory of mind. For example, relatively good understanding of intentional behavior in infancy predicts relatively good understanding of false belief at age 4.

AUTISM

All of the work discussed so far has been with typically developing children. As I noted in Chapter 1, there is also a large—and rapidly growing—research literature devoted to theory-of-mind understanding in children and adults with autism. I settle for briefly summarizing the first-order component of this literature here; we will return to autism in subsequent chapters in the discussion of more advanced forms of theory of mind. Among the sources for fuller reviews of the general autism literature are Baron-Cohen (2000, 2001), Rajendran and Mitchell (2007), and Yirmiya, Erel, Shaked, and Solomonica (1998).

Autism is a severe developmental disorder, almost certainly biological in origin, one of the defining characteristics of which is problems in social understanding and social interaction. An approach known as the *cognitive theory of autism* posits that deficits in theory of mind account for some of the features of autism. The claim is not that such deficits account for all of the features of autism, because they clearly do not, nor is the claim that theory-of-mind deficits are limited to the syndrome of autism, because they clearly are not. The claim is simply that theory of mind contributes to what we see in autism.

It did not take long after Wimmer and Perner's (1983) initial study of false belief for the false belief task to be applied to the study of autism. Baron-Cohen, Leslie, and Frith (1985) carried out the first such study. They compared the performance of three groups of participants on the Sally/Anne task described earlier in the chapter: children with autism (mean age = 11 years 11 months), children with Down syndrome (mean age = 10 years 11 months), and typically developing children (mean age = 4 years 5 months). The typically developing and Down syndrome children did well (85% and 86% correct, respectively); the children with autism, however, were correct only 20% of the time.

A flood of research followed the Baron-Cohen et al. (1985) study, and it provided clear support for their general conclusion. Many children with autism never master first-order false belief. This conclusion holds not only for the unexpected locations procedure (such as the Sally/Anne task used by Baron Cohen et al.) but also for the other main false belief paradigm, the unexpected contents task. When mastery does occur it typically comes several years later than the norm for typical development, and also later than what is found for groups (e.g., developmentally delayed individuals) who have been matched with the autism sample for mental age. Furthermore, the difficulties shown by people with autism are not limited to the false belief task but apply to theory-of-mind abilities more generally. They are evident, for example, on the appearance–reality task and also on measures of pretend play. They are also evident on measures of joint attention in infancy.

On the other hand, for some people with autism the difficulties are not absolute, because success on many first-order measures does eventually emerge. This is especially likely for individuals whose attributes (relatively good language abilities, IQs in the normal range) place them at the high-functioning end of the autism spectrum. This finding does not mean that the theory-of-mind profiles of such individuals match those found in typical development; delays of several years remain common, and there is also the suggestion that the underlying bases for correct response to tasks like false belief may be somewhat different for people with autism (Tager-Flusberg, 2007). Nevertheless, for many the problem seems to be one of delay rather than permanent deficit.

A conclusion that theory of mind is delayed rather than absent in autism would be of considerable significance for our understanding of the disorder. The preceding, however, is based on first-order measures, and thus on developments that are typically complete by about age 5. But theory of mind in general is not complete by age 5. A full assessment of the theory-of-mind hypothesis of autism must also encompass the more advanced forms of understanding that typically emerge in the post-preschool years. I therefore return to the subject of autism in both Chapter 3 and Chapter 4.

NEUROIMAGING OF THEORY OF MIND

For much of the twentieth century, our ability to see into the brain was limited to questions of anatomy and organization. Such is no longer the case. The development of various neuroimaging techniques (e.g., functional magnetic resonance imaging, or fMRI; positron emission tomography, or PET; electroencephalography, or EEG; event-related potentials, or ERPs) has for the first time allowed researchers and clinicians to view not just the static brain but also brain *activity*. (A special issue of *Developmental Science* [Casey & de Haan, 2002] describes how these and other techniques work.) Among the topics to which imaging techniques have been directed is theory of mind. A recent meta-analysis (Van Overwalle, 2009) cites over 200 studies of theory of mind using fMRI alone.

A number of daunting challenges accompany both the measurement and the interpretation of brain activity (for discussions of these challenges, see Apperly, 2011; Saxe & Pelphrey, 2009). I will mention two in the case of the most often used technique in the theory-of-mind component of this literature, fMRI. Both stem from the fact that participants in an fMRI study must lie motionless for an extended period with their heads encased within a noisy tube. This requirement constrains the kinds of situation and tasks that can be presented, limiting input to "abstracted and impoverished sources of social information" (Saxe, 2006, p. 60). It also means that the technique is unusable with preschoolers and of limited use with older children, and in fact only a handful of fMRI studies (Kobayashi, Glover, & Temple, 2007; Mosconi, Mack, McCarthy, & Pelphrey, 2005) have included children.

Most of the research, then, is with adults. What has such research shown? Perhaps the most basic question concerns the areas of the brain that are active when someone engages in theory-of-mind reasoning. Is there a single portion of the brain devoted to theory of mind, or is theory of mind perhaps spread across the entire brain? As is often the case when extreme alternatives are posed, the answer is somewhere in between, but probably closer to the specific than general end of the range of possibilities. Mitchell (2008, p. 142) provides the following summary: "The processes that occur during mentalizing are associated with a small number of brain regions, including the medial prefrontal cortex (MPFC), tempero-parietal junction, precuneous/posterior cingulate, amygdala, superior temporal sulcus, and temporal poles."

Although the findings just summarized may be primary data for the neuro-psychologist, for most of us they are just the starting point. What (apart from physiological underpinnings) can neuroimaging tell us about theory of mind? In particular, can neuroimaging help to answer questions about theory of mind that behavioral data alone have been unable to resolve?

Undoubtedly the most basic question is whether there is something special and distinct about theory of mind as a form of cognition or whether theory of mind is simply one expression of the general cognitive system. This, as we will see in the final section of the chapter, is a central issue for theories of theory of mind. The finding that theory of mind is limited to specific regions of the brain suggests that it may indeed be a special form of cognition. But such a conclusion cannot be reached without comparative data, for it may be that *any* form of cognition engages these same brain regions. What is needed, then, are studies in which theory-of-mind performance is compared with performance on tasks that are matched for general characteristics (e.g., linguistic demands, memory demands) but that lack a mentalistic component. Such matching is difficult to achieve, and the result is that there is no clear answer as of yet to the general versus specific question. Probably every researcher who has considered the issue agrees that theory of mind draws on a mixture of specialized and general brain regions. Researchers disagree, however, on the balance, with some (e.g., Saxe, Carey, & Kanwisher, 2004) stressing the specialized aspects and others (e.g., Apperly, 2011) coming down on the general side.

Another basic question concerns the relation between thinking about the self and thinking about others. As we will see in the concluding section of the chapter, this issue is central to an approach labeled simulation theory, which argues that our knowledge of others builds upon our awareness of our own mental processes. If this argument is valid, we would expect the same brain regions to underlie think-ing about self and thinking about others. Such is often the case, and some com-mentators (e.g., Mitchell, 2008) have therefore interpreted the neuroimaging work as support for simulation theory. Such self–other congruence is not always found, however, and other commentators (e.g., Abu-Akel, 2003) have therefore reached a different conclusion. As with the general versus specific issue, this is clearly an ongoing question.

Somewhat clearer conclusions emerge with respect to a third issue: differences among different mental states. As we saw, children master some basic aspects of intention and desire before they demonstrate much understanding of belief, especially false belief. Might differences in maturation of relevant brain regions account for this difference? Although there is as of yet no relevant work with children, several studies with adult participants suggest that the answer is yes. These studies come from different laboratories (Abraham, Rakoczy, Werning, von Cramon, & Schubotz, 2010; Liu, Meltzoff, & Wellman, 2009; Saxe & Powell, 2006; Zaitchik et al., 2010), they employ different imaging techniques (fMRI in three cases, ERPs in one), and in total they encompass a range of different nonbelief states (perception, intention, emotion, desire). Each reports that reasoning about beliefs engages different brain regions than does reasoning about other internal states. The physiological data thus complement and add to the behavioral data: Both indicate that there is something special about belief.

My brief treatment of neuroimaging has barely skimmed the surface of this large and growing literature. Among the sources for fuller treatments are Carrington and Bailey (2009); Van Overwalle (2009); and Zelazo, Chandler, and Crone (2010). I have also not attempted to review a related (and mostly congruent) literature: that concerned with the effects of brain injury on theory-of-mind performance. Apperly (2011) provides a good coverage of this work.

RELATIONS TO OTHER DEVELOPMENTS

Let us revisit Figure 2.3. As the figure indicates, identifying important milestones of development, such as false belief and appearance–reality, is just one of the tasks for the researcher of theory of mind. We also want to know what makes these achievements possible—what are the precursor skills and relevant experiences that underlie developments such as false belief? This is the Antecedents part of the figure. We also want to know what these developments themselves make possible—what can children now do that they could not do prior to mastering the concept in question? This is the consequences part of the figure. Questions such as these are central to the theory-of-mind enterprise, and there is therefore no shortage of further sources that go beyond the brief coverage provided here. Of the general books cited earlier, Carpendale and Lewis (2006) and Hughes (2011) provide especially good coverage. Other helpful sources include Astington (2003), Davies and Stone (2003), Harris (2006), and Hughes and Leekam (2004).

Antecedents of Theory of Mind

We begin with antecedents. I have not yet talked about theories of theory of mind. These theories vary in the emphasis they place on social experience as a source of theory-of-mind development. In any theory, however, there must be *some* role for experience—children could hardly come to understand the thoughts and feelings of others without experience interacting with others. And there are, in fact, multiple forms of evidence that tell us that experience plays a role.

One intriguing kind of evidence comes from research on the effects of siblings on theory-of-mind development. On the average—and, of course, with many exceptions—children with more siblings are faster to develop theory-of-mind skills than are children with no siblings or just one sibling. In some studies only older siblings have proved beneficial (Ruffman, Perner, Naito, Parkin, & Clements, 1998), whereas in other studies child siblings of any age have been shown to confer a benefit (McAlister & Peterson, 2007; Peterson, 2000). Presumably, growing up with siblings provides experiences (e.g., pretend play, being teased, being tricked) that help children learn about the thoughts and feelings of others. Studies that have looked directly at how siblings interact (e.g., Dunn, 1999; Randell & Peterson, 2009) provide support for this conjecture.

Siblings are not the only possible source for development-enhancing experiences. Family size in general has been shown to relate to theory-of-mind development (Jenkins & Astington, 1996; Lewis, Freeman, Kriakidou, Maridaki-Kassotaki, & Berridge, 1996). So has experience with peers (e.g., Astington & Jenkins, 1995). As with siblings, there is some evidence that interaction with older peers is especially beneficial (Lewis et al.).

Parents can also contribute to their children's theory-of-mind development. One line of study, initiated by Elizabeth Meins (e.g., Meins & Fernyhough, 1999; Meins et al., 2003), examines parents' *mind-mindedness*, that is, "the proclivity to treat one's infant as an individual with a mind, rather than merely an entity with needs that must be supplied" (Meins et al., p. 1194). Operationally, mind-mindedness is determined primarily (although not only) by how mothers talk to or about their children. Do they comment on the infant's mental states when interacting with the baby, or do they use a high proportion of mental state terms when describing their child to someone else? Relatively high maternal mind-mindedness in infancy and early childhood predicts relatively good theory-of-mind performance at age 4 or 5. Interestingly, measures of mind-mindedness also relate positively to security of attachment in infancy.

A second line of research focuses not simply on mothers' tendency to think of the child in mentalistic terms but specifically on their use of mental state terms when talking with the child. A common procedure is to have the mother and child look together at a wordless picture book, a task that provides mothers with frequent opportunities to make comments about the mental states of the characters. There turn out to be marked individual differences among mothers in how often they offer such comments, and these differences in turn relate to various aspects of theory of mind in their children (Doan & Wang, 2010; Peterson & Slaughter, 2003; Ruffman, Slade, & Crowe, 2002). Most such research has focused on mothers, but a recent study by Wellman and colleagues demonstrates effects of mental state talk for fathers as well (although, interestingly, somewhat different effects from those reported for mothers; Wellman, Olson, Lagattuta, & Liu, 2008).

More general aspects of parenting also show relations to theory of mind. The parent's general style of discipline and control can be important. Perhaps the clearest finding here is one that echoes the child rearing literature in general: Controlling the child primarily through threats and punishments (the so-called power-assertive approach to child rearing) does not work out very well, as such techniques are associated with relatively poor theory-of-mind development. Conversely, providing the child with reasons for behavior, especially reasons that stress the consequences for others, appears to nurture theory-of-mind skills (Pears & Moses, 2003; Ruffman, Perner, & Parkin, 1999).

My emphasis so far has been on various kinds of social experience that contribute to theory-of-mind development. Another approach to the antecedents question attempts to identify prerequisite abilities—that is, skills that must be in place for theory-of-mind understanding to emerge or to be expressed. Two presumed prerequisites have received special attention.

One is language. A large research literature is quite consistent in demonstrating positive relations between language and theory of mind: On average, children who are more advanced in language are also more advanced in theory of mind (Milligan, Astington, & Dack, 2007). In most instances the relation remains significant when other factors, most obviously chronological age, are controlled for statistically. No single aspect of language has emerged as critical in research to date; rather, a variety of measures have proved predictive, including vocabulary, aspects of syntactic development, and indices of overall language ability.

The second presumed prerequisite is executive function. Executive function is an umbrella term for general problem-solving resources (e.g., inhibition, planning, working memory) that contribute to performance in a variety of cognitive domains. Among the cognitive domains for which executive function has been shown to be predictive is theory of mind, especially performance on false belief tasks: Children who are relatively advanced in executive function tend to do better on false belief. The ability to inhibit a dominant response appears to be especially important in this regard (Moses, 2005; Moses, Carlson, & Sabbagh, 2005).

The preceding summary of links between theory of mind and both language and executive function leaves two issues unresolved. One is the causal direction for the relations. I have discussed both language and executive function as contributors to theory of mind. This is the usually assumed causal direction and one for which there is a good deal of empirical support. But it is also possible that the causality flows in the other direction: that theory of mind affects both language and executive function. Josef Perner, in particular, has argued for the causal priority of theory of mind in the theory of mind-executive function relation (e.g., Perner, 1998). There is no reason, of course, that both causal directions could not apply; the developments in question are extended, multipart ones, and each may feed into the other over time. On my reading of the literature this in fact is what occurs. The evidence to date, however, is probably stronger for theory of mind as outcome rather than cause.

The second issue concerns the way language or executive function affects theory of mind. This *is* an issue because there are two possibilities: Developments in these domains may affect the emergence of theory-of-mind abilities, or such developments may affect the expression of such abilities on the standard measures. Again, the two possibilities are not mutually exclusive, and the evidence suggests that both probably occur. The reviews cited earlier, however (Milligan et al., 2007; Moses, 2005; Moses et al., 2005), argue primarily for an emergence role for both language and executive function.

The role of language and executive function is an issue in the second-order literature as well. We will therefore return to these constructs in Chapter 3.

All of the kinds of evidence discussed in this section are correlational, in the sense that they examine naturally occurring variations among children (e.g., in social experience or in language ability) as possible contributors to theory of mind. As any student of psychology knows, correlations cannot establish cause-and-effect relations with certainty; for this we need experimental manipulation. The relevant manipulation in this case would be a training study: provision of some presumably beneficial experience in an attempt to instill some theory-of-mind ability such as false belief. Studies of this sort are just beginning to appear in the theory-of-mind literature (e.g., Hale & Tager-Flusberg, 2003; Lohmann & Tomasello, 2003), and it is too early to draw any general conclusions about training. If the earlier Piagetian literature is any guide, we can expect many more such studies in the years to come.

Consequences of Theory of Mind

I turn now to consequences. In a sense, much of the rest of this book has to do with the further developments that become possible once first-order theory of mind has been mastered. In this section I focus on contemporary consequences—that is, various developments outside the domain of theory of mind for which theory-of-mind abilities appear to be a prerequisite.

Astington (2003) is a good source on this issue. She identifies at least a dozen distinct aspects of children's social development that have been shown to relate to theory of mind. Again, in most instances the relations remain significant when other factors (age, language, executive function) are controlled for. Her summary provides a good overview of the particular relations that have been found, and I therefore quote from it here:

> There is clear evidence that false-belief understanding is related to some aspects of social functioning … communicative abilities, as seen in more connected and more informative conversation; imaginative abilities, as seen in more frequent and more sophisticated pretend play …; ability to resolve conflicts and to maintain harmony and intimacy in friendships; teacher ratings of global social competence …; contentedness in school; and peer-related empathy and popularity. (p. 32, reprinted with permission from Psychology Press)

As can be seen, children who are relatively advanced in theory of mind tend to be advanced in social interaction as well. Importantly, the outcomes that have been linked to theory of mind include not only specific social skills (e.g., ability to resolve conflicts) but also overall measures of social competence and social success.

It is worth noting, however, that not all the consequences of advances in theory of mind are positive ones. Children may use their theory-of-mind skills for bad as well as for good purposes, to tease, deceive, or manipulate others (see, e.g., Polak & Harris, 1999). In addition, theory-of-mind advances may sometimes bring new challenges and new difficulties in their wake. There is evidence, for example, that children with relatively good theory-of-mind understanding are more sensitive to criticism than are children in general (Cutting & Dunn, 2002). We will reencounter these conclusions about the mixed-blessing nature of theory of mind in the discussion of the second-order literature.

Astington's (2003) review makes several further, cautionary points. First, not all studies that have looked for expected consequences of theory of mind have been successful in finding them. I will add as well that her review, like most reviews, is limited to the published literature; there is no way to know how many unsuccessful attempts reside in file drawers somewhere.

A second point is that children sometimes show early and simple forms of social behaviors prior to the emergence of the presumed theory-of-mind prerequisite for the behaviors. Such is the case, for example, with early forms of deception, which may be evident well before success on the typical measures of false belief (e.g., Newton, Reddy, & Bull, 2000). More generally, the impressive skills that toddlers or preschoolers demonstrate in their everyday social interactions often seem out of line with their poor performance on laboratory measures of social understanding. As Judy Dunn (1991, p. 98) writes, "If preschool children are so limited in their ability to understand others, how do they manage to function effectively in the complex world of the family?" One possible answer, of course, is that children possess skills that do not come through on laboratory measures—a possibility for which, as we have seen, there is a good deal of empirical support.

A final point concerns the strength of the relations that have been demonstrated. Although theory-of-mind abilities have been shown to contribute to a wide range of different outcomes, the relations are almost always modest, leaving large proportions of the variance to be accounted for by other factors. Thus theory of mind is at best *one* contributor to outcomes that are multiply determined. This point is captured in the title of the Astington review (2003): "sometimes necessary, never sufficient." This, as we will see, is a conclusion that applies to the second-order literature as well.

CONCLUSIONS

Let me conclude the chapter by addressing a question that I will return to in Chapter 8. The question is: What is new in all this theory-of-mind work? As we have seen, theory of mind as a distinct topic dates back only to the mid-1980s. But researchers in psychology, including child psychology, certainly studied beliefs about the mental world long before this time. The most obvious predecessor of the contemporary research is Piaget's work, especially some of the first Piaget studies from the 1920s (Piaget, 1926, 1929). Indeed, the Piagetian notion of egocentrism, or difficulty in separating one's own perspective from those of others, would these days fall squarely under the heading of theory of mind. So too would many of the questions that Piaget explored in his early work, such as "What does it mean to think?", "What do you think with?", and "Where do dreams come from?"

Piagetian research is hardly the only source for related lines of study. Anyone who has ever taken a course in social psychology is familiar with a number of topics that have to do in some way with beliefs about people, both others and oneself: metacognition, social cognition, person perception, attribution. All of these topics, moreover, have been fruitful areas of study at the childhood as well as adult level.

So theory of mind is hardly totally new. The answer to the what *is* new question is, I would say, three things. One is the focus on young children—initially preschoolers, and in more recent research infants and toddlers. Piaget did study preschoolers, of course, but mainly to demonstrate the things they could not yet do. This, in fact, is one of the long-standing criticisms of the Piagetian enterprise: the negative picture of the preschool period (hence the "pre" in preoperational). Most research under the other headings listed in this chapter (e.g., metacognition) has seldom dipped below age 5, and when it has done so it has been mainly to document some lack-of-understanding starting point. In contrast, research under the heading of theory of mind identifies numerous important cognitive achievements that emerge during the first 5 years of life. These achievements, to be sure, are not instantaneous; one of the exciting things about theory-of-mind research is its ability to surprise us, just as Piaget's studies did, with what children do *not* yet understand. Still, in this case many basic forms of understanding do emerge very early.

The second distinctive aspect of theory-of-mind research is the creation of new experimental tasks to probe children's thinking about the mind. The field was certainly ready for some new tasks after two decades filled with thousands of studies of conservation and other Piagetian phenomena. The false belief task is the best known and most often used of these measures, but it is hardly the only one—I described a number of other commonly used tasks earlier in the chapter, and the list easily could have been made longer. And along with these new tasks, of course, have come new findings—all sorts of interesting things that we did not know about children's thinking prior to the advent of theory-of-mind research.

The third new aspect of theory of mind is the theories that direct research. In the 1980s, prior to the emergence of theory of mind, three broad theoretical positions directed most of the research in cognitive development: Piaget, information processing, and the Vygotsky sociocultural approach. These general positions continue to have some influence on contemporary work on theory of mind. As many commentators have noted, the topic itself probably would not exist had not Piaget come first—Piaget changed the way we think about and study children, and his legacy is clearly apparent in both the methods and the findings from research on theory of mind. The continued influence of the information-processing approach is evident in the emphasis on executive function as a contributor to theory of mind. Finally, Vygotskian ideas have always had some role in theorizing about theory of mind, and they have grown more prominent in recent years as it has become increasingly clear that social experience plays an important role in the development of theory-of-mind abilities (Carpendale & Lewis, 2004; Fernyhough, 2008; Hutto, 2008; Nelson, 2007).

Nevertheless, the major theories that frame most current research are not the old-line ones but new positions developed specifically for the topic of theory of mind. Three positions are predominant: simulation theory, modularity, and the theory theory approach.

Of the three positions, simulation theory is in a sense the oldest, because it has roots in philosophy that date back many centuries. The basic idea in the simulation approach is that we have privileged access to our own mental contents—thus our own immediate thoughts, feelings, percepts, and so forth. Our ability to make sense of others then depends on our ability to place ourselves, via an imaginative simulation process, in their position. For example, we may predict how someone else will respond to an emotion-arousing stimulus by imagining how we ourselves would respond. The difficulty of carrying out such simulations varies across different mental states and with how many "default settings" must be adjusted, which is why some developments (e.g., reasoning about beliefs) are slower to develop than others (reasoning about desires). Paul Harris is the psychologist who has developed this position most fully (Harris, 1991, 1992).

The modularity approach does not deny some role for simulation. Its emphasis, however, is on the biological bases for theory of mind. Any approach, of course, acknowledges that there must be some biological underpinning—specifically, a human brain—for development of any sort to occur. The modularity approach, however, makes a much stronger claim. In this view theory-of-mind reasoning is made possible by an innately specified portion of the brain dedicated solely to the task of theory of mind (and thus "encapsulated," that is, separate from other brain regions and cognitive functions). Developmental change then results primarily from biological maturation that brings more advanced modules online, although certain environmental "triggers" may also be necessary for change to occur.

Somewhat different versions of modularity theory have been proposed. Probably the most influential models are those developed by Alan Leslie (e.g., Leslie, 1994; Scholl & Leslie, 1999) and Simon Baron-Cohen (e.g., 1994, 1995).

My goal in this section is simply to sketch out the basic elements of the leading theories of theory of mind, not to review evidence relevant to the theories. I will note, however, that the work on autism has long provided what is probably the most compelling evidence in support of the modularity approach. Two claims are central to theorizing about modularity: that theory of mind has a strong biological basis and that theory of mind is largely independent of other cognitive abilities. Both claims find support in the study of autism.

The third position is labeled the theory theory approach. This is not—to quote a book review by James Russell (1992, p. 485)—because the theory was "so good they named it twice." Rather, the label denotes the central tenet of the position: that children's knowledge about the mind takes the form of an informal theory. Children's theories, to be sure, do not share all the features of scientific theories; they are not embodied in formal language, and they do not undergo testing by a larger scientific community. But they do have some theory-like qualities. They have a specific domain to which they are directed, and they identify specific entities within that domain—in this case, the mental world and various mental entities. They specify cause-and-effect relations among the entities with which they are concerned, and they are used for explanatory purposes—in this case, to make sense of people's behavior. And they change as experience provides evidence that an existing theory is not satisfactory. In this view, then, developmental change is theory change: the replacement of early theories by later, more satisfactory theories.

As with modularity, different theorists have developed somewhat different versions of the theory approach. Probably the most fully developed and influential are those by Josef Perner (e.g., Perner, 1991, 1995) and Henry Wellman and Alison Gopnik (e.g., Gopnik & Wellman, 1992; Wellman, 1990). An article by Karen

Bartsch (2002) provides both a helpful overview of the theory theory position and a review of relevant evidence.

As this discussion of theories suggests, the term *theory of mind* has two different meanings in the literature. One is as a substantive claim about the nature of development: that what children develop *is* a theory of mind. In this sense the term is limited to those who, like Perner and Wellman and Gopnik, subscribe to the theory theory point of view. The second sense in which the term is used is simply as a generally accepted, theoretically neutral label for the content area under study. This is the sense in which it appears in textbooks and other secondary sources, and this is the sense in which I use it in this book. I will add, however, that not everyone is comfortable with a label that seems, despite its professed neutrality, to endorse a particular theoretical orientation; thus, in some writings other general labels (e.g., *mind reading, commonsense psychology*) replace theory of mind.

The influence of both the theory theory approach and the modularity approach is not confined to the topic of theory of mind. Both have been applied to other aspects of children's cognitive development. Advocates of the theory theory approach talk about an early intuitive theory of physics (which encompasses the work by Baillargeon (e.g., 1994) and Spelke (e.g., Spelke & Kinzler, 2007) discussed earlier) and an intuitive theory of biology (Gopnik & Wellman, 1994). Modular accounts of the domains of perception and language have long existed.

The preceding is obviously a very brief overview of theories. Fuller treatments, of course, are available in the books cited in Chapter 1 (Doherty, 2009 is an especially good source) and in a number of other sources as well (e.g., Carruthers & Smith, 1996). I will return to theories at several later points in the book. Often, however, the return will be brief, and the discussion will consist more of needed future directions than of complete and testable theoretical claims. As we will see, research on advanced forms of theory of mind has often been a rather nontheoretical enterprise, largely empirical in orientation and with only limited attempts to integrate later developments with the theoretical positions developed to explain first-order achievements.

I conclude this chapter with an acknowledgment and a related source. The acknowledgment is that not everyone who studies children's social and mental understanding subscribes to the theory-of-mind approach to these issues that I present throughout the book (and here I am using theory of mind not in the theory theory sense but in a generic sense that encompasses all the work discussed). A book titled *Against Theory of Mind* (Leudar & Costall, 2009) presents an extended critique of the assumptions, methods, and conclusions of work carried out under the theory-of-mind heading. Obviously, I would not be writing an entire book on this work if I found these criticisms decisive. Still, the critique deserves attention from any serious student of theory of mind (see also Leudar, Costall, & Francis, 2004).

3

Second-Order False Belief

This chapter is devoted to the most popular task in the second-order literature: the second-order false belief task. Several dozen studies of second-order belief have appeared across the last 20 or so years; thus, we know a fair amount about both its development and its relation to other developments. At the same time, we will see that a number of the most informative lines of research at the first-order level (e.g., revised methods of assessment, formative experiences, relations to language, and executive function) have just begun to appear in the second-order literature. The result is that there is still much to be learned.

PRECURSORS

I noted in Chapter 1 that the second-order false belief task dates from a 1985 publication by Perner and Wimmer. Theirs, however, was not the first attempt to measure children's ability to think about thinking about thinking. Indeed, their report begins by reviewing, and critiquing, previous approaches to the issue.

These approaches had taken several forms. Some investigators had searched for signs of recursive thought in the ways children talk about interpersonal relations, either when asked to describe their friends (e.g., Barenboim, 1978) or in response to hypothetical social dilemmas (e.g., Selman, 1980). Do children realize, for example, that a child may be concerned about what a friend thinks about her ideas or that the success of a collaborative effort may depend on the extent to which each child is aware of what others think about his or her thinking?

Other researchers had devised competitive games in which success depended on taking into account what an opponent was thinking, including the opponent's thoughts about one's own thoughts. In one study, for example, children played a game involving two cups, one with a nickel inside and one with two nickels. The children were told that someone would soon enter the room and select one of the two cups and that he would get to keep whatever money he found (as Flavell, 1985, notes, two nickels were still worth something at the time the study was carried out). Their job was to attempt to fool the person by taking the money out of whichever cup they thought he would pick (Flavell, Botkin, Fry, Wright, & Jarvis, 1968).

ONE-LOOP RECURSION (Item no. 14)   **TWO-LOOP RECURSION (Item no. 15)**

Figure 3.1 The thoughts-bubbles approach to the study of recursive thinking. (From Miller, P. H., Kessel, F., & Flavell, J. H., *Child Development, 41*, 1970, p. 616. Copyright 1970 by John Wiley & Sons. Reprinted with permission.)

Various strategies of various levels of complexity are possible in such a situation. Perhaps he'll think that I'll take the two nickels so I should take the cup with one. But he may think that I'll think that, so maybe I should take the cup with two. But then he may think that I'll think that he'll think that, so I should....

Finally, Miller, Kessel, and Flavell (1970) devised a thought-bubbles procedure in which, similar to a comic strip, a character's thoughts were depicted in a bubble above his or her head and the child's task was to indicate what the character was thinking. Bubbles within bubbles then served to convey recursive thinking about thinking trains of thought. Figure 3.1 shows two examples. In the first the boy is thinking that he is thinking of himself. In the second the boy is thinking that the girl is thinking of the father thinking of the mother. I will note that with one exception (Eliot, Lovell, Dayton, & McGrady, 1979) the thought-bubbles method has not recurred in the second-order literature since this initial use; it has, however, been profitably applied to the study of first-order beliefs (e.g., Custer, 1996; Wellman, Hollander, & Schult, 1996).

A general conclusion from each of the paradigms just described was that recursive, thinking about thinking forms of reasoning were late to develop, typically not appearing until the late grade-school or early adolescent years. A study by Shultz and Cloghesy (1981) was a partial exception to this conclusion; they reported some success at their competitive game task among 5-year-olds, although not as much success as by age 7 or 9.

THE SECOND-ORDER TASK

Perner and Wimmer's (1985) approach differed in two ways from these predecessors, both of which reflected its grounding in the study of first-order false

TABLE 3.1 One of the Perner and Wimmer (1985) Scenarios Used to Assess Children's Understanding of Second-Order False Belief

This is a story about John and Mary who live in this village. This morning John and Mary are together in the park. In the park there is also an ice cream man in his van.

Mary would like to buy an ice cream but she has left her money at home. So she is very sad. "Don't be sad," says the ice cream man, "you can fetch your money and buy some ice cream later. I'll be here in the park all afternoon." "Oh good," says Mary, "I'll be back in the afternoon to buy some ice cream. I'll make sure I won't forget my money then."

So Mary goes home…. She lives in this house. She goes inside the house. Now John is on his own in the park. To his surprise he sees the ice cream man leaving the park in his van. "Where are you going?" asks John. The ice cream man says, "I'm going to drive my van to the church. There is no one in the park to buy ice cream; so perhaps I can sell some outside the church."

The ice cream man drives over to the church. On his way he passes Mary's house. Mary is looking out of the window and spots the van. "Where are you going?" she asks. "I'm going to the church. I'll be able to sell more ice cream there," answers the man. "It's a good thing I saw you," says Mary. Now John doesn't know that Mary talked to the ice cream man. He doesn't know that!

Now John has to go home. After lunch he is doing his homework. He can't do one of the tasks. So he goes over to Mary's house to ask for help. Mary's mother answers the door. "Is Mary in?" asks John. "Oh," says Mary's mother. "She's just left. She said she was going to get an ice cream."

Test question: So John runs to look for Mary. Where does he think she has gone?

Justification question: Why does he think she has gone to the ____?

Source: Perner, J., & Wimmer, H., *Journal of Experimental Child Psychology, 39,* 1985, p. 441. Copyright 1985 by Elsevier. Reprinted with permission.

belief. One was the focus not simply on second-order reasoning but specifically on second-order false belief, a concept touched on but not clearly examined in the earlier studies. The second change was methodological: the use of a story paradigm similar to those in first-order false belief tasks, in contrast to the varied procedures through which previous investigators had attempted to infer recursive thought.

The theoretical rationale for Perner and Wimmer's (1985) research was also grounded in arguments from the first-order literature (see also Perner, 1988). Just as first-order false belief was argued to mark an important conceptual advance in children's understanding of belief, so too was the capacity for second-order thought argued to be a major cognitive advance over the earlier system, an advance not only with regard to understanding of false belief but also with regard to recursive mentalistic reasoning more generally. Similarly, just as a first-order understanding of belief was seen as opening the way for new forms of social understanding and social behavior, so too was second-order reasoning argued to be a prerequisite for more complex forms of social behavior, forms of behavior not seen in early childhood. We will return, of course, to both of these claims.

The participants for Perner and Wimmer's (1985) research were 5- to 10-year-old children. Their report included six studies, each based on variants of two assessment scenarios. Table 3.1 presents one of the versions of the better known of these scenarios: the ice cream truck story. The other scenario was similar in structure but involved a playground that was moved by workers from one location to another.

Perner and Wimmer (1985) reported some variation in success across the six studies. In particular, helpful prompts during the scenarios led to some improvement in performance. The youngest children, however, showed little success under any of the procedural variants. Under the optimal conditions, some 6-year-olds and most 7- to 9-year-olds were successful at attributing second-order false beliefs. The studies thus suggested that second-order reasoning is indeed a later developmental achievement than the first-order reasoning tapped in the classic false belief task. But they also suggested an earlier emergence of such reasoning than had been indicated by the earlier studies of recursive thought.

As we will see, subsequent research has indicated that success on the second-order task probably emerges somewhat earlier than Perner and Wimmer (1985) reported. Nevertheless, their basic conclusion remains valid: Mastery of second-order false belief is a post-preschool development, a development that requires abilities beyond those sufficient for first-order success.

In what ways is second-order reasoning more advanced than first-order? I address the issue briefly now and then return to it after a review of the relevant evidence.

First-order theory of mind deals with children's ability to think about mental states in both themselves and others—thus to think about somebody thinking something, or feeling something, or wanting something, or whatever the relevant mental state may be. In symbolic terms, the task for the child confronted with a first-order problem is to judge the psychological relation between some person A and some event in the world X: A thinks X, A wants X, A intends X, and so forth. Doing so requires at least two basic realizations. One is that the mental world and the physical world are distinct and do not always correspond. They may diverge intentionally, as is the case with pretense, or they may diverge unintentionally, as is the case with false belief. Thus, A may think X when Y is actually the case. The second realization is that these two worlds, though distinct, are connected. Generally when we think X, X is in fact the case—that is why we have the belief that we do. Thus, what is in the world affects what is in the mind—what we think, perceive, desire, or whatever. And what is in the mind affects how we act upon the world; in particular, it is our beliefs that determine our actions.

Second-order reasoning goes beyond first-order reasoning in several, related ways. First, there is now another agent in the reasoning chain, a B as well as an A. There is also now another mental state, that of B, and it is B's mental state that serves as the target for A's belief. Thus A thinks that B thinks (or wants, intends, or whatever) X. In addition simply to the increase in complexity introduced by a second agent, there is a basic change in the nature of the belief to be judged. The child must now realize that beliefs can have other beliefs and not just events in the world as their target and that such beliefs about beliefs, like beliefs about the world, can sometimes be false. Finally, because of their propositional nature, beliefs can enter into recursive chains of potentially any length—thus, A thinks that B thinks that C thinks…. The ability to embed one proposition within another introduces a major expansion in the complexity and scope of the child's cognitive efforts.

These differences in content between first order and second order are paralleled by differences in methodology. Thus the scenarios through which the second-order task is conveyed are necessarily longer than in the first-order case, they contain more informational units, they put more demand on working memory, and they conclude with a more complexly worded test question.

In short, second-order tasks are more complex, both conceptually and procedurally, than are first-order tasks. On this point everyone agrees. The disagreement is whether complexity is the sole difference between the tasks or whether mastery of second-order belief entails a qualitative change in the underlying thought system—entails what is referred to in the first-order literature as a *conceptual change*. I will not be offering a definitive answer to this question, because work to date does not support a definitive answer. But we can consider the arguments on both sides after reviewing the relevant evidence.

DEVELOPMENTAL FINDINGS

In this section I present the basic descriptive picture for the development of second-order false belief. At what age does success on second-order tasks begin to emerge, and what factors influence children's performance? Results are considered under four headings: method of assessment, criteria for success, within-child comparisons of first-order and second-order, and content area for the final mental state in the A–B chain. (I will note that many of the conclusions reached here are developed at greater length, and with more thorough documentation, in Miller, 2009.)

Method of Assessment

All subsequent studies of second-order false belief have adopted the vignettes approach introduced by Perner and Wimmer (1985), and many have used the Perner and Wimmer vignettes or slight variations thereof. The other most often used set of vignettes was introduced by Sullivan, Zaitchik, and Tager-Flusberg (1994). Table 3.2 presents one of the Sullivan et al. stories. As a comparison of Table 3.1 and Table 3.2 suggests, the goal of the Sullivan et al. study was to offer a simpler, more child-friendly assessment than that provided by Perner and Wimmer. Thus, their vignettes are shorter, they have fewer characters and fewer scenes, and they contain frequent reminders and probe questions. They also include deception, an element that has been shown to have a facilitative effect when included in assessments of first-order false belief (Wellman et al., 2001).

The new approach did in fact prove easier. Perner and Wimmer (1985) reported little success before age 6 and less than perfect performance even by age 7 or 8. Sullivan et al. (1994) found some success even among 4-year-olds and close to perfect performance at age 5.

Research since Sullivan et al. (1994) confirms the greater ease of their procedure while at the same time suggesting some adjustment in details. In general, later studies using the Perner and Wimmer (1985) approach or modifications thereof have reported slightly better performance than that in the original research, and later studies using the Sullivan et al. approach or modifications thereof have reported slightly worse performance than that in the original research. (Interestingly, no study has obtained performance quite as good as that in Sullivan et al.) The gap between the two is approximately 1 year, with the Sullivan et al. approach suggesting mastery for most children by about age 5 or so and the Perner and Wimmer approach suggesting mastery a year or so later.

TABLE 3.2 One of the Sullivan, Zaitchik, and Tager-Flusberg (1994) Scenarios Used to Assess Children's Understanding of Second-Order False Belief

Scenario	Question
Tonight it's Peter's birthday, and Mom is surprising him with a puppy. She has hidden the puppy in the basement. Peter says, "Mom, I really hope you get me a puppy for my birthday." Remember, Mom wants to surprise Peter with a puppy. So, instead of telling Peter she got him a puppy, Mom says, "Sorry Peter, I did not get you a puppy for your birthday. I got you a really great toy instead."	*Probe question 1.* "Did Mom really get Peter a toy for his birthday?" *Probe question 2.* "Did Mom tell Peter she got him a toy for his birthday? *Probe question 3.* "Why did Mom tell Peter that she got him a toy for his birthday?"
Now, Peter says to Mom, "I'm going outside to play." On his way outside, Peter goes down to the basement to fetch his roller skates. In the basement, Peter finds the birthday puppy! Peter says to himself, "Wow, Mom didn't get me a toy; she really got me a puppy for my birthday." Mom does *not* see Peter go down to the basement and find the birthday puppy.	*Nonlinguistic control question.* "Does Peter know that his Mom got him a puppy for his birthday? *Linguistic control question.* "Does Mom know that Peter saw the birthday puppy in the basement?"
Now, the telephone rings, ding-a-ling! Peter's grandmother calls to find out what time the birthday party is. Grandma asks Mom on the phone, "Does Peter know what you really got him for his birthday?	*Second-order ignorance question.* "What does Mom say to Grandma?" *Memory aid.* Now remember, Mom does not know that Peter saw what she got him for his birthday.
Then, Grandma says to Mom, "What does Peter think you got him for his birthday?"	*Second-order false belief question.* What does Mom say to Grandma? *Justification question.* Why does Mom say that?

Source: Sullivan, K., Zaitchik, D., & Tager-Flusberg, H., *Developmental Psychology, 30,* 1994.

In a moment I will discuss possible reasons for the discrepancy. First, though, let me address what is perhaps a more basic question: When we have different methods of assessing some target, as we do in the case of second-order belief, how do we evaluate the methods and decide which is most appropriate to use?

Perhaps the most obvious criterion—and certainly the one that is most often invoked—is that the method elicits the child's optimal level of performance, what the child can do at his or her very best. If a method elicits optimal performance, then it is capable of revealing the first emergence of understanding with respect to the concept in question. First emergence is a basic question in the study of cognitive development, a question of both theoretical and pragmatic importance. When can children first demonstrate some cognitive capacity—object permanence, conservation, false belief, appearance/reality, or whatever? Because of its importance, first emergence has been the focus of scores of studies in both the first-order theory-of-mind literature and the Piagetian literature. I reviewed some of the attempts to identify the first inklings of first-order false belief in Chapter 2. If optimal performance is our criterion, then the choice of methods seems clear: The Sullivan et al. (1994) approach is preferable to that of Perner and Wimmer (1985).

TABLE 3.3   Differences Between the Perner and Wimmer (1985) and Sullivan et al. (1994) Assessment Procedures

Complexity	Deception	Question About Ignorance	Wording of Question
Greater in Perner & Wimmer	Sullivan et al.: yes	Sullivan et al.: yes	"think" in Sullivan et al.
	Perner & Wimmer: no	Perner & Wimmer: no	"look" in Perner & Wimmer

Why, once this point has been established, would any study *not* adopt the Sullivan et al. (1994) approach? The general answer to this question is that first emergence is not the only issue of interest in the study of cognitive development. Children's performance on maximally simplified assessment measures cannot tell us the range of situations in which they can apply their abilities, nor can it tell us what their *typical* level of responding is. It seems probable, for example, that most real-life instances of second-order reasoning do not, as in the Sullivan et al. scenarios, include three helpful reminders of the important information prior to the eventual judgment. This does not mean, of course, that the Perner and Wimmer (1985) scenarios are necessarily closer to real life. In general, however, a variety of assessment methods is preferable to a single method whatever the target for the assessment may be. If we use but a single method there is the danger that what we conclude may be at least in part specific to this method, a threat to validity labeled the *mono-operation bias* in discussions of experimental design (Shadish, Cook, & Campbell, 2002). In addition, the use of multiple methods provides more clues about the determinants of performance than could use of a single method alone, especially if, as is true in the second-order literature, performance varies across methods.

What, then, does a comparison of the Perner and Wimmer and the Sullivan et al. approaches suggest about the determinants of second-order performance? As Table 3.3 indicates, there are at least four potentially important differences between the two approaches.

The most obvious difference—and also the most certainly important one—is in complexity. The main goal of the Sullivan et al. (1994) study was to devise a simpler assessment procedure than that in Perner and Wimmer (1985). Thus, their scenarios are shorter than those in Perner and Wimmer, they contain less information, they put less demand on memory, and they provide helpful prompts and reminders at various points during the story.

Two kinds of evidence suggest that these differences do in fact make a difference. First, the division of assessment procedures is really more a continuum than a dichotomy, in that later researchers have modified both the Perner and Wimmer (1985) and the Sullivan et al. (1994) stories, generally in an attempt to make them simpler. The Sullivan et al. study included a simplified version of the ice cream truck story, and they reported better performance than had Perner and Wimmer. Other researchers (e.g., Coull, Leekam, & Bennett, 2006; Hayashi, 2007b) have added still further simplifications to the Sullivan et al. scenarios. As noted, neither these nor any other studies have produced better performance than that in Sullivan et al. Within-study comparisons, however, generally show that simplifications in procedure lead to improvements in performance.

The second kind of evidence for the role of complexity comes from relations to measures of executive function. We saw in Chapter 2 that executive function is a clear correlate of performance in the first-order domain. Measures of executive function also correlate with performance on second-order tasks.

Note the parallel between the two kinds of evidence for the role of complexity. Studies of the effects of task simplification show that performance improves when the information-processing demands of the task are reduced. Studies of executive function show that performance improves when the information-processing resources of the child are increased.

A second possible contributor to the difference in difficulty is the presence of deception in the Sullivan et al. (1994) scenarios. As I noted in Chapter 2, Wellman et al.'s (2001) meta-analysis concluded that deception is a facilitative factor in the study of first-order false belief. (I should add: not always and not strongly, although this remains a controversial issue—cf. Chandler, Fritz, & Hala, 1989; Sodian, Taylor, Harris, & Perner, 1991.) It is possible, then, that the mother's explicit attempt to deceive Peter helps children to recognize the possibility of a false belief in the second-order case. This was a suggestion that Sullivan et al. offered in their discussion. Note, though, that the deception–belief connection is less direct here than is the case with first-order false belief. In the first-order case it is the target for the belief attribution who is deceived, and thus it is plausible that children who have some grasp of deception would be helped to realize that this person holds a false belief. In the second-order case it is not the target for the belief attribution (e.g., the mother in the vignette in Table 3.2) who is deceived; rather, it is this person who attempts, initially successfully but ultimately unsuccessfully, to deceive the target for *her* belief. What may be more helpful here than the deception per se is the salience with which the mother's belief is presented to the child participant. The child, after all, hears the mother attempt to implant a particular belief in Peter; it may be relatively easy, then, to realize that this is the belief that she thinks he holds.

To date, there has been only one attempt to study the effects of deception on second-order reasoning free of the other differences that confound the comparison between the two main paradigms. It is some recent research of my own (Miller, 2011). In describing the study I will use the terminology introduced earlier. Thus, A refers to the protagonist whose belief must be judged (in the Sullivan et al., 1994, scenario this would be the mother) and B refers to the protagonist whose belief is the target for A's judgment (Peter in the Sullivan et al. scenario). My study presented three kinds of trials: a standard second-order trial with no deception; a second-order trial on which A deceived B (analogous to the Sullivan et al. procedure); and a second-order trial on which B deceived A (analogous to the deceptive manipulation in the first-order case). The results suggested that both kinds of deception were helpful, although only the A-deceives-B manipulation achieved significance in comparison to the standard trial. At present, the basis for these results (which, of course, will need to be replicated in future research) is not clear. It may be that deception produces its effects by somewhat different routes in the two cases: by the direct focus on the target's belief in the B-deceives-A case and by the focus on the belief that A intends to implant in the A-deceives B-case. Or it may simply be that a deceptive context of any sort is helpful because it sensitizes children to the possibility that a belief can be false.

A third possible contributor to the task differences is the inclusion of an additional question in the Sullivan et al. (1994) protocol. In their procedure the false belief question was preceded by a question directed to the knowledge or ignorance of the target for the belief (the "Does Peter know what you really got him for his birthday?" question). Several findings follow from the inclusion of such a question. First, the knowledge question turns out to be easier than the false belief question. Hogrefe et al. (1986) were the first to explore this issue, and they found approximately a 2-year gap between the two developments; other studies have typically reported a somewhat smaller discrepancy. This finding parallels a conclusion from the first-order literature, in which generally (although with occasional exceptions, e.g., Sullivan & Winner, 1991) children find it easier to judge ignorance in a target than to judge false belief (Wellman & Liu, 2004).

Why are attributions of ignorance easier than attributions of false belief? The generally accepted explanation was first put forth by Hogrefe et al. (1986). In the case of false belief the child must be able to entertain two incompatible representations about the same reality (e.g., John thinks that Mary thinks X, but the child knows that Mary thinks Y), whereas in the case of ignorance all that need be represented is John's lack of access to the critical information. In this view, false belief presents a more complex conceptual challenge than does knowledge/ignorance, and it is for this reason that the false belief question is more difficult (for an alternative explanation—one that so far has been applied only to the first-order literature—see Perner, 2000).

A further finding is that inclusion of the knowledge question is helpful: Performance on the second-order belief question is better when a question about knowledge or ignorance precedes the question about belief (Coull et al., 2006; Hogrefe et al., 1986). It is possible, then, that this procedural difference contributed to the difference between the Sullivan et al. (1994) and the Perner and Wimmer (1985) results. A further finding, however, is that the facilitative effect occurs for both the Sullivan et al. and the Perner and Wimmer paradigms, and the latter remains more difficult even when this aspect of the procedure is equated; thus, the inclusion of the knowledge question is not a complete explanation for the difference in difficulty.

Why is a question about knowledge or ignorance helpful? Presumably, reflecting on and verbalizing the fact that A does not know B's knowledge state reduces the probability of attributing a true belief to A, and the only alternative then is to attribute a false belief. Such an explicit focus on A's ignorance is not necessary (since children can succeed even when a knowledge question is not part of the procedure), nor is it sufficient (since many children pass the knowledge question and then fail the belief question). But it is helpful.

A final possible contributor to the task differences is the wording of the test question. Here the two dominant paradigms differ in two ways. One concerns the target for the belief question, or the A part of the A–B chain. Perner and Wimmer (1985) ask what does John "think"; Sullivan et al. (1994) ask what does Mom "say." The second difference concerns the target for A's belief, or the B part of the chain. Perner and Wimmer ask where Mary has "gone"; Sullivan et al. ask what does Peter "think."

Might these differences make a difference? Relevant data from the first-order literature suggest probably not. The contrast between "think" and "look" (a variant of "gone") appears often in this literature, albeit generally in across-study rather than within-study form. One conclusion from the Wellman et al. (2001) meta-analysis was that this variation has no effect on first-order performance.

The only systematic examination of the wording issue in the second-order literature reached a different conclusion. It comes in some research by Kamawar, Pelletier, and Astington (1998). Their focus was on the B part of the A–B chain, with a contrast between "A thinks that B will say…" and "A thinks that B will look…." The latter wording resulted in better performance—indeed, considerably better performance—than did the former. This difference had been predicted based on Russell's (1987) analysis of the explicitness with which different verbs express an underlying mental state. A communicative verb such as "say" falls between the extremes of "think" (maximally explicit) and "look" (purely physical, not mental). "Say" is more difficult than "look" because "to verbalize a belief, the child must hold an explicit representation of it.… No such demand is made for acting on a belief" (Kamawar et al., p. 1).

I will make two points about the Kamawar et al. (1998) analysis. First, their research is a nice example of the fact that sometimes what seems like a trivial procedural difference may turn out not to be trivial, and the resulting difference in response may tell us something interesting about children's thinking. Second, their findings do not provide an explanation for the greater ease of the Sullivan et al. (1994) procedure, given that the B part of the Sullivan et al. test question ("think") is more mentalistic than the B part of the Perner and Wimmer (1985) question ("look"). If anything, the results suggest that the Sullivan et al. approach is easier *despite* the specific wording that is used.

So why the difference in difficulty between the two paradigms? My own answer is that complexity undoubtedly contributes and deception probably does. We need more research on the latter possibility.

My focus to this point has been on studies that have used some variant of one or the other of the two dominant paradigms. As we saw in Chapter 2, research on first-order false belief quickly moved beyond the basic paradigms to explore a number of potentially facilitative factors (e.g., variations in wording, use of less demanding response measures, the presence of deception). For the most part these would-be facilitators remain unexplored in the second-order literature. Deception does appear in the Sullivan et al. (1994) approach and its variants, but not in a way that allows an isolation of its effects. As noted, the only attempt to do so (Miller, 2011) suggests that deception is also helpful at the second-order level; clearly, however, more research is needed.

The only other attempt to incorporate a procedural comparison from the first-order literature appears in the same set of studies (Miller, 2011). As I noted in Chapter 2, some studies of first-order false belief have found that children who are unable to succeed on the usual prediction measure are nevertheless able to explain a false belief when shown the relevant behavior. My study tested for a comparable effect at the second-order level. On half the trials the children responded to the standard test question about the protagonist's belief, whereas on the other half the false belief was provided and the children's task was to explain it. The study provided no evidence for an explanations benefit; indeed, the mean level of performance was higher on predictions than on explanations. As with deception, more research is needed to establish the generality of the conclusion (indeed, more research is needed at the first-order level, given the inconsistent results in research to date). Intuitively, however, it seems reasonable to expect that difficulties in translating incipient knowledge into explicit judgment might be greatest for young children. Thus, a simplification in response demands that makes a difference for 3-year-olds may no longer matter by age 5 or 6.

Several other modifications of the standard approach can be briefly mentioned. We saw that the study of false belief at the first-order level includes questions about false beliefs held by the self as well as those held by others. Homer and Astington (1995, 2001) developed a second-order version of a self question ("Did you think you knew what was inside the box before we opened it?"). Responses to the self and other questions were significantly related, and there was no difference in difficulty between the two. As part of a case study of a brain-damaged patient, Apperly and colleagues (Apperly, Samson, Carroll, Hussain, & Humphreys, 2006) devised a nonverbal version of the second-order task (not literally nonverbal in toto, but nonverbal in the presentation of stimuli and response required during the test phase). This procedure has yet to be used beyond their case-study application. Finally, Froese, Glenwright, and Eaton (2011) reported that an online version of the second-order task produced results comparable to those from the standard in-person, face-to-face version. As they note, this conclusion, if generally valid, could lead to an expansion in the range of populations that can feasibly be included in such research.

Criteria for Success

To this point I have been discussing findings from second-order false belief tasks without addressing a basic and logically prior question: What do we mean by success on these tasks?

This *is* a question because there are two possibilities. One possibility is to define success as correct judgments in response to the test question. Clearly, this has to be at least part of what we mean when we say the child has mastered the task. The question is whether a correct judgment is sufficient to infer mastery or whether the child must also provide an adequate explanation for the judgment.

The judgment-only versus judgment-plus-explanation issue was for many years a heated debate in the Piagetian literature. The debate was never really resolved, probably for the good reason that there is no clear right answer; rather, valid arguments exist on both sides. On one hand, a child—especially a young child—might well possess a basic understanding of a concept without being able to put the reasoning behind the understanding into words. Requiring the child to provide an explanation might therefore result in an underestimation of true competence.

On the other hand, children may sometimes come up with correct answers that do not reflect true understanding of a task, especially when the task presents essentially only two response alternatives (which is the case for both conservation and false belief). An adequate explanation along with the judgment serves to ensure that the understanding is genuine. The choice, then, is between avoiding false negatives as a result of too strict a criterion and avoiding false positives as a result of too lenient a criterion.

I have already noted a number of parallels between the theory-of-mind literature and the earlier Piagetian literature. The criterion issue is an exception, however. The judgment-only versus judgment-plus-explanation dispute has never entered the basic false belief literature. With only a handful of exceptions (e.g., Clements, Rustin, & McCallum, 2000; Ruffman, Slade, Rowlandson, Rumsey, & Garnham, 2003; Wimmer & Weichbold, 1994), the great majority of studies of first-order false belief have been judgment only.

The situation at the second-order level is in one respect similar and in one respect different. The similarity is that there has been little discussion, let alone debate, about the criterion issue. The difference is in the solution adopted. In contrast to the first-order literature, the great majority of studies of second-order false belief have elicited explanations along with the judgments. The reason for the difference between the two literatures is not clear. It may simply reflect historical precedent, in that both Perner and Wimmer (1985) and Sullivan et al. (1994) elicited explanations as part of their protocols. It may also reflect a belief that explanations are a more reasonable criterion with 5- to 8-year-olds than they are with 3- and 4-year-olds. In any case, the tendency of researchers to include explanations means that the second-order studies provide information that is for the most part not available in the first-order literature. Several findings emerge.

A first finding is that the majority of children who provide correct judgments on second-order tasks are also able to provide an adequate explanation for the judgments. The proportion who are able to do so varies some across studies, but it is always high and in some studies it reaches 100%.

A second finding is that the criterion adopted does not seem to affect the general conclusions that emerge from the second-order studies. The criterion does, of course, affect conclusions about level of performance: Performance is better, and mastery comes sooner, with a judgment-only criterion than with judgment-plus-explanation. For other issues, however (e.g., comparisons among tasks, relations to other developments), the same basic conclusions emerge whatever the criterion.

A third finding concerns the types of explanations that are offered. Perner and Wimmer (1985) distinguished three types of explanations: *belief–belief*, in which one epistemic state is nested within another (e.g., "he doesn't know that she knows"); *belief–information*, in which an information component is nested within a belief (e.g., "he doesn't know that she talked to the ice-cream man"); and *initial location*, in which the reference is to the initial location of the sought-after object (e.g., "because that's where she saw the ice cream truck"). Sullivan et al. (1994) added a fourth category of *deception* to cover instances in which children referred to the deceptive aspect of the story (e.g., "because Mom wanted to surprise Peter with the puppy"). Although the labels sometimes vary, all subsequent investigators have used some version of the same categories.

Whatever the specific labels and specific distinctions, adequate explanations for false belief judgments divide into two general categories: those that explicitly mention a mental state (Perner and Wimmer's, 1985, first two categories) and those that ground the judgment in aspects of the situation (the initial location and deception responses). Although either explanation provides a sufficient justification for the belief, mentalistic explanations are of special interest for two reasons. First, such explanations demonstrate unequivocally that the child is engaging in recursive reasoning about mental states. Second, they demonstrate as well that the child not only can employ recursive reasoning but also can reflect upon and verbalize such a train of thought.

The proportion of such explanations varies markedly across studies. In the original Perner and Wimmer (1985) studies some 80 to 90% of the adequate explanations were mentalistic; in other studies (Hayashi, 2007b; Parker, MacDonald, & Miller, 2007) the figure has been around 30%. At present, the reasons for this variation are not clear. Some of the variation probably reflects population differences, and some almost certainly reflects methodological differences—variations in how explanations are elicited and subsequently probed. Clearly, the failure to produce a mentalistic explanation does not mean that the child is incapable of doing so, especially given the availability of situational responses as a simple and sufficient alternative. Preschoolers sometimes (though typically not very often) provide mentalistic explanations for their first-order judgments (e.g., Clements et al., 2000). Indeed, in simple situations children as young as 3 can offer mentalistic explanations for behavior (Colonnesi, Koops, & Terwogt, 2008; Youngstrom & Goodman, 2001).

Within-Child Comparisons of First-Order and Second-Order

For the most part, conclusions about the relative difficulty of first-order false belief and second-order false belief have been based on across-study comparison of the two literatures: the large first-order literature that indicates mastery at about age 4 and the growing second-order literature that indicates mastery at about age 5 or 6. In this section I consider what is found when the same children respond to both first-order and second-order tasks.

In many such studies, unfortunately, what is found is limited by various procedural or analytical decisions. In some studies second-order problems are administered only if the child passes the first-order tasks, thus precluding a full test of the relative difficulty issue (e.g., Astington, Pelletier, & Homer, 2002; Hughes et al., 2000). In other studies first-order and second-order trials are combined into a single composite theory-of-mind score, without separate analyses of the two sorts of problem (e.g., Hughes et al., 2005; Pellicano, Murray, Durkin, & Maley, 2006).

A handful of studies do provide within-child comparisons of first-order and second-order performance (e.g., Hayashi, 2007b; Parker et al., 2007; Pellicano, 2007). Not surprisingly, these studies confirm the conclusions from the across-study, across-child comparisons. In all instances first-order judgments have proved to be easier than second-order judgments, in most instances substantially so. Across studies the success rate on first-order tasks is approximately 75% compared with approximately 50% on second-order.

In addition to mean levels of success, the within-child studies provide a kind of information that is not available in between-child comparisons: namely, information about individual patterns of performance. What we can ask, in particular, is whether first-order understanding and second-order understanding constitute an invariant developmental sequence: Do all children master first order before mastering second order? It could be argued, of course, that such an ordering is not an empirical question by a by-definition necessity, given that a first-order false belief (e.g., Mary thinks the ice cream truck is at the park) is embedded within the second-order question (e.g., What does John think Mary thinks?). Nevertheless, success on the second-order task does not guarantee that children will respond accurately when first-order understanding is explicitly elicited in the standard way. The evidence to date (which comes from three studies—Hayashi, 2007b; Lecce & Hughes, 2010; Parker et al., 2007) suggests that they will. Across the studies only a handful of children showed success on second-order in the absence of success on first-order, outcomes that are probably best attributed to measurement error.

I will add that Hayashi (2007b) provides an especially convincing demonstration of the first-order versus second-order difference. One goal of the study was to provide as close a match as possible between the first-order and second-order tasks. Table 3.4 shows the scenarios that were used. As can be seen, the scenarios were identical apart from an additional 19 words at one point in the second-order scenario, and the test questions differed by only four words (I base these counts

TABLE 3.4   Scenarios Used in the Hayashi (2007b) Study of First- and Second-Order False Belief

Episode	First-Order	Second-Order
1	These are a boy and a girl. The girl puts the chocolate into the refrigerator and then goes out of the room.	Same as first-order
2	While the girl is absent, the boy takes the chocolate out of the refrigerator. The boy eats a bit of it.	Same as first-order
3	Then, the boy puts it into the basket. The girl looks at the boy's action from outside the window, but the boy is not aware of this.	
4	The girl comes back into the room to eat the chocolate.	Same as first-order
Reality question	Where is the chocolate now?	Where will the girl look for the chocolate now?
Memory question	Where did the girl put the chocolate in the beginning?	Same as first-order
Test question	Where does the girl *think* the chocolate is?	Where does the boy *think* the girl will look for the chocolate?

Source: Hayashi, H., *Psychologia, 50*, 2007, p. 19. Copyright 2007 by the Psychologia Society. Reprinted with permission.

on an English translation of the original Japanese). Despite these similarities, children found first-order false belief much easier than second-order.

Content of the Belief

In all of the work considered so far the mental state for both A and B has been a belief—thus, A thinks that B thinks…. Beliefs are not the only mental states that can enter into recursive, second-order forms of thought. Other possibilities exist at both the A and B ends of the reasoning chain.

At the A end of the chain, second-order studies divide into two general categories. In some instances A's goal is to judge B's mental state, and the child's task is to indicate the judgment that A would form. This, of course, was the approach in all of the research considered to this point. In other instances A's goal is to manipulate B's mental state—that is, to instill a particular belief in B. The child's task is then to judge both the intent and the effect of A's manipulation. The distinction, thus, is between A *thinks* that B … and A *intends* that B…. Note that the examples with which I began the book fall in the second category. Iago does not merely attempt to judge Othello's belief; rather, his goal is to implant a particular belief in Othello. Similarly, the wolf does not simply hope that Red Riding Hood will happen to believe something that brings her within his grasp; rather, he works hard to create the necessary belief.

Studies of the intends-that sort speak to the functional side of second-order reasoning, that is, *why* one person might manipulate another person's belief. For this reason—and also because such studies constitute a fairly large literature—I defer their coverage to Chapter 6, "Consequences of Second-Ordering Reasoning."

What about the B end of the reasoning chain? Potentially, any psychological state might serve as a target for A's judgment about B. In fact, only two of the possibilities besides belief appear in the literature to date: judgments of intention and judgments of emotion.

Table 3.5 shows one of the scenarios used by Shiverick and Moore (2007) to test 5- to 10-year-old children's understanding of second-order intentions. Other scenarios were identical apart from alterations at certain critical points in the story. In some instances, for example, the little girl's intention was a positive one (as in the example in the table), and in some instances it was a negative one (to take the rabbit home). In some instances the teacher was aware of the prior intention (as in

TABLE 3.5   Example of a Scenario Used to Study Children's Understanding of Second-Order Intention

The teacher brought a pet rabbit to school. She told the children not to let the rabbit out of its cage. This little girl said that she was going to help care for the rabbit. The teacher heard what the girl said. She put the rabbit back in its cage and took the children to the playground. By accident, the latch on the cage was not closed, and the rabbit escaped from the cage. The same girl was the last person in the room. She saw the rabbit jump out, and she chased after it. The teacher came back in and saw her chasing the rabbit. The rabbit ran out the door and was gone.

Source: Shiverick, S. M., & Moore, C. F., *Journal of Experimental Child Psychology*, 97, 2007, p. 59. Copyright 2007 by Elsevier. Reprinted with permission.

the example), and in some instances she was not. The task for the children was to indicate both the belief that the teacher would form about the child's intention and the sociomoral evaluation ("how good or bad") she would offer for the child's behavior. With increasing age children showed an increasing realization that the teacher's belief would depend on her knowledge of the stated intention and not simply on the act itself. At all ages children showed the further realization that the teacher's sociomoral evaluation would depend on her belief about intention; impressively, many did so even when their own belief and evaluation differed from what they attributed to the teacher. The study thus demonstrated several accomplishments in second-order understanding that were in place by the early grade-school years: the ability to use informational access to make accurate attributions of one person's belief about another person's intention, the realization that such beliefs might differ across different perceivers, and the realization that such beliefs could be false.

Many of the same accomplishments were evident in some earlier research by Pillow and Weed (Pillow, 1991; Pillow & Weed, 1995). In these studies children heard scenarios in which one child observed an action by a second child and they were then asked to judge the first child's belief about the second child's intention—specifically, whether the child thought that the action was on purpose or accidental. In some instances the first child was presented as liking the second, and in some instances the relation was presented as one of disliking. The question was whether children would use the like–dislike information to guide their judgments about the first child's belief about the second child's intention. Preschoolers showed no ability to do so, and kindergarteners demonstrated only limited success. Second graders, however, were generally able to use the bias information in either direction, attributing a positive belief in the likes case (e.g., a belief that the action was accidental in the case of a negative behavior like knocking a toy to the floor) and a negative belief in the dislikes case. The studies thus demonstrated the same kinds of understanding shown by Shiverick and Moore's (2007) participants (beliefs about intention may vary across perceivers; beliefs about intention may be false) and added one other: the realization that beliefs about intention can be affected by prior experience with and beliefs about the target in question.

How does judging a false belief about an intention compare with judging a false belief about a belief? The studies just reviewed suggest that both developments emerge at about the same time. In neither set of studies, however, was an understanding of false belief explicitly elicited in a manner comparable to the usual second-order assessment, and in neither was a standard second-order belief-about belief task included for comparison. There is no reason to think that false beliefs about intentions would be any more difficult to judge than false beliefs about beliefs; this equivalence, however, remains to be demonstrated.

I turn now to the work on emotion. This work raises both a definitional question and a related theoretical question. If second-order reasoning is defined as one person's thoughts about another person's mental state, then beliefs about emotion would qualify as second order. If second-order reasoning is defined as recursive thinking about mental states, then the status of emotion is less clear. Recursive reasoning requires that the elements in the chain be in propositional form—a characteristic that typically is conveyed through a "that" clause in English. Beliefs and intentions clearly meet this criterion—thus, A thinks that B thinks that..., A intends that B thinks that..., A thinks that B intends that.... Note that the various terms that denote desire (*wants, hopes*) also can enter into propositional chains. Perner (1988) argued that the critical issue with respect to emotions is whether B is sad *that* something is the case or B is sad *because of* something: the former would be second order; the latter would not. Perner went on to acknowledge that it would be "extremely difficult" to test this distinction empirically, and indeed no one has attempted to devise a test.

What does research show? There is one relatively clear finding, along with a number of inconsistencies and uncertainties. The clear finding is that judging one person's beliefs about another person's emotions is not necessarily a second-order task. The clearest demonstration of this point comes in a study by Davis (2001). Her 3- and 4-year-old participants heard stories in which a story character was experiencing a particular emotion (e.g., felt sad) but attempted to hide the emotion by assuming a misleading facial expression (e.g., put on a happy face). The stories were accompanied by pictures that showed the facial display. The question was what a second character, not privy to the true emotion and thus dependent on the facial expression, would believe. Procedurally, therefore, the approach paralleled the unexpected contents task: a misleading exterior display that masked a very different underlying reality, with the child participant but not the target aware of the true nature of things. The results also proved similar to those of the unexpected contents task. Three-year-olds showed some success and 4-year-olds more success at judging the belief about emotion, and there was no overall difference in difficulty between the new task and a standard unexpected contents task.

The other studies with emotion as a target have reported less impressive performance. One method of study was developed initially by Landry and Lyons-Ruth (1980) prior to the advent of theory of mind as a distinct research area and later adopted by Jingxin, Jiliang, and Wenxin (2006). With this approach the emotion in question is a preexisting, dispositional one that is different from what most people would hold—for example, a fear of cats. The emotion is stated directly for the child; the question is then whether he or she realizes that someone without access to this knowledge (e.g., an uncle who has just delivered the gift of a cat) will have a false belief about the target's emotional response. In both studies it was only children from about age 6 on who showed such awareness. Although no standard first-order or second-order tasks were included for comparison, the relatively late age of mastery is more compatible with second-order timing. It is also compatible with the results from other studies that have required children to infer beliefs about emotion from story facts alone, without any accompanying physical cues (e.g., Gross & Harris, 1988). Again, however, the Davis (2001) study indicates that even preschoolers can handle such a task when helpful cues are provided.

Two studies by my colleagues and me provide the closest match between a second-order emotion task and the standard second-order belief task (Miller, 2011; Parker et al., 2007). In these studies children heard stories in which character B was initially either happy or sad but then received information that changed the emotion; character A, however, was unaware of the change in B's informational state. The question then was what A believed about B's emotion. Presumably, to answer this question the child must first infer A's belief about either B's belief (e.g., still thinks things are good) or B's knowledge (e.g., doesn't know about the bad news), then infer the emotion that follows (e.g., is still happy). Recall that in the first-order domain the additional infer-emotion step appears to add to the difficulty of the basic belief task. We did not find a comparable effect at the second-order level. In the Miller study the mean difference was in the same direction as with first-order tasks but fell short of significance; in the Parker et al. study the emotion task was actually easier than the standard belief task.

As promised, then, no clear or consistent picture emerges from the emotion studies to date. Davis (2001) demonstrated that inferring a false belief about an emotion is not inherently a second-order task. On the other hand, the other studies reviewed indicated that in many situations preschoolers are not at all good at judging beliefs about emotion; indeed, as we saw in Chapter 2, many preschoolers who pass the standard false belief task are unable to make comparable first-order judgments about emotions (e.g., realize that A is happy because he is not yet aware of some sadness-inducing event). Emotions, as mostly unobservable internal phenomena, may present special challenges to understanding. In most cases, however, the challenges probably do not involve the need for recursive thinking. Two exceptions may exist. One is the case in which inferring a second-order belief is a necessary step in inferring the emotion. The other is the situation postulated by Perner (1988) in which the emotion is understood as a propositional statement—thus not "sad because of…" but "sad that…." This distinction has yet to be operationalized.

ANTECEDENTS OF SECOND-ORDER UNDERSTANDING

In Chapter 2 I addressed two basic questions with respect to first-order understanding: What are the antecedents that lead to understanding, and what are the consequences that follow from understanding? The same two questions apply to second-order developments. In this section I consider the question of antecedents. The literature on consequences is considerably larger; indeed, most studies of second-order false belief have included at least one sort of putative consequence. That topic, consequently, will be the subject of a separate chapter.

Chapter 2 made a distinction between two kinds of antecedents: relevant experiences from which children acquire new knowledge and prerequisite skills that serve as building blocks for more advanced knowledge. I begin with the former.

Social Experience

There is not much work to consider. Presumably, the same sorts of social interactions that contribute to first-order developments remain important at the second-order level. As we will see in Chapter 6, correlational research has identified positive relations between second-order understanding and various aspects of children's social behavior. A correlational relation, however, does not specify causal direction, and the usual—and indeed generally plausible—assumption in this research has been that the direction is from second-order understanding to social behavior and not the reverse.

Some recent research of my own (Miller, 2011) provides a first attempt to look at one aspect of social experience: namely, possible effects of siblings on second-order development. Correlations between number of siblings and task performance were examined in two studies of second-order false belief. In neither study was there a hint of a relation. It is worth noting that the sibling effect at the first-order level is not a very robust one; although most studies have reported a relation, not all have (Cole & Mitchell, 2000; Cutting & Dunn, 1999; Peterson & Slaughter, 2003). In any case, the question of sibling effects at the second-order level is clearly another entry in the more-research-is-needed category.

Executive Function and Language

Earlier I noted that in many studies that include both first-order and second-order tasks only composite theory-of-mind scores are reported, with no separate analyses of the two sorts of task. Of course, this approach is taken for the good reason that an overall theory-of-mind score is all that is needed for the issues of interest in these studies. Still, it does frustrate the attempt to learn more about second-order reasoning per se.

Such is the case with respect to much of the research on executive function and language. Several studies have examined correlations between measures of executive function and composite theory-of-mind scores (Hughes, 1998; Jahromi & Stifter, 2008; McGlamery, Ball, Henley, & Besozzi, 2007; Pellicano, 2007, 2010). Other studies have done the same for measures of language (Lockl & Schneider, 2007; Pellicano, 2007). In both cases, such research verifies that the positive associations found in the first-order literature still remain when second-order measures are added to the theory-of-mind battery. But they provide no evidence about associations for second-order alone.

A few studies do provide such evidence. The evidence to date is clearer for language than for executive function. As with the first-order work, a variety of aspects of language have been shown to relate to performance. These include vocabulary (Filippova & Astingon, 2008; Hasselhorn, Mahler, & Grube, 2005), syntax (Hasselhorn et al.), and measures of overall linguistic competence (Astington et al., 2002; Astington, Pelletier, & Jenkins, 1998). Controlling for age or executive function does not change this conclusion. The Astington et al. (1998) study was longitudinal, and it provided further evidence in support of a causal role for language: Language at age 5 predicted false belief performance at age 6; early false belief, however, was not predictive of later language. The work on autism to be discussed shortly provides further evidence for the importance of language.

The fullest examination to date of executive function and second-order reasoning comes in a study by Perner and associates (Perner, Kain, & Barchfeld, 2002). The executive function measures were drawn from a general assessment battery labeled the NEPSY. The NEPSY assesses a variety of aspects of executive function, including inhibition, planning, self-regulation, and working memory. Most of the subtests in the battery correlated significantly and in some cases strongly with second-order false belief, and most of the correlations remained significant when age and IQ were partialled out.

Surprisingly, only three other studies with typically developing samples have provided evidence with respect to links between executive function and the second-order false belief task. Sodian and Hulsken (2005) found no relation between second-order false belief and performance on the Luria hand game (not an often used measure in this literature). Hasselhorn et al. (2005) reported relations between second-order false belief and working memory, relations that remained with age controlled but not when language was partialled out. Finally, Flynn (2010) reported a positive relation between the second-order belief task and a measure of planning and self-regulation.

As with language, studies of autism provide further evidence on the role of executive function. We will therefore return to executive function in the section on autism.

First-Order Performance

Earlier I discussed the handful of studies that have compared first-order and second-order performance in the same children. Three of these studies have done so longitudinally, testing children first during the preschool years and then testing them again either 1 year later (Hughes, 1998), 1 and a half years later (Astington, 2005), or both 1 and 2 years later (Lockl & Schneider, 2007). These studies allow us to address a question that cannot be answered with one-point-in-time data: Does relatively quick mastery of first-order abilities predict relatively quick mastery of second-order abilities? If the former serve as building blocks for the latter, we would expect a positive answer to this question.

The answer is in fact positive, although not very strongly so. In Hughes (1998) and Lockl and Schneider (2007) the correlations between first-order and second-order were in the .20s and .30s across the various ways of measuring the two developments; in the Hughes study, moreover, many of the correlations disappeared when age and verbal ability were controlled for statistically. Astington (2005) reported a stronger relation: a correlation of .57 between first- order and second-order. When general language ability and nonverbal IQ were controlled, first-order performance accounted for 8% of the variance in second-order success. There does, then, seem to be some relation; still, the fact that the relations are not stronger than they are is surprising. Relatively competent children, after all, tend to remain relatively competent. Even if there were no functional links between first-order competence and second-order competence we would expect some correlation between whatever we measure early and whatever we measure later. The issue of how and why first-order developments and second-order developments relate clearly deserves more study.

AUTISM

The literatures on autism and theory of mind have been closely linked for some 25 years now, ever since Baron-Cohen and colleagues (Baron-Cohen et al., 1985) carried out the first test of the theory-of-mind hypothesis of autism. As we saw in Chapter 2, this test yielded mixed results. In support of the hypothesis, Baron-Cohen et al.'s autism sample showed marked deficits in understanding of first-order false belief, falling well short of the performance shown by both typically developing and developmentally delayed controls. On the other hand, the deficits were not absolute, in that 20% of the sample did succeed on the first-order task. It appeared, then, that theory of mind might be delayed rather than absent in autism. Of course, whether delay rather than absence characterized the entire sample is not clear; it did, however, apparently characterize at least 20%.

Perner and Wimmer's (1985) invention of the second-order false belief task provided a natural further testing ground for the delayed versus absent issue. Even if first-order competencies are eventually attained, perhaps people with autism never develop second-order understanding. Baron-Cohen (1989) was again the first researcher to explore the possibility. As in his earlier study, he compared three groups: individuals with autism, individuals with Down syndrome, and typically developing children. In this case, however, all of the sample with autism had succeeded on a task of first-order false belief. The second-order task was a slightly modified version of the Perner and Wimmer ice cream truck story (in which, interestingly, the roles of John and Mary were reversed). A total of 9 of the 10 typically developing children and 6 of the 10 children with Down syndrome succeeded. In contrast, none of the 10 children with autism were able to pass the second-order task.

The average age of the autism sample in the Baron-Cohen (1989) study was 15.3 years and thus well beyond the typical age of mastery for second-order false belief. Still, the results do not rule out the possibility of delay; perhaps if we go still older, or simply sample more broadly, some individuals with autism would succeed. Several studies that followed soon after Baron-Cohen's demonstrated that this is in fact the case (Bowler, 1992; Ozonoff, Pennington, & Rogers, 1991; Ozonoff, Rogers, & Pennington, 1991). The age ranges in these studies extended from 8 to young adulthood, and the samples included diagnoses of both high-functioning autism and Asperger syndrome. Success was by no means universal; across studies only about half of the individuals with the autism diagnosis succeeded. Still, about half did succeed.

Second-order abilities, then, are not totally lacking in autism. The evidence, however (including further research since the early '90s), does suggest that they emerge considerably later than is true in typical development, that they are probably limited to the subset of the autism population that are labeled as high-functioning autism or Asperger syndrome, and that many individuals with autism never achieve second-order competence. It is worth noting as well—and this is a point that applies to the first-order literature also—that figures denoting the percentage of success on theory-of-mind tasks are limited to the segment of the autism population whose cognitive and linguistic abilities are sufficient to allow them to be tested. Thus, even if not designated as "high functioning," those who participate in research are toward the more positive end of the autism continuum.

What are the implications of the autism research for our understanding of theory of mind in general? Such studies provide two sorts of evidence with respect to the origins of theory-of-mind abilities. First, they indicate that theory of mind almost certainly has a substantial and at least somewhat domain-specific biological basis. The findings do not compel us to adopt a strong version of modularity theory, as indeed the continued viability of other theoretical positions demonstrates. Still, they do offer a challenge to which any theory must respond.

The autism studies also speak to the roles of language and executive function in theory of mind. Success on second-order tasks in autism samples is limited to individuals designated as high functioning autism or Asperger syndrome, and relatively good language ability is one criterion for both diagnoses. Within samples, moreover, consistent correlations are found between measures of language ability and performance on theory-of-mind tasks: the better the language, the better the performance (Happé, 1995a; Tager-Flusberg & Joseph, 2005).

The autism research also suggests an important role for executive function. There is, to begin with, a parallel between the two domains; just as deficits in theory of mind are pervasive in autism so too are deficits in executive function (Hill, 2004). In addition to this general convergence, the two domains are related at the individual level; performance on theory-of-mind tasks, including second-order tasks, correlates with measures of executive functioning in samples with autism (Harris et al., 2008; Ozonoff, Pennington, et al., 1991; Pellicano, 2007, 2010). As with typical samples, the ability to inhibit a dominant response and to shift bases for responding may be especially important.

Chapter 4 is devoted to the further higher-order reasoning tasks that researchers soon added to the second-order belief task. As we will see, many of the tasks were initially developed for the study of autism and as further tests of the delayed versus absent issue. We will consequently return to autism in the next chapter.

AGING

In some instances (although of course with many exceptions), aspects of cognitive functioning show impairments in old age. The two largest research literatures devoted to this issue are those directed to performance on IQ tests and those concerned with various forms of memory. In both cases many older people show no impairment at all. Some, however, do, and the problems are informative with respect to both the nature of aging and the nature of intelligence or memory.

Potentially, then, studies of aging could add to our knowledge of the nature and determinants of second-order reasoning. There is beginning to be a literature on theory of mind and aging, and it includes a dozen or so studies that have examined higher-order forms of theory of mind. For the most part, however, these studies have concentrated on the newer second-order measures that followed after the Perner and Wimmer (1985) task; they are a subject, therefore, for Chapter 4. Several of the studies have included the second-order belief task, but most have not analyzed it separately from the other higher-order measures. There are two exceptions. Gregory and colleagues (Gregory et al., 2002) reported perfect performance on the Perner and Wimmer task in their control sample of healthy older adults (the main focus of the research was on various clinical conditions). This sample had a mean age of 57, however, and so at best fell in the very early phases of the old-age continuum. McKinnon and Moscovitch (2007), working with nonstandard forms of first- and second-order tasks created for the study, found that older adults (mean age = 78) were equivalent to young adults (mean age = 20) on first-order performance; they lagged behind, however, on second-order. The work to be considered in Chapter 4 will tell us more about what happens as people age.

CONCLUSIONS

I address two general questions in this final section of the chapter: What do we now know about the second-order false belief task, and what do we still need to learn? The answers in both cases will be partial, with further discussion to come in later chapters.

One thing we know is the developmental timing for mastery of the second-order task. For most children, mastery comes at about age 5 or 6. For some, success comes a bit later, and for some (probably a smaller number) a bit earlier. The exact timing varies some across the two dominant methods of assessment, and it also varies some across the two possible criteria for mastery (judgment only or judgment plus explanation). By any measure, however, second-order false belief is an early grade-school achievement. And by any measure second-order false belief is more difficult than first-order false belief.

The preceding summary needs to be qualified in two ways. First, apart from a few studies in Japan and one in India (Patnaik, 2006), research on second-order false belief has been confined to a small range of Western industrialized societies. The study of first-order development also began as a Western literature, but it now includes a substantial amount of work in Asian countries (e.g., Liu, Wellman, Tardif, & Sabbagh, 2008) as well as some research in traditional, nonindustrialized societies (e.g., Avis & Harris, 1991; Vinden, 2002). It has also been extended to a range of different ethnic and socioeconomic groups (e.g., Holmes, Black, & Miller, 1996; Shatz, Diesendruck, Martinez-Beck, & Akar, 2003). Extensions of this sort remain a future task for second-order research.

The second qualification concerns the range of assessment procedures that have been attempted. The first-order literature has seen exploration of a wide range of potentially important procedural variations, some (but certainly not all) of which I reviewed in Chapter 2. Most of these approaches have yet to be tried at the second-order level. It is true that factors that might mask some underlying competence (most obviously, limited verbal ability) lessen with development and that the need for simplified assessment procedures probably lessens as well. Still, it is worth noting that what we know at present about the emergence of second-order false belief is based on a narrow range of highly verbal and somewhat artificial methods of eliciting the child's knowledge.

There is a further difference between the first-order and second-order literatures that is relevant here. Although most studies of first-order understanding involve experimental elicitation of the abilities in question, the first-order literature is not all laboratory-bound; rather, for many topics naturalistic data complement or extend the experimental work. Bartsch and Wellman's (1995) analyses of spontaneous speech discussed in Chapter 2 are one obvious example. As we will see in Chapter 6, the second-order literature does contain a number of demonstrations of the relevance of second-order abilities for children's real-life social functioning (albeit generally via laboratory analogs rather than naturalistic study). No researcher, however, has attempted to identify second-order reasoning per se in children's naturally occurring behavior.

One of the central issues in the first-order literature concerns how and why theory of mind relates to executive function and to language. This is also a central issue for second-order developments. One surprising aspect of the second-order literature is how few studies have examined this question (again, some potentially relevant studies are made uninformative by the decision to use composite theory-of-mind scores). The evidence that does exist suggests a parallel to the first-order case: Both executive function and language relate positively to performance on second-order false belief. We will see in Chapter 4 that the same conclusion holds for the other higher-order measures that followed after Perner and Wimmer's (1985) invention of the belief task.

Of course, the existence of a relation does not tell us why it occurs. Are relatively good executive function and linguistic abilities a contributor to theory of mind, or is relatively good theory of mind a contributor to executive function and language? In addition, to the extent that executive function and language are the causal forces in the relation, do they affect the emergence of theory-of-mind abilities, or do they make possible the expression of already existing abilities on the typical measures? These questions have yet to be resolved in the first-order literature, and they are certainly no closer to resolution in the much smaller second-order literature. I will, however, hazard a couple speculations with respect to the second-order case.

The first is that the causal direction for the relation is primarily from executive function or language to theory of mind and not the reverse. This speculation is based partly on theoretical analysis and partly on the available evidence. I take the latter basis first. Beyond simply demonstrating correlational relations between the constructs, the first-order literature contains several forms of evidence that can help to specify the causal direction for the correlations. These forms of evidence include across-time tracing of the relations via longitudinal study, experimental induction of one of the abilities to see if the other follows, and dissociation of the abilities in clinical cases (the logic being that the cause can exist without the effect but not the reverse). On my reading, these forms of evidence (more extensive to date for language than for executive function) suggest a bidirectional causal flow but one in which the primary causal direction is from executive function or language to theory of mind and not the reverse.

Of course, even if this is a valid conclusion for first-order abilities the picture may be different at the second-order level. The second-order literature does contain some work on dissociation of abilities in clinical cases, though not any that as of yet leads to any clear conclusions (cf. Pellicano, 2007; Perner, Kain, et al., 2002). It also contains two longitudinal studies (Astington et al., 1998; Lockl & Schneider, 2007), both of which suggest that language is the causal factor in the relation between language and theory of mind. Training studies are at present entries in the needed-future-research category.

The posited causal direction also seems, at least to me, to be the more likely one from a theoretical point of view. At the first-order level it is plausible that advances in theory of mind could in some way nurture the emergence of basic executive function skills, and Perner has in fact made this argument in a number of places (e.g., Perner, Kain, et al., 2002; Perner & Lang, 2000). At the second-order level it is difficult—again at least for me—to see how the development of recursive reasoning could contribute to working memory, or to the ability to inhibit a dominant response, or to at least most of the aspects of language that have been shown to be related. In contrast, it is not at all hard to see how memory or inhibition or language could be important for second-order reasoning.

The second speculation is that executive function and language affect primarily the expression rather than the emergence of second-order abilities. Again, the bases for the speculation are in part empirical and in part theoretical. Empirically, this was the conclusion that Lockl and Schneider (2007) reached in the one explicit consideration of how language relates to second-order competence. Based on the across-time pattern of correlations in their longitudinal research, they argued that language primarily affects emergence of abilities in first-order development and expression of abilities in second-order development. It is also—to anticipate research that will be reviewed in Chapter 4—the conclusion that follows from work on theory of mind and aging. We will see in Chapter 4 that some older adults show parallel and correlated deficits in executive function and in performance on higher-order theory-of-mind tasks. It is not plausible that either ability is affecting the other in an emergence sense at this point in development, and it is also not plausible, at least in most instances, that older individuals have actually lost their basic theory-of-mind abilities. The problem almost certainly is one not of competence but of performance—a failure to express abilities because of declines in the necessary executive functions.

Theoretically, it is certainly possible that either language or executive function or both contribute to the emergence of second-order abilities, although no researcher has spelled out exactly how this might occur. The expression role, however, seems more certain. Even in their simplest possible form, second-order tasks are verbally demanding, and understanding the language must be a necessary part of successful response. Such tasks also require children to hold a substantial amount of information in working memory and to inhibit the naturally dominant response (i.e., to judge in terms of reality and their own true belief) in order to attribute a false belief. Thus a certain level of executive function also seems necessary for successful performance.

Conclusions about the role of language and executive function are central to the question of whether the transition from first-order competence to second-order competence entails a conceptual change. There is no need to posit a conceptual change if domain-general advances in executive function and language can explain the movement from failure to success on second-order tasks. This is the conclusion that Sullivan et al. (1994) reached in light of the precocious success revealed by their simplified measures: "These findings support the view that once children understand the representational nature of mental states, which emerges at around the age of 3 or 4 … no further conceptual development is needed to recursively embed mental states" (p. 401). Lockl and Schneider (2007) offered a similar conclusion with regard to language: "We assume that, once children have acquired basic language abilities that help them to create a representation of the character's representation, their performance on second-order belief tasks might depend largely on their comprehension of the complex stories and the test questions that are used in second-order theory-of-mind assessments" (p. 151).

Is such a complexity-only position justified? I would say that at present the position is possible but by no means established. It is clear that language and executive function do contribute to second-order performance, and that performance improves when these ancillary demands are reduced. On the other hand, the Sullivan et al. (1994) study remains the only one to show much success among 4-year-olds, and within-study comparisons consistently find marked differences between first-order and second-order false belief. Again, Hayashi (2007b) is especially convincing in this regard, given the close matching of the first-order and second-order scenarios. In addition, Chapter 4 will discuss a number of further second-order developments that emerge well after first-order success.

Of course, the existence of a consistent age difference between early and later developments is at best a necessary condition to posit a conceptual change; it is not a sufficient condition. What else needs to be true? The fullest discussion of this issue in the first-order literature comes in the Wellman et al. (2001) meta-analysis and the accompanying commentaries (see also Wellman & Cross, 2001). Wellman et al. summarize the further criteria as follows:

> To begin with, a task is needed that plausibly assesses a target conceptual understanding, and performance on that task must change from incorrect to systematically above-chance judgments with age. Confidence in both good and poor performance on the task must additionally be bolstered by correct judgments on control tasks or on control questions that demonstrate memory for key information and grasp of the task format…. Conceptual change accounts are also subject to a general multi-method approach to construct validity: a variety of tasks, all conceptually similar but varying in their task specifics, should lead to similar developmental changes. (p. 672)

The work reviewed in this chapter indicates that the second-order case meets the first two criteria. In Chapter 4 we will see that a variety of conceptually similar higher-order achievements all emerge at about the same time in development. Thus, second-order developments could be argued also to meet the third criterion. These empirical criteria, however, are not sufficient to specify a conceptual change. What must be added to them is a conceptual criterion: a clear specification of exactly what the conceptual change *is*. This criterion is met in the first-order case; indeed, multiple versions have long existed across the various forms of the theory theory, simulation, and modularity approaches. It also was met in the earlier Piagetian literature. Whatever the doubts about the accuracy of Piaget's model of concrete operations, no one disputes the fact that the model does what a theory of developmental change should do—namely, provide a detailed account of how middle-childhood thought differs from preschool thought.

The fullest discussion of conceptual change at the second-order level remains Perner's (1988) suggestion that:

> Second-order attributions require understanding of the recursive nature of mental states (repeated embeddings of propositions). It is plausible that this possibility for recursion is understood at a particular point in development and that, once understood, it is then widely applied for making social distinctions. (pp. 272–273)

This statement provides the beginnings of a theoretical account but leaves a number of points to be worked out. Why does the change occur? What role do language and executive function play in the transformation? How does the child come to understand which mental states lend themselves to recursive chains and which do not? And how does understanding of recursive mental states relate to understanding of other forms of recursion? The most obvious entry for this final question is language, for which recursion is a central, even defining, property. Various authors (e.g., Corballis, 2011) have discussed the general dependence of both language and theory of mind on recursion; at a more specific level, however, the relation between the two domains is by no means straightforward. Children master various forms of linguistic recursion years before they become capable of reasoning about second-order mental states. Furthermore, there is no further linguistic development in mastery of recursion—at least none that has been identified to date—that coincides with the emergence of second-order mentalistic competence.

A further complication is that recursion, at least by some analyses, is not limited to the grammatical aspect of language. Various aspects of communicative interchanges have been argued to depend on each partner's knowledge of the other's mental state, including what the other thinks the self thinks. In Tomasello's (2008, pp. 94–95) words:

> The creation of common ground and/or joint attention between two persons requires that each of them sees, knows, or attends to things that she knows that the other sees, knows, or attends to as well—and knows that the other knows this about her as well, and so on recursively potentially ad infinitum.

Tomasello goes on to acknowledge that most acts of communication do not require lengthy recursive chains; rather various heuristics and agreed-upon conventions are sufficient to get the job done. Nevertheless, recursive thinking is available when needed—for example, to repair a breakdown in communication. As with recursion in the grammatical realm, the relation of recursive communicative competence to second-order reasoning has yet to be specified.

At present, therefore, the literature on second-order false belief offers no clear answer with respect to the complexity-only versus conceptual change issue. Arguments exist on both sides; further work is necessary on both sides. We will revisit the question in subsequent chapters as further developments under the "higher order" heading are discussed.

4

Other Higher-Order Developments
Part 1

Although it has been the most thoroughly explored, the second-order false belief task is not the only measure developed for the study of higher-order theory of mind. Across the next two chapters I add the results from a number of other higher-order tasks. This chapter reviews work under the theory-of-mind heading that followed directly out of the research on second-order false belief. Chapter 5 adds work from a variety of other perspectives, some explicitly labeled theory of mind and some not. The common element is a focus on post-preschool forms of mentalistic understanding.

We saw in Chapter 2 that only a couple years elapsed between the invention of the first-order false belief task and its application to the study of autism. We saw in Chapter 3 that the second-order task was also quickly extended to samples with autism. With a couple exceptions, the measures to be considered now reverse this sequence: These are tasks developed for the study of autism and only later extended to typically developing samples.

AN OVERVIEW OF MEASURES

Strange Stories

The first such measure was developed by Francesca Happé (1994). Happé had two goals in creating the Strange Stories test. The first goal stemmed from what we saw were the results of the initial false belief studies in samples with autism (Baron-Cohen et al., 1985; Bowler, 1992). In the case of both first-order and second-order false belief, many children with autism apparently never mastered the ability in question, and when mastery did come it was delayed by several years. Nevertheless, for a subset of the sample mastery *did* eventually come. For these individuals, therefore, theory-of-mind abilities were not absent in autism; they were simply delayed. A delayed-rather-than-absent conclusion would be important for our understanding of both autism and theory of mind. Still, the conclusion held only for abilities that typically emerge in the first 5 or 6 years of life. Perhaps if we focus on more advanced forms of theory of mind we will find developments that remain beyond the reach of people with autism, thus demonstrating for the first time a general absence and not simply a delay in development. One goal of the Strange Stories was to probe for more advanced forms of understanding.

A second goal followed from a cautionary point that I noted briefly in Chapter 2. Although some individuals with autism do succeed on false belief tasks, they may not arrive at their answers in the same way as do typically developing participants. Rather, various sorts of evidence suggest that people with autism may solve such tasks through a "hacking through" strategy, relying on general logical reasoning abilities rather than the social-cognitive insights that underlie typical response (Frith, Morton, & Leslie, 1991). The Strange Stories were intended to offer a more naturalistic, and therefore more challenging, context from which to infer mental states. In Happé's words (1994, pp. 130–131), "The aim … was to extend the range of tasks involving theory of mind to a more contextually embedded and realistic form, which might be expected to trip up even those subjects who succeeded on the previous, simplified tasks."

Table 4.1 shows a sampling of items from the Strange Stories measure. As can be seen, the focus of the measure is on nonliteral statements of various sorts—that is, statements whose correct interpretation requires going beyond the surface of the utterance to infer the speaker's underlying motive and intended meaning. It is in this respect that they require second-order reasoning; the participant must realize that the speaker intends to implant a particular belief in the listener—thus A intends that B thinks that…. In addition to the examples in the table, the other speech forms included are white lie, misunderstanding, appearance–reality, sarcasm, forgetting, contrary emotions, persuasion, and double bluff. Also included as a control are several stories that require physical rather than social-cognitive reasoning. Such stories serve to demonstrate that the participant is capable of the level of information processing and reasoning required by the stories, and that any failures on the psychological items therefore denote a specific problem in thinking about mental states. (As it happens, however, the original Happé stories were too simple to serve this purpose; later researchers have therefore devised more complex control stories—see, for example, White, Hill, Happé, & Frith, 2009.)

The issue in scoring the Strange Stories is whether response to the Why question demonstrates understanding of the intention behind the speaker's utterance. Consider the Lie story. An indication that Anna did not break the vase (a factual error) or that she is joking (an incorrect mental state) would be scored as incorrect. Note, with respect to the latter example, that reference to a mental state is not sufficient; it must be the right mental state. In contrast, an indication that Anna is trying to deceive her mother would clearly be scored as correct. Such references to the relevant mental state are one of two general categories of explanation that are credited. In some instances reference to a relevant physical state can also be adequate. For example, a child might explain the Pretend scenario in terms of the resemblance between a banana and a phone or might explain the Joke by noting the dog's elephant-like size. As would be expected, however, references to mental states are of special interest in scoring the measure.

TABLE 4.1 Examples of Scenarios From the Strange Stories Measure

Story Type	Scenario	Questions
Pretend	Katie and Emma are playing in the house. Emma picks up a banana from the fruit bowl and holds it up to her ear. She says to Katie, "Look! This banana is a telephone!"	Is it true, what Emma says? Why does Emma say this?
Joke	Today, James is going to Claire's house for the first time. He is going over for tea, and he is looking forward to seeing Claire's dog, which she talks about all the time. James likes dogs very much. When James arrives at Claire's house Claire runs to open the door, and her dog jumps up to greet James. Claire's dog is huge; it's almost as big as James! When James sees Claire's huge dog he says, "Claire you haven't got a dog at all. You've got an elephant!"	Is it true what James says? Why does James say that?
Lie	One day, while she is playing in the house, Anna accidentally knocks over and breaks her mother's favorite crystal vase. Oh dear, when mother finds out she will be very cross! So when Anna's mother comes home and sees the broken vase and asks Anna what happened, Anna says, "The dog knocked it over; it wasn't my fault!"	Was it true what Anna told her mother? Why did Anna say that?
Figure of speech	Emma has a cough. All through lunch she coughs and coughs and coughs. Father says, "Poor Emma, you must have a frog in your throat!"	Is it true, what Father says to Emma? Why does he say that?
Irony	Ann's mother has spent a long time cooking Ann's favorite meal: fish and chips. But when she brings it to Ann, she is watching TV, and she doesn't even look up, or say thank you. Ann's mother is cross and says, "Well that's very nice, isn't it? That's what I call politeness!"	Is it true, what Ann's mother says? Why does Ann's mother say this?

Source: Happé, F., *Journal of Autism and Developmental Disorders*, 24, 147–151, 1994. Copyright 1994 by Plenum Publishing Corporation. With kind permission from Springer Science & Business Media.

Stories from Everyday Life

The Stories from Everyday Life measure (Kaland et al., 2002) is patterned closely after Strange Stories. As with Strange Stories, the measure consists of a series of vignettes, each of which ends with a statement whose interpretation depends on going beyond the literal words to take into account the speaker's mental state and thus actual intended meaning. The mental states and corresponding speech forms at issue are also similar, encompassing most of the those examined in Strange Stories (e.g., irony, lie) and a few others as well (e.g., misunderstanding, social blunder). The difference is that the Everyday Stories are more complex and the eventual inference of intended meaning more difficult than is the case for Strange Stories. The measure thus continues the tradition in the autism literature of progressively more challenging assessment instruments over time.

Table 4.2 gives an example that makes the greater complexity clear. It can be seen that the stories are longer than those in Strange Stories and that they contain many more informational units. There are also more questions following the story—a dozen for this example, in contrast to the two questions that follow

TABLE 4.2   Example of a Scenario From the Stories from Everyday Life Measure

Scenario

The Hanson family, Mrs. Elsie, her husband Gerald and their children, Emma and Dan, have a large, kind, fowl-hunting dog called Fido. Both Emma and her brother Dan are very fond of Fido. Every day Fido sits on the doorstep, looking out for Emma and Dan when they come home from school, and wags his tail when he sees them.

When Emma and Dan's mother was young, she was bitten by a dog. Since then she has never liked dogs, and she is not particularly fond of Fido. Also, she complains that Fido regularly runs after birds in the muddy ground close by.

When the dog isn't outside, it is usually to be found in the kitchen. Elsie has to wash the kitchen floor almost daily. Even though she knows that her husband and her children are fond of the dog, she has several times said to her husband that she would like to get rid of Fido. Her husband is against this, especially because the children are extremely fond of Fido.

Emma has asthma, and suffers sometimes from asthma attacks, generally when she is at school. One day she has an attack and is almost unable to breathe. Luckily, she has her asthma spray in her school bag, so she soon recovers. When her mother hears about this she says to her husband: "I am quite sure that Emma's asthma attack was caused by an allergy to dogs, and that this is Fido's fault. It is therefore time to get rid of this dog before it ruins Emma's health!"

Questions

1. What is the Hanson family's dog called?
2. What do Emma and Dan think of Fido?
3. Why does Fido sit and wait for Emma and Dan to return from school?
4. What does Emma and Dan's mother think of dogs?
5. Why does she wash the kitchen floor almost daily? (PI)
6. What does she want to do with Fido?
7. What do her husband and children think of this?
8. What kind of illness has Emma?
9. What does Emma's mother say to her husband after hearing about Emma's asthma attack at school?
10. Where is Emma when she normally has her attacks?
11. Is Fido normally present when Emma has her asthma attacks?
12. Why does Emma's mother say that Fido is the cause of Emma's asthma attacks, even though she has her attacks when the dog is not present? (MI)

Source: Adapted from Kaland, N., Moller-Nielsen, A., Callsen, K., Mortensen, E. L., Gottlieb, D., & Smith, L., *Journal of Child Psychology and Psychiatry, 43*, 2002, pp. 527–528. Copyright 2002 by John Wiley & Sons. Adapted with permission.

each of the Strange Stories. Many, indeed most, of the questions are control items designed to ensure that the participant remembers the details of the story. Two test questions provide the basis for scoring the measure. One, which comes partway through, tests for the ability to draw a physical-state inference from the information provided in the story. In the example this is the "Why does she wash the kitchen floor almost daily?" question. The other, which comes at the end, tests for the relevant mental-state understanding. In the example this is the question that asks why Emma's mother said what she did. It is this latter question, of course, that is the measure of greatest interest.

Faux Pas

The next measure to be considered is somewhat narrower in scope than either Strange Stories or Stories from Everyday Life. The Faux Pas measure (Baron-Cohen, O'Riordan, Stone, Jones, & Plaisted, 1999) presents, as its name suggests, a series of vignettes that illustrate various sorts of faux pas. The authors define faux pas as follows:

> A working definition of faux pas might be when a speaker says something without considering if it is something that the listener might want to hear or know, and which typically has negative consequences that the speaker never intended. Utterances of this type are suitable for inclusion in an advanced theory of mind test because detecting a faux pas requires both an appreciation that there may be a difference between a speaker's knowledge state and that of [the] listener, and an appreciation of the emotional impact of a statement on the listener. (p. 408, reprinted with kind permission from Springer Science & Business Media)

Table 4.3 gives three examples (out of the 10 vignettes that were used). The first two questions that follow each story establish that the participant has recognized that a faux pas occurred. The third question verifies that important story information was understood. Finally, the fourth question tests whether the participant realizes that the faux pas resulted from the speaker's false belief and not, for example, from some malicious intent. To be credited with passing an item the participant must answer all four questions correctly.

The Eyes Test

All of the measures discussed to this point are fairly verbal at both the input and the output end. Thus, the situations to be judged are conveyed through words, and the participant's response also occurs via language. Presumably, though, not all real-life instances of mentalistic understanding depend on language. What might be the nonverbal cues that help us to figure out what someone else is thinking or feeling or wishing?

The Eyes Test—another measure developed by Simon Baron-Cohen and colleagues (Baron-Cohen, Jolliffe, Mortimore, & Robinson, 1997; Baron-Cohen, Wheelright, Hill, Raste, & Plumb, 2001)—makes use of facial expressions. Specifically, the measure focuses, as the name indicates, on the eyes region of the face. Participants are shown a series of photographs of the eyes of various adult faces and are asked in each case to judge the mental state that the target is experiencing. The format is forced-choice: presentation of the correct alternative along with three other choices. A total of 36 mental states are assessed; examples include playful, upset, worried, regretful, doubtful, friendly, confident, and nervous. Note that the mental states are not so-called basic ones (e.g., happy, sad) that most people find easy to judge; rather, they are more subtle conditions whose identification may require an inference of the target's belief or intention. Figure 4.1 shows two sample items. The alternatives in the first case are serious, ashamed, alarmed, and bewildered. The alternatives in

TABLE 4.3   Examples of Scenarios From the Faux Pas Measure

Scenario	Faux Pas Detection Question	Identification Question	Comprehension Question	False Belief Question
Kim helped her Mom make an apple pie for her uncle when he came to visit. She carried it out of the kitchen. "I made it just for you," said Kim. "Mmm," replied Uncle Tom, "that looks lovely. I love pies, except for apple, of course!"	In the story did someone say something that they should not have said?	What did they say that they should not have said?	What kind of pie had Kim made?	Did Uncle Tom know that the pie was an apple pie?
James bought Richard a toy airplane for his birthday. A few months later, they were playing with it, and James accidentally dropped it. "Don't worry," said Richard, "I never liked it anyway. Someone gave it to me for my birthday."	In the story did someone say something that they should not have said?	What did they say that they should not have said?	What did James give Richard for his birthday?	Did Richard remember James had given him the toy airplane for his birthday?
Sally has short blonde hair. She was at her Aunt Carol's house. The doorbell rang. It was Mary, a neighbor. Mary said, "Hello," then looked at Sally and said, "Oh, I don't think I've met this little boy. What's your name?" Aunt Carol said, "Who'd like a cup of tea?"	In the story did someone say something that they should not have said?	What did they say that they should not have said?	Whose house was Sally at?	Did Mary know that Sally was a little girl?

Source: Adapted from Baron-Cohen, S., O'Riordan, M., Stone, V., Jones, R., & Plaisted, K., *Journal of Autism and Developmental Disorders*, 29, 1999, p. 416. Copyright 1999 by Plenum Publishing. Adapted with kind permission from Springer Science & Business Media.

Figure 4.1   Example of items from the Eyes Test. (From Baron-Cohen, S., Wheelwright, S., Hill, J., Raste, Y., & Plumb, I., *Journal of Child Psychology and Psychiatry, 42*, 2001, p. 242. Copyright 2001 by the Association for Child and Adolescent Mental Health. Reprinted with permission from John Wiley & Sons.)

the second case are reflective, aghast, irritated, and impatient. It would be a good exercise to try these items yourself. I give the correct answers shortly.

The Eyes Test comes in various forms. The items depicted in the figure are from a second, revised version of the measure (Baron-Cohen, Wheelright, Hill, et al., 2001). There is also a children's version (Baron-Cohen, Wheelright, Spong, Scahill, & Lawson, 2001). The children's version is similar to the adult version but has fewer items and uses somewhat simpler wording. Finally, some researchers (e.g., Back, Ropar, & Mitchell, 2007) have presented dynamic versions of the test, in which the static photos are replaced by animated faces.

A basic question with regard to the Eyes Test—and indeed for all the measures considered in this section—is that of test validity. How can we determine that the test really measures what it is intended to measure—in this case, that it measures understanding of mental states as conveyed through facial expression? Your response to the examples in Figure 4.1—assuming that you responded correctly by selecting serious in the first case and reflective in the second—is one source of evidence. If the eyes really do convey usable information about mental states, then normal adults should show a good deal of accuracy and agreement in their response to the items. Such in fact is the case. A further source of evidence offered by Baron-Cohen and colleagues (Baron-Cohen et al., 2007) came from comparisons with the Strange Stories measure; they reported that the Eyes Test produced the same pattern of group differences and similarities as is found with Strange Stories. Strangely, though, they did not report the correlation between the two measures; other studies have sometimes (e.g., Botting & Conti-Ramsden, 2008) but not always (e.g., Brent, Rios, Happé, & Charman, 2004) reported significant correlations. Finally, Baron-Cohen and colleagues (1997) showed that response to the test was, as predicted, largely independent of two other measures of facial decoding: gender recognition and emotion recognition. (For a critical evaluation of the Eyes Test, see Johnson, Miles, & McKinlay, 2008.)

Preadolescent Theory of Mind

Although they have (as we will see) applications to typical development, all of the measures described to this point were initially developed for the study of autism. The final two examples come out of the basic theory-of-mind literature.

Table 4.4 shows one of the items from the Preadolescent Theory of Mind measure (Bosacki, 2000; Bosacki & Astington, 1999). The general format that the measure takes should by this point be familiar: a vignette that presents a snapshot of social life, followed by a series of questions that assess the participant's

TABLE 4.4   Example of a Scenario From the Preadolescent Theory-of-Mind Measure

Scenario

Nancy and Margie are watching the children in the playground. Without saying a word,
Nancy nudges Margie and looks across the playground at the new girl swinging on the swing set.
Then Nancy looks at Margie and smiles. Margie nods, and the two of them start off toward the girl at the swing set. The new girl sees the strange girls walk toward her. She'd seen them nudging and smiling at each other. Although they are in her class, she has never spoken to them before. The new girl wonders what they could want.

Comprehension Questions

1. Does the new girl see Nancy and Margie nudging and smiling at each other? Yes/No
2. Has the new girl ever spoken to Nancy and Margie before? Yes/No
    A. *Conceptual Role-Taking*
        1. Why did Nancy smile at Margie?
        2. Why did Margie nod?
        3a. Why did Nancy and Margie move off together in the direction of the new girl?
        3b. Why do you think this/How do you know this?
        4. Does the new girl have any idea of why Nancy and Margie are walking toward her? Yes/No
    B. *Empathic Sensitivity*
        5a. How do you think the new girl feels?
        5b. Why? Does she feel anything else? Why?
    C. *Person Perception*
        6. Choose a character in the story and describe her. What kinds of things can you think of to describe her? What kind of person do you think she is?
    D. *Alternative Explanations*
        7. Is there another way that you can think about this story? Yes/No If so, how?

Source: Bosacki, S. L., & Astington, J. W., *Social Development, 8,* 1999, p. 255. Copyright 1999 by John Wiley & Sons. Reprinted with permission.

understanding at both a surface and a deeper level. In this case, however, there is nothing "strange" about the behavior depicted, nor is there some nonliteral utterance to be interpreted (indeed, there are no utterances at all). Nor is there a single correct answer that furnishes the criterion for understanding. The interest, rather, is in the level of reasoning displayed in attempting to make sense of a familiar but also challenging-to-judge social situation. As the table indicates, four aspects of reasoning are scored, summarized by the authors as follows:

> The ability to understand multiple perspectives (conceptual role-taking), the ability to recognize and understand emotional states (empathic sensitivity), the ability to understand the concept of a person as a psychological being with stable personality characteristics (person perception) … and the ability to imagine multiple perspectives and alternatives. (Bosacki & Astington, 1999, p. 240)

Because of its open-ended and wide-ranging format, the Preadolescent measure presents more of a scoring challenge than do the other measures reviewed in this section. The emphasis in the coding system—a system for which the authors report good reliability—is on the cognitive complexity of the participant's response. Consider the "Why did Nancy and Margie move off together in the direction of the new girl?" question. An "I don't know" or irrelevant response would receive 0 points, and a response in terms of behavioral or situational factors (e.g., "to play on the swings") would receive 1 point. In contrast, the maximum of 3 points would be awarded to responses that identify and integrate two or more relevant mental states (e.g., "because I've seen kids on the playground who look lonely and you don't want them to feel bad, so you try to be their friend because you know it's the right thing to do").

I will note that one of the theoretical bases for the Preadolescent measure is the work of Michael Chandler and colleagues on post-preschool developments in theory of mind (e.g., Chandler, 1987). This is work to which I return in Chapter 5.

Third- and Fourth-Order Reasoning

Although one starting point for all of the approaches considered thus far is the second-order belief task, each departs in various ways from Perner and Wimmer's (1985) methodology. That, in a way, is the point of the general enterprise: to explore other methods—generally more naturalistic and more challenging methods—from which to infer understanding of higher-order mental states. The work to be considered now returns us to vignettes a la Perner and Wimmer. The difference is that the vignettes are more complex and thus so is the level of reasoning required. Rather than a single recursive chain (A thinks that B thinks), we now have recursive chains of potentially any length.

We have already seen one example: the multiple mental states depicted in the right-hand side of Figure 3.1. Miller, Kessel, and Flavell (1970) dubbed such "thinks that … thinks that … thinks that…" constructions *two-loop recursion*. Deciphering such constructions proved challenging for their participants: Young grade-school children showed little success, and even 11-year-olds were correct only about 30% of the time.

TABLE 4.5   Example of a Scenario From the Liddle and Nettle (2006) Study of Higher-Order Reasoning

Scenario

There was a little girl called Anna who had a big problem on her mind. It was her mum's birthday the very next day. Anna wanted to get her mum a birthday present, but she just didn't know what to buy. She thought and thought. Tomorrow was nearly here! Anna remembered that her brother, Ben, had already asked Mum what Mum would like most of all for her birthday. Ben was out riding his bike so Anna decided to look around his room to see if she could find what present he had got for mum. Anna went in and found a big bunch of beautiful flowers with a little card that said: "Happy Birthday Mum, love from Ben." Anna thought to herself, "Mum must want flowers for her birthday!" Just as Anna was leaving the room, Ben was coming up the stairs, but he didn't see Anna leaving his room. Anna didn't want Ben to know that she had been snooping around his room, so she said to Ben, "Ben, have you got Mum a birthday present?" Ben thought for a minute, he didn't want Anna to copy him and get Mum the same present, so he said, "Yes, Anna, I have. I have got Mum some perfume. What have you got for her?" Anna replied, "Erm, nothing yet, Ben," and she walked away.

Memory:

  a. Anna's mum's birthday is tomorrow.

  b. Anna's mum's birthday is next week.

ToM Level 1:

  a. Anna thinks Ben has bought Mum some perfume.

  b. Anna knows Ben has bought Mum some flowers.

Memory:

  a. Ben was Anna's friend.

  b. Ben was Anna's brother.

ToM Level 4:

  a. Ben thinks that Anna believes that he knows that Mum wants perfume for her birthday.

  b. Ben thinks that Anna knows that he knows that Mum wants flowers for her birthday.

Source: Liddle, B., & Nettle, D., *Journal of Cultural and Evolutionary Psychology, 4,* 2006, pp. 240–241. Copyright 2006 by Akadémiai Kiadó. Reprinted with permission.

Table 4.5 presents another example, in this case one grounded in the vignettes approach. In the study from which the example is taken, the level of reasoning required varied across the different vignettes that were used; the example includes a first-order question and a fourth-order question. Other vignettes tapped second-order and third-order understanding. The format was forced-choice: selection between the correct answer and an alternative incorrect answer.

My goal in this section has been to summarize methodologies, with discussion of findings to come in the remaining sections of the chapter. I will make an exception, however, for the work under the present heading, both because there is not much such work to discuss (one study to date with children) and because the results are not easily integrated with those from the other measures.

A handful of studies (Kinderman, Dunbar, & Bentall, 1998; Rutherford, 2004; Stiller & Dunbar, 2007) have explored higher-level forms of recursive reasoning with adult participants. Adults do fairly well up to chains that are four items in length, but performance drops off markedly at more complex levels.

The example in Table 4.5 is from the one such study with children (Liddle & Nettle, 2006). The participants were 10- and 11-year-olds, and they responded close to perfectly on the first-order and second-order problems, certainly an expectable finding given the previous research literature. Response to the more complex problems was much less impressive. Performance on third-order problems was marginally above chance (59% correct); performance on fourth-order problems was at chance level. As we would expect, then, children's capacity for higher-order recursive reasoning falls short of that shown by adults.

An obvious question that arises in evaluating this work is that of ecological validity. How often do we engage in four- or five-item chains of recursive thought? On the other hand, it is not difficult to imagine plausible instances of three-item chains, and it would be good to have more research that examines children's ability to handle such problems. At issue is not only the descriptive picture but also the bases for difficulties when difficulties arise. Once recursive reasoning at any level is understood, there is no obvious reason to think that further levels would present a new conceptual challenge; rather difficulties with higher-level forms most likely result from the lengthy and complex scenarios that must be understood and remembered. If so, performance on such tasks should relate to relevant measures of language and of executive function. Such relations remain to be demonstrated.

Other Measures

The measures just discussed do not exhaust the possible entries under the "Other Higher-Level" heading. The Baron-Cohen group continues to generate new instruments; the Reading the Mind in the Voice Test-Revised was published in 2007 (Golan, Baron-Cohen, Hill, & Rutherford, 2007), the Reading the Mind in Films task appeared in 2008 (Golan, Baron-Cohen, & Golan, 2008), and the Moral Dilemmas Film task followed in 2009 (Barnes, Lombardo, Wheelwright, & Baron-Cohen, 2009). Recent years have also seen the creation of the ATOMIC (which stands for Animated Theory of Mind Inventory for Children; Beaumont & Sofronoff, 2008) and the MASC (which stands for Movie for the Assessment of Social Cognition; Dziobek et al., 2006). As of this writing, these measures have had limited use, and I therefore settle for simply citing the sources here.

DEVELOPMENTAL FINDINGS

The majority of studies with the measures just described have been with samples with autism, and most of the remaining studies have been directed to other clinical conditions. Research whose focus is typical development has been rare. On the other hand, interpreting the results in clinical cases requires information about what happens in typical development, and thus almost all of the clinical studies include a typically developing control group. Not all such studies provide descriptive information about typical development, but many do. Table 4.6 provides a quick overview of the basic findings that emerge.

Changes With Age

A first finding is that these measures do in fact require abilities more advanced than those tapped by the standard first-order tasks. Indeed, few studies have even

TABLE 4.6   Samples, Methods, and Findings in Studies Employing Higher-Order Measures of Theory of Mind With Nonclinical Child Populations

Study	Sample	Method	Findings
Adrian et al. (2007)	4- to 7-year-olds	Strange Stories (reduced version)	59% of possible points
Banerjee (2000)	6-, 8-, and 10-year-olds	Faux Pas (reduced version)	38% of possible points at age 6, 93% at 8, 93% at 10
Banerjee et al. (2011)	6- through 11-year-olds	Faux Pas (reduced version)	28% of possible points at age 6, 75% at age 11
Barlow et al. (2010)	8- to 10-year-olds	Faux Pas	69% of possible points
Baron-Cohen et al. (1999)	7-, 9-, and 11-year-olds	Faux Pas	34% of possible points at age 7, 59% at 7, 82% at 9
Baron-Cohen, Wheelright, Spong, et al. (2001)	7-, 9-, and 11-year-olds	Eyes Test	48% of possible points at age 7, 64% at 9, 74% at 11
Bosacki & Astington (1999)	11-year-olds	Preadolescent Theory of Mind	67% of possible points
Botting & Conti-Ramsden (2008)	15- and 16-year-olds	Eyes Test, Strange Stories (reduced version)	71% of possible points on Eyes Test, 88% on Strange Stories
Brent et al. (2004)	5- to 13-year-olds (M = 8)	Eyes Test, Strange Stories (reduced version)	63% of possible points on Eyes Test, 72% on Strange Stories
Charman et al. (2001)	8- to 10-year-olds	Strange Stories	93% of possible points
Colvert et al. (2008)	11-year-olds	Strange Stories	62% of possible points
Dorris et al. (2004)	7- to 17-year-olds (M = 11)	Eyes Test	72% of possible points
Dyck et al. (2001)	9- to 16-year-olds (M = 12)	Strange Stories	87% of possible points
Dyck et al. (2006)	12-year-olds	Strange Stories	86% of possible points
Filippova & Astington (2008)	5-, 7-, and 9-year-olds	Strange Stories, Faux Pas	29% of possible points on Strange Stories at age 5, 71% at 7, 77% at 9, 44% on Faux Pas at 5, 82% at 7, 85% at 9
Gillot et al. (2004)	8- to 12-year-olds	Strange Stories	67% of possible points
Gini (2006)	8- to 11-year-olds	Strange Stories (modified version)	69% of possible points
Happé (1994)	8-year-olds	Strange Stories	88% of possible points
Hayward (2011)	8-, 10- and 12-year-olds	Strange Stories, Faux Pas, Eyes Test	76% of possible points on Strange Stories at age 8, 79% at 10, 83% at 12, 63% on Faux Pas at 8, 68% at 10, 64% at 12, 68% on Eyes Test at 8, 70% at 10, 72% at 12
Henderson et al. (2009)	8- to 16-year-olds (M = 13)	Strange Stories, Eyes Test	89% of possible points on Strange Stories, 73% on Eyes Test

TABLE 4.6 (continued)   Samples, Methods, and Findings in Studies Employing Higher-Order Measures of Theory of Mind With Nonclinical Child Populations

Study	Sample	Method	Findings
Kaland et al. (2008)	9- to 20-year-olds ($M = 15$)	Eyes Test (modified version), Strange Stories, Stories From Everyday Life	83% of possible points on Eyes Test, 94% on Strange Stories, 95% on Everyday Life
Loth et al. (2010)	8- to 16-year-olds ($M = 11$)	Strange Stories	78% of possible points
Meins et al. (2006)	7- to 9-year-olds	Strange Stories (reduced version)	39% of possible points
Meristo et al. (2007)	6- to 15-year-olds ($M = 10$)	Faux Pas (reduced version)	69% of possible points
O'Hare et al. (2009)	5- to 12-year-olds	Strange Stories (revised scoring)	19% of possible points at age 5, 79% at age 12
Qualter et al. (2011)	8- to 10-year-olds	Faux Pas (reduced version)	69% of possible points
Shaked et al. (2006)	4-year-olds	Strange Stories (reduced version)	26% of possible points
Sobel et al. (2005)	10-year-olds	Strange Stories (modified version)	81% of possible points
Sutton et al. (2000)	12-year-olds	Eyes Test	64% of possible points
Turkstra et al. (2008)	13- to 21-year-olds ($M = 18$)	Strange Stories, Faux Pas	73% of possible points on Strange Stories, 86% on Faux Pas

attempted to apply any of the measures prior to age 7 (and the few exceptions to this rule have used simplified versions of the tasks). As the table indicates, adolescent samples do sometimes approach ceiling performance on some of the measures, perhaps especially Strange Stories. Performance within the span of childhood, however, is well below ceiling.

A second finding is that performance on such tasks shows the expected improvement with age. The available evidence on this point is not all that one would hope, given that many studies, even those with a wide range of ages, fail to include a breakdown by age. Those that do, however, generally find (the Hayward, 2011, research being an exception) that performance gets better as children grow older.

I will add a point not evident in the table, and that is that performance often continues to get better into adulthood as well. Each of the first four measures described in this chapter has been utilized in the study of a range of clinical conditions in adult participants—most commonly autism but other syndromes as well. Most such studies include a comparison group of unimpaired adults, and such groups typically perform at high levels that exceed those found in childhood or adolescence. It is interesting to note, however, that performance is not necessarily at ceiling even in adult samples. This conclusion is probably clearest with respect to the Eyes Test, and it is this measure, probably not coincidentally, that has been the most often used of the various tests in research with adults.

Comparisons Among Tasks

As Table 4.6 indicates, only a minority of studies have employed more than one of the newer higher-order measures. When multiple measures have been employed, the focus has generally been on their individual or joint prediction of some clinical condition such as autism and not on the relative difficulty of the tasks. Indeed, none of the multimeasure studies summarized in the table include any inferential tests that compare performance on the different measures. An eye-balling of means suggests that Strange Stories is a bit easier than the Eyes Test (a conclusion that also emerges in the adult literature). In general, however, the similarities among tasks appear greater than the differences.

What about comparisons with the second-order false belief task? A general goal behind the development of the newer measures was to probe for forms of reasoning more complex than those sufficient for success on the second-order task. These tasks, then, were designed to be more difficult, and the evidence indicates that they are. Age-of-mastery data provide support for this conclusion, and so also do the handful of within-study comparisons. In some studies, in fact, success on the second-order task has been used as a selection criterion: Only children who pass the task go on to receive the newer measures.

Relative difficulty is one issue when two or more measures are included in the same study. The other issue is association among the measures. If the measures are all tapping into the same general construct, as is the goal with the tasks described here, then we would expect responses to them to correlate positively.

Such is sometimes, although not always, the case. Several studies have reported significant correlations among measures, a finding that emerges in both child (e.g., Botting & Conti-Ramsden, 2008) and adult (e.g., Speck, Scholte, & Van Berckelaer-Onnes, 2010) samples. On the other hand, not all researchers have found significant relations (e.g., Ahmed & Miller, 2011; Hayward & Homer, 2011), and when correlations do emerge they are seldom large. There is also the question of the basis for the correlations: whether they reflect the common content tapped by the various measures (which, of course, is the explanation of interest) or whether they result simply from shared methods variance, given the highly verbal nature of most of the instruments. Evidence of divergent validity remains a task for future research.

The greater ease of the second-order belief task militates against the likelihood of its correlating with the newer measures. For two measures to correlate there must be sufficient variation in response to each. Results are mixed in the handful of studies that meet this criterion. The most extensive examination of the issue (Hayward, 2011; Hayward & Homer, 2011) found no correlation between second-order false belief and either Faux Pas or the Eyes Test and only a weak relation ($r = .25$) with Strange Stories. In contrast, Banerjee (2000) reported a partial correlation (controlling for age) of .35 between the second-order task and a reduced version of Faux Pas, and Qualter, Barlow, and Stylianou (2011) obtained a partial correlation (controlling for both age and language) of .25 between the two measures. In addition, both Farmer (2000) and Meristo and Hjelmquist (2009) reported significant and fairly substantial (around .50) correlations between second-order belief and both Strange Stories and Faux Pas.

Sex Differences

The discussion of first-order developments in Chapter 2 made no mention of sex differences. In this respect it paralleled most treatments of this literature. For example, the four general theory-of-mind books cited in the opening chapter (Carpendale & Lewis, 2006; Doherty, 2009; Hughes, 2011; Moore, 2006) devote a total of half a dozen sentences to the issue of sex differences.

This is not to say that no differences exist. It is true that the great majority of first-order theory-of-mind studies either report no difference between boys and girls or are silent on the issue. Charman, Ruffman, and Clements (2002) argued, however, that the relatively small sample sizes in most such studies may make it difficult to detect a genuine but small difference between the sexes. They report some support for this conjecture: When they pooled the samples from different studies in their laboratories, thus greatly increasing the overall N, they found a difference favoring girls on both the contents and the locations forms of first-order false belief. This finding of girls outperforming boys is compatible with the occasional reports of sex differences that have appeared in individual studies (e.g., Banerjee, 1997; Cutting & Dunn, 1999).

Having made the case for sex differences, Charman and colleagues (2002) go on to acknowledge that such effects are small, are far from universal, and are limited to a narrow time window in the cases in which they do occur (boys, after all, are eventually perfect on first-order false belief). In their words, "Gender effects are weak and might perhaps be best construed as general tendencies with exceptions being the norm" (p. 8). And certainly anyone who has done much theory-of-mind research has seen data sets in which boys perform at least as well as girls.

What about the higher-order measures at issue here? As in the first-order literature, many reports provide no information about sex differences. In addition, sample size is again an issue, probably more so, in fact, than in first-order studies. Most of the evidence comes from control samples in studies whose main focus is on some clinical syndrome, and these samples are often the minimal size necessary to serve their comparative function.

With these qualifications, a fairly clear conclusion is that there *are* sex differences in this literature. Differences have been found for three of the measures. One is the Eyes Test. The original application of the measure (Baron-Cohen et al., 1997) reported a sex difference in favor of females, and many, although not all, later studies have confirmed this finding. Differences have been found for both child and adult samples.

Sex differences in favor of girls also appear on the Preadolescent Theory of Mind measure (Bosacki, 2000; Bosacki & Astington, 1999). In this case the difference remained significant when language ability was controlled; thus girls' on-the average superior verbal ability was apparently not the basis for the difference.

The final entry is Strange Stories. The original Happé (1994) study did not report a sex difference, and some later studies have also failed to do so. Other studies, however, have found a difference, and the direction is the same as that for the other measures: Females outperform males. Again, the difference has been reported for both children and adults.

The findings just discussed provide an interesting contrast with the first-order literature. As we saw, reports of sex differences are the exception rather than the rule in this literature, at least for sample sizes of less than several hundred. They also contrast with work on second-order false belief. It is no accident that Chapter 3 was also silent on the issue of sex differences—such differences simply do not occur in this literature. In contrast, sex differences appear fairly frequently in the studies reviewed here, and they might appear even more frequently if the typical samples were not so small (or, in some cases, all male or all female). It is true that differences are not inevitable (some studies do not contain even the hint of a difference) and that they are not large when they do occur. Still, this work constitutes the one aspect of the theory-of-mind literature for which sex differences could be argued to be a characteristic feature.

Why are sex differences more likely here than in theory-of-mind research more generally? Two factors, not clearly pulled apart in work to date, probably contribute. One is the age of the participants. Sex differences, especially in the cognitive realm, generally become more likely with increased age, and the measures discussed in this chapter have most often been used with adolescent or adult samples. Age, however, is not sufficient to explain the contrast. Some differences appear even in child samples; conversely, a move to adult samples does not produce sex differences on first- or second-order false belief. Such findings indicate that the content of the task is also important. By definition, any theory-of-mind task is at least somewhat social in nature, in that it involves some sort of understanding about people. The first- and second-order belief tasks could be argued to be minimally social, however. The entire focus of such tasks is on the cognitive processes necessary to arrive at a correct answer; it does not matter who the targets for belief ascription are, and nothing need be done with these targets other than to figure out what they (or anyone) would think in the situation presented. In contrast, measures such as Strange Stories or Preadolescent Theory of Mind come closer to real-life social reasoning and social interaction. Sex differences in social understanding and behavior are not common, but when they do occur they generally favor girls. The differences in higher-order theory of mind may be another entry in the girls-more-advanced category.

The preceding argument leaves unanswered the question of why girls should be more advanced than boys in social reasoning. Charman and colleagues (2002) discuss two, not mutually exclusive, explanations. One is differences in socialization history. Family studies indicate that girls, on the average, receive more supportive talk than do boys and more talk about emotions than do boys (e.g., Kuebli, Butler, & Fivush, 1995; Leaper, Anderson, & Sanders, 1988). We saw in Chapter 2 that aspects of family interaction and family talk can nurture theory of mind. Girls may receive more of these development-enhancing experiences than do boys.

TABLE 4.7   Baron-Cohen's Model of Different Brain Types

Brain Type	Cognitive Profile
The cognitively balanced brain	Folk physics = folk psychology
The normal female brain	Folk physics < folk psychology
The normal male brain	Folk physics > folk psychology
Asperger syndrome	Folk physics >> folk psychology
Autism	Folk physics >>> folk psychology

Source: Baron-Cohen, S., in Tager-Flusberg, H. (Ed.), *Neurodevelopmental disorders*,
MIT Press, Cambridge, MA, 1999, p. 415. ©1999 Massachusetts Institute
of Technology, by permission of The MIT Press.

The second possible explanation is biological. Simon Baron-Cohen (2003) proposed the best-known such theory in a book titled *The Essential Difference: The Truth About the Male and Female Brain* (see also Baron-Cohen, 2010). In very brief synopsis, the theory proposes that there are two biologically given brain types, with variations within each. The female brain is relatively good at empathizing—that is, thinking about and feeling for other people. The male brain is relatively good at systematizing—that is, organizing and reasoning about the physical world. Although there are many exceptions, females on the average are more likely to have the female brain type, and males on the average are more likely to have the male type. Females, therefore, tend to be better at theory of mind or folk psychology, and males tend to be better at reasoning about the physical world or folk physics.

What about autism? In Baron-Cohen's (2003) theory autism reflects the extreme of the male brain type, thus the maximum difference between physical reasoning, which tends to be unimpaired in autism, and social reasoning, which is very much impaired. Table 4.7 provides a summary of the different brain types.

One implication of the theory is that there should be more males than females with autism. Such in fact is the case: Approximately four times as many boys as girls are diagnosed with autism. For Asperger syndrome the ratio is nine to one (Baron-Cohen, 1999).

Special Populations

Most of the measures that I have been discussing were developed for the study of autism, and most of their uses have come in that context. I consider the work on autism shortly. In this section I review findings from three other populations that provide data of interest. Sprung (2010) provides a more general overview of the use of these and other theory-of-mind measures with a range of clinical syndromes.

One population is relatives of people with autism. Although much remains to be learned about the etiology of autism, there is little doubt that the disorder has a strong genetic basis (Brown, 2010; Curran & Bolton, 2009). If genes are important for autism, then we would expect similarities among people who share a substantial proportion of their genes, in particular first-order relatives (parents and children, siblings). Furthermore, if autism represents the extreme end of a continuously distributed set of traits—as most researchers of the topic now believe—then the similarities among relatives would not have to take the form of a common autism diagnosis. Rather, first-order relatives might show a "lesser variant" of the disorder, that is, some autism-like qualities even in the absence of the full clinical syndrome.

The theory-of-mind literature (which, of course, is just one approach to the question) provides mixed support for this prediction. The first examination of the issue focused on parents of children with Asperger syndrome (Baron-Cohen & Hammer, 1997). Compared with a matched control group, these parents performed more poorly on the Eyes Test but at a superior level on the Embedded Figures Test (a measure of speed of perceptual processing). This was exactly the autism-like pattern that had been predicted.

Most of the more recent theory-of-mind studies have been with siblings of children with autism. Most of this work, in turn, has examined infant siblings. In some, although not all, studies the infant siblings have differed from control samples in ways suggestive of an autism-like pattern—for example, they are less responsive to bids for social interaction (Goldberg et al., 2005), and they are delayed in the development of joint attention (Presmanes, Walden, Stone, & Yoder, 2007). Rogers (2009) provides a review of this work.

What about more advanced forms of theory of mind? Only two studies have explored the higher-order tasks discussed in this chapter, and they have produced conflicting results. Dorris and colleagues (Dorris, Espie, Knott, & Salt, 2004) reported that the siblings of children with autism performed more poorly on the children's version of the Eyes Test than did a matched control group. In contrast, Shaked and colleagues (Shaked, Gamliel, & Yirmiya, 2006) found no difference between siblings of children with autism and a control sample on a subset of the Strange Stories. The children were young, however (mean age of 4½), and performance was poor; it is possible that differences might have emerged later in development. More generally, more work is clearly needed to determine whether the "lesser variant" pattern holds for older children and more advanced forms of theory of mind.

The second population is children adopted from Romanian orphanages. Such children constitute a "natural experiment": an opportunity to study the effects of severe early deprivation in a way that would be ethically impossible in a controlled experimental study. A research team headed by Michael Rutter has been following a United Kingdom sample of Romanian adoptees longitudinally for over a decade now (Colvert et al., 2008; Rutter et al., 2010). Among the problems that became evident early in the project was a pattern of "quasi-autism" identified in a subset of the children. As the label suggests, the behaviors shown by these children, although not meriting a diagnosis of autism, did mirror some aspects of the syndrome—for example, stereotyped behaviors, difficulties with communication, difficulties in forming relations with others.

Might the quasi-autistic pattern extend to the children's theory-of-mind performance? At age 11 the children were given the Happé Strange Stories measure. Their performance was compared with that of the two control samples utilized throughout the research: an adopted sample born in the United Kingdom and Romanian children growing up in their families of birth. Although the differences among groups were not large they were significant: The Romanian orphans performed more poorly than either of the other two samples. These results suggest that the cognitive deficits long known to result from early deprivation (most obviously, lowered IQs) may extend to the domain of theory of mind.

Interestingly, the detrimental effects of traumatic experience on theory of mind are not limited to childhood. Schmidt and Zachariae (2009) administered the Eyes Test to a sample of adult Bosnian war refugees. The refugees' scores were well below those of a control sample and also well below the level of performance typically shown by adult participants.

The third population is admittedly of less general interest than the first two; still, the research is intriguing enough to merit brief mention. Dziobek and colleagues (Dziobek et al., 2005) wondered whether professional psychics might have mind-reading skills that outstrip those of the general population. They therefore compared a sample of psychics with a matched control group on two measures: the Eyes Test and a test of empathy labeled the Interpersonal Reactivity Index. The results were mixed. The groups did not differ on the Eyes Test; the psychics did prove superior, however, on the measure of empathy.

Whatever may prove to be the case for psychics, the question of the origins of individual differences in higher-order theory of mind deserves more attention. Both Chapter 2 and Chapter 3 discussed various antecedent factors that appeared to contribute to the outcomes being discussed. Most of these factors have not been explored with respect to the developments considered in this chapter. Two exceptions exist. Humfress and colleagues (Humfress, O'Connor, Slaughter, Target, & Fonagy, 2002) examined the possible contribution of various parenting factors to performance on Strange Stories. The quality of attachment to the parent related positively to performance, an outcome in accord with findings in the first-order literature. The particular measures of parental practices that were included showed no relation, however.

The second exception concerns the possible contribution of executive function and language. I turn to that work now.

EXECUTIVE FUNCTION AND LANGUAGE

A look back at the first five tables in the chapter is sufficient to explain why executive function and language might be of interest in this literature. Most of the measures require that the participant understand a lengthy verbal scenario and then respond in words to a series of verbal questions. Even the one less purely verbal measure, the Eyes Test, assumes understanding of the relevant mental-state vocabulary. In addition, some degree of working memory seems necessary to keep track of relevant information, and inhibitory control may be necessary to suppress a dominant response (e.g., the literal interpretation of an utterance) en route to the true meaning.

Executive function and language are in fact important. The evidence is more extensive with respect to language. Probably because of their clinical focus, most studies have included some sort of measure of overall language ability, typically either receptive vocabulary or subtests from the verbal section of an IQ test. With only a few exceptions, such tests relate positively to the measures reviewed in this chapter: The better the language, the better the theory-of-mind performance. Because of the global nature of the language assessments, these studies do not tell us which aspects of language, if any, are especially important. In addition, in most such studies language has been included as a variable to be controlled rather than as something of interest in its own right; thus there has been little theorizing about the basis for the correlations. At the least, however, it seems likely that language plays an expressive role with regard to performance on tests such as Strange Stories or Faux Pas. The better the language ability, the more quickly and accurately the participant can take in the material to be judged, and the better the language ability, the more readily the participant can translate his or her underlying reasoning into the words necessary to answer the test questions.

As with first- and second-order false belief, further evidence for the importance of language comes from the study of special populations. Children with specific language impairment (SLI) perform more poorly than matched controls on both Strange Stories and the Eyes Test (Botting & Conti-Ramsden, 2008; Gillot, Furniss, & Walter, 2004). In deaf samples there is a clear relation between age of exposure to sign language and performance on theory-of-mind measures, including Strange Stories and Faux Pas (Meristo et al., 2007; Meristo & Hjelmquist, 2009). Finally, samples with autism provide the same sorts of evidence for the importance of language that were discussed in earlier chapters: Only those with sufficient language abilities are even testable in such research, and within tested samples there is a positive relation between language ability and level of performance.

The evidence with respect to executive function is both more limited and less consistent than that for language. Several studies, however, have reported positive relations for both Strange Stories and Faux Pas, albeit for only a subset of the executive function measures examined (Charman, Carroll, & Sturge, 2001; Filippova & Astington, 2008; Meristo & Hjelmquist, 2009). Both working memory and inhibition have been shown to relate.

AUTISM

There are now several dozen studies that examine the performance of people with autism on the measures described in this chapter. I settle here for a brief summary.

A first finding is that performance is impaired in samples with autism. There are occasional exceptions (e.g., Back et al., 2007); in the great majority of studies, however, people with autism have been found to lag behind whatever comparison sample or samples are included. Lags have been demonstrated for each of the first four measures described in this chapter; they also have been shown on the newer tests cited in the Other Measures section. In some instances, moreover, the deficit appears specific to theory of mind, in that group differences are absent or reduced on tasks that do not involve social reasoning.

Studies of false belief, whether first-order or second-order, lend themselves to a present or absent conclusion. It is therefore possible to talk about whether people with autism "have" or "do not have" theory of mind, at least to the extent that "having" is defined as success on these tasks. In contrast, the measures being considered now offer a range of scores rather than a pass/fail conclusion. The Eyes Test is a partial exception, given that its multiple-choice format permits a determination of whether performance is above chance level. Some people with autism fail to exceed chance level on the test, an outcome that is virtually never found in comparison samples. Many people with autism, however, are above chance in their responses. The difference, then, is not one of presence/absence but of degree—some success, just not as much success as that shown by typically developing samples. The same conclusion holds for Strange Stories, Stories from Everyday Life, and Faux Pas.

It has become clear that the answer to the question of whether people with autism have a theory of mind must be of the "it depends" sorts. It depends, to begin with, on the sample. As I noted earlier, many people with autism are not even testable with theory-of-mind measures. For those who are, the answer depends on the aspect of theory of mind that is examined. Some people with autism fail first-order tasks and thus show no evidence of theory-of-mind ability. Some have mastered first-order false belief but fail the second-order task. Finally, some can pass the second-order task but still have difficulty with the more challenging, and more naturalistic, measures reviewed here—thus show (to quote various recent summaries by Simon Baron-Cohen) "subtle theory of mind deficits" and "milder manifestations" and "residual difficulties."

As with first- and second-order false belief, the question arises as to the basis for success when successes do occur—that is, whether people with autism arrive at their answers in the same way as do typically developing individuals. Various kinds of evidence suggest that at least in some cases they do not. Neuroimaging studies indicate that somewhat different brain regions are activated during theory-of-mind problem solving in people with autism compared to typically developing samples (Frith & Frith, 2003). Even when they can solve the standard tasks, people with autism are less likely than typical samples to show implicit forms of understanding, for example, anticipatory eye movements based on an actor's false belief (Senju, Southgate, White, & Frith, 2009). Finally, people with autism take longer to answer theory-of-mind questions than do control samples, a finding that has been demonstrated for the Eyes Test, Stories from Everyday Life, and second-order false belief (Bowler, 1997; Kaland, Calleson, Moller-Nielsen, Mortensen, & Smith, 2008; Kaland, Smith, & Mortensen, 2007). In some cases, although not always, the response-time differences are greater for mental than for physical content. All of these findings suggest that people with autism may in fact take a different, and less spontaneous, route to solving theory-of-mind tasks, one based more on general reasoning abilities than on social-cognitive understanding. In Tager-Flusberg's (2007, p. 313) words:

> Some more able children with autism develop a linguistically mediated theory of mind that provides them with the facility to reason correctly about the social world, but their theory of mind is not based on the same foundational insights that are provided by a domain-specific theory-of-mind mechanism.

I will add, with respect to the last of the forms of evidence, that response-time measures are not limited to autism samples. Such measures have long been common in the study of aging, including recent work on theory of mind and aging. They also play a prominent role in theory-of-mind research with adults (e.g., Apperly, Back, Samson, & France, 2008). And they are beginning to appear in the basic child literature (e.g., Atance, Bernstein, & Meltzoff, 2010; Kikuno, Mitchell, & Ziegler, 2007).

AGING

The title of the first study of theory of mind and aging was "The Getting of Wisdom: Theory of Mind in Old Age" (Happé, Winner, & Brownell, 1998). As this title suggests, theory-of-mind performance, in this case on the Strange Stories measure, did not decline in old age; rather, just the reverse was true—the older adults (mean age = 73) outperformed a young adult comparison sample. In their Discussion the authors tied this finding to the notion, for which there is some although limited empirical support, that wisdom may sometimes increase in old age. Social sensitivity is a core component of many conceptions of wisdom, and response to the Strange Stories clearly involves social sensitivity.

Later studies have not replicated the Happé et al. (1998) finding. Two studies do report equivalent performance of old and young participants, in one case on Strange Stories (Slessor, Phillips, & Bull, 2007) and in one case on Faux Pas (MacPherson, Phillips, & Sala, 2002). In most studies, however, the age effect is a negative one. An apparent decline in old age has been demonstrated for both Strange Stories (e.g., Castelli et al., 2010; Charlton, Barrick, Markus, & Morris, 2009) and the Eyes Test (e.g., Pardini & Nichelli, 2009), as well as on similar theory-of-mind measures created for specific studies (e.g., McKinnon & Moscovitch, 2007). Furthermore, many such studies report no decline on control measures that do not require social reasoning, suggesting that the deficit may be specific to theory of mind.

Why the disparity in results across studies? Sampling differences seem the most likely explanation. Happé et al.'s (1998) older participants may have been an exceptionally able group, a possibility that Happé and colleagues in fact noted themselves. This speculation, however, raises two important points about this literature. The first is that there are marked individual differences at any point in the life span, including old age, and any on-the-average pattern of decline does not apply to all older people. The second is that all studies to date are cross-sectional, and what they show therefore are age differences and not necessarily age changes. No researcher of aging and theory of mind has carried out a longitudinal examination of stability or change in the same people over time.

I noted that there is some evidence that the difficulties shown by older participants may be especially great on tasks of social reasoning. This does not mean, however, that general processes do not also play a role. Various kinds of evidence indicate that executive function makes a contribution to the young adult–old adult differences. There is, to begin with, a parallel developmental course for theory of mind and executive function, in that both show apparent declines in old age (e.g., German & Hehman, 2007). This general pattern is reflected in within-person relations; with only a few exceptions, measures of executive function correlate with theory-of-mind performance in older samples (e.g., Charlton et al., 2009; Maylor, Moulson, Muncer, & Taylor, 2002). As with child samples, both working memory and inhibition emerge as important. A final piece of evidence comes from task manipulations. Manipulations that increase executive function demands (for example, increase the demands on working memory) negatively impact theory-of-mind performance, and they typically do so more strongly for older than for younger participants (e.g., German & Hehman, 2007; McKinnon & Moscovitch, 2007).

The Conclusions section of Chapter 3 discussed the question of whether executive function plays an emergent or an expressive role with regard to theory of mind. As noted then, the effects in old age almost certainly fall in the expressive category. In the absence of some sort of illness or pathology, it is doubtful that older adults have actually lost their basic theory-of-mind knowledge. What may be missing are the executive function skills necessary to express such knowledge.

CONCLUSIONS

In Chapter 3 I noted the atheoretical nature of most work on second-order false belief. If anything, that conclusion applies even more strongly to the work considered in this chapter. There is one exception. The Preadolescent Theory of Mind measure (Bosacki, 2000; Bosacki & Astington, 1999) has a grounding in Michael Chandler's writings, and it specifies a set of theoretically motivated components (conceptual role-taking, empathic sensitivity, person perception, alternative thinking) that underlie the forms of reasoning being examined. To date, however, this approach has not been employed beyond its single initial use, nor has anyone attempted to extend the theoretical analysis to measures such as Strange Stories.

Most of the measures reviewed here were devised for clinical/pragmatic purposes—specifically, as further, more advanced examinations of the cognitive component of autism. Although the enterprise is definitely an ongoing one, there is no doubt that the newer measures have added to our understanding of autism—and, indeed, to our understanding of the dozen or so other syndromes to which they have been applied. But their contribution is not limited to the pragmatic domain. Such measures also add to our understanding of typical development, for they demonstrate some of the ways in which theory of mind improves beyond the preschool and early grade-school years.

What exactly are these improvements? In particular, why are these measures more difficult than the second-order false belief task? Several factors probably contribute. One is the need not only to have mastered a particular form of knowledge (such as second-order false belief) but also to access and apply this knowledge within a particular social context. Like cognitive assessments in general, the vignettes approaches described in Chapter 3 are intended to be optimal assessments of the ability in question—that is, to draw out the relevant knowledge if it is present at all. As such, the scenarios are stripped down to the basic informational units that the child needs to arrive at a judgment, and this information is presented in as clear and helpful a manner as possible. It is doubtful that most real-life contexts are this accommodating. Furthermore, tests such as Strange Stories or Faux Pas require that the child not only infer the relevant belief but also something about the effects of the belief—embarrassment, deception, or whatever. This is a point that we will return to in Chapter 6 on the consequences of higher-order understanding. A recurring conclusion there will be that understanding of second-order false belief is often necessary but seldom sufficient for various real-world applications.

A second likely contributor is the multipart nature of these assessments. The second-order belief task requires judgment of a single mental state held by a single target. The measures considered in this chapter often require that the participant think about two or three targets simultaneously. Furthermore, a full understanding of the scenario may require an inference not just of beliefs but of other mental states as well—in particular, the intentions that underlie the actions described and the emotions that follow from those actions. There is, in short, simply more that has to be done.

The Eyes Test is a partial exception to the point just made. The Eyes Test requires judgment of a single mental state in a single target. In itself, this is a first-order task, a judgment about what X thinks or feels or whatever. Why, then, is the task so difficult? Two factors are probably important. One is the nature of the mental states that must be judged. As note, the Eyes Test focuses on complex mental states (e.g., suspicious, preoccupied, tentative) whose mastery in development may depend on an appreciation of the beliefs and emotions that can produce such states. The other is the available evidence from which these states must be inferred, namely, a single, static view of part of an unfamiliar face. Even though the task is a first-order one, the ability to make such subtle inferences on the basis of such limited evidence may depend on a backdrop of experience that is simply not available prior to middle childhood or later.

The discussion to this point does not suggest that success on the tasks reviewed here requires any further structural or qualitative change beyond mastery of second-order recursive thought. Such may not always be the case. It is possible, for example, that in some instances third-order reasoning (she thinks that they think that she thinks....) may contribute to the most mature responses that are found. For the most part, however, the advances demonstrated by tasks such as Strange Stories and Faux Pas seem more quantitative than qualitative: an ability to make not just one but several mental state inferences simultaneously; the ability to do so across a variety of contexts, including naturalistic ones; and the ability to do so across a variety of kinds of evidence, including limited and subtle forms. Advances in language and executive function may be necessary contributors to such developments, perhaps in an emergence sense and almost certainly in an expressive sense. It may be, however, that the main contributor—and the main impediment to faster development—is simply the need for extensive social experience that furnishes the necessary evidence about how people think about each other.

5

Other Higher-Order Developments
Part 2

As the title indicates, this chapter continues the discussion of higher-order tasks that probe for competencies beyond those found at the preschool level. The distinction between the approaches considered now and those reviewed in Chapter 4 is perhaps at least as much historical as substantive. All of the studies discussed in Chapter 4 were carried out explicitly under the theory-of-mind heading, most had a common starting point in the second-order false belief task, and most had the pragmatic goal of illuminating the condition of autism. The work reviewed in this chapter reflects a diversity of starting points and theoretical orientations, and it clearly falls more in the basic-science than the applied side of the field. The similarity with the work in Chapter 4 is that both help to fill in the later phases of the theory-of-mind developmental story.

Although no one (to my knowledge) has brought together all of the work that I consider here, there have been reviews of portions of this literature. Among the helpful sources are Chandler and Birch (2010), Keenan (2003), Kuhn and Franklin (2006), and Pillow (2008).

INTERPRETIVE DIVERSITY

Chandler's Work

One theme of this book is that most theorists and researchers of theory of mind have paid relatively little attention to what happens beyond about age 5. There is, however, at least one seminal figure in the theory-of-mind field for whom this indictment clearly does not hold, and that is Michael Chandler (1982; Chandler & Sokol, 1999). Chandler has long argued against the notion that theory-of-mind development is essentially defined by and complete with the mastery of false belief at age 4 or 5, a position he dubs the "one miracle" view of development. His contention, rather, is that many important developments both precede and follow success on the standard false belief tasks. It is the latter that I concentrate on here.

What further developments might there be? As noted, the answer is many—Chandler is certainly not advocating a "two miracle" view in place of the "one miracle" model he decries. Still, one post-preschool development is especially emphasized in his research and writing, and that is mastery of interpretive diversity. Interpretive diversity refers to "the appreciation that one and the same thing can be assigned different meanings by different persons" (Carpendale & Chandler, 1996, p. 1703). This appreciation is seen as part of a more general understanding that the mind is active and constructive in its encounters with the world and not merely a passive recipient of whatever information comes along. Clearly, in anybody's theory such understanding must be a central component in theory-of-mind development.

Although we can all agree that understanding of interpretive diversity is important, not everyone has seen it as a relatively late developmental achievement. Mastery of false belief, after all, could be argued—and indeed has been argued by many theorists—to demonstrate an appreciation of interpretive diversity. The child who has mastered false belief realizes that Maxi believes one thing about the location of his chocolate while the mother believes something different—thus different meanings for the same aspect of reality. In the false belief case, however, the two thinkers are not dealing with "one and the same thing"; rather, the mother has information that Maxi does not have. False belief, therefore, demonstrates only a limited, albeit important, appreciation of diversity: the understanding that different information can lead to different beliefs. It does not demonstrate the understanding that the same information can lead to different beliefs.

Chandler and Sokol (1999) illustrated the distinction just made with the following example:

> Imagine that two couples, the Wimmers and the Perners, both go to a movie. At some disadvantageous moment in the plot line of the film, one of the Wimmers goes out for popcorn. Later they end up arguing over the meaning of what they saw. By contrast, the Perners remained glued to their seats throughout the film, but also exit in sharp disagreement about what they had both seen together from curtain to credits. The Wimmers...are in a situation not unlike that of Maxi and his mother who have access to differing amounts of information, and the basis of any disagreement ... that they may have is easily laid at the door of the fact that going out for popcorn at the wrong moment often leads to false beliefs. By contrast, the Perners, who are also in disagreement ... closely approximate the kind of ideal test case we are looking for. They both have equivalent access to the "facts," they sharply disagree about the meaning of their common experience, and their disagreement has real epistemic content—that is, their disagreement is about what they hold out as matters of fact (rather than about some matter of taste or personal preference). (p. 222; reproduced with permission of Taylor & Francis, LLC, a division of Informa plc.)

This example suggests the kind of methodology that is needed to study the form of interpretive diversity emphasized by Chandler and associates: namely, require the child either to predict or to explain different responses to the same stimulus or event. The Chandler group has taken two general approaches to this task.

One approach makes use of ambiguous stimuli, that is, stimuli that lend themselves to at least two equally valid interpretations. In the visual realm reversible

Figure 5.1   Examples of ambiguous stimuli.

figures meet this criterion. Figure 5.1 presents two of the most often studied examples. With a bit of concentrated attention you should be able to see a rabbit and a duck in the first case and a rat and an old man in the second. It is doubtful, however, that you were able to do so when you were 3 or 4, for the ability to perceive both versions of a reversible figure is a developmental achievement, and most preschoolers show little success at the task (Gopnik & Rosati, 2001). The research to be considered now is limited to children who themselves can see both interpretations of such pictures.

The auditory realm also presents instances of ambiguous stimuli. Homophones (e.g., *pair–pear*, the different meanings of *ring*) are one example. Ambiguous sentences are another—for example, the instruction "Pick the big block" when there are in fact two big blocks in the array. Such would-be communications are undoubtedly the most important real-life form of ambiguity. Most of us spend little time puzzling over reversible pictures, but we have all struggled with messages that lend themselves to more than one possible interpretation.

Figure 5.2 shows an example of the second approach taken by the Chandler group (Lalonde & Chandler, 2002). The drawings are examples of Droodles, a form of cartoon popularized by Roger Price in the 1950s. As can be seen, Droodles are amorphous forms that do not lend themselves to any single, definite interpretation (Rorschach ink blots are another example). On the other hand, once an interpretation is provided—and every Droodle comes with an explanatory caption—it is hard *not* to see the specified interpretation. The caption for the first Droodle is "ship arriving too late to save a drowning witch." That for the second is "spider doing a handstand."

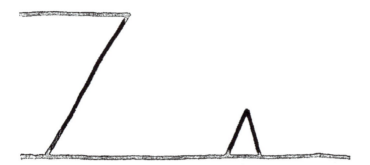

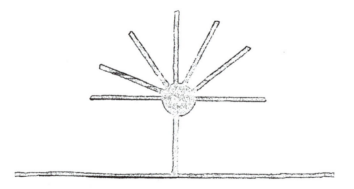

Figure 5.2 Examples of Droodles. (From *Droodles: The Classic Collection*, by Roger Price, pp. 8, 38. Copyright 2000 by Tallfellow Press. Used by permission. All rights reserved.)

Both ambiguous stimuli and Droodles have been used in two ways in research. In some cases the child participant first receives some disambiguating information about the stimulus. In the case of the Droodles task, for example, the child sees a picture that incorporates the Droodle into a complete and easily interpreted rendering of the full scene. Figure 5.3 shows the picture used in the drowning witch case. The question then is whether the child can predict the response of a target who was not privy to the information that he or she has received—someone, for example, who sees only the original Droodle. Procedurally, this approach is quite similar to the false belief task; in both cases situational cues create an informational

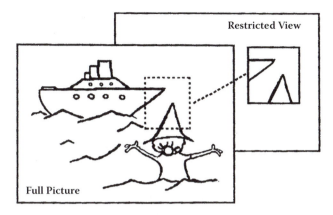

Figure 5.3   A Droodle disambiguated. (From Lalonde, C. E., & Chandler, M. J., *New Ideas in Psychology, 20,* 2002, p. 169. Copyright 2002 by Elsevier. Reprinted with permission.)

difference between self and other that the child must appreciate to judge correctly. Given this similarity, it is not surprising that success on this form of the ambiguity task emerges (usually—there is some variation across studies) at about the same time as success on false belief, namely, at around age 4 (Perner & Davies, 1991; Ruffman, Olson, & Astington, 1991).

The second approach to the study of ambiguity is more relevant to the Chandler conceptualization of interpretive diversity. In this case two targets (typically puppets) receive the same insufficient information about the stimulus—thus they see the same Droodle or the same ambiguous picture. The question now is whether the child realizes that two people can form different beliefs given the same information to work with. This realization turns out to be more difficult than the realization that people can form different beliefs given different information. It is only at about 7 or 8 that children succeed at tasks that require them either to predict or to explain different responses to the same stimulus (Carpendale & Chandler, 1996; Lalonde & Chandler, 2002). This conclusion is a general one, holding for visual ambiguity, lexical ambiguity (i.e., homophones), and ambiguous messages. It occurs, moreover, despite the fact that most of the children in these studies had succeeded on standard measures of false belief and most had no difficulty in acknowledging that two people might have different tastes or preferences. It was only different beliefs that gave them difficulty.

A possible caution with respect to this research may have occurred to you. Ambiguous pictures and Droodles are obviously rather unusual stimuli, and puppets are not among the real-life targets of interest. If conclusions about interpretive diversity were confined to such situations they might be of limited interest. Research by Ross and colleagues (Ross, Rechia, & Carpendale, 2005), however, makes clear that this is not the case. The task for the participants (4- to 9-year-olds) in their study was to make sense of conflicts between siblings, conveyed via scenarios that provided information about each protagonist's point of view but left the interpretation of the disagreement up to the child. Response to the conflict task showed the same developmental pattern as that found in the original diversity studies, with the youngest children showing little realization that two defensible positions might exist and older children better able both to identify and to justify different points of view. In addition, children's reasoning about conflict correlated with their reasoning on the standard measures of diversity.

A recent study by Lagattuta and colleagues (Lagattuta, Sayfan, & Blattman, 2010) provides an interesting addendum to the Chandler research. They presented problems on which two characters first received different but irrelevant information about the identity of an object, followed by a full view that made the identity of the object apparent. Despite the irrelevance of the initial experience, many 6- and 7-year-olds judged that the two characters would form different beliefs about the object. They thus applied their newfound knowledge of diversity too broadly, predicting difference even when no differences would occur. In the authors' words, they showed an *over*interpretive theory of mind.

The Lagattuta et al. (2010) study demonstrates that mastery of interpretive diversity is not complete by age 7. Chandler, in fact, has always been careful to acknowledge that the understanding of diversity demonstrated in his research is an early and simple form. There is still much for children to learn about where beliefs come from and how and why beliefs may differ among different people. In the rest of this chapter we will see what some of these further advances are. Nevertheless, the Chandler research does identify an important early achievement in the move beyond preschool competence: the realization that the mind does not simply copy reality; rather, two minds may impose different interpretations upon the same aspect of the world.

Sources of Diversity

Informative though they are, the Chandler studies leave one basic question about interpretive diversity unanswered, and that is exactly what differences two thinkers might bring to a particular task. Realizing that differences in belief are possible—the achievement focused on by the Chandler group—is a necessary condition for attempting to infer what the differences may be. It is not a sufficient condition, however, and the typical ambiguity study gives the child no basis for attaching particular beliefs to particular targets.

When might there be a basis for predicting how different people will interpret the same situation? The general answer is that prediction becomes possible when the child has prior information about at least one of the targets. Two approaches to the provision of such information have been explored. In some cases (e.g., Barquero, Robinson, & Thomas, 2003; Pillow & Henrichon, 1996) the child is given information about a target's previous experience with the stimulus in question. The child might watch, for example, as a puppet receives partial views of an object that suggest a plausible but (as the child knows) mistaken interpretation of its identity; the question then is whether the child can use this information to predict the puppet's response. The answer varies some across different studies and different ways of posing the interpretive question; for the most part, however, it is only at about

TABLE 5.1   Examples of Scenarios Used in the Pillow Research on Understanding of Biased Interpretation

Scenario

Ann doesn't like Linda. Ann thinks Linda is mean, and starts fights, and gets into a lot of trouble. Mary likes Linda. Mary and Linda are friends. One day Linda was throwing a ball outside. When Linda threw the ball, it went over the other girl and smashed right through a window. The window broke into pieces.

Cathy likes Sarah. Cathy thinks Sarah is nice, and helpful, and always does good things. Joan does not like Sarah. Joan thinks Sarah is mean, gets in trouble a lot, and always does bad things. At Christmas time, the teacher told the class about the poor children who wouldn't have any toys for Christmas. The teacher asked the children in the class to give toys to the poor children. Then the teacher put a big box at the back of the classroom for them to put toys into for poor children. Some of the children brought toys to school and put them in the box. One morning before school, Cathy and Joan saw Sarah holding a doll in front of the box. The box was open and its top was on the floor.

Source: Pillow, B. H., *Developmental Psychology, 27,* 1991, p. 551.

age 6 or 7 that children succeed in using a target's informational history to predict the specific response to an ambiguous stimulus.

The second general approach was touched on in Chapter 3 in the discussion of Brad Pillow's research. The focus in this case is on the child's ability to use general characteristics of the target to predict how the target will respond to an ambiguous stimulus or event. In the Pillow studies (Pillow, 1991; Pillow & Weed, 1995) children heard scenarios of the following sort: Character A likes Character C but Character B dislikes C; C then performs some damaging action, in some cases accidentally and in some cases with ambiguous intent. The child's task is to predict A and B's interpretation of C's behavior. Table 5.1 presents two of the scenarios that were used.

As we saw in Chapter 3, preschoolers showed little ability to use the information about the targets to predict their response, and kindergartners were only slightly more successful. By second grade, however, most children were able to make sensible use of the information about bias. They could do so, moreover, whether the bias was positive or negative and whether the response to be predicted was evaluation of the target's action or judgment of the intent behind the action (see also Mills & Grant, 2009; Mills & Keil, 2005, 2008).

The Pillow studies (Pillow 1991; Pillow & Weed, 1995) extend the Chandler research in three informative ways. The first extension is the one I have already noted. The Chandler studies demonstrate that children realize that diverse views are possible. The Pillow studies demonstrate that children can also use relevant evidence to figure out what the different views are.

A second extension concerns the situations with respect to which children can apply their newfound knowledge. As I noted, most ambiguity studies have focused on the interpretation of limited and somewhat artificial stimuli, typically partial views of two-dimensional pictures. Ross et al. (2005) is one exception to this statement. The Pillow research is another, given its focus on a topic that is clearly of real-life importance: understanding other children's social behavior (see also Wainryb, Shaw, Langley, Cottam, & Lewis, 2004).

The third extension concerns the types of evidence that children can use to make sense of differences in belief or behavior. I will draw here from a distinction raised by Higgins (1981) in a discussion of the perspective-taking literature. As he noted, the challenges in perspective taking are of two general sorts. In some cases the differences between self and other are situational in origin. This is the case, for example, when the child attempts to describe a referent to a peer who does not share his or her visual perspective. In other cases the differences between self and other reflect what Higgins labels the individual dimension, that is, general status differences that cut across different situations. This would be the case, for example, when an older child attempts to explain the rules of a game to a younger child.

Most studies of ambiguity have focused on the situational dimension. More generally, most theory-of-mind studies have concerned children's ability to use situational information (Miller, 2000). This is true, for example, of the typical false belief task, as well as most of the other frequently used measures at the pre-school level (e.g., appearance-reality, origins of knowledge). The Pillow research adds some relatively rare information about children's ability to use the individual dimension—specifically, to take into account positive or negative biases that may affect how children evaluate their peers. I return to the situational–individual distinction later in the chapter.

Relations to Other Developments

One issue with respect to any higher-order task is whether it correlates with other higher-order tasks. Of course we never expect a perfect relation; different tasks exist in order to assess abilities that are at least somewhat different. Still, if there is a common underlying core then responses to different higher-order tasks should show some relation.

The limited evidence to date with respect to interpretive diversity is mixed. Two studies provide data. Hayward and Homer (2011) assessed understanding of diversity via both an ambiguous figures task and a Droodles task. Response to the Droodles task correlated significantly, albeit weakly, with second-order false belief; neither the ambiguous figures task nor the Droodles task showed any relation to Strange Stories, Faux Pas, or the Eyes Test. I should add—given that this summary singles out the diversity measure—that an absence of relations was a general finding of the study; only 2 of 15 correlations among the various higher-order measures were significant.

More positive results were reported by Comay and Astington (Comay, 2011; Comay & Astington, 2011). Again, the assessment of diversity was based on both ambiguous pictures and Droodles; first- and second-order false beliefs were also assessed. A composite diversity score correlated .49 with a composite belief score; when age and language were partialled out the correlation remained significant at .31. In Comay and Astington's analysis the common core that links second-order belief and diversity is that both require an appreciation of two divergent perspectives on the same reality: John's belief and Mary's belief, a belief that the picture is a rat and a belief that the picture is an old man.

OPACITY

The notion of opacity is most easily introduced through example. Imagine that you hear the following pair of sentences (adapted from Kamawar & Olson, 2009):

> Jane knows that her cat is in her favorite tree.
> Her favorite tree is the oldest tree in town.

You are then asked to evaluate the truth status of this pair of sentences:

> The cat is in the oldest tree in town.
> Jane knows that her cat is in the oldest tree in town.

The first sentence is true. *Favorite tree* and *oldest tree* are coreferential terms; that is, they refer to the same aspect of reality. Any statement about the world that is true of one term is therefore also true of the other. Such contexts are said to be transparent. In contrast, the second sentence is not necessarily true, for we have not been told whether Jane knows that the favorite tree is also the oldest. The context in this case is said to be opaque.

Kamawar and Olson (2009, p. 286) define opacity as follows: "Opaque contexts are linguistic contexts in which one cannot see through a description to the referent itself…; hence the metaphorical name 'opaque'…. Opaque contexts, more formally, are those that contain both a proposition and a mental attitude toward the proposition." It is the inclusion of the mental attitude (e.g., knows that, thinks that, wishes that) that places opacity in the domain of theory of mind. Children must realize that the truth value of such utterances does not depend on what is true in the world but rather depends on the speaker's attitude toward what is said about the world.

There is an overlap between work under the heading of opacity and that just discussed under the heading of interpretive diversity. In both instances the core understanding—an understanding that is not present in early childhood but rather must develop—is the realization that the same object or event can be represented in different ways. In the case of opacity, however, the different representations are not imposed by different thinkers. The distinction, rather, is between a representation of reality and a representation of a mental attitude toward reality.

As can be guessed from its inclusion in this chapter, the notion of opacity poses problems for young children. The first demonstration of this point was reported by James Russell (1987). In the Russell study children heard a story in which a man named George saved up money to buy a beautiful watch, only to have the watch stolen by a red-headed thief as he lay sleeping. An initial question verified that the children realized that George did not know that the thief had curly red hair. Two further questions followed: "Can we say that George was thinking: 'I must find the thief who stole my watch'?" "Can we say that George was thinking: 'I must find the man with the curly red hair who stole my watch'?" The 5- to 7-year-old participants had no difficulty answering "yes" to the first question. Many, however, also answered "yes" to the second, despite having agreed moments before that George did not know the color of the thief's hair. They thus treated an opaque context as if it were transparent, focusing on the reality in question rather than George's knowledge about the reality.

Research since the Russell (1987) study has had two general goals. One has been to determine whether preschoolers' difficulties with opacity are genuine and not the result of some methodological artifact. The error, after all, is a surprising one—the child has just stated that George does not know what the robber looks like yet seconds later goes on to credit George with knowledge about the robber's looks. Perhaps performance would be better if the vignettes were shorter and simpler or the test question was not so complexly worded. Various attempts at simplification have been explored; examples from different laboratories include Apperly and Robinson (1998); Hulme, Mitchell, and Wood (2003); Kamawar and Olson (2009); and Sprung, Perner, and Mitchell (2007). These studies have led to a clear conclusion. Although the procedural simplifications have sometimes proved helpful, the effects are limited and success prior to age 5 remains rare. Preschoolers' difficulties with opacity are indeed genuine.

This conclusion leads to the second general goal: to determine why preschoolers find the opacity task so difficult. Why, in particular, is opacity more difficult than false belief? The two concepts, after all, would seem to depend on the same basic cognitive advance: the realization that a representation of reality is not necessarily the same thing as reality. Indeed, mastery of false belief could be argued to imply a beginning-level understanding of opacity: The child must realize that Maxi's belief about reality does not reflect reality, that is, is opaque with respect to the true state of the world. Beginning-level, however, is not mature form, and full mastery of opacity requires something more than just false belief.

One possibility is that this something more is linguistic. This was Russell's (1987) explanation for the results in the original opacity study, a position reflected in the title of his article: "Can we say...?" In Russell's view the main difficulty faced by the young child is in handling linguistic descriptions—specifically, in realizing that a description picks out only some and not all aspects of the real-world referent. Kamawar and Olson (1999, 2009) offer a somewhat similar explanation. In their view the key development is metalinguistic awareness, that is, the ability to reflect on language as an object of thought in itself—to "*see* the description, and not just *see through it* to the referent" (Kamawar & Olson, 2009, p. 287; italics in original). Such metalinguistic awareness is not sufficient for an understanding of opacity; developments in representational understanding are also required. It may be necessary, however. The Kamawar and Olson (2009) study provides empirical support for this hypothesis: a positive correlation between a measure of metalinguistic awareness and performance on the opacity task. The study also reported a positive correlation between understanding of false belief and performance on opacity, a finding that has emerged in other studies as well (e.g., Kamawar & Olson, 2011).

Other positions, while not necessarily denying a role for metalinguistic awareness, stress the representational advances that make success on opacity tasks possible. Apperly and Robinson (1998, 2003) and Robinson and Apperly (2001) have argued that the main challenge for the young child comes in understanding partial information. Suppose, for example, that Heinz knows that there is a ball in the box but does not know that the ball is a present. When asked, "Does Heinz know that there is a present in the box?" the child must answer not in terms of a full representation of the situation (i.e., that there *is* a present in the box) but rather in terms of Heinz's partial representation, which includes no information about a present. It is true, of course, that on the false belief task the child must also answer in terms of the protagonist's knowledge rather than the actual situation. With false belief, however, the protagonist is working with outdated information and all that need be represented is his or her ignorance of the current situation. Representing partial information presents a more difficult challenge.

I should add that Hulme et al. (2003) raised doubts about the generality of Apperly and Robinson's (1998) argument. In their view scenarios such as the one about George and his stolen watch do not entail simply a difference in amount of information; rather there is a qualitative difference between the information available to George and that available to the child participant. Research by Sprung and colleagues (2007) also suggests an addendum to the partial information argument. When they presented stimuli that could be represented in two ways (e.g., an eraser in the shape of a dog) they found what Apperly and Robinson had found: Young children answered in terms of their own knowledge rather than in terms of the information available to the protagonist. Children did much better, however, when the missing information had to do with a property of an object rather than its identity. Told, for example, that Heinz wished to find a red block, they predicted that he would go to the box in which he had seen a red block, rather than to a second box, also containing a red block, for which only the child had seen the color. Children's difficulties with partial information, therefore, do not seem to be across the board. They are limited to cases of dual identity.

Sprung and colleagues (2007) go on to offer their own explanation for the difficulty of the opacity task, an explanation that is grounded in the more general second-order literature. As we saw, the first question in an opacity task tests the child's understanding of the protagonist's knowledge—for example, "Does Heinz know that the dog is an eraser?" Judging someone else's knowledge is a first-order task, and thus it is not surprising that even 4-year-olds are fairly successful on this question. The opacity test question, however, requires that children recognize the difference between their own perspective on a dual identity situation (e.g., know that the object is both a dog and an eraser) and the protagonist's perspective on the situation (knows only that the object is a dog). This, according, to Sprung et al., is a second-order task. In their words (Sprung et al., p. 238), "The use of dual identities in … partial knowledge stories requires an understanding of different perspectives created by the dual identities in relation to another person's … perspective, which is different from the child's own. This becomes a second-order perspective problem." And it is because the task is second-order that success is not seen until about 6 or 7.

I have quoted Sprung et al.'s (2007) analysis so that readers can decide for themselves how compelling the argument for second-order competence is. Personally, I believe that the argument needs at the least some further development. I will note also that Sprung et al. attempted to provide some empirical support for their position by relating performance on opacity to performance on a task (taken from Perner & Howes, 1992) that tested understanding of second-order ignorance.

Although the two tasks proved to be at about the same level of difficulty, there was no within-child correlation between the two measures.

Three conclusions follow from the work reviewed in this section. First, mastery of opacity is an important developmental achievement, reflecting a major advance in the child's understanding of both language and representation. Second, such mastery is not a single developmental achievement but rather takes different forms, and even preschoolers may be capable of simple levels of understanding. Full mastery, however, is a post-preschool developmental achievement. Finally, research and theorizing have identified a number of contributors to this achievement; thus far, however, we do not have a fully satisfactory theory of why young children struggle with opacity and how they eventually overcome their difficulties.

ORIGINS OF BELIEFS

The work to be considered now is addressed to one of the basic issues in theory of mind: the child's understanding of where beliefs come from. It is part of the more general question of where mental states of any sort (e.g., desires, emotions, intentions) come from. Beliefs, however, have been by far the most often studied mental state, especially beyond the preschool period, and it is therefore beliefs on which I concentrate here.

I begin with some distinctions. Table 5.2 provides an overview of the points to be made.

As a starting point, consider one of the sources mentioned briefly in Chapter 2, a study by Pratt and Bryant (1990). In the Pratt and Bryant study 4-year-olds watched as one adult looked inside a closed box and a second adult merely lifted the box. When subsequently asked who knew what was in the box, most were able to judge that the first adult would know and the second adult would not. Note that both judgments are important. Children need to be able both to attribute knowledge when appropriate and to withhold such attributions when experience is insufficient to support a belief. The children in the Pratt and Bryant study were able to do so, thus demonstrating a basic understanding of how experience leads to belief.

The Pratt and Bryant (1990) task is perhaps the simplest possible test of the experience-belief relation: perception as the source of information, a simple empirical fact as the target for judgment, and either knowledge or ignorance as the outcome to be judged. In a sense, most other research under this heading—in particular, research directed to developments beyond the preschool period—involves various complications of this basic paradigm. The source of the information may vary. Perception is not the only experiential source for beliefs; communication and inference also contribute. The outcome may vary. Knowledge and ignorance are

TABLE 5.2   Relevant Dimensions in the Study of Origins of Beliefs

Source of Information	Recipient of Information	Nature of Target	Outcome
perception, communication, inference, guess	e.g., self or other, adult, child, or baby	e.g., empirical fact, word meaning, conceptual principle	true belief, false belief, ignorance, uncertainty

not the only possible outcomes; some kinds of experience result in false beliefs, and other kinds lead to uncertainty. The kind of belief at issue certainly may vary. Simple and arbitrary empirical facts, such as the contents of a box, are not the only beliefs to be formed, and most real-life beliefs of interest are considerably more complex than this maximally simple case. Finally, it may be important to take into account not only what kind of belief is involved but also who it is who is forming the belief. In a simple situation such as the Pratt and Bryant task the recipient of the information really does not matter—anyone looking in the box should come away with the knowledge in question. In more complex situations the nature of the recipient may be a critical determinant of the eventual outcome.

A difficulty in focusing on any of these dimensions in isolation—either in research or in summaries such as the present one—is that the dimensions never occur in isolation. Any belief-forming situation necessarily includes a source of information, a recipient of the information, a content area for the belief, and a particular outcome such as knowledge or ignorance. In what follows I organize the discussion in terms of source of information, beginning with perception and moving on to communication and inference. Each of the other dimensions, however, will also receive consideration.

Perception

As Pratt and Bryant (1990) and other studies show, a basic understanding of the relation between perception and belief develops quite early. By age 4 most children can make appropriate judgments of knowledge or ignorance based on the targets' perceptual access to the relevant information. Most can do so, moreover, for both self and other, although some show a tendency to overrate their own knowledge relative to that of another (Miller, 2000). Children who are 4 years old also typically succeed on the standard false belief tasks, thus demonstrating understanding of a third important outcome of perceptual experience in addition to knowledge or ignorance: namely, false beliefs that result from misleading perceptual information. What they do not yet appreciate, at least usually, is a fourth possible outcome: uncertainty in the face of ambiguous perceptual information. This, as the first section of this chapter indicates, must wait for the early grade-school years.

In studies such as Pratt and Bryant's (1990) the perceptual information is visual. Children must also come to understand the contribution of other perceptual senses, in particular hearing and touch, as well as the different kinds of information provided by the different senses. As we saw in Chapter 2, preschoolers initially struggle with tasks that require them to differentiate among the senses; they have difficulty reporting the source for things they have just learned (e.g., O'Neill & Chong, 2001), and they are also poor at selecting particular senses when seeking particular kinds of information (e.g., Robinson, Haigh, & Pendle, 2008). These problems, however, are short-lived, and by age 5 performance on such tasks is typically at or close to ceiling.

The gist of the preceding is that many basic forms of understanding with regard to the perception-belief relation are in place by age 5. Tasks with ambiguous information provide an exception. Are there any others?

The situational–individual distinction raised by Higgins (1981) is relevant here. In the tasks considered thus far the relevant information is all situational—what matters is the particular perceptual experience, not who is receiving that experience. It is worth noting that preschoolers seem to appreciate the irrelevance of the particular target in such situations; with rare exceptions they offer the same judgments for self and other, child and adult, friend and stranger, and so forth (Miller, 2000). But what about situations in which the particular target makes a difference?

There is not much relevant work with regard to perception. A study by Taylor, Cartwright, and Bowden (1991) provides the clearest example. They first verified that their participants (4- and 6-year-olds) realized that babies know some things (e.g., what rattles and bottles look like) but not others (e.g., what elephants and bicycles look like). A series of trials followed on which a baby observer received partial views of the objects in question and the children judged whether the baby would know what the object was. Despite having accurately judged babies' ignorance of the nonbaby items, many 4-year-olds believed that the baby would be able to identify all of the objects; 6-year-olds were better but not yet perfect at making such judgments. The children thus demonstrated an understanding of the situational basis for knowledge formation, namely, adequate perceptual access, but not of the individual basis: a cognitive system capable of utilizing the information. This is a conclusion that we will see again in the work on communication.

Several recent studies (Barrett, Newman, & Richert, 2003; Barrett, Richert, & Driesenga, 2001; Knight, 2008; Makris & Pnevmatikos, 2007) provide a novel approach to the issue of possible differences among targets in response to perceptual input: namely, questions about how God would respond to the typical theory-of-mind tasks. Although the results are not perfectly consistent, the data do suggest an interesting developmental pattern. Three- and 4-year-old children tend to treat God in the same way as any other target. By 5 or 6, however, a view of an omniscient God has emerged; thus God is judged as incapable of forming a false belief or of remaining ignorant even in the face of patently inadequate evidence about an object's identity. Obviously, determining the accuracy of such judgments is a tricky issue. But they do signal a developmental change in children's thinking between the preschool and grade-school years.

Communication

As with perception, a basic understanding of communication as a source of information is evident by the preschool period. Such a conclusion emerges from laboratory studies of the issue (e.g., Montgomery, 1993), and it is also implied by various naturally occurring behaviors (question asking, question answering) that are common by the preschool years.

The evidence suggests, however, that children's initial understanding of communication is probably shakier than their understanding of perception. They have difficulty in particular in recognizing the inadequacy of unclear or ambiguous messages, often overestimating the knowledge that can be gained from such communications (e.g., Sodian, 1988). In addition, within-study comparisons of the two sources, although not perfectly consistent, generally report better performance on perception than on communication (e.g., Miller et al, 2003; Montgomery, 1993).

Limitations in children's understanding of communication become more apparent when they must take into account not only the situational dimension (the adequacy of the message) but also the individual dimension (who is receiving the message). As in the Taylor et al. (1991) study, difficulties are especially evident when babies are the target. Montgomery (1993) found that most 4-year-olds and even many 6- and 8-year-olds believed that a baby could acquire knowledge from a verbal communication; this finding occurred despite the fact that the children realized that the babies did not know the words involved in the message. Miller et al. (2003) reported similar results; indeed, in their research the attributions of knowledge for the baby actually increased between ages 4 and 8.

The preceding is based on laboratory study. I should note that children's adjustments to different targets, including different-aged ones, are often more impressive in the natural setting. Even 2- and 3-year-olds, for example, direct simpler speech to younger siblings than they do to their mothers (Dunn & Kendrick, 1982). Miller (2000) discusses possible explanations for the lab-field discrepancy.

A more positive picture of preschoolers' ability also emerges from a recent line of research directed to children's selective learning from different would-be informants (e.g., Birch, Vauthier, & Bloom, 2008; Corriveau, Meints, & Harris, 2009; Robinson & Nurmsoo, 2009). The basic paradigm for these studies is some version of the following. Children watch as two adults perform some task, one quite well and the other quite poorly. For example (and this has been the most often studied content domain), Adult A might label a series of objects correctly whereas Adult B makes a number of labeling errors. Shortly afterward the children are presented with some novel objects for which they do not yet know a label. Adult A provides one label and Adult B provides a different label, and the question is which adult is more influential. A consistent finding, now reported across two dozen or so such studies, is that children place more credence in the previously reliable adult. This finding has been shown for several different content domains in addition to word learning and for several different ways of establishing informant reliability. And it has been shown in children as young as 2 (Birch, Akmal, & Frampton, 2010).

The findings just summarized provide impressive evidence of preschoolers' ability to use their knowledge of others to take in information in a selective and adaptive fashion. Also surprising evidence, given that in most settings preschoolers are not at all good at people-reading skills. It should be pointed out, therefore, that the learning situation in these studies is set up to be as simple and as helpful as possible: two simultaneously present adults who offer clearly contrasting responses to some task, followed by an immediate test of the child's ability to use this information in some closely related setting. The real-life settings in which children observe and learn from others are almost certainly not this helpful. It seems likely that a major developmental change beyond age 4 consists of a progressively improving ability to extract relevant information about others from the hubbub of everyday life. This point is not purely speculative; there is in fact an older research literature under the heading of "information seeking" that documents changes across the grade-school and adolescent years in children's ability to seek out and utilize informational sources differentially (e.g., Bar-Tal, Raviv, Raviv, & Brosh, 1991; Nelson-Le Gall & Gumerman, 1984). So far there has been no attempt to integrate the newer studies with this older literature.

Inference

Conclusions about when children understand inference as a source of knowledge are somewhat controversial. The question, it should be noted, is not whether they can use inference themselves; it is whether they recognize that inference can be a source of knowledge for others. Most examinations of the issue have concluded that children show little such recognition prior to age 6 (e.g., Miller et al., 2003; Pillow, 1999; Sodian & Wimmer, 1987), a phenomenon known as *inference neglect* (Varouxaki, Freeman, & Peters, 1999). In the within-child comparison in Miller et al., inference proved more difficult than either perception or communication. Studies in which children have to identify the sources of their own knowledge have also generally found inference to be more difficult than perception or communication (Bruell & Woolley, 1996; O'Neill & Gopnik, 1991).

Not everyone agrees with the conclusion that understanding of inference is a post-preschool development. Using simplified procedures (memory aids, heightened salience of the important information), Keenan, Ruffman, and Olson (1994) reported some success in judging inferential knowledge even among 4-year-olds (though see Pillow, 1999, for a critique of their conclusions). In addition, the type of inference may be important. In most studies the inference has been of the logical syllogism sort: All X are Y, this in an X, therefore it is a Y. Rai and Mitchell (2006) explored children's ability to recognize inferences based on elimination—specifically, if the target knows the names of two out of three characters, then he or she will assume that any new name belongs to the third character (an assumption that children in fact show in their early word learning). Children who were 5 were above chance, although well short of ceiling, in making this attribution.

A reasonable conclusion from the preceding is that inference comes in various forms and various contexts and that some forms and contexts are easier than others. Such, of course, is also the case for perception and, more strongly so, for language. Recall from the Strange Stories measure that children's understanding of speech forms such as irony or metaphor lags well behind their mastery of more literal, direct messages.

A further question about origins of beliefs cuts across the specific sources of information. It concerns the certainty with which the resulting belief can be held, including the relative certainty of the different informational sources. Do children trust some sources more than others?

One way to study this question is to pit two sources against each other. Suppose that the child sees one thing but is told something else. Not surprisingly, children as young as 3 tend to weight the perceptual information more heavily in such a case (Clement, Koenig, & Harris, 2004; Mitchell, Robinson, Nye, & Isaacs, 1997). They do so, moreover, whether judging for themselves or judging for another.

Another approach to the issue is to teach children to use simple rating scales to express the degree of certainty with which a particular conclusion can be held.

Research adopting this approach by Pillow and colleagues reveals definite developmental changes in feelings of certainty, especially with regard to inference (Pillow, 2002; Pillow, Hill, Boyce, & Stein, 2000; Pillow, Pearson, Hecht, & Bremer, 2010). Although 6-year-olds can recognize inference as a source of information for others, they judge the resulting belief as no more certain than a belief achieved through guessing. It is only at about 8 or 9 that children draw distinctions between the two sources. Children are better at judging the certainty of their own knowledge than that of others; when their own belief is the focus, children as young as 6 realize that inference results in more certain conclusions than does guessing. Finally, by 8 or 9 children recognize that different kinds of inference vary in the certainty of the conclusions that they yield. They rate deductive inferences as more certain than inductive inferences and strong inductive inferences (those with much supportive evidence) more certain than weak inductive inferences (those with less supportive evidence). Such judgments mirror the judgments made by adults.

In summary, three general developmental changes are evident in children's understanding of informational sources beyond the preschool years. First, although preschoolers understand simple forms of perception, communication, and (perhaps) inference, the variety of forms that they can handle expands with development. Second, developmental changes are especially marked with regard to children's ability to use the individual dimension in inferring belief. Even preschoolers have a fairly good understanding of the situational bases for belief formation; what they still need to learn is how different people make use of this information. Finally, with development children become capable not only of inferring beliefs accurately but also of reflecting on the nature of the beliefs—in particular, of realizing that some beliefs are more certain than others.

The last point prefigures material to be discussed in Chapter 7. As we will see, reflection about beliefs, including differences among beliefs, is a central theme of work in epistemology.

UNDERSTANDING OF MENTAL ACTIVITIES

The following passage from Flavell, Green, and Flavell (1995, p. 3) summarizes the kind of knowledge that is at issue now:

> Much of the research in this area has focused on young children's understanding of mental *states*, such as beliefs, knowledge, desires, emotions, and intentions.... In contrast, there has been little investigation of their knowledge about mental *activities*, that is, mental things that we could be said to *do* rather than just *have*. (italics in original; copyright 1995 by John Wiley & Sons; reprinted with permission)

The preceding section did provide some initial coverage of children's understanding of mental activities. Inferring, for example, is certainly a mental activity, and we saw that children's understanding of inference undergoes definite changes as they develop. The present section takes up the topic of mental activity more fully.

Flavell's Work

As is true of many topics in the study of cognitive development, John Flavell and colleagues are responsible for some of the first and the most influential research on children's understanding of mental activities. I therefore begin with some findings from the Flavell program of research.

The Flavell studies have concentrated primarily on thinking—"broadly and minimally defined as mentally attending to something" (Flavell et al., 1995, p. v). It will be a useful exercise, before reading further, to think about what you know or believe about thinking. Here and in general in cognitive-developmental research, the starting point for work with children is often knowledge of the adult end state—what are the developments that we are attempting to document and explain?

A first finding from the Flavell et al. (1995) studies is that even preschool children demonstrate some understanding of thinking. They realize, for example, that only animate beings think. Indeed, preschoolers, more than older children or adults, tend to deny that animals can think, reserving the ability only for humans. Preschoolers also show some realization that thinking is an internal act, and some are able to localize it in the head or brain. They show some ability as well to distinguish thinking from overt actions to which it is often related, such as seeing or touching something. Although they are not very good at doing so, they can sometimes make some use of available cues to infer when someone is thinking. Finally, they realize that thinking is *about* something, that it has some target, even though they are not very good at figuring out what the target is.

The preceding account should be qualified in several ways. First, "some" understanding is not complete understanding, and all of the developments mentioned show improvement into the grade-school years. Second, although 3-year-olds show some success on some measures, in many instances it is only at age 4 or 5 that above-chance performance emerges. Finally, the assessment procedures throughout the Flavell program of research are designed to be as clear, simple, and undemanding as possible (something that the Flavell group is very good at). The fragile competence elicited by such measures may not be evident very often in the child's everyday cognitive efforts.

A further point, of course, is that many forms of understanding are not even minimally present in preschoolers but rather emerge only later in development. As a sampling, I discuss two such developments here.

One is an aspect of thinking first identified by William James more than a century ago (James, 1890, p. 239):

> Consciousness, then, does not appear to itself chopped up in bits. Such words as "chain" or "train" do not describe it fitly as it presents itself in the first instance. It is nothing jointed; it flows. A "river" or a "stream" are the metaphors by which it is most naturally described. *In talking of it hereafter, let us call it the stream of thought, of consciousness, or of subjective life.* (italics in original; copyright 1890 by Holt; reprinted with permission)

This passage expresses the famous Jamesean notion of the stream of consciousness—an essentially unending flow of mental activity that characterizes the mental life of a sentient human being. It is a notion, research reveals, with which most adults agree (Flavell, Green, & Flavell, 1993). What about children? For preschoolers the answer is clear. Preschool children have difficulty identifying thinking even when the clues seem maximally obvious (e.g., a problem to be solved, a pensive look, relevant verbalizations). Most are loath to credit any sort of mental activity to someone who is just sitting silently. In Flavell et al.'s words (1995, p. 32), "4-year-olds are apt to believe that a person who is doing nothing overtly may also be doing nothing covertly." This judgment extends to their own mental life—preschoolers are no better at introspecting about their own mental activities than they are at judging the mental activities of others.

Although they are not yet at adult level, 6- and 7-year-olds are a good deal more likely than preschoolers to believe that some sort of ongoing mental activity is the norm rather than an exception. They also show some understanding of how one mental activity can lead to another, a phenomenon known as cognitive cuing (Gordon & Flavell, 1977). By 8 or 10 children are also able to *withhold* attributions of thinking when doing so is relevant; in particular, they realize that someone who is asleep and not dreaming is not thinking or engaging in any other consciousness-requiring mental activity (Flavell, Green, Flavell, & Lin, 1999). Finally, by the grade-school years children begin to show some appreciation of the fact that different thinkers may have diverse trains of thought—that two people looking at the same object, for example, may be thinking quite different things (Eisbach, 2004). Note the convergence of this last conclusion with findings from the Chandler work on understanding of interpretive diversity.

The second development to be discussed is related. One implication of the stream of consciousness is that we have limited ability to control our mental activity. We cannot, for example, simply will ourselves to think of nothing for an extended period of time. Many preschoolers do not realize this. When asked, for example, whether someone can keep her mind free of thoughts for 3 minutes many respond yes (Flavell et al., 1993); indeed, some believe that it is possible to do so for 3 days (Flavell, Green, & Flavell, 1998)! Older children are more likely to share the adult intuition that an extended stretch with no mental content is simply not possible.

Children also come to realize that different mental activities vary in how controllable they are. Table 5.3 shows some of the items used in the Flavell group's examination of this issue (Flavell & Green, 1999). The first three items (Knowing, Fearing, Wanting) were intended as examples of hard-to-control mental activities; the other entries in this category were Liking and Believing. The last three items (Thinking, Imagining, Changing One's Mind) were included as examples of relatively easy-to-control mental activities; the other entries in this category were Looking and Paying Attention. The basic question following each scenario was whether it would be easy or hard for the story character to change the mental activity. As with other studies in the Flavell program of research, the results showed a clear age difference. Seven-year-olds (the youngest group tested) did fairly well but not as well as 10-year-olds who in turn were (by some measures) not yet at the level of adults. Interestingly, the main difficulty shown by the youngest children came on the easy-to-control items. Only a third, for example, judged that Clara would be able to change what she was thinking about. These results indicate

TABLE 5.3   Examples of Items From the Flavell and Green Study of the Controllability of Mental Activities

Cognitive activity	Example
Knowing	"This is about Mary. Mary knows her name. She knows that her name is Mary. Now suppose she doesn't want to know that her name is Mary any longer. So, she is going to try very hard to forget that her name is Mary. Will it be kind of easy or kind of hard for her to forget that her name is Mary? Why would that be kind of easy (kind of hard)?"
Fearing	"This is about Julia. Julia was bitten by a big dog one time. Now she is very afraid of big dogs. She is really really afraid of big dogs. Now suppose she doesn't want to feel afraid of big dogs any longer. She is going to try very hard to stop feeling afraid of big dogs."
Wanting	"This is about Jane. Jane doesn't have a computer at home. She wants very much to have a computer. She has wanted one for a very long time. Now suppose she would like to stop wanting a computer. She is going to try very hard to stop wanting a computer."
Thinking	"Now I'll tell you about Clara. Clara is walking along one morning and suddenly, she starts to think about the cereal she just ate for breakfast. So, she is thinking about that cereal. Now suppose she doesn't want to think about that cereal any longer. She is going to try very hard to stop thinking about that cereal."
Imagining	"This is about Wendy. Wendy is sitting quietly in her room. Suddenly, she starts to imagine that she is someplace else. She is imagining that she is sitting in a tree. Now suppose that she doesn't want to imagine that she is sitting in a tree any longer. She is going to try very hard to stop imagining that she is sitting in a tree."
Changing one's mind	"This is about Hannah. Hannah has decided to take her parrot out of his cage. So, she has made up her mind to take her parrot out of his cage. Now suppose she wants to change her mind about taking her parrot out and decide not to do that after all. She is going to try very hard to change her mind about taking her parrot out of his cage."

Source: Flavell, J. H., & Green, F., *Cognitive Development, 14,* 1999, pp. 137–139. Copyright 1999 by Elsevier. Reprinted with permission.

that children face two, related challenges as they develop: coming to realize that mental activities are often uncontrollable but at the same time also developing an appreciation for the exceptions to this rule.

In some instances children's knowledge about the controllability of mental states may have clinical implications. Some recent research by Sprung and colleagues (Sprung, 2008; Sprung & Harris, 2010; Sprung, Lindner, & Thun-Hohenstein, 2011) provides an example. The primary participants for their research were children who had recently undergone a traumatic experience; some had been exposed a few months earlier to Hurricane Katrina, and some had been hospitalized because of injury or maltreatment. The primary measure was the frequency and nature of intrusive thoughts, defined as when "we start to think about something we don't really want to think about." Two main findings emerged. As would be expected, the children who had recently been traumatized reported more negative intrusive thoughts than did a nonexposed control group. In addition, it was children whose theory-of-mind understanding was greatest (as determined primarily by response to a subset of the Flavell questions) who showed the greatest awareness of negative thoughts. If, as many clinicians believe, reflecting about traumatic experience is a necessary step in overcoming such experience, then these results suggest that theory-of-mind understanding may play an important role.

Even more than is true for most theory-of-mind research, the preceding summary is based largely on the study of Western, mostly middle-class children. It is worth noting, therefore, that many of the same findings, especially those concerning preschoolers' difficulties with the concept of thinking, emerged in an independent project with a sample of Filipino children (Liwag, 1999). (For other related work, see Amsterlaw, 2006; Wellman & Hickling, 1994.)

Schwanenflugel and Fabricius's Work

A helpful review by Pillow (2008) draws a distinction among three kinds of understanding with regard to mental activities. One kind is labeled *occurrence knowledge*, defined as "knowledge that particular cognitive activities occur" (p. 299). It is this sort of knowledge to which the Flavell studies were directed. The other two forms of understanding are *organizational knowledge* ("knowledge of relations among cognitive activities"—p. 299) and *epistemological thought* ("reflection on the nature of knowledge and relation between knowledge and reality"—p. 299). The present section addresses the topic of organizational knowledge. Epistemological thought is one of the topics addressed in Chapter 7.

The main program of research directed to the issue of organization is that of Schwanenflugel, Fabricius, and colleagues (Fabricius, Schwanenflugel, Kyllonen, Barclay, & Denton, 1989; Schwanenflugel, Fabricius, & Alexander, 1994; Schwanenflugel, Fabricius, & Noyes, 1996; Schwanenflugel, Henderson, & Fabricius, 1998). They have taken two, related approaches to the task. One has been to have participants rate the similarity of mental verbs (e.g., "deciding," "explaining," "guessing," "knowing," "memorizing") with respect to how they would use their mind for each. The other has been to ask participants to rate the similarity of different cognitive activities. Table 5.4 presents a subset of the items used in one of the latter studies (note that the category labels—for example, List Memory, Prospective Memory—do not appear in the information provided to the participant). The items were presented in pairs, and participants rated their similarity on a seven-point scale ranging from "use your mind in completely the same way" to "use your mind in completely different ways." With both approaches, the similarity judgments were then subjected to various statistical procedures (e.g., multidimensional scaling) designed to reveal the underlying organization of a set of items.

As with the Flavell research, it will be a useful exercise to think about your own probable response to such an assessment before reading the developmental findings. Each of the studies in the research program does in fact include a sample of adult participants. Several emphases characterize adults' thinking about mental organization. Perhaps strongest is an emphasis on memory; cognitive activities that involve the use of memory (such as the first three examples in the table) tend to be seen as similar. Adults also distinguish a dimension of inference (including in particular the Inference and Recognition Memory items) and one of attention. Finally—and cutting across the content areas that characterize the first three dimensions—adults identify two more general dimensions. One is information

TABLE 5.4   Examples of Items From the Schwanenflugel et al. Study of Organization of Cognitive Activities

Cognitive activity	Example
List memory	Telling your friend everything you had to eat today in the school cafeteria.
	Writing down the names of the states you learned about in social studies last year.
Prospective memory	Being sure to turn on the TV to watch your teacher on the evening news.
	Making sure to stop by your classroom after playing to pick up your sweater before you go home.
Recognition memory	Identifying a song by the first few notes that your teacher plays on the piano.
	Seeing a mitten in the lost and found and knowing that it's the one you lost last week.
Comprehension	Feeling like you know how to do an assignment after the teacher explains it.
	Investigating a Lego building to see how it is built during recess.
Inference	Figuring out that your teacher is going to give you a test when she says "Put your books away."
	Knowing that your mother baked cookies for your school party by seeing the dirty dishes.
Planning	Deciding with your mom where she is going to pick you up after school.
	Choosing what you need to make your costume for the school Christmas play.
Selective attention	Listening to the announcements being made at lunch time in a noisy cafeteria.
	Finding where the rabbit is when it's the same color as the background in a picture in a science class.
Comparison	Listening to two different songs in music class and deciding if they were sung by the same person.
	Deciding if two crayons are the same color out of your art box at school.

Source: Adapted from Schwanenflugel, P. J., Fabricius, W. V., & Alexander, J., *Child Development, 65,* 1994, p. 1550. Copyright 1994 by John Wiley & Sons. Adapted with permission.

processing, which encompasses activities at both the input end (e.g., seeing, attending) and the output end (e.g., deciding, inventing) of the decision-making process. The other dimension concerns the certainty with which the resulting knowledge can be held. This means, for example, that "knowing" and "understanding" are seen as highly similar, "guessing" comes at the other end of the certainty continuum, and "thinking" falls somewhere in between. Note the congruence of this last finding with the research by Pillow discussed in the Origins section.

Children's ratings proved in some ways similar to those of adults and in some ways different. Eight-year-olds (the youngest group tested) did distinguish a memory dimension; they did not do so as strongly or consistently as older children or adults, however, and they showed little differentiation among different types of memory. In addition, 8-year-olds tended to group items along dimensions that from an adult point of view are relatively superficial—whether the activity involved going somewhere or staying where you are, for example, or whether the activity was something that you wanted to do or something someone else wanted you to do (perhaps understandably, a salient dimension for many children). By age 10 the memory dimension was both more firmly established and more differentiated in children's evaluations, and the more superficial dimensions had begun to recede in importance. At both ages there was some evidence, as with adults, for both an information-processing dimension and a certainty dimension; the latter, however, figured less importantly in children's judgments than was the case for the adult participants.

What is the overall message from this work? In the view of Schwanenflugel and colleagues, the most general finding to emerge from their research concerns the movement with development toward a progressively constructivist theory of mind—a conclusion, of course, that is in keeping with other research reviewed in this chapter. As children develop they place less emphasis on the external aspects of problem-solving situations and more emphasis on what the mind does to make sense of those situations. In the researchers' words (Schwanenflugel et al., 1996, p. 288, italics in original):

> A constructive theory of mind is achieved when children consolidate the following insights: (a) that knowledge can be more or less certain, (b) that feelings of uncertainty are important in evaluating information, (c) that things can have multiple meanings, and (d) … that those meanings can derive solely from differences in *interpretive mental processes*.

VARIATIONS OF THE FIRST-ORDER PARADIGM

We saw in Chapter 2 that the typical pattern of performance on the first-order false belief task is one of the most solidly established, often replicated outcomes in the literature. We saw also that there is general agreement that success on the task marks an important milestone in children's understanding of belief; questions typically have focused on the possibility that other, simpler measures might reveal success at an earlier point in development.

The work to be discussed now has an opposite emphasis: the possibility that variations in the typical procedures might result in *poorer* performance and thus provide evidence of aspects of development that are not complete by age 4 or 5. I address this possibility first with respect to children and then with respect to adults. In both cases a variety of different approaches will be considered, but the general message will be the same: Things are more complicated than we might have thought, and there are indeed further developments beyond those that the typical measures reveal.

Studies With Children

In a typical false belief task of the unexpected locations sort the target character has a desire to find a particular object. Thus, Maxi wants to find his chocolate, Sally wants to find her marble, and so forth. Suppose, however, that the desire is just the opposite—to avoid rather than go to a particular location. Perhaps, for example (to take one of the examples used in this literature), Sally does not like frogs and wants therefore to avoid the box that has a frog hiding under it.

Logically, the task for the child participant is the same in an avoidance scenario as it is in the typical approach scenario: namely, infer the belief held by the target character and then predict the behavior that will follow from this belief. Thus if

Sally believes (falsely) that the frog is under the red box, she should avoid the red box and select the green box instead. And she should do so despite the fact that the frog (as the child participant knows) is actually under the green box. It turns out, however, that the two tasks are not of equal difficulty; rather, children find avoidance more difficult than approach (Cassidy, 1998; Friedman & Leslie, 2004, 2005; Keenan & Ellis, 2003; Leslie, German, & Polizzi, 2005). The difference, moreover, is not trivial; only a minority of preschool children who pass the standard task succeed on the avoidance task (the exact percentage varies across studies). Younger children's difficulty is not in predicting avoidance under all circumstances, for if the character holds a true belief they have no trouble predicting that she will avoid the unwanted location. Nor is their difficulty with the ascription of the false belief, for if the question is "think" rather than "look" they do fine. The difficulty, then, is specific to the behavioral prediction: predicting that the character will go to a location that she actually wishes to avoid.

Why might reasoning about avoidance be more difficult than reasoning about approach? The most general explanation is offered by Friedman and Leslie (2004, 2005). The explanation is part of Leslie's general theory of modularity, a position touched on in Chapter 2. According to this model, to reason about an agent's action the child must select a content for the agent's belief and an action for the agent's desire. The default assumption for belief is that beliefs are true. In the case of false beliefs this assumption must be inhibited, which is why young children find the false belief task difficult. The default assumption with respect to desire is that action will be directed toward a known location. On the standard task this assumption poses no further problem; on an avoidance task, however, it must be overcome. Avoidance thus requires a double inhibition, which is why children find it more difficult than the standard approach task.

Keenan and Ellis (2003) offer a different, although not necessarily incompatible, explanation for the difficulty of the avoidance paradigm. Their position is narrower in scope than that of Friedman and Leslie, in that it applies to only some kinds of avoidance situations—specifically, to those in which a prey is attempting to avoid a predator. In one of their scenarios a thirsty zebra goes to a pond to get a drink, aware that the lion that she is attempting to avoid is resting behind the trees. While the zebra is drinking, the lion moves to a hiding place behind the tall grass. The question then is what route will the zebra take in going home: past the trees or past the grass? Most 4-year-olds indicate that she will go past the trees, thus ignoring her false belief about the lion's location; they do so, moreover, even when they are capable of passing a standard version of the locations task. Some recent research by Ellis and colleagues (Ellis, Bjorklund, & King, 2011) verifies this effect and shows that even 5- and 6-year-olds have difficulty with the avoidance task.

Why is the predator–prey situation so difficult? Keenan and Ellis (2003) argue that the task activates an evolutionarily provided instinctual response system that has evolved to promote survival and that this automatically evoked system, even in vicarious form (for the child, after all, is not the prey), overrides the more deliberate cognitive processing of which the child would otherwise be capable.

Intriguing though the evolutionary argument is, further research is clearly needed to establish both its validity and its generality. This question aside, the

Keenan and Ellis (2003) study does introduce another feature of potential importance: namely, an animate being as the target for the protagonist's thought and
action. Such a focus is rare; in the great majority of false belief studies it is some
inanimate object (e.g., chocolate, a marble, a toy) that serves as the object of
thought. Again, from a logical point of view the variation should not make a difference; people as well as objects may be in different locations, and beliefs about their
whereabouts may be either true or false. Several studies, however, have indicated
that the nature of the target does make a difference, with poorer performance for
animate (specifically human) targets than for inanimate targets (Rai & Mitchell,
2004; Symons & Clark, 2000; Symons, McLaughlin, Moore, & Morine, 1997). The
effect holds, however, only under certain conditions. What turns out to be important is the nature of the human's movement from the original to the new location.
If the movement is involuntary—for example, made in response to someone else's
command—then the task is no more difficult than the standard object displace-
ment problem. If the movement is voluntary, however, then keeping track of a
human is more difficult than keeping track of an object.

Why should this be? The explanation offered by Symons and colleagues (1997)
is that voluntary movement by an animate object introduces a second set of mental states for children to consider—not only the belief of the target for the false
belief question but also the thoughts and intentions of the self-moving agent. Even
though only the former belief is relevant in this context, children who are in the
process of mastering false belief apparently find the inclusion of additional mental
states confusing and thus perform more poorly. (Not always, I should add—Ahn
and Miller, in press, failed to confirm the voluntary-movement effect.)

Nguyen and Frye (1999) provide some further evidence that reasoning about
the actions of others may be more difficult than reasoning about inanimate objects.
Their study contrasted a standard unexpected locations scenario with scenarios that
involved a change in activities rather than a change in locations. Thus in an initial
scene Child A and Child B were shown to be engaged in activity X; B then left for a
while, and in his absence A switched to activity Y; Child B prepared to return; and
the question for the participant was what B believed that A was now doing. The correct answer, of course, is activity X—having no knowledge of the change, B should
have a false belief about A's activity. This question turned out to be more difficult
than the standard change-of-location question, with a substantial number of misses
even among 5-year-olds. (Again, however, I must note that the research evidence is
not perfectly consistent—cf. Garner, Curenton, & Taylor, 2005.)

The procedural variations discussed to this point have all retained a focus on
false belief; what has varied from the standard task has been either the content
of the belief or the action that follows from it. Zhang et al. (2010) add a different
emphasis: children's ability to reason about uncertain beliefs. Their participants
heard a story in which a dog placed his toy in a red house and left the scene;
in his absence a rabbit moved the toy to a blue house. The dog then returned,
and the question was where he would search for the toy. So far we have standard
false belief, and all of the participants who continued to the next phase of the
study answered the search question correctly. The next phase introduced the novel
element. The dog was shown to search unsuccessfully in the red house, and the

question was where he would look next. This *was* a question because there were three other houses: not only the blue one but a green and yellow one as well.

If your own answer to the look-next question was some version of "any of the other three," then you responded in the same way as the adult participants included in Zhang et al.'s (2010) study. Also the 8-year-olds. Not the younger children, however. Most 4-year-olds and a substantial number of 6-year-olds indicated that the dog would search in the blue house—that is, in what they themselves knew to be the true location. Note that all of the children had been able to set aside their own knowledge in the false belief case; many, however, proved unable to do so when judging an uncertain belief. As Zhang et al. noted, their results show some similarity to findings from the opacity literature, in which children also have difficulty realizing that someone may share some but not all of their knowledge. There is also an obvious overlap with work on ambiguity, in that in both cases a key development is the realization that not all problems have a single correct answer. Each of the three paradigms leads to the same general conclusion: Reasoning about uncertainty is a more difficult, later developing ability than is reasoning about false belief.

Studies With Adults

As we saw in Chapter 4, advanced theory-of-mind tasks such as Strange Stories or the Eyes Test are sometimes used with adult samples. For adults with clinical impairments first-order tasks may also be informative, and such tasks have in fact been applied across a range of clinical conditions (see Apperly, Samson, & Humphreys, 2009, for an excellent summary of such work). Presumably, however, there is no point in administering first-order measures to a sample of normal adults. What could be the point of asking adults to respond to a task that they had all mastered by age 4 or 5?

If standard tasks with standard measures are used then there is in fact no point. Suppose, however, that we introduce some change in the typical approach, perhaps a variation in the usual experimental procedure, or perhaps a change in the response required of the participant, or perhaps both. In this case we may pick up some variability in how even normal, unimpaired adults respond, some way in which performance, at least for some, is not yet at ceiling.

Figure 5.4, taken from Birch and Bloom (2007), shows one example. As can be seen, the task introduces three changes from the usual unexpected locations problem. First, there are four possible locations rather than the usual two. Second, the containers themselves and not just the object of interest are moved in the protagonist's absence. Finally, the response is not a simple choice between the alternatives; rather the task is to assign a probability to each of the possible search locations.

Not shown in the figure is a final feature: an experimental condition comparison. Some of the participants heard the wording shown in the figure: "moves the violin to the red container." Others heard simply "moves the violin to another container." Thus, the former but not the latter knew the true location.

This manipulation proved to be important. Those who were ignorant of the true location assigned an average probability of 71% to the original location of the blue container; thus they regarded the typical false belief error as Vicki's most likely

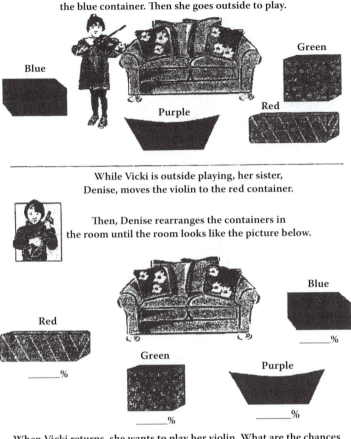

This is Vicki. She finishes playing her violin and puts it in the blue container. Then she goes outside to play.

Green

Blue

Purple

Red

While Vicki is outside playing, her sister, Denise, moves the violin to the red container.

Then, Denise rearranges the containers in the room until the room looks like the picture below.

Blue

Red

_____%

Green

Purple

_____%

_____%

_____%

When Vicki returns, she wants to play her violin. What are the chances Vicki will first look for her violin in each of the above containers? Write your answers in percentages in the spaces provided under each container.

Figure 5.4   False belief task used to test the curse-of-knowledge effect in adult participants. (From Birch, S. A. J., & Bloom, P., *Psychological Science, 18*, 2007, p. 384. Copyright 2007 by SAGE Publications. Reprinted by permission of SAGE.)

response. The only other container to receive an appreciable probability rating (23%) was the red one, the container that now occupied the spatial position where the violin had been left. Participants who knew the true location also rated these two outcomes as most likely, but their ratings differed significantly from those in the ignorance condition: 59% for the original container and 34% for the red container. Why the higher ratings for the red container? The only possible explanation is that these participants knew that this container actually held the violin, and they allowed their own knowledge to color their predictions of Vicki's response.

Birch and Bloom (2007) refer to the biasing effects of one's own knowledge as "the curse of knowledge," defined as the "difficulty appreciating a more naïve perspective as a result of being biased by one's own knowledge" (Birch, 2005, p. 25). As they note, this concept overlaps with the notion of egocentrism; indeed, most commentators would probably classify their findings as an example of egocentrism. The curse of knowledge, however, is a more specific and directional bias, in that it applies only to judgments of a more naïve perspective. As their research shows, both children and adults can often (although of course not always) appreciate a more knowledgeable perspective; the more difficult task is to realize that someone knows less than the self. (For another curse-of-knowledge effect on adults' first-order performance, see Bernstein, Thornton, & Sommerville, 2011.)

The Birch and Bloom study illustrates two of the possible ways to pick up some variability in adults' theory-of-mind performance: modify the task (four locations rather than two) and modify the response (probability ratings rather than a categorical judgment). A third possible approach is to give adults something else to do in addition to the theory-of-mind task. Newton and de Villiers (2007) provided an example of such a "dual task" approach. Their adult participants responded to a nonverbal false belief task of the unexpected contents sort while simultaneously performing either a verbal (shadowing sentences) or a nonverbal (rhythmic tapping) interference task. The nonverbal task had little effect on false belief performance, and neither interference task affected performance on a true-belief trial that was included for comparison. False belief performance, however, was markedly impaired by the imposition of the sentence-shadowing task; fewer than half of the participants were successful on the locations task, a task, recall, that most 4- and 5-year-olds have mastered.

Most of us, of course, do not engage very often in sentence-shadowing or rhythmic tapping tasks. Still, it *is* a common experience to have two or more cognitive activities in play at the same time, and it is in this respect that dual-task studies are informative. What the Newton and deVilliers (2007) study and others like it (e.g., McKinnon & Moscovitch, 2007) suggest is that theory-of-mind reasoning, even in adults, is not so effortless and automatic that it can proceed unimpeded and error-free when there are other demands on cognitive resources. A further, more specific conclusion from the Newton and deVilliers study follows from the differential effects of the two interference tasks. The fact that only the verbal task disrupted performance suggests that language is important not only for mastery of theory-of-mind skills; it remains important for mature theory-of-mind performance (though see Apperly, 2011, for a dissenting view).

Let us return to the curse-of-knowledge effect. The false belief task is by no means the only context in which such effects have been demonstrated in adults. Epley and colleagues provide an example from the domain of communication (Epley, Morewedge, & Keysar, 2004). The task for the participants in their study was to move a set of objects to various places in a spatial array in response to instructions from a "Director." Participant and Director were seated on opposite sides of the array, and the Director (as the participant knew) could see only some of the objects that were visible to the participant. One contrast, for example, was that the participant could see a small, a medium-sized, and a large truck, whereas the Director could see only the medium and large trucks. One of the Director's instructions was to "move the small truck." To respond nonegocentrically, the participant must realize that "small" from the director's perspective corresponds to the medium-sized of the three trucks that he or she sees. The adults proved fairly, although not perfectly, successful at directing their reach toward the appropriate object; reaching errors were considerably more common in the children (mean age = 6) included for comparison. Reaches, however, were not the only dependent variable in the study; eye movement data were also recorded. In this case there were no adult–child differences; the adults were just as likely as the children to direct their first look toward the object that only they could see—thus the small truck in the example. Adults, then, were just as prone to an initial curse-of-knowledge bias as the children; where the two groups differed was in the speed with which they were able to correct the error and respond appropriately.

The studies just discussed are just a few examples from a growing literature devoted to theory-of-mind performance in adulthood. No one, of course, suggests that adults no longer possess the first-order knowledge that they developed as preschoolers. What this research shows, however, is that applying this knowledge is not always as easy or as certain as we might have expected. Apperly (2011) is a good source for this work.

It may seem strange to spend a section on adult shortcomings in a book devoted to the positive developments that occur beyond the preschool period. But of course any shortcomings shown by adults are simply the lingering and relatively minor vestiges of problems that are much more marked earlier in development. Part of development beyond preschool consists of the acquisition of new knowledge. Part, however, is a matter of getting better at using the knowledge one already has.

CONCLUSIONS

This chapter, much more than the preceding two chapters, has dealt with a wide range of different topics. For each, significant advances in understanding occur beyond the preschool years, which, of course, is the reason for their inclusion in this book. But is it possible to extract any further, more specific themes that cut across the diversity of approaches? In this final section I attempt to identify several such themes.

One theme concerns children's growing ability to free themselves from their own knowledge and perspective. Some such ability, of course, is present in the preschool period; it is a necessary contributor to mastery of first-order false belief. As we saw in this chapter, however, the same child who easily handles first-order false belief may respond in terms of his or her own knowledge on an ambiguity or opacity task. Indeed, under some procedural variations the child may respond egocentrically to a first-order belief task. And not just children—adults also may struggle to overcome their own perspective. We can see here a message that emerged in the earlier Piagetian research: Breaking away from egocentrism is not a one-time process but a continual, perhaps lifelong challenge.

A second theme concerns understanding of cognitive activities—thus the processes and not simply the products of the cognitive system. Preschoolers are fairly good at judging various mental states. In simple situations, they are also good at figuring out where those states come from. As we have seen, however, a full appreciation of the constructive nature of the mind is a later developmental achievement. Understanding of thinking (the most thoroughly studied cognitive activity) is rudimentary at best in early childhood and continues to develop into the adult years. Finally, children's understanding of how others form beliefs shows one of the most general and important developmental changes. Even preschoolers are fairly successful at recognizing the situational determinants of belief formation, such as informative perceptual input or an adequate verbal message. What they struggle with—and what accounts for most developmental change beyond age 5—is the individual dimension: the contribution of the cognitive system to formation of beliefs.

A third theme concerns the expansion in the range of beliefs that are targets for children's thinking. The great majority of studies at the preschool level have examined understanding of beliefs of two sorts: where is an object located, or what is in a closed container. There are exceptions, some of which were discussed in Chapter 2 and some of which appeared in this chapter (in particular, the work on learning from different sources). The exceptions, however, are limited. It is no accident that the label for the most often studied concept in this literature is "false belief," not "false beliefs." The attempt has been to identify what children know about belief in general, not about particular beliefs. And as part of this attempt, most studies have presented the simplest sort of belief possible.

Each of the lines of research discussed in this chapter goes beyond beliefs about simple and arbitrary empirical facts. The work on thinking, for example, encompasses beliefs of a wide range of different sorts. The research discussed in the preceding section adds beliefs about people to the usual focus on beliefs about objects. We will see a further expansion in the kinds of beliefs that are the targets for thought with the work on epistemology discussed in Chapter 7. Together, these various research literatures broaden the traditional theory-of-mind focus on children's understanding of belief to a focus on children's understanding of beliefs

A final theme that emerges from the work reviewed here is diversity, in two senses. Each of the paradigms reviewed here documents children's growing awareness that people may differ in their mental contents. Even preschoolers realize that people with different information may form different beliefs. The Chandler research identifies an important next step: the realization that people with the same information may form different beliefs. The work on understanding of the origins of beliefs reveals further developments. Young children have limited understanding of the ways in which differences among people may lead to differences in what they take from experience. And even when they are aware of relevant cognitive differences (e.g., babies can't talk), they may at first fail to apply their knowledge.

The first sense of diversity, then, concerns children's appreciation of diversity. The second sense concerns ways in which children themselves differ. Of course work on first-order theory of mind demonstrates individual differences among children. Furthermore—and as discussed in Chapter 2—much productive research has been directed to the question of where these differences come from and what implications they have for other aspects of children's development. Nevertheless, the differences studied at the first-order level are almost all of one sort: differences in the rate of development. Except in clinical cases, first-order developments are universal developments; children vary in how quickly they develop such skills, not in whether they develop them. Furthermore, most first-order assessments are dichotomous; the child either passes or fails and thus either possesses the knowledge or does not yet possess it. Work on advanced forms of theory of mind offers the possibility for, and in fact demonstrates, a much wider range of individual differences. This is a point to which I return in the concluding chapter.

6

Consequences of Higher-Order Understanding

The preceding three chapters discussed a number of developments in theory-of-mind understanding that follow upon the well documented achievements of the preschool period. As its title indicates, this chapter is concerned with the consequences of these further developments. What are the advances in children's social and cognitive functioning that are made possible by the emergence of higher-order forms of theory of mind? The importance of exploring such consequences has been recognized since the advent of work on advanced theory of mind. Perner and Wimmer (1985) concluded the initial article about second-order false belief with the following statement: "Investigations into children's attribution of higher order epistemic states will achieve theoretical importance only if a developmental link with children's understanding of other social domains can be established" (p. 469). The purpose of this chapter is to review the links that have been identified.

We saw in Chapter 2 that the question of the consequences of theory-of-mind understanding is a long-standing issue in the first-order literature. In relative (although not absolute) terms, the issue has been even more prominent in the higher-order literature, in that a high proportion of studies have explored some would-be consequence of children's newfound cognitive abilities. This concentration on consequences has both a positive and a negative side. On the negative side, it is undoubtedly a contributor to the atheoretical nature of much of this work. Most research has concentrated on what second-order reasoning makes possible, with less attention paid to the nature of the reasoning per se. More positively, this concentration on outcomes means that we know a fair amount about how advances in social-cognitive understanding contribute to other aspects of children's development.

At least two dozen somewhat distinct outcomes have been explored in this literature. In what follows I divide the coverage into three general (and sometimes overlapping) categories: lying and other deliberately false statements, social outcomes, and cognitive outcomes.

A general methodological point should be made before beginning. All of the studies to be reviewed are correlational—that is, they measure both some aspect of children's social-cognitive understanding and some other aspect of their development and then examine the relation between the two measures. Because the studies are correlational, questions of causality arise. It is possible that the direction of effect is the reverse of that usually assumed—that is, that social-cognitive understanding is the outcome rather than the cause in the relationship. In most instances such a causal direction is implausible; as we will see, however, it may sometimes apply. The second possibility is that some third factor or set of factors is driving any correlation that is found, and that there therefore is no causal link in either direction between the measures being correlated. As a test of this possibility many studies include statistical controls for some potentially important third factor or factors; the most commonly examined such factors are chronological age, language, and executive function. In what follows I will not always indicate whether such controls have been employed (more study-by-study detail is provided in Miller, 2009). In most cases they have, however, and unless otherwise noted, none of the relations I report disappears when such controls are imposed.

DELIBERATELY FALSE STATEMENTS

Sometimes the intended meaning of a message is different from the literal meaning of the utterance. Such is the case with lies, for example, or jokes or sarcasm—to name just a few examples. Understanding the intent of such utterances is a theory-of-mind task. The child must realize that the speaker intends to create a particular effect in the listener—to implant a false belief, induce guilt about a misbehavior, or whatever. The mental states of two interacting partners must be taken into account.

We have already had some coverage of children's understanding of deliberately false statements. The Strange Stories measure discussed in Chapter 4 is directed to precisely this kind of understanding. As we saw, the youngest children tested with this measure (typically 5- or 6-year-olds) show only limited understanding of such nonliteral statements. Performance improves with age, although it typically remains short of ceiling even by adolescence.

The work to be considered now differs in two ways from the Strange Stories studies. First, the Strange Stories measure typically yields one overall score summed across the dozen or so speech forms that are included. The focus in the research at issue now is on specific speech forms (e.g., lies, irony) considered independently. The second difference—one that reflects the "Consequences" of the present chapter's title—is that most of the studies to be considered have the goal of relating understanding of such utterances to second-order competence, most commonly to performance on the second-order false belief task.

Lying

Of all the possible consequences of false belief mastery, an understanding of lying is perhaps the most direct. The purpose of a lie is to implant a false belief; thus it is difficult to see how lies could be either produced or understood without some realization that beliefs can be false. As Talwar, Gordon, and Lee (2007, p. 804) put it, "Lying, in essence, is theory of mind in action."

Although lying may be theory of mind in action, by most analyses it is first-order theory of mind. Knowledge that beliefs can be false is a first-order achievement, and such knowledge would seem to be both a necessary and a sufficient underpinning for both the production and the comprehension of lies. Reasonable though this hypothesis seems, the evidence in support of it is mixed. On the positive side, understanding of false belief has been shown to relate to the frequency and sophistication of children's lies (Evans, Xu, & Lee, 2011; Polak & Harris, 1999) as well as to the ability to distinguish between lies and mistakes (Wimmer, Gruber, & Perner, 1984). On the other hand, not all examinations of the issue have reported relations between false belief understanding and production of lies (Newton et al., 2000). In addition—and as noted in Chapter 2—children tell simple lies as early as age 2 ½ and thus well before mastery of the standard false belief task. Exactly what underlies such early acts of deception is a much debated and still unresolved issue (Chandler et al., 1989; Meis, Call, & Tomasello, 2010; Reddy & Morris, 2004; Sodian et al., 1991).

However this issue is eventually resolved, first-order competence seems sufficient (if perhaps not always necessary) to account for what children can do up to about age 5 or 6. What more becomes possible once the child can engage in second-order reasoning? Research to date has examined three developments. One concerns the ability to engage in acts of deception more prolonged than an initial false statement. A second concerns the distinction between lies and other forms of deliberately false statement. Finally, the third concerns understanding of different kinds of lies.

The first topic has been labeled *feigning ignorance* (Polak & Harris, 1999) or *semantic leakage control* (Talwar, Gordon, et al., 2007; Talwar & Lee, 2008). The method of study is simple: Children are told not to look inside a closed container or not to touch an attractive toy, they are left alone with a chance to peek or to touch, and upon the experimenter's return they are asked whether they have complied with the instructions. Three findings emerge. First, most children disobey. Second, most children lie about doing so. Finally, there is a positive relation between understanding of false belief and the tendency to lie.

So far we are at the first-order level. Suppose, however, that the adult's questioning extends beyond the initial "did you look?" The adult might ask, for example, "What color is the writing on the back of this card?"—a card that the child supposedly has not looked at. It is here that second-order competence enters in. To feign ignorance successfully the child presumably must represent the adult's false belief about the initial noncompliance ("she thinks I didn't look") and then the second-order false belief that follows from this belief ("she thinks I don't know the color"). Research by Talwar and associates provides support for this assumption. They reported a positive relation between second-order understanding and success either at feigning ignorance (Talwar, Gordon, et al., 2007) or at providing a plausible explanation when caught in an apparent lie (Talwar & Lee, 2008).

Lies by definition are deliberately false statements. Even preschoolers show some awareness of the importance of the "deliberately," in that they distinguish between lies and mistaken utterances (although this distinction is shaky in young children, as Piaget, 1932, long ago demonstrated). Doing so is a first-order achievement. Lies and mistakes do not exhaust the category of deliberately false statements, however. Many jokes are deliberately false statements, and the same holds true for ironic or sarcastic statements. The distinguishing characteristic in these instances is not, as in the lie-mistake contrast, the speaker's belief about the statement (since the speaker disbelieves all such utterances) but rather two further factors: the speaker's belief about the listener's knowledge and the speaker's intention in making the utterance. With lies the speaker believes that the listener does not know the truth, whereas with jokes or irony the speaker believes that the listener knows the truth. With lies the intention is that the listener believe the statement, whereas with jokes or irony the intention is that the listener not believe. We have, then, a prototypic form of second-order cognition: A thinks that B knows … and A intends that B thinks……

Various kinds of evidence suggest that distinguishing among different kinds of false statements is indeed a second-order achievement. Although results are not perfectly consistent (cf. Leekam, 1991; Winner & Leekam, 1991), age-of-mastery data generally support this conclusion. Young children do show some ability to make the distinction under maximally simple circumstances; the ability to do so, however, increases as children grow older. Correlational data provide further support. Performance on tasks of second-order reasoning relates positively (although sometimes rather weakly) to the ability to distinguish lies from other false statements (Sullivan, Winner, & Hopfield, 1995; Winner, Brownell, Happé, Blum, & Pincus, 1996). Understanding of both second-order false belief and second-order ignorance has been shown to relate.

In addition to distinguishing lies from other utterances, children come to distinguish among different types of lies. By definition, all lies involve an intention to deceive. Lies vary, however, in the motivation behind this intention. In so-called white lies the motivation is a positive, prosocial one: to protect the feelings of the recipient of the message. Theoretically, such lies could be argued to involve second-order reasoning ("If I say … she'll think that I think…"), and there is in fact evidence for a link between second-order competence and understanding of white lies (Broomfield, Robinson, & Robinson, 2002; Naito & Seki, 2009). Any strong version of the argument, however, runs up against an embarrassing empirical fact, and that is that children as young as 3 can produce white lies (Talwar & Lee, 2002). Preschoolers also show some success at using facial display rules to convey false emotions to others (Cole, 1986). The usual explanation for such precocious deceptive efforts—an explanation with some empirical support (Talwar, Murphy, & Lee, 2007)—is that parents and other adults socialize such behaviors directly, thus bypassing the need for much theory-of-mind understanding. Plausible though such an explanation may be, it does raise the question of how testable theory-of-mind accounts are, if specific experience can be invoked as an explanation for any precocious, contra theory outcome. This is an issue to which I return in the Conclusions section.

Whatever the contribution of second-order understanding to white lies, such understanding appears integral to another form of deception, namely self-presentational lies. A self-presentational lie is one whose one goal is to enhance others' evaluation of the self. Common childhood examples might include denying pain in front of one's peers ("It didn't really hurt") or denying disappointment in the face of failure ("I didn't really want that prize"). Robin Banerjee (2002; Banerjee & Yuill, 1999a, 1999b) has argued that an understanding of self-presentation requires second-order competence. With prosocial lies there is a direct behavior–outcome connection; smile or say "I like it" and the other will be happy. Self-presentational lies, however, do not have this sort of one-to-one relation; rather, their particular form will vary depending on the particular belief being instilled. Such lies can therefore be understood only in terms of one person's intent to manipulate the beliefs of another.

Two sorts of data support this argument. One is the developmental timing of self-presentational understanding. Banerjee's research program (Banerjee, 2002; Banerjee & Watling, 2010; Banerjee & Yuill, 1999a, 1999b) demonstrates that preschool children have little understanding of such lies, that understanding improves across the grade-school years, and that self-presentational understanding lags behind understanding of both prosocial, white lies and self-serving lies that do not involve self-presentation. Table 6.1 shows a subset of the scenarios used in one of the studies. The entries under the "Evaluative" heading are examples of self-presentational lies, whereas those under the "Factual" heading manipulate beliefs about objective facts rather than about the self.

The second kind of supportive evidence comes from the finding that mastery of second-order false belief is significantly related to understanding of self-presentation. The correlation does not mean that the two developments necessarily emerge in synchrony. Children typically demonstrate second-order understanding before they master self-presentation, a finding that suggests that the cognitive competence is a necessary but not sufficient condition for the social understanding. This necessary-but-not sufficient conclusion is one that we will encounter again.

A recent study by Naito and Seki (2009) adds some complications to the conclusions just noted. As in the Banerjee research, they found improvements with age in understanding of self-presentational behavior, with little understanding among preschoolers, moderately good performance by age 6, and better performance by age 8. They also found a positive relation between understanding of self-presentation and measures of second-order competence. In their study, however, the positive relation was not evident in younger children but emerged only at age 8, leading to the conclusion that "children base their second-order theory of mind and display rules understanding on distinct reasoning until middle childhood" (p. 150). Exactly what this reasoning is and why their results diverge from those of Banerjee are at the moment open questions.

The work considered thus far has been with typically developing samples. If second-order understanding is important for self-presentation, then we would

TABLE 6.1 Examples of Scenarios Used in the Banerjee Study of Self-Presentational Behavior

Behavior Type	Scenario	Question
Evaluative	Simon is in the playground. Some big children are playing ball and they let Simon join their game. They're all playing together when one of the children kicks the ball right up in the air, and when it lands it hits Simon on the arm. It really hurts. But when one of the big children says, "Are you all right?" Simon smiles and says, "Of course I am. That didn't hurt at all."	Why does Simon say to the big children that it didn't hurt?
	Julie is playing with her friends next to a very high wall. They all climb up on top of the wall. Julie climbs on the wall as well. Julie is very scared about being on the wall because she's frightened of falling off and hurting herself. But when they all get down and the other children say, "Did you enjoy climbing on the wall?" Julie says "Yes, I loved climbing on the wall."	Why does Julie say to the other children that she loved climbing on the wall?
Factual	Alex is at the fair. Alex really wants to go on the roller coaster, but Alex is only 9 years old and you have to be at least 10 years old to go on the roller coaster. So Alex is upset. But then Alex decides to join the queue for the roller coaster anyway. Alex gets to the front to buy his ticket, and the ticket man says "Hello." Then Alex smiles and says to the ticket man, "Do you like my coat? I got it for my tenth birthday."	Why does Alex say to the ticket man that he got the coat for his tenth birthday?
	Tina's mum has been making a special dinner and she asked Tina not to eat any snacks in the afternoon so that Tina would be hungry at dinner time. But Tina ate some crisps in the afternoon. When she gets home, she doesn't really feel hungry at all. But when her mum asks her if she's feeling hungry for her dinner, Tina smiles and says, "Yes, I'm feeling very hungry."	Why does Tina say to her mum that she feels very hungry?

Source: Copyright 2002 by Robin Banerjee. Reprinted with permission.

expect children with autism to lag behind typically developing children. Such is in fact the case. Children with autism are less likely to engage in self-presentation than are typically developing children and less skillful at doing so when they do attempt such behavior (Barbaro & Dissanayake, 2007; Begeer et al., 2008; Scheeren, Begeer, Banerjee, Terwogt, & Koot, 2010).

Research on understanding of modesty (Banerjee, 2000) provides an interesting addendum to the work on self-presentation. Although the general goal (positive evaluations from others) is the same for modesty and self-presentation, the behavioral strategies necessary to achieve the goal are opposite, in that modesty requires a self-denying, self-depreciating response (e.g., "I was just lucky to win the prize"). As with self-presentation, understanding of modesty increases with age across the grade-school years, and as with self-presentation such understanding relates to second-order competence—specifically, in the Banerjee study, to performance on the Faux Pas measure.

TABLE 6.2   Example of an Irony Scenario

Scenario	Question Type	Questions
Robert is a new player on his school's soccer team. He is really excited about being on the team. Robert's best friend Oliver also plays on the team. During his first game, Robert misses the chance to score several easy goals. His team loses the game. After the game, Oliver says to Robert, "You sure ARE a GREAT scorer!"	Comprehension	1. Did Robert help his team to win the game? 2. What did Oliver say to Robert?
	Meaning	3.1 Does Oliver mean that? 3.2 What does he mean?
	Belief	4. Does Oliver think that Robert is a great scorer?
	Communicative intention	Oliver said to Robert, "You sure ARE a GREAT scorer!" 5. Does Oliver want Robert to believe that he thinks that?
	Motivation/attitude	Oliver said to Robert, "You sure ARE a GREAT scorer!" 6. Why did he say that?

Source: Filippova, E., & Astington, J. W., *Child Development, 79*, 2008, p. 137. Copyright 2008 by John Wiley & Sons. Reprinted with permission.

Irony, Metaphors, and Idioms

Lies have been the most often studied form of false statement in the child litera-ture. In this section I consider children's understanding of three other types of nonliteral statement. There is no attempt to review all of the work on these speech types (indeed, metaphor has been the subject of enough research to merit its own journal—*Metaphor and Symbol*!). My focus, rather, is on attempts to relate such speech types to second-order understanding.

I begin with irony. As an example, consider the scenario in Table 6.2. Understanding of ironic statements such as the example has been argued to be a four-step process (Filippova & Astington, 2008). To start with, the hearer must realize that the statement is false and that it is intentionally false—that is, the speaker is not mistaken but is deliberately saying something that is not true. These two steps are necessary but not sufficient, for lies also satisfy these two criteria. A third step is to infer the communicative intent behind the utterance—what is the speaker attempting to accomplish with the message. It is here that lies and irony pull apart. With lies the speaker is attempting to implant a false belief, whereas with irony the speaker is attempting to convey a particular opinion with regard to the behavior commented on. Inferring the nature of this opinion, or what is labeled the speaker's attitude, is the fourth step. In some cases the attitude is a positive one, with the irony used to convey a compliment in a humorous fashion. This would be the case, for example, if Robert had scored the winning goal and Oliver had told him, "Terrible job, Robert!" In most cases, however, the attitude is a negative or critical one, which is what makes the remark sarcastic and not merely ironic. This, of course, is what applies in the actual Robert–Oliver example.

Mastering the nuances of irony is a multifaceted and extended process, with some elements evident by age 5 or 6 and others typically not seen until adolescence or adulthood (Pexman & Glenwright, 2007). As noted, I concentrate here on the role of second-order understanding. It is at the third step in Filippova and Astington's (2008) model that such understanding becomes necessary. To appreciate irony, according to their analysis, the child must realize that A intends to create a particular mental state in B—thus must understand second-order intention. In support of this argument, performance on second-order tasks correlates with success at recognizing irony (Filippova & Astington, 2008; Nilsen, Glenwright, & Huyder, 2011; Winner & Leekam, 1991). Relations have been shown for understanding of second-order intention, for understanding of second-order false belief, and for a composite index that included the Faux Pas measure.

Once again, studies of autism provide further evidence for the importance of second-order understanding. Samples with autism lag behind typically developing samples in their understanding of irony, and within such samples it is those who have mastered second-order false belief who show the greatest success (Happé, 1993). There is also evidence for a point we have seen before, and that is that the successes that do occur for children with autism may be based on somewhat different underlying processes than those that characterize typical development (Pexman et al., 2011).

That irony requires second-order understanding (among other things) is generally agreed. There is less consensus with regard to metaphor. Suppose a child hears the statement "Julian was hiding behind the tree and not moving. He was a statue." What theory-of-mind skills are necessary to interpret the metaphor correctly?

As with any nonliteral statement, a minimal requirement is some understanding of first-order intention, that is, a realization that the speaker intends to convey a meaning that is different from the literal words in the utterance. Happé (1993, 1995b) argued that first-order skills are not only a necessary but a sufficient theory-of-mind contributor. Theoretically, she based the argument on an approach to pragmatics labeled relevance theory (Sperber & Wilson, 1995), wherein (in very brief summary) metaphor is a descriptive comment that requires only knowledge of the speaker's intention to communicate a message, whereas irony is an interpretive comment that requires a realization that the speaker intends to share an opinion and thus influence another's mental state. Empirically, she reported poor performance on metaphors by an autism sample that lacked first-order false belief but better, and equivalent, performance by groups with either first-order or both first- and second-order competence. Metaphors differed from irony in this respect, for it was only the second-order group that showed an understanding of irony. A similar metaphor-irony contrast has been reported in a study of adult schizophrenics (Langdon, Davies, & Coltheart, 2002).

As is often the case, further research has complicated the picture. Norbury (2005), working also with autism samples, reported success at understanding metaphors only for those who had passed the second-order false belief task. At present, the reasons for the difference in findings are not clear. Assuming that other contributors (in particular, the requisite semantic knowledge) are in place, it may be that second-order competence is helpful with respect to metaphors, because it sensitizes the child to the possibility of different meanings, but not necessary. Research with typically developing samples might help resolve the discrepancy.

I turn finally to idioms. Idioms come in two forms. In so-called decomposable idioms the elements that make up the idiom retain at least some of the meaning that they have in literal language use. A literal reading thus provides some clues as to how the idiom is to be interpreted. "She was play acting" or "He lay down the law" would be examples in this category. In contrast, in a nondecomposable idiom the elements retain none of their typical meaning, and thus they provide no clues with respect to the meaning of the idiom. "That broke the ice" or "He kicked the bucket" would be examples in this category.

Two main findings emerged in a study of idioms by Caillies and Le Sourn-Bissaoui (2008). First, the 5- to 7-year-old participants found nondecomposable idioms more difficult than decomposable ones. Second, there was a positive relation between understanding of second-order false belief and success at interpreting nondecomposable but not decomposable idioms. The latter finding contradicted the authors' predictions. Decomposable idioms offer a possibility for multiple interpretations that is not found with nondecomposable ones, and second-order reasoning was therefore expected to be more helpful for the former than for the latter. Why it was not at least somewhat helpful is not clear. To the extent that success on the second-order task does relate to understanding of idioms the basis may be the same as that suggested for metaphors: Such success may be a general marker of the ability to resist an immediate interpretation when necessary and to think about alternatives. As with metaphors, more research is clearly needed.

SOCIAL OUTCOMES

Clearly, lying is a social behavior, and white lies and social presentational lies have definite social consequences. In this section I take up the issue of social outcomes more broadly. The discussion is divided into several broad categories, beginning with understanding of emotions.

Emotions

So-called social emotions refer to emotions such as embarrassment, shame, and pride—emotions that depend on the actual or anticipated reactions of other people to the self's characteristics or behavior. The topic is tied in closely to that of self-presentation. The purpose of many self-presentational efforts is to minimize negative social emotions (e.g., I won't be embarrassed if no one knows I was trying) and to maximize positive ones.

Mark Bennett (Bennett & Gillingham, 1991; Bennett & Matthews, 2000) has argued that in some instances social emotions themselves require second-order competence. The "some instances" qualifier is important. Even toddlers may show shame or pride in simple situations (Stipek, Recchia, & McClintic, 1992), and by age 5 children can make accurate judgments about how the reactions of others can elicit various social emotions in story characters. Suppose, however, that there are no explicit reactions of others upon which to base response. It is here, according to Bennett, that second-order understanding enters in. To feel embarrassment in the face of failure, for example, the child who has no social feedback for guidance must be able to anticipate how others will react to him or her (they'll think that I think....)—must, in other words, be capable of second-order reasoning.

The evidence in support of this argument takes the same two forms that we have seen for other developments. First, there is developmental improvement across the grade-school years in understanding of social emotions. Second, there is a positive relation between understanding of social emotions and performance on the second-order false belief task, a relation that has been found not only for typically developing samples but also in samples with autism (Hillier & Allinson, 2002). It is interesting to note, however, that in the Bennett and Matthews (2000) study the relation with false belief held only for emotions stemming from violations of social conventions (e.g., wearing pajamas to school); there was no relation for emotions based on moral violations (e.g., stealing something). This difference (which had been predicted) was explained on the basis of a posited difference in parents' socialization practices: an emphasis on others in the case of moral rules, an emphasis on the self in the case of social conventions.

The most pervasive social emotion is social anxiety: a general tendency to feel anxious in social settings or when merely contemplating social interaction. At the extreme, such anxious responses shade into the clinical syndrome known as social anxiety disorder. As with the more specific emotion measures, social anxiety is related to self-presentation: Children who are high in social anxiety engage in more self-presentational efforts than do less anxious children (Banerjee & Watling, 2010). At the same time, highly anxious children are less skilled at differentiating among different audiences, that is, at tailoring their self-presentations appropriately for different listeners. The result is that such efforts are less likely to succeed, which in turn exacerbates the child's social anxiety.

Does social anxiety also relate to second-order understanding? The answer depends on the type of second-order understanding being examined. Banerjee and Henderson (2001) found no relation between understanding of second-order false belief and level of social anxiety; in contrast, relatively low scores on the Faux Pas measure were related to higher levels of anxiety. The conclusion drawn was that socially anxious children do not suffer from a general deficit in higher-order, recursive reasoning, as shown by their false belief performance. They do, however, have difficulty in "understanding the links between emotions, intentions, and beliefs in social situations" (p. 558)—that is, a deficit in the sorts of skills that the Faux Pas measure assesses.

In some circumstances the emotion experienced depends not only on the particular outcome but also on knowledge of how that outcome might have been different. Winning 5 dollars would generally be a positive experience, but it may be perceived as a disappointment if one had expected to win 20. Losing 5 dollars is a negative event, but it may be experienced as a relief if there had been danger of losing 20. Emotions such as disappointment or relief that depend on taking alternatives into account are referred to as counterfactual emotions.

To date, only one study has examined the possible contribution of second-order reasoning to the understanding of counterfactual emotions (Ferrell, Guttentag, & Gredlein, 2009). As with some of the research reviewed earlier, the second-order component of the study appears to have been included mainly as a general measure of higher-level cognition, and not because of any strong theoretical links between the two developments being correlated. In any case, relations turned out to be limited. Success on second-order false belief related positively, but modestly, to understanding of counterfactual emotions. The relation remained significant when age was statistically controlled, not, however, when verbal ability and short-term memory were partialled out.

Peer and Sibling Relations

The work on social emotions has emphasized emotions that arise in the context of peer interaction. In this section I consider peer relations, as well as relations between siblings, more generally.

As I noted in Chapter 2, the first-order literature has documented links between theory-of-mind understanding and various aspects of children's relations with their peers. Such work is a relatively recent addition to a much larger and more longstanding literature directed to the cognitive contributors to peer interaction (Rubin, Bukowski, & Parker, 2006). The question now is whether second-order understanding is also among these contributors. Relevant studies divide into two groups: those that focus on the child's success in the peer group and those that measure the social skills that children bring to their encounters with peers.

The most commonly used method for measuring success in the peer group is the sociometric approach, that is, peer-based assessments of the extent to which children are liked or disliked by their peers. Four studies have explored possible relations between second-order competence and children's sociometric status, although across different measures of second-order ability and with somewhat varying results (Banerjee & Watling, 2005; Bosacki & Astington, 1999; Hoglund, Lalonde, & Leadbeater, 2008; Jingxin, Wenxin, & Li, 2005). In the Banerjee and Watling (2005) study relatively poor performance on the Faux Pas measure was associated with both peer rejection (the most negative sociometric category) and the sociometric category labeled *controversial* (used for children who receive a mixture of positive and negative evaluations). In the Jingxin et al. (2005) study understanding of second-order false belief was related to positive evaluations from the peer group, in this case in a sample from mainline China (a rare non-Western entry in this literature). Strangely, though, the effect held only for the younger half of their 40- to 79-month-old sample. In Bosacki and Astington (1999) relatively good performance on the Preadolescent Theory of Mind measure was predictive of positive evaluations from peers; the relation was no longer significant, however, when language was controlled. Finally, in Hoglund et al. (2008) understanding of interpretive diversity showed a borderline negative correlation with peer rejection and peer neglect; again, however, the relation disappeared when other factors were taken into account.

A recent report from Banerjee and associates (Banerjee, Watling, & Caputi, in press) adds some valuable longitudinal information to the picture: follow-ups at 1 and 2 years of the original Banerjee and Watling (2005) sample. One finding—a novel one, given the rarity of longitudinal study—is that individual differences in faux pas understanding are fairly stable over time (correlations of around .50). With respect to peer relations, the longitudinal data suggest a bidirectional relation between theory-of-mind understanding and success in the peer group. Thus, across parts of the 5-year span encompassed by the project it is early theory-of-mind understanding that predicts later social success, whereas across other parts of the span it is early peer relations that predict later theory-of-mind performance. This bidirectional conclusion is probably a general one for the research considered in this section—and indeed, as we saw in Chapter 2, for the first-order literature as well.

If second-order competence relates to social status, it is presumably because children's theory-of-mind abilities help them to behave in effective ways with their peers. A handful of studies provide support for this assumption. Banerjee and Henderson (2001) reported a positive correlation between teacher ratings of social skills and a composite theory-of-mind score based on the Faux Pas test and a measure of self-presentational understanding. In Liddle and Nettle (2006) performance on higher-level reasoning problems (such as the example shown in Table 4.5) showed a "substantial correlation" with teacher ratings of 10- and 11-year-olds' social competence (although, strangely, the actual correlation is not reported). In Bosacki and Astington (1999) performance on the Preadolescent Theory of Mind measure related positively to peers' evaluations of children's social competence—not, however, to evaluations offered by teachers. Finally, another recent longitudinal report from the Banerjee group (Caputi, Lecce, Pagnin, & Banerjee, 2012) provides evidence that prosocial behavior mediates the across-time relation between theory-of-mind understanding (in this case, a composite of first- and second-order measures) and success with peers.

What about relations with siblings? The focus of a study by Recchia and Howe (2009) was a topic of interest to any parent with at least two children: How do siblings resolve conflict? The study explored two possible theory-of-mind contributors to conflict resolution: second-order false belief and the conflict-interpretation measure from Ross et al. (2005) that was described in Chapter 5. The latter is closer in content to the sibling-conflict target and therefore might be expected to be more predictive of children's conflict resolution strategies. This proved to be the case, although with the qualifier that neither cognitive measure turned out to be very predictive. Among the younger siblings false belief understanding was actually negatively related to constructive resolution strategies, a finding that suggests that children may sometimes use their theory-of-mind abilities for negative rather than positive ends (a possibility to which I return shortly). Performance on the conflict-interpretation measure did relate in the expected way to positive conflict resolution strategies—primarily, however, when the siblings' relationship quality was high. And in general, and perhaps not surprisingly, relationship quality was the best predictor of conflict resolution.

Moral Reasoning

By definition, moral reasoning encompasses the cognitive aspect of morality and attempts to link morality and basic aspects of cognitive development have a long, and mostly Piagetian, history. Attempts to identify links with theory of mind are more recent and more limited (Baird & Sokol, 2004), and most to date have concentrated on first-order competence. Baird and Astington (2004), for example, showed that understanding of first-order false belief predicted children's ability to take into account motives in judging the morality of identical actions that had different motives underlying the behavior. Other studies (e.g., Dunn, Cutting, & Demetriou, 2000) have also demonstrated relations between first-order understanding and aspects of moral reasoning.

When might second-order competence be important? The Shiverick and Moore (2007) study discussed in Chapter 3 provides one example. Sometimes the task in moral reasoning is to make sense of someone else's moral evaluation—to figure out, for example, why Mommy is mad about older brother's behavior, or why a teacher is punishing a group of students. Doing so requires taking into account what A thinks about B's mental state—for example, Mommy thinks that he did it on purpose; teacher thinks that they don't want to learn. The Shiverick and Moore study demonstrated that children as young as 5 have some ability both to judge beliefs about intention and to use such judgments to predict another's moral evaluations. It also found, as would be expected, that the ability to engage in this sort of thinking about thinking increased as children grew older.

A further context for second-order reasoning occurs when an evaluation of A's action with respect to B depends on taking into account what A thinks B knows or believes. The task in a study by Yuill and Perner (1987) was to judge responsibility for a traffic accident in which a bicyclist (A) ran into a car door opened by a motorist (B). In some instances B was aware that A was approaching and in some instances he was not aware; similarly, in some instances A believed that B had seen her and in some instances she believed that he had not seen her. Three main findings emerged. First, 6-year-olds (the youngest group tested) showed some ability to judge second-order false beliefs in the instances in which A had a mistaken belief about B's knowledge, and by age 9 performance on the second-order task was close to perfect. Second, by age 7 children showed some success at using their belief attributions to make sensible judgments of responsibility for the accident; in particular, A was judged as less culpable when she believed that she had been seen than when she believed that B had not seen her. Finally, the ability to make appropriate attributions of responsibility lagged behind the ability to judge second-order beliefs, the same necessary but not sufficient pattern seen for various developments considered earlier. Similar results, although on a slightly later time schedule, were reported by Hayashi (2007a) working with a Japanese sample.

In some instances A's knowledge of B's belief can be assumed, because it is A whose action created the belief in B. Such is the case with promises or commitment. A promise is a prototypical second-order situation: If A makes a promise to B, then A thinks that B thinks that A will perform the promised action. Two studies have examined children's understanding of the moral commitment entailed by promises (Maas, 2008; Mant & Perner, 1988). Do children realize, for example, that it is the sincerity of the stated intention and not the eventual act that distinguishes between a promise and a lie? Do they realize that a failure to act as intended is more blameworthy if someone else is counting on the action to be performed than if this is not the case? Do they regard failure to act as more blameworthy if the failure was under the actor's control rather than forced upon him or her?

In both studies the youngest children (4-year-olds in Maas, 2008; 5-year-olds in Mant & Perner, 1988) showed little ability to make distinctions of this sort. The ability to do so improved across the grade-school years, and in the Maas study showed some relation to success on the second-order false belief task. Still, some lingering difficulties were evident even among the oldest children. Some 9-year-olds, for example, judged a failure to perform an intended act as equally blameworthy whether someone was counting on the act or not, a clear failure to take into account A's belief about B's belief.

All of the work considered so far in this section has used the second-order false belief task as a correlate. There have been two attempts to relate the Chandler concept of interpretive diversity to children's moral reasoning. One is by the Chandler group (Chandler, Sokol, & Hallett, 2001). They presented a version of a Punch and Judy show in which Punch threw a box over a cliff, not realizing that Judy was inside the box. The infliction of harm was therefore unintentional, but it occurred under one of two circumstances. In some cases Punch was unaware that Judy had fallen into the box and therefore held a false belief that the box was empty. In other cases Punch knew that Judy was in one of two boxes but misinterpreted her ambiguous message with respect to which one (specifically—she cried "check the green one," meaning that she was in the box adorned with a green letter "one"; Punch, however, assumed she was in the green box). The children's task was to judge the blameworthiness of Punch's actions. For the subset of the sample who had not yet mastered interpretive diversity the particular scenario did not matter—both actions were judged as equally worthy of blame. For the subset who understood diversity, however—as well as for a comparison sample of adults—this equivalence no longer held; Punch was evaluated more negatively when he was confused rather than merely ignorant. Having themselves arrived at a constructivist theory of mind that allowed for diverse interpretations of ambiguous input, the children apparently blamed Punch for not being similarly constructivist, and thus for deciding too soon on just one of the two possibilities.

The other attempt to relate an understanding of diversity to moral judgment worked out less successfully. Malti and colleagues (Malti, Gasser, & Gutzwiller-Helfenfinger, 2010) did find one significant correlation between the two sets of measures, but the relation was a negative one—children who were relatively high in understanding of diversity were relatively low in moral reasoning. As they note, their measures of moral reasoning were geared to fairly early developments, and it may be that most of the differences among children in such reasoning were in place prior to mastery of diversity. The negative relation, however, remains unexplained.

The Negative Side: Bullying, Machiavellianism, Teasing

Negative outcomes are, of course, part of any study of social development—not everyone is popular, not everyone can keep emotions within bounds, not everyone shows high levels of moral reasoning. And, as we have seen, theory of mind, including second-order theory of mind, contributes to such outcomes, in that relatively low levels of theory-of-mind ability place the child at risk for various problems in development.

Much of the research to be considered now has been inspired by the possibility that *high* levels of theory of mind may at times lead to negative outcomes—that children may sometimes use their theory-of-mind skills for maleficent rather than beneficent purposes. As we will see, there is some support for this possibility, along with a fair amount of uncertainty and controversy.

Bullying has been the topic for which the maleficent-use hypothesis has been most thoroughly explored. The starting point was some research and accompanying analysis by Sutton and colleagues (Sutton, Smith, & Swettenham, 1999a, 1999b). At the time of their writing, most conceptions of bullying portrayed bullies as lacking in social-cognitive skills—as "physically powerful yet intellectually simple or backward, resorting to violence and aggression in their interactions almost because they know no other way" (Sutton et al., 1999a, p. 118). Sutton and colleagues presented three arguments against this model of the cognitively inept bully.

The first argument concerned the evidence in support of the model. Much of the support came from the well known work of Dodge and Crick (Crick & Dodge, 1994; Dodge & Crick, 1990), which had clearly established that various kinds of cognitive biases and distortions can contribute to children's aggression. Little of this work was with bullies, however. Furthermore, most of it concerned reactive or retaliatory aggression and not the more proactive forms of aggression that characterize bullying.

A second argument came from an analysis of what occurs in bullying. Many incidents of bullying, especially bullying that is verbal in nature or has a verbal component, hardly look like mindless expressions of power. Rather, bullies may be quite skilled at identifying and exploiting the specific vulnerabilities of their victims. In addition, bullying often occurs in a group setting, and bullies may play successfully to the audience in various ways. It is hard to see how they could operate so effectively without some ability to read and manipulate the mental states of others.

Finally, the third argument was empirical. Sutton et al. (1999b) assessed theory of mind (via a revised version of Strange Stories) in a sample of 7- to 10-year-old children who represented all of the various roles that have been identified in bullying episodes. Specifically, the sample included bullies, assistants (children who aided in the bullying), reinforcers (children whose responses reinforced the bullying), victims, defenders (children who tried to help the victim), and outsiders. Not only did the bullies prove not to be cognitively deficient; their overall theory-of-mind scores were the highest of all the groups.

With one partial exception, subsequent research has not reproduced this finding of the cognitively superior bully. Other studies, however, do support the conclusion that bullies are not necessarily cognitively *inferior*. Gini (2006), using the same six groups and the same theory-of-mind measure as Sutton et al. (1999b), found no differences between the bullies and any of the other groups. Gasser and Keller (2009) examined second-order false belief in four groups: bullies, victims, bully-victims (children who participated in both roles), and a group identified as highly prosocial. The bully-victims performed most poorly, but the bullies were comparable to the other groups, even the highly prosocial children. Caravita, Di Blasio, and Salmivalli (2010), also using a modified version of Strange Stories, reported a positive relation between theory of mind and bullying for boys but not for girls. Theory of mind was positively associated with participation in the defender role for both boys and girls. Finally, Sutton and colleagues (Sutton, Reeves, & Keogh, 2000), focusing on disruptive behavior rather than bullying per se, found no relation between such behavior and performance on the Eyes Test.

If bullies are (at least by certain theory-of-mind measures) cognitively indistinguishable from other children, why then does their behavior differ? The answer must be that they are relatively low on other factors that militate against the decision to act aggressively—feelings of empathy for others, for example, or mature forms of moral reasoning. This, in fact, is what research suggests. In the Gini (2006) study, for example, bullies were high on a scale that measured moral disengagement. In the Gasser and Keller (2009) study bullies were low on a measure of moral motivation. (My brief treatment has glossed over some uncertainties and disagreements in this literature. For further discussion, see Arsenio & Lemerise, 2001; Crick & Dodge, 1999.)

I turn now to Machiavellianism. Machiavellianism is one of the few psychological constructs to take its name from a person. The person is the Italian philosopher Machiavelli, and the construct refers to a personality type that embodies the characteristics that Machiavelli made famous in *The Prince*: namely, self-interested, cunning, manipulative, deceptive—in short, an ends-justifies-the-means approach to life. Since the formulation of the construct in the 1960s by Richard Christie (Christie & Geis, 1970), Machiavellianism has been explored in more than 2,000 studies in the adult personality literature (Jones & Paulhus, 2009).

Can Machiavellianism be identified in childhood? And if so, how? Table 6.3 shows one approach, a test known as the Kiddie Mach. The table indicates the responses that would or would not count toward a high score on the measure; probably, however, you could block off the left side of the table and fill in the plusses or minuses yourself.

One finding from use of the Kiddie Mach is that a childhood version of Machiavellianism does in fact seem to exist. Thus, not only does the test identify individual differences among children, but also the differences relate in sensible ways to behaviors that would be expected of a Machiavellian personality (e.g., low levels of prosocial behavior, high levels of aggression). Indeed, there is some evidence, gleaned from a teacher-report measure, that at least the precursors of Machiavellianism can be identified as early as preschool (Repacholi, Slaughter, Pritchard, & Gibbs, 2003).

Machiavellianism could be argued to have a by-definition relation to theory of mind, in that the ability to read and manipulate mental states seems central to so much of what a Machiavellian does. Still, we can ask whether standard theory-of-mind

TABLE 6.3   The Kiddie Mach Test

Item number	Statement
+1.	Never tell anyone why you did something unless it would help you.
−2.	Most people are good and kind.
+3.	The best way to get along with people is to tell them things that make them happy.
−4.	You should do something only when you are sure it is right.
+5.	It is smartest to believe that all people will be mean if they have a chance.
−6.	You should always be honest, no matter what.
+7.	Sometimes you have to hurt other people to get what you want.
+8.	Most people won't work hard unless you make them do it.
−9.	It is better to be ordinary and honest than famous and dishonest.
−10.	It is better to tell someone why you want him to help you than to make up a good story to get him to do it.
−11.	Successful people are mostly honest and good.
+12.	Anyone who completely trusts anyone else is asking for trouble.
+13.	A criminal is just like other people except that he is stupid enough to get caught.
−14.	Most people are brave.
+15.	It is smart to be nice to important people even if you don't really like them.
−16.	It is possible to be good in every way.
−17.	Most people cannot be easily fooled.
+18.	Sometimes you have to cheat a little to get what you want.
−19.	It is never right to tell a lie.
+20.	It hurts more to lose money than to lose a friend.

Source: From Christie, R., & Geis, F. L., *Studies in Machiavellianism*, New York, Academic Press, 1970, p. 327. Copyright 1970 by Susan Nachamie. With permission.

measures relate to the Machiavellian classification. The answer, for the most part, is no, both in adults (e.g., Paal & Bereczkie, 2007) and in children. Thus, two studies with preschoolers found no relation between Machiavellianism (as assessed by teacher report) and first-order false belief (Repacholi et al., 2003; Slaughter, 2011). The Slaughter article also reports a study with 9- to 13-year-olds who responded to the Strange Stories measure. Scores on Strange Stories showed no relation to the two Machiavellianism scales that were included. Finally, Barlow, Qualter, and Stylianou (2010) found a relation between Machiavellianism and the Faux Pas measure for girls but not for boys; the relation, however, was a negative one.

The same general conclusion seems to emerge for both bullying and Machiavellianism, and that is that children who fit these designations do not differ from other children in theory of mind per se; rather, they differ in how they use their theory of mind. This conclusion must be qualified by the admission that the theory-of-mind measures that have been used in these literatures (false belief, Strange Stories, Faux Pas) are not optimally constructed to reveal differences in the *kind* of theory of mind that children hold. Perhaps some children do have a "nasty" theory of mind (Ronald, Viding, Happé, & Plomin, 2006); to this point, however, this construct has been inferred from its putative effects rather than measured directly.

The final entry in this section is less clearly negative than the outcomes considered to this point. Teasing certainly can be negative, but it can also be affectionate and predominantly positive in nature. One developmental change, in fact, is that teasing becomes, on the average, more positive and prosocial as children grow older (Heerey, Capps, Keltner, & Kring, 2005).

Whatever its valence, teasing is another example of a nonliteral utterance, and both the production and the comprehension of an act of teasing require that each conversational partner take into account the mental state of the other. A study by Heerey and colleagues (Heerey et al., 2005) provides two kinds of evidence that theory of mind plays a role in teasing. First, a sample with autism lagged behind a typically developing sample in both their production and their comprehension of teasing. Second, differences in theory-of-mind understanding between the two groups (as assessed by the Strange Stories test) accounted for most of the group differences on the teasing measures.

Other Social Outcomes

The construct of agreeableness is one of the so-called Big Five—a set of personality dimensions identified by Costa and McCrae (1992) that have been the focus of a large body of research across the last 20 or so years. Agreeableness is characterized by high levels of warmth, friendliness, and altruism and low levels of anger and aggression. Operationally, it is shown by endorsement of statements such as "I believe that most people are basically well-intentioned" and "I would rather cooperate with others than compete with them."

Defined this way, agreeableness certainly sounds as though it should be related to the ability to think insightfully and empathically about other people—that is, to theory of mind. This was the hypothesis of a study with college students by Nettle and Liddle (2008). They measured agreeableness in a standard way in personality research and also administered two theory-of-mind measures: the Eyes Test and a set of higher-level recursive reasoning tasks similar to the example shown in Table 4.5. The prediction (the bases for which, I must admit, I do not find totally clear) was that the "social-cognitive" skills tapped by the recursive reasoning measure would be more strongly related to agreeableness than the "social-perceptual" abilities assessed by the Eyes Test. This, in fact, is what was found: Agreeableness showed a moderately strong correlation with the recursive reasoning measure but no relation at all with the Eyes Test.

The remaining entry under this heading also examined the predictive power of higher-level reasoning tasks like those in Table 4.5, in this case in an adult sample ranging in age from 18 to 65 (Stiller & Dunbar, 2007). The outcome of interest was the size of the participant's social clique, defined as "the number of individuals from whom one seeks support" (p. 97). The two measures proved to be related: On the average, the higher the level of reasoning of which the participant was capable, the larger the support clique. Furthermore, the mean values for the two measures were similar (five levels of recursive reasoning, five members of the support clique), leading to the speculation that reasoning ability set a limit on clique size—that "the limit is set on the innermost circle (average five individuals) by the fact that

… humans can cope only with five levels of intentionality (i.e., the mental states of five individuals)" (p. 101). I will add that this analysis, although intriguing, does leave an obvious question unanswered, and that is how often we need to reason simultaneously about the mental states of five people.

COGNITIVE OUTCOMES

Reasoning from Evidence

Although Perner and Wimmer (1985) referred to links with "other social domains" in their discussion of the implications of second-order competence, the specific example they offered was a cognitive one: children's ability to understand the typical questioning in a Piagetian assessment. Their particular focus was on the request for an explanation (e.g., "Why do you think so?") that typically follows the child's judgment on tasks such as conservation. To respond appropriately to this question, according to Perner and Wimmer, the child must realize that the point of the question is not to learn about the phenomenon itself (e.g., that quantities are conserved) but rather to learn about the child's thinking about the phenomenon. Perner and Wimmer suggested that the inability to understand such "second-order epistemic intention" might contribute to the failures on Piagetian tasks typically seen prior to age 6 or 7.

No one has followed up this specific suggestion. Research by Astington, Pelletier, and Homer (2002), however, speaks to children's ability to distinguish between the cause of an outcome and the reason for believing in the outcome (see also Kuhn & Pearsall, 2000). Five- to 7-year-old children heard the scenario presented in Table 6.4, followed by the questions about the cause of the wetness

TABLE 6.4   Example of a Scenario Used to Test Children's Understanding of Evidence

Scenario	Question Type	Question
This is a story about Frank and his sister Sally. This is Frank and this is Sally. One morning, Frank is getting water for the cat. He spills the water on the floor. It was a lot of water and the floor got very wet. But instead of cleaning up the water, Frank goes to his friend's house to play. Sally was upstairs and she did not see Frank spill the water. A little while later, Sally comes downstairs. She doesn't see the water and steps right in it! The floor was very wet and her feet got all wet.	Cause	Why is the floor wet?
	Evidence	How does Sally know the floor is wet?
	Control/cause	What did Frank do when he was getting water for the cat?
	Control/evidence	Does Sally know what Frank did?

Source: Astington, J., Pelletier, J., & Homer, B., *New Ideas in Psychology, 20*, 2002, p. 143. Copyright 2002 by Elsevier. Reprinted with permission.

and the evidence for Sally's belief. The cause question proved easier than the evidence question. Most children could cite the spill as the cause of the wetness, but many gave the same answer in response to the "How does Sally know?" question. A further finding was that performance on tasks of second-order false belief was a significant predictor of success on the evidence question

Why should children have difficulty distinguishing the evidence for a belief from the cause of the outcome being explained? According to the analysis by Astington and colleagues, doing so requires second-order competence. In their words, "In order to understand reasons, one needs to represent second-order beliefs, since a reason is essentially a belief that provides the evidence for another belief" (p. 134). Thus in the Sally scenario, for example, children must realize that the point of the "How" question is not to learn what they think about the wet floor but to learn what they think about Sally's thinking—thus Sally's belief as evidence for their belief.

I will add two points here. The first is that the ability to answer questions of the "Why does X think…?" sort cannot always be dependent on second-order competence. Even 4-year-olds can often give appropriate explanations for their first-order judgments—can explain, for example, why Maxi thinks that the chocolate is in the green cupboard. In the first-order case, however, the belief (green cupboard) and the outcome (blue cupboard) diverge; there is therefore no possibility of confusing outcome and evidence, and no need for second-order reasoning to pull the two apart.

The second point is one that applies also to some of the other work considered in this chapter. Although the theoretical analyses make a persuasive case for the importance of second-order understanding, it is sometimes not clear why the focus of research is on second-order *false* belief. In the reasoning-from-evidence case it is a true belief that needs to be understood. Similarly, in most instances of social emotions it is the true beliefs of the audience that are at issue. Mastery of false belief may be predictive as a kind of marker—a clear indication (clearer than any true-belief measure would be) that the child has developed the second-order competence necessary for the development in question.

Memory

Three forms of memory have been examined in relation to second-order competence. In two cases the focus has been on possible differences between samples with autism and typically developing individuals.

As the label suggests, the term self-referenced memory refers to memories regarding the self. One well established finding from the basic memory literature is that of superior memory for self-related content (e.g., words descriptive of the self vs. words descriptive of others). If the mentalizing difficulties in autism apply not just to thoughts about others but also to thoughts about the self (a point, interestingly, that is still in some dispute; see Hobson & Bowler, 2010), then the self-referenced memory effect should be reduced in samples with autism. Such has proved to be the case in two studies, one with children (Henderson et al., 2009) and one with adults (Lombardo, Barnes, Wheelwright, & Baron-Cohen, 2007). Both studies, moreover, found a positive relation between performance on the Eyes Test and self-referenced memory, although in the Henderson et al. study the relation held only for the autism sample. The latter study also reported no relation between the memory measure and performance on the Strange Stories test.

The next term from the memory literature is also a self-defining one. Event memory is memory for the typical sequence of actions that make up familiar events. Commonly studied examples in childhood include eating at a restaurant, making cookies, and going to a birthday party. There are two reasons to think that memories for activities such as these might be impaired in individuals with autism. First, much of the content of event memories is social in nature—who is involved, who does what. If interest in people is reduced in autism, then the chances to learn the structures of social events are also reduced. Second, the settings in which children consolidate and remember familiar experiences are themselves often social as well—pretend play, for example, or conversations with family members. Children with autism are less likely to have these memory-retaining experiences than are typically developing children.

Event memories are in fact impaired in samples with autism (Loth, Gomez, & Happé, 2008; Loth, Happé, & Gomez, 2010; Trillingsgaard, 1999). Furthermore, the degree of impairment correlates with theory-of-mind ability. Best performance is shown by those who demonstrate some second-order competence, as assessed either by Strange Stories (Loth et al., 2008, 2010) or by the second-order false belief task (Trillingsgaard, 1999). Conversely, those who lack even first-order ability demonstrate the poorest event memory.

The remaining entry in this section is not memory per se but rather beliefs about memory, or what is called *metamemory*. Lockl and Schneider (2007) administered a battery of metamemory measures to their 5-year-old participants. The battery included questions about how best to perform various memory tasks (e.g., remember to carry out a future activity, remember the location of a misplaced object) and about the effects on memory of variables such as study time and list organization. Also included were measures of both first-order and second-order false belief. Significant relations emerged between the false belief measures and the metamemory measures; thus relatively good false belief performance was predictive of relatively good metamemory. Unfortunately, the analyses used composite false belief scores, which means that there was no indication whether second-order understanding made a separate contribution beyond that provided by first order. It makes intuitive sense that the kind of ability to think about thinking tapped by the second-order false belief task would relate to measures of metacognitive understanding, including metamemory; metacognition, after all, *is* thinking about thinking. This relation, however, remains to be demonstrated (although links with other aspects of theory of mind *have* been shown—Leche, Zocchi, Pagnin, Palladino, & Taumoepeau, 2010). In the next chapter I consider general similarities between work under the heading of metacognition and work on theory of mind.

Communication

Obviously, the research discussed earlier under the Deliberately False Statements heading falls under the general rubric of communication. Here I consider three further, admittedly disparate, studies that also fit this general designation.

Myers and Liben (in press) were interested in children's ability to use non-linguistic symbols to communicate. Specifically, their focus was on possible differences between two kinds of symbols: iconic and abstract. Iconic symbols are those that have some physical resemblance to their referent; the small drawings on a set of how-to instructions would be an example. Abstract symbols, in contrast, have no resemblance to what they stand for and thus are completely arbitrary; any word would be an example in this category. Although the symbol-referent similarity in the iconic case might at times be helpful, it also carries the possibility of misunderstanding, for many icons are subject to more than one interpretation. It is important, therefore, that the user of such symbols not assume that the recipient will necessarily arrive at the intended interpretation based solely on the symbol. This argument should sound familiar, for it is an application of the Chandler (Carpendale & Chandler, 1996) concept of interpretive diversity: An ambiguous stimulus may be subject to two or more equally valid interpretations. Myers and Liben predicted, therefore, that children who had mastered interpretive diversity would be more successful at conveying the meaning of iconic symbols than would children who had not yet attained such understanding. And this is exactly what they found. In contrast, when abstract symbols were involved, and thus no possibility of overestimating the recipient's understanding, performance on the diversity task had no relation to children's communicative success.

Less positive results, at least with regard to the second-order component of the research, were reported in the remaining two studies. The focus of research by Meins and colleagues was on 8-year-old children's production of internal state language, that is, the frequency of their references to beliefs, intentions, and other mental states (Meins, Fernyhough, Johnson, & Lidstone, 2006). Such references were measured across two contexts: describing a friend and narrating a wordless picture book. The expectation was that the use of internal state terms would relate to second-order competence, an outcome that was assessed with the Strange Stories measure. Sensible though this expectation seems, it was not confirmed; there was no correlation between the internal state measure and the second-order measure. The authors suggest a version of the necessary-but-not-sufficient position that we have seen before—in this case, that theory of mind makes possible mental state talk but does not determine individual differences in the frequency of such talk. In their words, "having a ToM is different from using one's ToM capacities" (Meins et al., p. 194).

The final example to be discussed also focused on the use of language, although in a different sense. The term *speech act* refers to the pragmatic aspect of language—to all the uses to which we put our language. Examples of speech acts include asserting, questioning, promising, requesting, thanking, apologizing, praising, and congratulating. Speech acts involve the speaker's intention to produce a particular effect in the listener, and they would seem, therefore, to have a clear, almost definitional, relation to theory of mind. Empirically, however, there was no relation in a study by Patnaik (2006). The sample consisted of 5- to 7-year-old Indian children, the second-order measure was the second-order false belief task, and the speech acts assessed, via an elicited production procedure, were the eight types previously listed.

The Patnaik (2006) study raises the question—an important and a difficult one—of exactly what sort of theory-of-mind ability is necessary for different kinds of communicative action. I return to this issue in the Conclusions section.

Other Cognitive Outcomes

In this section I add two further outcomes that fall under the general Cognitive heading.

As with the memory research, an interest in autism motivated the first study. One of the many cognitive problems that have been identified in individuals with autism is difficulty in drawing inferences, that is, in forming conclusions that follow from but also go beyond the available information (Norbury & Bishop, 2002). Central to communication are so-called pragmatic inferences, that is, inferences that can be derived from the particular language used in a communication (the realization, for example, that *think, know,* and *hope* imply different things about the speaker's mental state). LeSourn-Bissaoui and colleagues tested the role of second-order understanding (specifically, performance on the second-order false belief task) with respect to such inferences in both adolescents with Asperger syndrome and typically developing adolescents (LeSourn-Bissaoui, Caillies, Gierski, & Motte, 2009). As expected, the typically developing sample outperformed the Asperger sample, and those who succeeded on the second-order task were most successful at drawing the relevant inferences.

One of the most direct possible applications of children's theory-of-mind abilities occurs when children are attempting to learn from each other—thus in situations of peer tutoring or collaborative learning. It makes sense to predict that how successfully children teach each other or work together toward some common goal should depend, among other things, on how well they can think about each other's thoughts, including child A's ability to think about child B's thinking about child A. Furthermore, there has long been an influential theoretical analysis, Tomasello, Kruger, and Ratner's (1993) cultural learning theory, that makes exactly this argument. After explaining what is meant by second-order reasoning, these authors go on to say, "Collaborative learning as we conceptualize it relies on precisely this kind of thinking in which the partner's acts toward me and mine toward him are simulated recursively at the same time in an integrated fashion" (p. 501).

To date, relevant work is limited to teaching–tutoring interactions. A number of recent studies have shown that first-order understanding can contribute to one child's ability to teach another child (Davis-Unger & Carlson, 2008; Strauss, Ziv, & Stein, 2002; Ziv, Solomon, & Frye, 2008). A study by Flynn (2010) demonstrates that second-order understanding can also be important. The task set for her 6- and 7-year-old tutors was to teach an age mate how to complete a construction task. Half of the children assigned to the tutoring role had succeeded on two second-order false belief tasks and half had failed on both tasks. There were no differences between the two groups of tutors in the number of demonstrations offered or the amount of verbal instruction provided. The group of false belief passers, however, was over twice as likely as the other group to provide contingent instruction, that is, instruction that was geared to the level of the learner and that was adjusted appropriately as the learner's behavior changed. Such "scaffolding" is generally regarded as the most effective form of teaching, and it is precisely the sort of instruction for which theory of mind should be important.

OTHER OUTCOMES

I conclude with a potpourri of outcomes that do not fit clearly under any of the general headings.

Classifying the first entry as an outcome of advanced theory of mind is admittedly speculative. Sabbagh and Seamans (2008) administered the Eyes Test to a sample of parents and a battery of theory-of-mind measures to the parents' 3-year-old children. The two sets of scores turned out to be related: On the average, parents who scored high on the advanced test had children who scored high on the first-order measures. As Sabbagh and Seamans note, it is possible that the basis for the correlation is genetic; theory of mind has been shown to be moderately heritable (Hughes et al., 2005). It is also possible, however, that the basis is at least in part environmental: that parents who are high in theory-of-mind ability are more sensitive to and supportive of similar developments in their children. Such a possibility would be compatible with the work on childrearing origins of theory of mind discussed in Chapter 2. And if this interpretation of the correlation is valid, the cross-generation transmission of ability would certainly be one of the more important outcomes of advanced theory of mind.

In contrast to the work just discussed—and indeed to all of the other developments reviewed in this chapter—the final two outcomes to be considered are of little importance in themselves; they are of interest, rather, as markers of a more general construct. Several studies have explored possible relations between theory of mind and the ability to perceive both versions of a reversible figure (such as the stimuli shown in Figure 5.1). Success at this task has been of interest as an indicator of the general ability to consider multiple representations of the same aspect of reality. Although results are not perfectly consistent, research provides some support for this interpretation. Gopnik and Rosati (2001) reported a positive correlation between children's understanding of first-order false belief and their ability to see both interpretations of an ambiguous picture when informed that two interpretations exist. A more advanced development than such "informed" reversal is spontaneous reversal: seeing both interpretations without any prompting. This ability has been shown to be related to second-order competence, both understanding of second-order false belief (Mitroff, Sobel, & Gopnik, 2006) and performance on the Strange Stories measure (Sobel, Capps, & Gopnik, 2005).

The final entry is contagious yawning. In this case the more general construct of interest is emotional contagion: the tendency to encode and to mimic the emotional displays of those around us. Sensitivity to the emotions of others has a theory-of-mind sound, and three kinds of evidence suggest that theory of mind does in fact make a contribution to contagious yawning. First, 1- to 3-year-olds show little evidence of the behavior, but there is a substantial increase in the frequency of contagious yawns at age 4 (Helt, Eigsti, Snyder, & Fein, 2010). Second, individuals with autism show lower levels of contagious yawning than do typically developing individuals (Helt et al., 2010; Senju et al., 2007). Finally, in adults there is a positive relation between contagious yawning and performance on the Faux Pas measure (Platek, Critton, Myers, & Gallup, 2003).

CONCLUSIONS

I began this chapter with a quotation from Perner and Wimmer (1985) concerning the importance of higher-order reasoning. Here is another quotation, in this case from Perner alone: "The social significance of human interaction depends on the mental states of the interacting parties, in particular their higher-order mental states" (Perner, 1988, p. 271).

"The social significance of human interaction" is a broad target. Research across the last 20-plus years has certainly made significant strides toward filling in the various developments that fall under this general heading. Predicted effects of higher-order competence have been demonstrated across a wide range of outcomes in both the social and the cognitive domains. It is true that none of the forms of evidence for such effects (correlational studies, developmental comparisons, group comparisons) establishes causality with certainty. Nevertheless, the convergence of evidence from the different approaches, coupled with theoretical analyses of the importance of higher-order understanding, makes the case for causality persuasive.

Once these gains in knowledge are recognized, it remains true that the standard "more research is needed" conclusion clearly applies to the work considered in this chapter. Here I suggest several directions that such research might take.

The first is obvious, and that is more study of the majority of outcomes that have been explored in research to date. There are a few relatively well plumbed topics—lying is perhaps the main example. For no topic, however, can the research literature be considered extensive, and many topics have been the subject of only a single study or two. The result is a literature with a high proportion of intriguing suggestions relative to firm conclusions. Beyond simply the basic issue of replication, further study is often necessary to test for generality across methods and across samples. Given the ubiquity of the necessary-but-not-sufficient conclusion, research is also needed to specify what else, in addition to second-order competence, underlies the developments in question. In the case of negative outcomes such as aggression, further study is needed to distinguish between two possible bases for differences among children: differences in theory of mind per se, or differences in how theory-of-mind-skills are deployed. Both, of course, could be the case, but at present we simply do not know.

The second suggestion for future research is also an obvious one. Diverse though the outcomes reviewed in this chapter are, they obviously do not exhaust the possible contributions of higher-order theory of mind to children's social and cognitive development. In Miller (2009) I suggested three possible targets for future study.

One suggestion, which was grounded in the work of Tomasello and colleagues noted earlier (Tomasello et al., 1993), was to explore the contribution of second-order understanding to collaborative learning. The recent appearance of the Flynn (2010) study provides an initial step in this direction. Flynn's study, however (despite the article's title), dealt with tutoring, not true collaborative learning. The emphasis in Tomasello et al.'s cultural learning theory is not on the one-way transmission of knowledge; it is on the interplay of two minds, each trying to understand what the other is thinking, including thoughts about one's own thoughts. This interplay remains to be examined from a theory-of-mind perspective.

A second suggestion was to explore the possible contribution of second-order competence to an understanding of persuasion. Like a lie, a persuasive message has the goal of implanting a belief in another, although in this case not a false belief but rather a belief congruent with that of the speaker. For such an attempt to be successful the speaker must take into account the initial belief of the listener, including potentially different beliefs across different listeners (e.g., Mommy thinks X, but Daddy thinks Y). Doing so would seem to require a first-order understanding of belief, and research by Karen Bartsch and associates (Bartsch & London, 2000; Bartsch, London, & Campbell, 2007) in fact demonstrates relations between performance on first-order tasks and understanding of persuasion. These studies and others, however, also make clear that understanding of persuasion is far from complete by age 5 or 6. It seems likely that further developments depend in part on understanding of second-order mental states, including the ability to take into account what one message recipient thinks about another ("Mommy thinks that Daddy thinks….") and what the recipients think about the self ("they think that I think…."). Just as such understanding may contribute to children's ability to construct persuasive messages, so may it underlie their response when they are targets of persuasive attempts by others ("they want me to think…."). These links, too, remain to be explored.

Finally, the third suggestion concerned the breadth of the outcomes that have been targets for study in the higher-order literature. As I indicated in Chapter 2, first-order theory of mind has been shown to relate not only to specific social behaviors but also to indices of social competence and social success more broadly. As we saw in this chapter, most work on second-order understanding has been directed to specific and rather narrow outcomes. It is reasonable to predict, a la Perner's "social significance" claim, that the quality of second-order thinking will affect the skill with which children navigate through the social world and the success they achieve in relations with both adults and peers. The handful of studies discussed in the Peer Relations section provides some initial support for this prediction. For the most part, however, the wider implications of differences in higher-order theory of mind remain to be explored.

I conclude this chapter with two further points. One was prefigured by some discussion in Chapter 5, and the other was touched on briefly earlier in the chapter.

Chapter 5 made the point that most theory-of-mind research has focused on the situational determinants of mental state attribution (e.g., differences in informational access), with relatively little concern for the individual determinants (e.g., differences in how people use the same information). The same neglect of the specific targets for children's thinking applies to the research considered here. Whatever the outcome examined (moral reasoning, peer relations, etc.), what we are most interested in is how children think about and behave toward the familiar people in their lives—friends, family, teachers. This, however, is seldom what is actually studied. Rather, theory-of-mind understanding is assessed through response to generic story characters (John and Mary and the ice cream truck, the participants in the Strange Stories vignettes), and the application of this understanding is assessed through response to further story characters (e.g., the protagonists in a moral reasoning vignette). There are exceptions, at least at the outcome end—studies of children's social skills, for example, concern real-life encounters with familiar peers. These are exceptions, however. And there is virtually no research that examines children's ability to think differently about different targets.

That the particular target being thought about may matter is suggested by an intriguing study by O'Connor and Hirsch (1999). The participants in their research were young adolescents (mean age = 13), and the task set for them was to respond to vignettes (created for purposes of the study) that elicited explanations for commonly occurring teacher behaviors seen in the school setting. The adolescents did so with respect to two targets: their most liked teacher and their least liked teacher. The specific target proved to be important. The level of mental state reasoning was higher for the most liked than for the least liked teacher. In addition, negative bias in the reasoning (as shown by incongruity and distortions) was greater for the least liked than for the most liked teacher.

The O'Connor and Hirsch (1999) study included another dimension as well. In half the cases the vignettes referred to "a student" and in half the cases they referred to "you"—that is, the participant himself or herself. Although the result did not achieve statistical significance, the difference in level of reasoning between the most liked and the least liked teacher was greater in the self than in the "student" condition. Thus, both participants in the interaction turned out to be important.

The finding just noted raises another point about the typical study in this literature. Whoever the others may be in the child's real-life deployment of theory of mind, the child himself or herself is a constant element. Certainly in most discussions of second-order reasoning it is the self who is the critical target in the recursive chain. Thus discussions focus on children's newfound ability to engage in self-presentational behavior, or to express social emotions, or to produce and distinguish among various forms of false statement. Occasionally in research it is in fact the child participant who does these things; this is true in some of the studies of lying, for example (e.g., Talwar, Gordon, et al., 2007) as well as in the research on social emotions (Bennett & Matthews, 2000—although in this case the situations asked about are hypothetical rather than real). Such child-as-target studies are the minority, however. In most studies the child participants are in a passive, third-person role, making judgments about someone else's second-order intentions or beliefs. How well these judgments map onto beliefs and behaviors regarding the self remains to be determined.

The final point addresses a very general issue. The subject of this chapter is theory-of-mind explanations for social and cognitive behavior. The question I address now concerns the testability of such explanations. This issue arises in two different senses.

One is the question whether the role of theory of mind is in some instances even an empirically testable matter. Consider, again, Machiavellianism. If (as is typical) part of our definition of Machiavellianism includes something along the lines of "the ability to manipulate the mental states of others for one's own purposes," then theory of mind is involved by definition. It may still be of interest to determine whether individual differences on a particular measure of theory of mind (e.g., second-order false belief) predict individual differences in Machiavellianism; a null result, however, would not—indeed could not—imply the irrelevance of theory of mind more generally. As another example, consider irony. By any definition, understanding of irony requires understanding of the speaker's intent and the speaker's attitude—requires, in short, theory of mind. Some behaviors, to quote a phrase used earlier, are "theory of mind in action." In such cases the issue with respect to theory of mind is not whether it is involved, but exactly what form the involvement takes.

The second sense in which the testability issue arises concerns the scope of theory-of-mind explanations. Perner (1988) addresses this issue. As he notes, if second-order intention is defined as one person's attempt to affect another's belief, then virtually any act of communication would qualify. Thus, the toddler who says "juice" could be credited with an attempt to instill a particular belief in her mother. Clearly, no one wants to credit such competence to a toddler; the question is how do we avoid doing so? Perner's answer (see also Patnaik, 2006; Tomasello, 2008) is that the agreed upon conventions of communication—conventions into which children are socialized from the start of language learning—remove the need for any sort of mentalistic analysis in the great majority of communicative interchanges, including those found in early childhood. Note that a version of this argument was used earlier in the chapter to explain the early appearance of white lies and misleading facial displays.

Plausible though Perner's (1988) argument may be in the "juice" context, in its more general form it raises the question in a skeptic's mind of the disconfirmability of mental-state explanations of behavior. If any precocious behavior in the absence of the presumed mentalistic underpinning (such as early lies and facial displays) can be explained on some simpler, lower-level basis, then it is difficult, at least some would argue, to see how the mental state-position can ever be proved wrong. For those who wish a fuller version of this argument, as well as a more general critique of work under the theory-of-mind heading, two sources cited in Chapter 2 (Leudar & Costal, 2009; Leudar et al., 2004) provide extensive treatment.

7

Historical Connections
What Did We Know
Before Theory of Mind?

The goal of this chapter is to review—selectively and at a general-summary level—the 60 or so years of research on social and mental understanding that preceded the advent of theory of mind. I will draw some comparisons between the older and newer research literatures as I go; the concluding chapter, however, will take up the question of the fit between old and new more fully.

Two of the most helpful sources from which I will be drawing are review chapters by Flavell (1985) and Shantz (1983). These sources appeared right at the cusp of the theory-of-mind era; they thus provide good overviews of where the field stood prior to the emergence of theory of mind.

I begin with the oldest of the various literatures: research on perspective taking, beginning with Jean Piaget's studies from the 1920s.

PERSPECTIVE TAKING

Piaget's Studies

Piaget's first studies of perspective taking, and of its converse egocentrism, appeared in his first book, *The Language and Thought of the Child* (Piaget, 1926). Two methods of study were used. One was to record the naturally occurring speech of 4- to 7–year-old children in school across a span of several weeks (apart from the infancy work, the only extended use of naturalistic observation in Piaget's writings). The second was to present experimental tasks in which one child had to convey information to another, either retelling a story or explaining the operation of a simple machine. By both measures much of the speech the children produced was categorized as egocentric speech, defined by Piaget (1926, p. 32) as follows:

The child ... does not bother to know to whom he is speaking nor whether he is being listened to. He talks either for himself or for the pleasure of associating anyone who happens to be there with the activity of the moment.... He does not attempt to place himself at the point of view of his hearer. (copyright 1926 by Harcourt Brace; reprinted with permission)

For Piaget, egocentric speech was just one manifestation—although arguably the most important manifestation—of the young child's general cognitive egocentrism. Although it was frequently so interpreted, egocentrism does not refer to selfishness or concern only with the self. The reference, rather, is to the child's failure to break away from his or her own perspective to take the point of view of another. As the quoted material suggests, the emphasis in Piaget's early discussions of egocentrism was on failure even to attempt to decenter and communicate—young children talk for the pure pleasure of talking. In later writings the emphasis was less on the attempt to communicate than on the ability to do so (Piaget, 1962). Thus, even when young children are trying their best to make themselves understood, their egocentrism often frustrates their efforts. Failing to take into account the listener's perspective, they operate as though the listener already knows everything that they are attempting to convey.

In addition to the speech that young children produce, the other main context in which Piaget studied egocentrism was on tasks of visual or spatial perspective taking (Piaget & Inhelder, 1956). Figure 7.1 illustrates the so-called three mountains problem. The child was first given an opportunity to see how the display looked from various vantage points. He or she was then seated on one side of the display, and a doll was placed at various points around the perimeter. The child's task was to indicate what the doll saw from her vantage point, either by constructing the view with cardboard pieces that represented the mountains or by selecting a photograph that showed the view. Whatever the method, Piaget reported that children younger than 9 or 10 generally failed the task. The youngest children tested (4- to 6-year-olds) typically reproduced or selected their own view, thus responding in a literally egocentric fashion. Older children were less likely to be totally egocentric, but their responses were still colored by their own perspective and thus at best tended to be only partially correct.

Figure 7.1   Piaget's three mountains problem.

Later Research

As John Flavell (1963) noted in *The Developmental Psychology of Jean Piaget* (still the best summary of Piaget's work), Piaget's early books were quickly translated into English, and they elicited a flood of follow-up research. The surprising claims about young children's egocentrism were by far the most popular focus for this research effort. At a general level this work confirmed the basic Piagetian claim—young children *are* often egocentric, and the ability to decenter and take the perspective of another increases with age. At a more specific level the later work identified a number of corrections or additions to the Piagetian picture. I will discuss five such modifications here (for fuller reviews, see Flavell, 1992; Shantz, 1983).

The first is a conclusion that applies in general to Piaget's work (the studies of formal operations being the only exception), and that is that young children are more competent than Piaget's studies indicated. With respect to perspective taking this conclusion proved true in two senses. First, there are simple and basic forms of perspective taking, not examined in Piaget's work, that emerge very early in development. The Flavell studies of Level 1 perspective taking discussed in Chapter 2 are the clearest example (Flavell, Everett, Croft, & Flavell, 1981). Even 2-year-olds realize that two people may have different visual experiences—that the fact, for example, that they see something does not mean that someone else also sees it. Second, the use of simpler tasks, stripped of the extraneous demands that often characterize Piaget's procedures, has revealed earlier success at the kinds of perspective taking discussed by Piaget. When spatial arrays simpler than the three mountains are used, even preschoolers may succeed in taking the visual perspective of another (e.g., Borke, 1975). When the task demands are sufficiently simplified, children as young as 2 may succeed in constructing nonegocentric communications that take into account the knowledge of the listener. For example, 2-year-olds who need mother's help to obtain an out-of-reach object provide fuller and more informative requests when the mother was absent during the object's placement than when she was present and hence already knows where the object is (O'Neill, 1996).

Just as later work has revealed earlier developments than those identified by Piaget, so have later studies documented forms of perspective taking more advanced than those that he studied. The Miller et al. (1970) research discussed in Chapter 3 is one example. In most perspective-taking studies, including Piaget's, the task is a first-order one; the child must figure out what a single target sees, thinks, or whatever. With a recursive chain such as the one illustrated in Figure 3.1, the child must be able to reason about multiple perspectives—not only what A thinks but what A thinks that B thinks that C thinks….

Another example of more advanced development comes in the work of Robert Selman (Selman, 1980; Selman & Byrne, 1974). Selman identified five stages of perspective taking that span the age range of preschool through adolescence. The method of study was Piagetian: presentation of a series of vignettes that posed some social dilemma, followed by semistandardized questioning directed to how the central character should behave. Table 7.1 presents one of the vignettes and also summarizes the Selman stages. As can be seen, the progression is from the

TABLE 7.1   Selman's Levels of Perspective Taking

Sample Dilemma	Questions
Holly is an 8-year-old girl who likes to climb trees. She is the best tree climber in the neighborhood. One day while climbing down from a tall tree she falls off the bottom branch but does not hurt herself. Her father sees her fall. He is upset and asks her to promise not to climb trees anymore. Holly promises. Later that day, Holly and her friends meet Shawn. Shawn's kitten is caught up in a tree and cannot get down. Something has to be done right away or the kitten may fall. Holly is the only one who climbs trees well enough to reach the kitten and get it down, but she remembers her promise to her father.	1. Does Holly know how Shawn feels about the kitten? 2. How will Holly's father feel if he finds out she climbed the tree? 3. What does Holly think her father will do if he finds out that she climbed the tree? 4. What would you do in this situation?

Level	Level Description
0: Egocentric perspective taking (3 to 6 years)	Children do not distinguish their own perspective from that of others. They fail to recognize that others may interpret the same situation differently.
1: Differentiated perspective taking (6 to 8 years)	Children now realize that other perspectives may differ from their own but have limited ability to judge what the differences are.
2: Reciprocal perspective taking (8 to 10 years)	Children can now accurately judge others' perspectives, including others' perspectives on the self, but cannot yet consider different perspectives simultaneously.
3: Mutual perspective taking (10 to 12 years)	Children can now take different perspectives simultaneously. They can reflect on their own viewpoint from the perspective of another person.
4: Social and conventional perspective taking (12 years to adulthood)	Children now relate specific points of view to those prevalent in society in general (the "generalized other").

Source: Selman, R. L., in Lickona, T. (Ed.), *Moral Development and Behavior: Theory, Research, and Social Issues,* Holt, Rinehart and Winston, St. Louis, 1976, pp. 299–316. Copyright 1976 by Thomas Lickona. With permission.

egocentrism of the preschool child through an initial ability to recognize different perspectives to the eventual ability of the adolescent or adult to relate different perspectives to those prevalent in society in general ("the generalized other"). (For recent discussions of the Selman approach, see Martin, Sokol, & Elfers, 2008; Selman, 2008.)

In addition to its extended developmental scope, Selman's research demonstrates another emphasis in the post-Piaget study of perspective taking: namely, an emphasis on drawing relations between perspective taking and other aspects of children's development. Thus, the delineation of developmental stages was for Selman just a starting point; the further goal was to identify the contribution of perspective taking to other developments—or, in Selman's words, to get "research in social development out of the laboratory and into the lives of children" (Selman,

1980, p. xi). Selman's own research included examinations of the contribution of perspective taking to concepts of friendship and of parent–child relations, as well as various clinical applications. Other researchers have added a range of other developmental outcomes. It is worth noting that the evidence amassed for the importance of perspective taking was not only correlational (children who are advanced in perspective taking tend to be advanced in other aspects of develop-ment) but also experimental. For example, training in perspective taking skills has been shown to lead to decreases in aggression and increases in altruism (Chandler, 1973; Iannotti, 1978). In this respect the perspective-taking literature devoted to consequences outstrips the parallel theory-of-mind literature. The latter has yet to move beyond correlational study.

I do not mean the preceding to suggest that Piaget was unconcerned with the broader implications of perspective taking. In fact, he argued that egocentrism and its eventual decline were related to a number of other developments, most notably, changes in how children reason about moral issues (Piaget, 1932). His own research, however, did not go beyond the documentation of parallel developmental changes in the two domains. The demonstration of within-child links between per-spective taking and its putative effects thus became a task for later research, one, as noted, that dozens of studies have taken on not only for moral reasoning but also for a host of other outcomes as well.

Note that the work just discussed reveals a basic similarity between the study of perspective taking and the study of theory of mind. Both topics have been of interest for two reasons. One is an important aspect of children's cognitive develop-ment. The other is as a contributor to other important aspects of cognitive and social development.

A fourth way later studies have gone beyond Piaget's concerns the content of the perspective taking—that is, exactly what about the other is the child attempt-ing to infer? Piaget's studies addressed two forms of perspective taking. The three mountains task is a measure of spatial (or visual or perceptual—the labels are used interchangeably) perspective taking. The communication studies, in con-trast, require cognitive perspective taking. To construct an adequate message, the speaker must take into account both what the listener knows and what the listener does not yet know and thus needs to be told—must, in short, assume the cognitive perspective of the other.

What other aspects of a target might a perspective taker attempt to infer? The main category added by later research has been inference about what the target feels—thus affective perspective taking. Can children figure out whether another is happy, sad, angry, or whatever, particularly in situations in which the other's emotion differs from their own? Do they show a tendency as well to share the emotional experience of the other—to feel sad, for example, when the other is sad? Although the cognitive understanding of the other and the empathic response to the other often go together, they are potentially separable. A child might realize, for example, that a peer is sad without feeling at all sad himself.

Like other forms of perspective taking, affective perspective taking is limited (although not nonexistent) among preschool children and shows clear increases as children develop (Eisenberg, Murphy, & Shepard, 1997). Also like other forms of perspective taking, affective perspective taking relates to other aspects of children's development. Of particular interest have been possible relations to prosocial behavior. It makes sense to predict that the tendency to help or comfort others should be greatest in children who recognize and are saddened by another's distress. Although results are not perfectly straightforward or consistent, such in general seems to be the case (Underwood & Moore, 1982).

I will add that thoughts, percepts, and emotions are not the only psychological states that might serve as targets for perspective taking. Much research has also been directed to children's ability to infer the intentions of others. Such work, however, has generally been discussed under the heading of attribution rather than perspective taking; I therefore defer its coverage for a later part of the chapter.

The final way in which later research has extended its Piagetian beginnings concerns the situational-individual distinction discussed in both Chapter 5 and Chapter 6. The three mountains task clearly falls in the situational category. It is situational because the characteristics of the target being judged do not matter; all that matters is the difference in spatial perspective between self and other. The communication tasks on which one child must convey information to another are also situational. In such a case there are no naturally occurring differences between the two children; the only difference is that one has been given information that the other lacks.

Probably the majority of later research on perspective taking has also had a situational focus, including all work on spatial perspective taking (differences in spatial perspective being inherently situational rather than individual). Some research, however, has also addressed the individual dimension. Perhaps the most interesting such research has concerned children's ability to adjust their communications for targets of different ages. Here, there is a striking contrast between conclusions from laboratory studies and conclusions from naturalistic observations (Miller, 2000). In lab studies children as old as 7 or 8 may be surprisingly inept at constructing an appropriate message for a younger child (e.g., Flavell et al., 1968; Sonnenschein, 1988). In contrast (as noted briefly in Chapter 5), when observed in the natural setting even preschoolers may adjust their speech appropriately when talking to younger listeners (e.g., Sachs & Devin, 1976; Shatz & Gelman, 1973). It seems likely that the developmental truth with regard to perspective taking lies somewhere between the two extremes: that the unfamiliarity and artificiality of the lab approach may lead to an underestimation of what children can do, whereas cues available in the natural setting (e.g., parental modeling, responses from the listener) may remove the need for much perspective taking in children's naturally occurring conversational efforts. Despite this caveat, the speech adjustments shown by young speakers stand as one of the most striking findings of preschool competence in the older research literature.

We saw that Piaget's initial approach to the study of perspective taking was to analyze children's spontaneous speech when talking to other children. This work does not divide clearly along the situational-individual dimension. Presumably, here and in most such settings, most of the differences between self and other to which young speakers must adjust are situational in origin—the listener cannot see the speaker's focus of interest, was not present during the event being discussed, or whatever. Some, however, may be individual—for example, the need to simplify a message for a younger child. Piaget's analyses do not tell us what sort of perspective taking was involved in the speech that he recorded. Most of the examples he quotes are of communication failures, and in most of these it is not clear that an attempt at perspective taking even occurred; rather the children seem to be speaking for the pure pleasure of speaking.

METACOGNITION

I noted earlier that if perspective taking were a newly emerging research literature it would undoubtedly fall under the heading of theory of mind. The same point applies to our next topic. Flavell (2000, p. 16) defines metacognition as "any knowledge or cognitive activity that takes as its cognitive object, or that regulates, any aspect of any cognitive activity." "Knowledge about cognitive activities" certainly sounds like theory of mind, albeit only the epistemic aspect and not everything that the term encompasses.

In fact, the literature on metacognition emerged a decade or so before that on theory of mind, and the two literatures have remained largely separate. Shortly I will discuss possible reasons for the separation. First, however, I provide an overview of the basic developmental findings that emerge from research on metacognition.

Some Distinctions

It is necessary to begin with some distinctions, for several different aspects of metacognition can be identified. Deanna Kuhn is one of the foremost developmental researchers of the topic, and she draws a distinction between two general components (e.g., Kuhn, 1999). She uses the term *metacognitive knowing* to refer to explicit, conscious knowledge about cognition, with a further division into knowledge about task goals and knowledge about strategies to address the goals. The term *metastrategic knowing*, in contrast, refers to the knowledge necessary to carry out cognitive processes—to execute whatever strategies one has decided on for the task at hand. Important in this regard is the capacity both to regulate and to monitor one's cognitive activities, adjusting one's approach as necessary depending on the feedback received.

As Kuhn (1999) notes, the distinction she draws between metacognitive and metastrategic is not a novel one. The division is simply a specific instance of a well known distinction in cognitive psychology: that between declarative (knowing that) knowledge and procedural (knowing how) knowledge.

John Flavell is another major developmental researcher of metacognition, and he adds some further distinctions (e.g., Flavell, 1979). First, he divides the metacognitive category into three components. Two are similar to components identified by Kuhn: knowledge about tasks and knowledge about strategies. The third component, knowledge about persons, encompasses what we know about persons as cognitive actors, both ourselves and others and both similarities and differences among people. All three types of knowledge may act together in a particular cognitive endeavor. For example, a young girl's realization that she has difficulty remembering spatial locations (a form of person knowledge), coupled with the realization that the task confronting her requires exactly this sort of ability (task knowledge), may impel her to activate various techniques (e.g., consult a map, ask a friend for help) that she knows are likely to help (strategy knowledge).

Flavell makes one further distinction. He uses the term *metacognitive experiences* to refer to "any conscious cognitive or affective experiences that accompany and pertain to any intellectual enterprise" (Flavell, 1979, p. 906). Having studied some need-to-learn material, for example, you may feel that you now know it perfectly (and thus have what is known as a feeling-of-knowing experience) or you may feel confused and far from your learning goal. Either sort of experience is likely to affect your subsequent behavior, although presumably in somewhat different directions. In general, metacognitive experiences play an important role in the monitoring of cognitive activity.

A final distinction concerns the content area for the child's metacognitive efforts. The content area certainly may be cognition in general, and thus metacognition in its broadest sense. But it may also be limited to one particular type of cognition—thus metamemory, or meta-attention, or metacommunication. These three content areas are, in fact, among the ones that have received research attention, although disproportionately so—there has been more work on metamemory than on any other topic under the meta heading. Much of the research that I will discuss, therefore, will come from the domain of metamemory.

Developmental Findings

In what follows I move back and forth between the metaknowing and metastrategic categories. I begin with some research on metamemory.

Table 7.2 gives a sampling of items from one of the earliest and most comprehensive studies of metamemory. As can be seen, the questions were directed to knowledge that falls under the task category, that is, what children know about the demands of different memory tasks. Response to the questions, however, necessarily brings in the other two components of metaknowing: knowledge about strategies to perform the tasks and knowledge about both one's own and others' mnemonic abilities and limitations. In addition to the items shown in the table, other aspects of memory that were examined included memorization of related versus unrelated items, the relative ease of rote versus gist recall, and the phenomenon of retroactive interference.

The sample for the Kreutzer, Leonard, and Flavell (1975) research spanned the age range of kindergarten through fifth grade. Even the youngest children showed some knowledge of how memory works. Most basically, most knew that there *is* such a thing as memory, and most also demonstrated the fundamental realization that memory is fallible—that we do not always remember our experiences, even in cases in which we attempt to do so. Most also appreciated an important point that follows from this fallibility: that it may be necessary to do things to help ourselves remember, that is, generate some mnemonic strategy or strategies. It is interesting to note, however, that most of the strategies proposed involved external mnemonic aids (e.g., write a note, ask a parent for help), as opposed to the

TABLE 7.2   Examples of Items From the Kreutzer et al. Study of Metamemory

Item	Example
Savings	Jim and Bill are in grade_____ (subject's own grade). The teacher wanted them to learn the names of all the kinds of birds they might find in their city. Jim had learned them last year and then forgot them. Bill had never learned them before. Do you think one of these boys would find it easier to learn the names of all the birds? Which one? Why?
Immediate-delay	If you wanted to phone your friend and someone told you the phone number, would it make a difference if you called right away after you heard the number or if you got a drink of water first? Why? What do you do when you want to remember a phone number?
Study time	The other day I asked two children to look at and learn some pictures [gestures at 20 pictures] because I wanted to see how well they could remember. I asked them how much time they would like to learn the pictures before I would take them away and ask them how many they could remember. One child said 1 minute. The other child said a longer time, 5 minutes. Why do you think he wanted as long as 5 minutes? Which child remembered the most, the one who studied 1 minute, or the one who studied 5 minutes? Why? And what would you do, study 5 minutes or study 1 minute? Why?
Preparation: object	Suppose you were going ice skating with your friend after school tomorrow and you wanted to be sure to bring your skates. How could you be really certain that you didn't forget to bring your skates along to school in the morning? Can you think of anything else? How many ways can you think of?

Source: Adapted from Kruetzer, M. A., Leonard, C., & Flavell, J. H., *Monographs of the Society for Research in Child Development, 40,* 1975, pp. 8, 9, 18, 25. Copyright 1975 by John Wiley & Sons. Adapted with permission.

in-the-head strategies (e.g., verbal rehearsal, clustering) that have dominated the study of children's memory. Finally, even the 5-year-olds showed some awareness of how different memory tasks differ—knew, for example, that relearning something is generally easier than learning it for the first time.

Not surprisingly, fifth graders demonstrated all of the competencies shown by kindergartners and added a number of others as well. We would expect, of course, that any aspect of cognition should improve with development, and other studies confirm that such is in general the case for metamemory (Schneider & Pressley, 1997). Among the improvements is the ability to gauge one's own mnemonic limitations. When asked, for example, how many items out of an array of 10 they will be able to remember, most kindergartners indicate that they will be able to remember all 10, a performance that no child comes close to achieving. Older children are both more pessimistic and more accurate in judging their own memory (Flavell, Friedrichs, & Hoyt, 1970). Older children are also more skilled at other aspects of memory monitoring—at allocating study time, for example, and at judging what has been learned and what still needs to be mastered (Schneider, 2010).

Young children's difficulty in monitoring performance and assessing knowledge are not limited to the domain of memory. Work on comprehension monitoring (a form of metacommunication) paints a similar picture. Imagine a communication situation in which one young child tells another "pick the red block"; the array,

TABLE 7.3   Examples of Items From Markman's Study of Comprehension Monitoring

Example

Many different kinds of fish live in the ocean. Some fish have heads that make them look like alligators, and some fish have heads that make them look like cats. Fish live in different parts of the ocean. Some fish live near the surface of the water, but some fish live way down at the bottom of the ocean. Fish must have light in order to see. There is absolutely no light at the bottom of the ocean. It is pitch black down there. When it is that dark the fish cannot see anything. They cannot even see colors. Some fish that live at the bottom of the ocean can see the color of their food; that is how they know what to eat.

One of the things children like to eat everywhere in the world is ice cream. Some ice cream stores sell many different flavors of ice cream, but the most popular flavors are chocolate and vanilla. Lots of different kinds of desserts can be made with ice cream. Some fancy restaurants serve a special dessert made out of ice cream called Baked Alaska. To make it they put the ice cream in a very hot oven. The ice cream in Baked Alaska melts when it gets that hot. Then, they take the ice cream out of the oven and serve it right away. When they make Baked Alaska, the ice cream stays firm and it does not melt.

Source: Markman, E. M., *Child Development, 50,* 1979, pp. 645–646. Copyright 1979 by John Wiley & Sons. Reprinted with permission.

however, contains two red blocks. Does the listener respond with confusion and a request for a clearer instruction? By age 7 or 8 such responses begin to appear, but they are unlikely before this point. Younger children are likely to assume that they have understood, and if it becomes clear that they have not, they are likely to blame themselves for the communication failure rather than the inadequate message, thus demonstrating a basic deficiency in communication monitoring (Flavell, Speer, Green, & August, 1991). I should add that young children's performance as listeners is not always as dismal as this description suggests, especially when more naturalistic situations are used (Flavell et al., 2002). Still, it is often pretty dismal, a conclusion that holds across a range of experimental paradigms and research laboratories.

Not only is comprehension monitoring important for conversation; it is also an essential element of successful reading. Consider the passages shown in Table 7.3. Assuming that you read each passage with sufficient care, you probably ended up puzzled and in need of a second look, for each contains a blatant contradiction. Young children, however, are unlikely to spot the inconsistency. Even when the prerequisites for doing so were clearly in place (reading ability, motivation, memory), Markman (1979) reported that most 8-year-olds and even many 11-year-olds required a number of probes and prompts before they expressed awareness of the contradiction. As in the case of conversation, child readers often fail to engage in comprehension monitoring as they take in information and thus often fail to realize what they do not understand. Comprehension monitoring is in fact just one of a number of meta skills that underlie successful reading and that develop gradually across the school years (Garner, 1988).

Each of the types of research discussed to this point demonstrates improvements in metacognition as children develop; none, however, tells us where the improvements come from. Why are older children more knowledgeable about cognition than are younger ones, and why are they more skilled at selecting and executing cognitive strategies?

Research by Kuhn and colleagues (Kuhn, 2001; Kuhn, Garcia-Mila, Zohar, & Andersen, 1995; Kuhn & Pearsall, 1998) provides some evidence on these questions. The task set for their fifth-grade participants was a problem in scientific reasoning, drawn from either the physical sciences (for half the children) or the social sciences. One of the physical science problems, for example, concerned the factors that affected the speed of a model boat, with a variety of both causal (e.g., boat size, boat weight) and noncausal (e.g., sail color, sail size) features available for experimentation. Various measures were taken of the children's response to the tasks, including their ability to explain the strategies they were using to another child (included as an index of metastrategic knowledge). In addition, the design of the study was microgenetic: seven sessions of experimentation spread across a 7-week period. The microgenetic approach has emerged in recent years as a favored method for many researchers interested in the study of cognitive change. The essence of the approach is close, repeated observations of problem-solving behavior across a period of transition, the goal being to observe the process of change as it occurs (Miller & Coyle, 1999; Siegler, 1996).

Change did in fact occur for most of the participants and did so with respect not only to the sophistication and effectiveness of the strategies used but also at the meta level: thus, knowledge of task goals and metastrategic knowledge about strategies. Although the metastrategic–strategy relation was complex, for the most part it was the meta understanding that seemed to lead to strategy change. In part the change involved the creation of new strategies that were not initially available. In part, however, change occurred through selection among strategies, as less effective strategies were gradually replaced by more effective ones. The notion that children often have multiple strategies for a task, and that much of cognitive change therefore consists of strategy selection, has emerged in other domains of study as well (e.g., Siegler, 1996).

Effects of Metacognition

As we have seen, children's metacognitive knowledge increases with development, a conclusion that applies to both declarative, knowing-that knowledge and procedural, knowing-how knowledge. The examples discussed were from the domains of memory, communication, and scientific reasoning, but the conclusion applies to other content areas as well. Studies of meta-attention, for example, document clear developmental improvements across the grade-school years (Miller & Bigi, 1979). So too does research on metacognition with respect to a variety of academic subjects (Hacker, Dunlosky, & Graesser, 2009).

Although the descriptive picture of development is important, it is not all that most researchers want to know about metacognition. The further question is what effects does all this metaknowledge have? Does metaknowledge about a domain contribute to performance in that domain? In the case of memory, for example, both metamemory and memory performance improve as children grow older. Does one change contribute to the other?

The answer is yes, although with the proviso that the contribution of meta factors is not necessarily large and for no domain, memory or otherwise, is metacognition a complete explanation for the developments that we are attempting to explain. Memory is the topic with the largest research base. Schneider and Pressley (1997) reported a meta-analysis of memory–metamemory relations based on 60 studies and 7,097 participants. The average correlation was .41, indicating a modest but still noteworthy relation between the two developments. Relations were somewhat stronger for measures of memory monitoring than for measures of explicit knowledge about memory. Although most of the evidence was correlational, the database included some training studies of metamemory and thus an experimental and not solely correlational approach to the issue (e.g., Pressley, Borkowski, & O'Sullivan, 1985). The experimental approach, of course, provides clearer evidence for a causal role for metamemory than does correlational study alone.

Training efforts are by no means limited to the domain of metamemory. Nor are such efforts purely of basic-science interest. The possibility of training metacognitive knowledge and skills relevant to performance in school provides a clear pragmatic basis for an interest in metacognition. Such efforts began with the pioneering work of Ann Brown and colleagues in the 1980s (Brown, Palincsar, & Armbruster, 1984; Palincsar & Brown, 1984), and they continue today (Hacker et al., 2009; Waters & Schneider, 2010). Although success is neither easily come by nor inevitable, positive results have been reported across a range of subject areas, including reading (McKeown & Beck, 2009), writing (Harris, Santangelo, & Graham, 2010), math (Carr, 2010), and science (White, Frederiksen, & Collins, 2009).

Some Concluding Points

As noted, the research literatures on metacognition and theory of mind, despite an obvious overlap in issues of concern, have for the most part proceeded independently. Why this separation? My discussion draws from several authors who have addressed this question (Flavell, 2000; Kuhn, 2000; Misailidi, 2010) and also adds a few points of my own.

One obvious difference concerns the age period of interest: mostly preschool children for theory of mind, mostly grade-school children, adolescents, and adults for metacognition. This difference, in turn, follows from the primary goals underlying the two sorts of research. For theory of mind a major goal has been to identify what children know about a wide range of mental states, including the earliest forms of knowledge that can be identified. For metacognition, in contrast, the focus has been less on mental states than on mental actions—how, for example, do children choose among various strategies to complete a task? Metacognition is more goal-directed than is theory of mind—is, in Flavell's (2000) words, "applied theory-of-mind" (p. 17). As we saw in Chapter 5, some recent research under the theory-of-mind heading does address children's knowledge of cognitive activities; recall the discussion of the Flavell and the Schwanenflugel and Fabricius programs of research. For the most part, however, cognitive activity has been the province of metacognition, not theory of mind.

A further contrast concerns the self–other distinction. Although research on theory of mind may encompass knowledge about the self (e.g., the self question on the unexpected contents task), its main thrust is knowledge about people and the mental world in general. Research on metacognition may also address knowledge about people in general (e.g., Flavell's persons category); its main thrust, however, is knowledge about the self, especially self-knowledge in the service of some cognitive goal.

Because metacognition (by definition) involves beliefs about cognition, the nonepistemic mental states (e.g., desire, emotion, pretense) that make up much of the theory-of-mind literature are simply outside of its purview. In this sense the scope of theory of mind is a good deal broader than that of metacognition. On the other hand, the aspects of behavior to which metacognition has been applied far exceed the applications of theory of mind, and thus in this sense the metacognitive literature is the broader one. I quote a passage from Flavell et al. (2002, p. 164) to make this point:

> Metacognitive skills are believed to play an important role in many types of cognitive activity that are related to problem solving. Examples are oral communication of information, oral persuasion, oral comprehension, reading comprehension, writing, language acquisition, perception, attention, memory, logical reasoning, social cognition, and various forms of self-instruction and self-control…. Metacognition has also seen service in the fields of cognitive psychology, artificial intelligence, intelligence, human abilities, social-learning theory, cognitive behavior modification, personality development, gerontology, and education. (copyright 2002 by Prentice Hall; reprinted with permission)

I conclude this section with two final points. Although I have discussed metacognition under the "older literature" heading, research on metacognition is very much an ongoing enterprise. It is also, despite my emphasis on childhood developments, a topic for research in adulthood as well. A number of recent books on metacognition make both points (e.g., Efklides & Misalidi, 2010; Larkin, 2010; Shaughnessy, Veenman, & Kleyn-Kennedy, 2008; Tarricone, 2011). So too does the existence of a journal devoted to the study of metacognition: *Metacognition and Learning*.

EPISTEMOLOGICAL CONCEPTIONS

The Mental Activities section of Chapter 5 included a definition of the topic under consideration now. Epistemology refers to "reflection on the nature of knowledge and relation between knowledge and reality" (Pillow, 2008, p. 299).

Defined this way, epistemology, like metacognition, has a clear overlap with theory of mind. Indeed, epistemology is simply another label for what was referred to earlier as the epistemic component of theory of mind, that is, mental states directed to the nature of reality. Despite this commonality, the two research literatures show the same historical separation that we saw applies to metacognition and theory of mind. In Kuhn's (2000) words, "Work on epistemology … has remained curiously isolated from other cognitive developmental research … especially the theory-of-mind work to which it is most closely related" (pp. 316–317).

Undoubtedly one of the reasons for the separation is the difference in chronological emphases. Theory of mind, as we have seen, began as a preschool literature and is still predominantly a preschool literature. In contrast, the starting point for modern discussions of epistemology is a young adult study published in 1970 by William Perry, and most subsequent work has been with adolescent or young adult samples. In what follows I begin with the Perry study and then move on to two other approaches that focus on earlier parts of the developmental span. The particular approaches discussed are by no means the only relevant work; other examples include Belenky, Clinchy, Goldberger, and Tarule (1986); Chandler, Boyes, and Ball (1990); and King and Kitchener (1994). Among the sources for general coverage of this work are Burr and Hofer (2002), Chandler and Birch (2010), and Hofer and Pintrich (1997, 2002).

The Perry Study

The young adults in the Perry (1970) study were not exactly a random sample of young people; rather they were Harvard undergraduates in the late 1950s and early 1960s. They were studied first as freshmen and then followed longitudinally through the 4 years of college, the goal being to trace changes in their thinking across the college years. The method consisted of open-ended and flexible interviews, beginning with "Why don't you start with whatever stands out for you about the year?" and then followed up as necessary. In the author's words:

> Our original purpose in the study—to obtain from students their own reports of their college experience, in their own terms—demanded that we leave the student as free as possible to speak from his own ways of perceiving himself and his world. (p. 18)

(I will add that the masculine pronouns reflect the practice at the time of the writing; in fact, however, the Perry sample was overwhelmingly male.)

Perry's (1970) original assumption—an assumption in keeping with the dominant thinking in the 1950s—was that differences among the students would stem primarily from individual differences in their personalities. This assumption, however, had to be abandoned once comparisons among the age groups became available, for what turned out to be especially striking were the changes in students' thinking about knowledge across the 4 years of college. These changes, moreover, proved to have a systematic, directional, upward-moving quality—proved, in short, to be stage-like. Perry himself eschewed the term *stage* in favor of the softer *position*, and later researchers of epistemology have only sometimes talked explicitly about stages. Nevertheless, the notion of a directional, stage-like developmental progression is common to work on epistemology, and it is one difference between this literature and the literature on theory of mind. The earlier chapters did not talk about stage theories of theory of mind because no such theories have been proposed.

Perry (1970) identified nine developmentally ordered positions in all. These positions, in turn, can be grouped into four more general categories, each comprising two or more of the positions. The developmentally earliest of these categories, a form of thinking most characteristic of the freshmen in the sample, is labeled *dualism*. This label reflects the dichotomous nature of thinking at this point in development; problems have either a right or a wrong answer, and authorities can be counted on to supply the right answer. In the words of one student: "When I went to my first lecture, what the man said was just like God's word.... I believed everything he said, because he was a professor, and he's a Harvard professor, and ... this was a respected position" (p. 61).

As anyone who has taught college students knows, most do not continue to view their professors as the deliverers of God's word. The developmentally next category is *multiplicity*. As the label suggests, the one-right-answer mode of thinking has now given way to the view that most problems have many possible answers. Early in this phase the student may still believe that a single best answer exists; authorities simply have not yet determined what the answer is. Eventually such thinking is supplanted by the belief that many problems have no answer and all views are therefore equally valid.

To this point the student's thinking about knowledge has focused on the various problems that the knowledge system attempts to solve. Now, as Chandler (1987, p. 150) summarizes the next transition, "the border of responsibility begins to shift away from the objects of thought and toward the subjects that are doing the thinking." The next phase, that of *relativism*, is characterized by "the radical reperception of all knowledge as contextual and relativistic" (Perry, 1970, p. 109). Problems are no longer seen as having right or wrong answers that can be gleaned from reality; rather different thinkers impose different constructions upon the world. The different thinkers include the self; the student now perceives himself or herself as an active maker of meaning, a position that carries with it the responsibility to make choices among different beliefs and courses of action.

The notion of commitment, which is incipient in the phase of relativism, is central to the final phase, which is labeled *commitment within relativism*. Although the relative nature of knowledge is still acknowledged, not all positions are seen as equally valid, and the main task for the developing individual is to make an informed commitment to the beliefs and values that best fit his or her own ideals. In Perry's (1970) view, the advances that define this final phase are at least as much ethical as cognitive.

The preceding is a brief summary of a complex theory. Moore (2002) provides a fuller description, as well as a review of relevant research and of changes in the model since the 1970 book.

Mansfield and Clinchy's Work

If changes in epistemological beliefs were limited to the college years—let alone to Harvard undergraduates—they would be of limited interest in a book like this. Research since Perry's (1970), however, makes clear that there are important changes in how children think about knowledge well before the age of 18.

TABLE 7.4   Examples of Questions from the Mansfield and Clinchy Study of Epistemological Conceptions

Domain	Question	Vignette
Objective "fact"	*Do those clouds mean rain?*	It's almost lunchtime. These two friends are planning to go on a picnic. They've brought the picnic basket up from the basement, and they're about to make sandwiches. Then, the boy looks out the window. "Oh, no!" he says. "Those are rain clouds. We can't go on our picnic. It's going to rain." But the girl looks out the window and says, "No, those aren't rain clouds. It's not going to rain. We can go on our picnic."
Mixed objective and subjective	*Would a juju be a good pet?*	It's a beautiful sunny day, and these two friends are at the zoo. They walk around the zoo for a while, and then they come to a cage with an animal they've never seen before. The sign on the cage says that the animal is a baby juju from Australia. This boy looks at the juju and says, "I wouldn't want a juju for a pet." But this girl says, "I would! A juju would make a great pet."
	Is that teacher nice or mean?	These two girls are swinging on the swings on the school playground. A new student-teacher came to teach their class this morning. One girl says to her friend, "That new teacher is mean." Her friend looks at her in surprise and says, "No, she's not mean. She's nice."
Subjective "value"	*Who is the better artist?*	These two girls are looking at a picture painted by a boy named John in their class. One girl says, "John is a terrific painter. He's the best painter in our class." But the other girl says, "Oh, he's not such a great painter. Billy's a better painter than John is."

Source: Mansfield, A. F., & Clinchy, B., *New Ideas in Psychology, 20*, 2002, p. 232. Copyright 2002 by Elsevier. Reprinted with permission.

Furthermore, in a very general sense, the developmental progression that emerges at earlier ages often seems similar to that identified by Perry, albeit in an earlier and simpler form: thus an early absolutist perspective about knowledge; followed by a subjective, no-right-answers position; and succeeded finally by a more balanced position that acknowledges different perspectives but also judges some positions more favorably than others.

Table 7.4 presents a subset of the items used in a study by Mansfield and Clinchy (2002). Like the Perry (1970) research, the Mansfield and Clinchy study was longitudinal; children were tested first at age 10 and then again at 13 and 16. (The table shows the wording of the items that was used for the 10-year-olds. The wording was adjusted some at the older ages, but the content of the problems remained the same.) A series of questions followed each vignette, including "Why do you suppose they disagree like that?" "Who is right, do you think?" "Is there a way they could find out for sure?" And "Could they both be right at the same time, or does one have to be right and does one have to be wrong?"

Mansfield and Clinchy (2002) identified three general categories of reasoning in response to their vignettes. Answers coded as *objective* indicated that the problem had a single right answer with which everyone would, or at least should, agree.

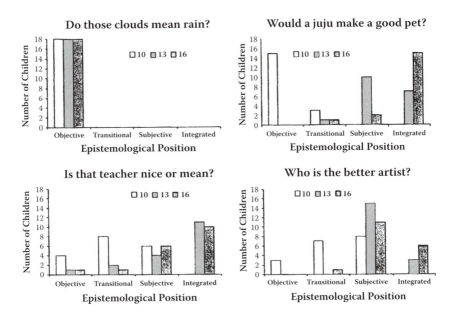

Figure 7.2 Findings from Mansfield and Clinchy's study of epistemological development. (From Mansfield, A. F., & Clinchy, B., *New Ideas in Psychology, 20,* 2002, p. 238. Copyright 2002 by Elsevier. Reprinted with permission.)

Those coded as *subjective* espoused exactly the opposite opinion: No single right answer existed, and therefore all views were equally valid. Finally, the *integrated* category, as the name suggests, combined elements of the first two forms of reasoning. Those reasoning at this level acknowledged that some problems had no clear, single right answer; they also argued, however, that answers grounded in evidence and logic were superior to those that lacked such grounding. In the words of one respondent, "I don't think that most questions have right answers. They have better solutions than other solutions" (p. 234).

Figure 7.2 presents the main results of the study. Two findings are noteworthy. The first concerns developmental changes. It can be seen that the objective responses were most characteristic of the youngest children; indeed, for two of the four vignettes they were the only age group to offer an objective response. Conversely, the integrated responses grew more likely with increased age. They were, in fact, completely absent at age 10 but became moderately common by 13 and 16.

The second finding concerns differences among the vignettes. Every participant at every age provided an objective response to the Clouds vignette, thus treating the issue as one of verifiable fact. In contrast, even the 10-year-olds tended to see the Artist question as a subjective matter of taste, conducive to different opinions but not to any single solution. What emerged as important, therefore, was not only the age of the child but also the type of belief at issue. Children reasoned differently about different types of beliefs, and the ability to do so increased with age.

I will note one more finding from the research. The types of justifications that children offered for their judgments also varied as a function of both age and type of belief. Justifications coded as personal experience and personal opinion were common in response to the Teacher and Artist vignettes, whereas reason and appeals to authority figured more prominently in the other two cases. In addition, the ways in which children talked about authority changed with age, moving from authority as a source of right answers to authority as a source of information to be used for one's own reasoning—a movement, in Mansfield and Clinchy's (2002, p. 246) words, "from source to resource."

Kuhn's Work

The age span for the final program of research to be considered was broader than that in either the Perry (1970) or the Mansfield and Clinchy (2002) study. Kuhn (1991) examined (cross sectionally) four age groups: teens (14- and 15-year-olds) and adults in their 20s, 40s, and 60s. The focus of the research was argumentative thinking—that is, "thinking that takes the form of an argument" (Kuhn, p. 2). Often, of course, "argue" means a dispute between two people, but the term can also apply to the justifications that an individual offers in support of his or her beliefs. It was the latter form of thinking that interested Kuhn.

The questions that Kuhn (1991) posed to elicit such thinking provide another good context for introspection, that is, a chance to think about one's own likely answers. There were three questions: What causes prisoners to return to crime after they're released? What causes children to fail in school? What causes unemployment? As these questions suggest, a further emphasis of the research was on reasoning about issues of considerable real-life importance. A series of follow-up questions followed the presentation of each issue, including how the participant had arrived at the answer and what he or she could say to convince someone who held an opposed position. Of particular importance with regard to conclusions about epistemology were questions directed to the certainty with which the position was held and the issue of expertise (e.g., "Do experts know for sure what causes prisoners to return to crime?" "Would it be possible for experts to find out for sure if they studied this problem long and carefully enough?")

Kuhn (1991) identified three levels of reasoning, levels that bear an obvious similarity to those that emerged in the Perry (1970) and Mansfield and Clinchy (2002) research. Reasoning at the *absolutist* level was defined by two criteria: a belief that a correct answer to the problem existed and a belief that experts knew with certainty what the answer was. Many participants who reasoned at this level were also quite certain about the correctness of their own answer to the question. The *multiplist* level, in contrast, was characterized by a denial of expert certainty. Participants at this level saw the questions as matters with multiple possible answers on which experts would probably never agree, and they also perceived their own knowledge as equal to or perhaps even greater than that of the experts. Finally, those at the *evaluative* level also recognized the existence of different viewpoints on the issues. Now, however, not all viewpoints were considered equal; experts were acknowledged to know more than the self, and some positions could be better justified and thus were more tenable than others.

Kuhn (1991) reported some consistency in participants' reasoning across the three questions. On each question the absolutist category was most frequent and evaluative responses were least common. It is worth noting that the highest levels of possible response were also infrequent in the Perry (1970) study. Interestingly, for the most part Kuhn reported no differences in levels of reasoning among the four age groups. There were, however, definite individual differences within an age, something that was also true in the Perry and the Mansfield and Clinchy (2002) research. The identification of marked individual differences among respondents of the same age is another respect in which work on epistemology differs from most research under the theory-of-mind heading. (For related research by Kuhn, see Kuhn, Amsel, & O'Laughlin, 1988.)

ATTRIBUTION

Attribution has long been a central topic in social psychology, dating from seminal publications by Heider (1958) and Kelley (1967). The term refers to the causal explanations that people generate for behavior. The explanation may be for our own behavior (why did I forget that appointment?) or for the behavior of someone else (why did my child fail that test?). Attributions are arguably one of the most frequently activated and important ways in which we attempt to make sense of human behavior.

Like metacognition, attribution is both a large and an ongoing research literature. It is, moreover, a research literature that is less easily separated from that on theory of mind, given the fact that issues once studied under the heading of attribution have in recent years often been examined from a theory-of-mind perspective. My coverage will mix together work from the two perspectives.

Attributions for Interpersonal Behavior

It will be helpful to have an example to work from. Imagine that Child A bumps into Child B in the cafeteria lunch line. How might an on-looking Child C explain A's behavior?

A first question is whether the behavior was accidental or intentional. We saw in Chapter 2 that an initial understanding of intentional behavior emerges in infancy and that further advances in understanding are evident by the toddler years. Nevertheless, in many circumstances making the accidental–intentional distinction is a challenge for young children. Preschool children tend to judge most actions as intentional, even ones (e.g., sneezing) that to an adult clearly fall in the unintentional category (e.g., Smith, 1978). The ability to distinguish the two types of action develops gradually across the preschool and grade-school years, with a number of factors (e.g., the valence of the outcome, the match between motive and outcome) that affect the ease of making the distinction (Zelazo, Astington, & Olson, 1999).

The accidental-intentional question has seldom been a focus in adult work on attribution, for the good reason that understanding of the distinction has long ceased to be an issue. What *has* been a focus is whether the target behavior is seen as internal or external in origin, as arising from something in the person or from something in the situation. This dimension is orthogonal to the accidental-intentional dimension. Perhaps A bumped into B because he wanted to hurt B (thus an intentional action with an internal origin), or perhaps the bump occurred because A is generally a clumsy person (thus an accidental action with an internal origin). Perhaps A slipped on the wet cafeteria floor and thus was propelled into B (an accidental action with an external origin), or perhaps he was goaded into behaving aggressively by another child in the setting (an intentional action with an external origin).

Early work on children's attributions concluded that young children prefer situational explanations for behavior, with little or no ability to take into account internal causes (e.g., Higgins & Bryant, 1982). Such a conclusion fit with the Piagetian zeitgeist of the time, with its emphasis on the perception-bound, surface-oriented reasoning of the young child.

Subsequent work makes clear that this conclusion is at best only partly correct. Under some testing circumstances young children do in fact appear to be situation theorists. More generally, however, even preschool children show a preference for psychological over physical causes in their descriptions and explanations of behavior (Montgomery, 1994; Youngstrom & Goodman, 2001). When asked, for example, to describe a picture of a boy mopping up spilled milk, 3-year-olds prefer "sad about his spilled milk" to "wiping up his spilled milk" (Lillard & Flavell, 1990). When asked to choose between psychological causes for performance on a task (e.g., "likes to do," "tries hard") and physical or external causes (e.g., "quiet room," "mother makes him do"), 4-year-olds prefer the psychological explanations (Miller, 1985). Note that the young child's tendency to view all behavior as intentional also implies a belief in psychological causation, albeit in this case a sometimes incorrect belief. In Miller and Aloise's (1989, p. 267) words, "The main developmental task seems to be learning when not to use the psychological causes that the child has preferred since toddlerhood."

What the research just discussed shows is that even young children appeal to psychological states (e.g., sad, angry) when attempting to make sense of behavior. A further question is whether they also appeal to psychological traits. A trait is an enduring disposition to behave in a particular way. A psychological state (e.g., angry) tells us what the person is like now; a psychological trait (e.g., aggressive) tells us what the person is like in general.

Understanding of traits lags behind understanding of psychological states (Miller & Aloise, 1989). How much behind has yet to be resolved. Recent research makes clear that under optimal circumstances even preschool children show some understanding of traits—they can use relevant information to infer traits, and they can use traits to predict future behavior (Heyman, 2009; Heyman & Gelman, 1999; Liu, Gelman, & Wellman, 2007). Young children are less likely to use trait-relevant information than are older children, however, and the inferences that they do draw are sometimes overly broad. A "smart" peer, for example, may be expected not only to do well on school tasks but also to excel at jumping and to share readily with others (Stipek & Daniels, 1990). Children's initial use of traits also tends to be categorical rather than dimensional. They can make judgments, for example, about nice versus not nice but do not yet reason in terms of degree of niceness

TABLE 7.5   Factors That Govern Attribution

Factor	Description
Covariation principle	attribute an outcome to the cause with which it covaries over time
Consistency information	extent to which an individual responds to a given situation in the same way over time
Distinctiveness information	extent to which an individual responds in the same way to different situations (similar response equals low distinctiveness)
Consensus information	extent to which others respond to the same situation in the same way as the individual being judged
Augmenting principle	attach greater importance to a potential cause if the behavior occurs despite the presence of other, inhibitory causes
Discounting principle	attach less importance to a potential cause if other potential causes are also present

(Gonzalez, Zosuls, & Ruble, 2010). They are also better at using trait information to predict behavior than they are at using such information to predict emotional response—to predict, for example, that a shy child will be sad rather than happy if selected to be the leader in a game (Gnepp & Chilamkurti, 1988). Finally and most generally, it is difficult to determine whether young children's understanding of traits extends beyond a recognition of behavioral regularities to a conception of traits as internal, stable, causal factors that underlie behavior. Indeed, this is a difficult determination at any age.

Children's understanding of traits is a central issue in work on person perception. I therefore return to the topic in the next section of the chapter.

Let me return to the A-bumps-B example to make several further points. The preceding discussion assumed that Child C's attributional efforts could focus solely on Child A. There are, however, two participants in the interaction. Suppose it turns out that child B is a target for aggression from virtually every other child in the class. Such a finding would suggest that the causal locus for the bumping incident may lie as much in B as is it does in A.

It is time to introduce some basic principles that have emerged from attribution theory and research. Table 7.5 provides a summary of several (although by no means all) of the factors that seem to govern how people make attributions. Of these the most basic is the covariation principle: attribute an outcome to the causal factor with which it covaries over time. The next three entries—consistency, consensus, and distinctiveness—are particular forms of covariation information that may apply in different situations. Suppose, for example, that consistency is high and consensus and distinctiveness are low. Such a pattern suggests that some factor internal to the actor is causing the outcome (given that the actor consistently behaves this way and others do not). Suppose, in contrast, that all three dimensions are high. A pattern of this sort suggests that there is something about the target that is eliciting the behavior (given that the actor is less likely to show the behavior toward other targets, and that others behave the same way toward the target).

In simple situations children as young as 5 or 6 can use covariation information to make attributions about others (Ruble & Rholes, 1983). Told, for example, that Ed consistently shares not only with Ralph but also with other children, they infer that Ed is a generous person (Leahy, 1979), a conclusion based on a combination of consistency and distinctiveness information (and one example of the early ability to infer traits from behavior). Other studies (e.g., Divitto & McArthur, 1978) have also reported use of consistency and distinctiveness information as early as age 5. Both these studies and others (e.g., Boseovski & Lee, 2008) indicate that children are less likely to use consensus information. This finding is perhaps not surprising, given that adults too often fail to make use of consensus information (Harvey & Weary, 1984). Because they do not take into account such information, young children's attributions tend to focus on the actor only, without considering the possible contribution of the target of the behavior (consensus information being most informative with respect to target effects).

What about the augmenting and discounting principles? To reason in terms of these principles the child must take two causal factors into account simultaneously. Are young children capable of doing so? As is often true in research with children, the answer depends on the method of study. When standard approaches to the study of augmenting are used it is not until adolescence that children show much success (Shultz, Butkowsky, Pearce, & Shanfield, 1975); with maximally simplified procedures (specifically, a geometric shape that moves to a goal with or without an obstacle to overcome), even 5-year-olds show augmenting in their responses (Kassin & Lowe, 1979). The age at which discounting appears is similarly variable, although in most research success emerges sometime between the ages of 7 and 9 (Miller & Aloise, 1990). Prior to this point children sometimes show an additive effect when presented with two sufficient causes, judging that the presence of cause B makes cause A more rather than less important.

A particularly interesting form of discounting is a phenomenon known as the overjustification effect. It is a phenomenon seen at a behavioral rather than conscious-judgment level. Imagine two children who are given the opportunity to do some drawing with some new magic markers. One child is promised a reward for every drawing she produces; the other is simply given a chance to draw. Which child is more likely to seek out the markers on a future occasion? If you guessed the child who was rewarded for the activity you would be wrong. Later interest is more likely for the child who did the drawing on her own, without any external incentive for doing so (Lepper, Green, & Nisbett, 1973). When rewards are given, the behavior is overjustified in the sense that two causal attributions are possible: an internal one (I'm drawing because I like to) and an external one (I'm drawing because I'm getting a reward). The external cause apparently results in a discounting of the internal one, thus diminishing future interest when the reward is no longer in place. This effect has been shown in children as young as 3.

Let us return to the A-bumps-B example to make one further point. So far the example has concerned a generic Child A and Child B. Suppose, however, that A is known to be a highly aggressive child. In this case both Child C and others may be more likely to judge A's behavior as an intentional act of aggression. Or suppose that B is himself an aggressive child. In this case B may be more likely than most children to interpret A's behavior as aggressive, and may therefore be likely to respond aggressively himself.

The outcomes just sketched are not merely hypothetical. Research by Dodge and colleagues (e.g., Dodge, 1980; Dodge & Crick, 1990) makes clear that both effects occur. Aggressive children are more likely than are children in general to interpret the behaviors of others as hostile, especially when the behavior is in itself ambiguous (as is true of the cafeteria bump). And the behaviors of aggressive children are more likely to be interpreted as hostile by others than are the behaviors of children in general, even when there is no objective difference between the behaviors being judged. Both effects serve to exacerbate the aggressive child's aggressive behavior.

Attributions for Academic Performance

Accidental–intentional and internal–external are not the only dimensions of interest in attribution research. An influential theoretical formulation by Weiner (1986) adds two further dimensions: stable–unstable and controllable–uncontrollable. Again, the dimensions are orthogonal. The fact, for example, that a particular factor is controllable does not in itself tell us whether it is stable.

It is with respect to attributions for academic performance that the dimensions of controllability and stability have been most thoroughly explored. In most discussions of academic performance four possible determinants are considered: ability, effort, task difficulty, and luck. Table 7.6 shows how these determinants are usually considered to divide along the dimensions of internal–external, stable–unstable, and controllable–uncontrollable. I should add that these distinctions, despite the either–or wording, are not absolute; some qualifier such as "usually" or "for the most part" should be assumed. I will also note shortly an exception to the view that ability is a stable, uncontrollable factor.

Just as in the work considered earlier, one question in research on academic attributions has concerned children's ability to reason simultaneously about multiple causes. Imagine two students who received the same score on a test. One studied hard; the other did not study at all. What can we conclude about their ability? Most adults view effort and ability as compensatory in such a situation: the higher the level of one, the less need there is for the other. They would conclude, therefore, that the second child has greater ability. Note that this is a form of discounting: downplay the role of one factor if another factor is sufficient to account for the outcome. We saw earlier that young children tend not to discount, and such is the case here as well. Children younger than 7 or 8 are more likely to see the two factors as positively related: the greater the effort, the greater the ability (Kun, 1977; Nicholls, 1978). Young children are also less likely than older children

TABLE 7.6   Attributions for Academic Performance

	Internal–External	Stable–Unstable	Controllable–Uncontrollable
Ability	Internal	Stable	Uncontrollable
Effort	Internal	Unstable	Controllable
Task difficulty	External	Stable	Uncontrollable
Luck	External	Unstable	Uncontrollable

or adults to apply the augmenting principle—to realize, for example, that success on a difficult task implies greater ability than does success on an easy task.

Although general reasoning principles such as discounting and augmenting are of interest, most research on academic attributions has concentrated on children's attributions for their own academic performance. How do they explain their successes and failures? And what effects do these attributions have on their subsequent performance?

Probably the best known approach to these issues is that of Carol Dweck, and it is her work that I will concentrate on here. Both Dweck's research (Dweck, 1999; Dweck & Leggett, 1988) and that of others make clear that the attributions that children draw for their successes and failures *are* important—indeed, in some respects more important than the successes and failures themselves. In general, the most adaptive attributional pattern is one that does not view failure as an unchangeable outcome and thus as a reason to abandon any future attempt. Instead, failures are seen as momentary transition points, resulting either from insufficient effort (and thus changeable with more effort) or from a temporary but correctable lack of the requisite ability. In this view, then, ability is not necessarily a stable, unchangeable quality; rather, ability can change, and so, therefore, can performance. As Dweck and Leggett (1988, p. 269) put it, "Controllability is in the eye of the perceiver."

Why do some children adopt such an attributional pattern? In Dweck's (1999) model the attributions that children make for their intellectual performance follow from their general theory of exactly what intelligence is. Two theories are identified. Children who hold an entity theory of intelligence believe that intelligence is a fixed quantity—different people have different amounts, and nothing can be done to change that fact. Given such a view, there is little reason to persist at a task if one has tried one's best and has failed. In contrast, children who hold an incremental theory believe that intelligence can and does change—with more effort and more experience abilities can grow, and as abilities grow, failure can turn into success.

I conclude this section with a brief consideration of the most often discussed finding with regard to academic attributions and academic performance. The finding is of a gender difference in attributions for success or failure in math. The qualifiers that apply to gender differences in general apply here as well: The difference is an on-the-average outcome that does not apply to all cases, it does not apply under all circumstances, and it may not apply in the future. This said, on the average boys attribute their successes in math to ability and their failures to lack of effort; girls attribute their successes to effort and their failures to lack of ability (Dickhauser & Meyer, 2006). Such attributional differences may contribute to the finding (in some although not all research—see Lindberg, Hyde, Peterson, & Linn, 2010) that girls, who often outperform boys in math during the elementary school years, eventually lag behind boys in both interest and achievement in math. If so, the gender difference in attributions would rank as one of the more important examples of how children's social-cognitive understanding can affect other aspects of their development.

PERSON PERCEPTION

Although the term is probably self-defining, I will begin this section with a formal definition of what is meant by person perception. The definition is from an early and influential developmental study of the topic by Livesley and Bromley (1973). According to these authors, person perception is "the area of psychology concerned with how we 'perceive' or 'cognize' other persons—their intentions, attitudes, traits, emotions, ideas, abilities, and purposes, as well as their overt behavior and physical characteristics" (p. 1). It is, in short, all-encompassing—however we think about people.

I will make one addition to Livesley and Bromley's (1973) definition. In some discussions of the topic, including the one I will present here, the scope is not limited to "other persons." The self is also a target for person perception.

Perceptions of Others

How might we study person perception? The most common method has been to ask the child to provide open-ended descriptions of people whom he or she knows. In Livesley and Bromley's (1973) study the children provided eight such descriptions: one each for a liked and disliked boy, girl, adult man, and adult woman. Other examples of the free-description approach include Barenboim (1981); Scarlett, Press, and Crockett (1971); and Secord and Peevers (1974).

Not all studies of person perception concern familiar others. In some studies children are shown films of children or adults behaving in particular ways, after which they are asked to provide descriptions of the people they have seen (e.g., Feldman & Ruble, 1988; Flapan, 1968). The open-ended response format thus remains, but the particular target varies.

The Livesley and Bromley (1973) study produced some striking examples of how children think about other people. Yuill (1997, p. 274) notes that it has become a "venerable tradition" to begin discussions of person perception by quoting some of these examples. My presentation will be no exception. Table 7.7 presents several examples drawn from different parts of the developmental span (including the one—I will let you guess which—that every secondary treatment reproduces).

A number of questions can be asked about data of this sort. A main question, however—and the one on which I will concentrate—concerns developmental change. How does the thinking of older children and adolescents differ from that of younger children?

The examples in the table suggest some obvious differences. As children develop, their descriptions become longer, more varied, more nuanced, and more psychological as opposed to physical in their content. Livesley and Bromley's (1973) scoring system (a detailed and complex one) identified two general categories of description: peripheral statements, which included information such as age, sex, physical appearance, and possessions; and central statements, which included more abstract and psychological information such as motives, attitudes, habits, and traits. The proportion of central statements rose from 20% at age 7 to close to 50% at age 15.

TABLE 7.7   Examples of Responses from the Livesley and Bromley Study of Person Perception

Situation	Description
Seven-year-old boy describing a girl he likes	She is shy. She is blonde and she likes working. She likes playing. She was born in Liverpool. She is small. She is active. She does not get hot. She is kind and she does not need much sleep.
Seven-year-old boy describing a boy he dislikes	He is very tall. He has dark brown hair, he goes to our school. I don't think he has any brothers or sisters. He is in our class. Today he has a dark orange jumper and grey trousers and brown shoes.
Nine-year-old boy describing a boy he dislikes	He smells very much and is very nasty. He has no sense of humor and is very dull. He is always fighting and he is cruel. He does silly things and is very stupid. He has brown hair and cruel eyes. He is sulky and eleven years old and has lots of sisters. I think he is the most horrible boy in the class. He has a croaky voice and always chews his pencil and picks his teeth and I think he is disgusting.
Fourteen-year-old girl describing a boy she dislikes	I dislike this boy because he is very rude, ignorant, cheeky, and thinks he is the best. Although he can sometimes be very nice, his poorer qualities outnumber his better qualities which are not very good to start with. He is very rude to his friend who is nice and this leads to an argument. I think he is very ignorant by the way he ignores things when he wants to. He is exceptionally cheeky to his mother when his friends are there especially.
Fifteen-year-old boy describing a woman he likes	She is always kind to strangers. She is not old-fashioned and stodgy but is fairly modern. She always seems calm and yet she always seems to be doing something or going somewhere. She is a very jovial person, good tempered and good-humored and very easy going and lively. She is fairly intelligent but does not boast.

Source: Livesley, W. J., & Bromley, D. B., *Person Perception in Childhood and Adolescence*, Wiley, London, 1973, pp. 126, 198, 213, 217, 220, 221. Copyright 1973 by John Wiley & Sons. Reprinted with permission.

Although the specific terminology may vary, other studies of person perception have come to similar conclusions with respect to developmental change. Barenboim (1981), for example, identified a transition from behavioral comparisons as the earliest developmental level to psychological constructs by middle childhood to psychological comparisons, or comparisons of the constructs, by adolescence. Secord and Peevers' (1974) participants moved from "simple differentiating" (physical characteristics, groups memberships, global evaluations) at the youngest age to "dispositional" responses (use of trait-like terms) by adolescence and young adulthood.

As in attribution research, a question of particular interest concerns children's tendency to impute traits in their thinking about others. As the quoted examples indicate, even the youngest children in the Livesley and Bromley (1973) study included some trait terms ("shy," "kind") in their descriptions. Such responses were not very frequent, however; indeed, almost half of the 7-year-olds provided no trait terms at all. In addition, the traits that were mentioned at the youngest ages tended to be global and evaluative in nature (e.g., "nice," "bad"). With development, both the frequency and the sophistication of trait terms increased, and by adolescence children were averaging approximately two and a half trait terms per description.

Again, other studies of this sort have reported similar results. The conclusion that use of traits increases with development is, of course, in accord with the findings from attribution research discussed in the preceding section.

The Feldman and Ruble (1981, 1988) study provides an interesting addendum with respect to the issue of traits. As noted, in this study the descriptions were not of familiar others but rather of children viewed on videotape. Half of their participants were led to believe that they would be interacting with the target children in the future; half received no such expectation. Those who anticipated future interaction produced significantly more trait-like descriptions than did the comparison group—two to three times as many, in fact. Feldman and Ruble (1981, p. 202) offer the following examples:

> (No expected interaction) She was throwing balls into the bucket. She was throwing Frisbees at the target. She has dark hair. She went into another room.

> (Expected future interaction) She is good at games and she is probably nice. She tries very hard. I think she likes to play games.

This study makes the point—perhaps obvious in retrospect but seldom discussed—that how we think about people depends on *why* we are thinking about them. It seems likely that many real-life instances of person perception are like Feldman and Ruble's (1988) anticipated–interaction condition: Our perceptions of others are guided by the attempt to learn things that will help us to interact successfully with them. Such a goal apparently motivates a deeper, more psychological level of processing than would otherwise obtain.

Self-Perceptions

The question now is what children know or think about themselves. The most common method of study has been the same as that used for perceptions of others: namely open-ended description. The approach may be maximally general ("Tell me what you are like.") or more focused ("Tell me what you are like at school." "Tell me what you are like with your friends.").

At a general level, the developmental picture for self-perceptions parallels that for perceptions of others (Damon & Hart, 1982; Harter, 2006). Preschoolers' self-descriptions focus on tangible, observable qualities—physical appearance, possessions, favorite activities. Different aspects of the description are not well integrated, and any evaluative components are typically unreservedly positive (e.g., "good singer," "fastest runner"). Recall that work in metacognition has also identified a positivity bias in young children's self-evaluations. As in the metacognitive studies, one developmental change is that self-descriptions become less positive and therefore also more realistic as children grow older. Part of the basis for the change is the child's increasing use of social comparison—that is, comparing the self to others and drawing conclusions about the self from the comparison. Children eventually come to realize, for example, that earning an 80

What I am like with Different People

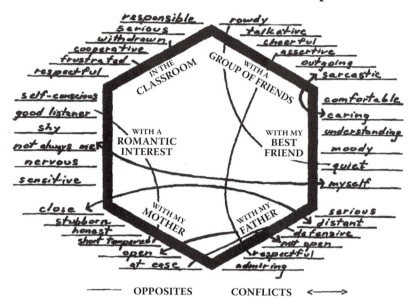

Figure 7.3 The multiple selves of a prototypical 15-year-old girl. (From Harter, S., *The Construction of Self*, Guilford Press, New York, 1999, p. 70. Copyright 1999 by Guilford Press. Reprinted with permission.)

on a test is good if everyone else is scoring 70—not, however, if everyone else gets 100.

As with perceptions of others, children's self-descriptions come to focus less on physical characteristics and more on abstract, psychological features as they develop. Trait terms increase in both frequency and complexity. Different aspects of the description no longer stand in isolation but rather become progressively integrated over time, and apparent inconsistencies are often resolved under some higher-level concept. Descriptions also become more differentiated, as the child comes to realize that aspects of his or her self may vary across different contexts or different relationships. An impressive example of such differentiation is pictured in Figure 7.3. Note that the figure also conveys the variety and sophistication of trait terms that characterize the self-perception by adolescence.

The preceding comparison of self and other is based on separate study of the two targets. What happens if the same child offers descriptions for both the self and others? Both the Livesley and Bromley (1973) and the Secord and Peevers (1974) studies elicited self-descriptions in addition to the descriptions of others that were the main focus of the research. In both studies the similarities in the descriptions of self and others were more marked than the differences; in particular, children seemed to operate at the same general level with respect to both targets. Other studies (e.g., Hart & Damon, 1985) have reported similar conclusions. The main difference noted by Livesley and Bromley was that participants made more use of the Preferences and Aversions (i.e., likes and dislikes) category in their self-descriptions—a perhaps expectable finding, given that we all have more self- than other-knowledge with respect to likes and dislikes. Secord and Peevers reported a similar finding: more reference to specific interests, beliefs, and values when describing the self.

All of the conclusions to this point have been based on the free-description methodology, and this fact raises an obvious concern. The concern is that use of such a highly verbal procedure may cause us to underestimate what children actually know about the self, especially at the younger, less verbal end of the age range. Two studies by Eder (1989, 1990) suggest that such is in fact the case. Both studies adopted simplified, minimally verbal procedures intended to uncover whatever trait-like thinking young children might be capable of showing. In one study (Eder, 1990), for example, children saw a pair of puppets who presented opposing trait-like statements, for example, "I get mad a lot" and "I usually don't get mad," after which they indicated which puppet they were most like. As in other research, the Eder studies found that thinking in terms of traits increased with age, in this case across the span of 3 to 8. But they also showed that even preschoolers seem to possess some trait-like knowledge about themselves. And not just about themselves—the Eder (1989) study reported comparable results when the target was another child. The latter finding fits with conclusions from the attributional approach to traits discussed earlier. Work under both the attribution and person perception headings makes clear that young children do not think in terms of traits as readily or as frequently as do older children or adults. But both approaches tell us that they are sometimes capable of doing so.

I conclude this section on the self by acknowledging its incompleteness. Learning about the self does not begin at the point when my coverage begins, with the ability to talk about the self at age 3 or so; it begins, rather, very early in life. The fascinating literature on forms of self-understanding in infancy is outside my scope; good reviews of this work include Legerstee (2006) and Rochat (2009).

RELATIONSHIPS AND GROUPS

The topics considered to this point in the chapter all overlap to varying degrees with work on theory of mind. Such is not the case for the final topic to be discussed. In most theory-of-mind studies the target for the participant's thinking is a single mental agent—sometimes the self, sometimes a specific other, sometimes a generic other. In higher-order studies it may be necessary to take into account at least two mental agents (John and Mary in the ice cream truck story, the various protagonists in the Strange Stories); the focus remains, however, on the individual actor. The work to be discussed now addresses a topic not yet examined from a theory-of-mind perspective: how children think about people together, with a focus first on relationships and then on larger, more formal groups.

Relationships

Shantz (1983) discusses three entries under this heading: friendship, conflict, and authority. I settle here for the first and third of these topics.

The question with respect to friendship is not friendship in general (a very large topic) but the cognitive aspect of the topic. How do children think about friendship, and how does their thinking change as they develop? As with thinking about the self, the main method of study has been verbal report. Children may be asked "What is a friend?" or "What makes someone a best friend?" or "How do children become friends?" Questions may also address more specific aspects of friendship—for example, how to repair a breach between friends. In any case, what we conclude about children's thinking about friendship comes from how they talk about friendship.

As noted, a main question is that of developmental change. A number of researchers have addressed this question, and there is a good deal of concurrence in what they report. I draw my summary from Damon (1977), who in turn bases his account partly on his own research and partly on work by Selman (1976) and Youniss (1975); see also Youniss & Volpe (1978).

Damon identifies three developmentally ordered levels of reasoning with respect to friendship. At the earliest level, which characterizes children of pre-school and perhaps early grade-school age, friends are seen as playmates who are nice and fun to be with and who share material things. Friendships are momentary and transient affairs, and there is little concern with the personal qualities of the friend. By middle childhood friends come to be seen as people who help and trust each other in an enduring reciprocal relationship. Friendship is now seen as a subjective rather than objective affair, and the specific qualities of the friend are therefore recognized as being important. Finally, by adolescence comes an emphasis on mutual understanding, communication, and intimacy as the hallmarks of friendship. Compatibility of interests and personality are the main bases for becoming and remaining friends.

The description just provided should not sound surprising, for it has obvious parallels in conclusions from work on person perception and on self-perception. All three topics involve how children think about people; we would therefore expect some similarities, in addition to the differences elicited by the different kinds of target.

The work on friendship raises two related points that I will return to in the final chapter. First, this literature shows a consistent attempt to relate thinking about friendship to general theories of children's cognitive development, especially Piagetian or neo-Piagetian approaches. Second—and not coincidentally—stage models are common in the friendship literature. Neither point is true of research in theory of mind.

Friendship is a symmetrical relationship between two same-aged or close to same-aged peers. Authority, in contrast, is an asymmetrical relationship that typically involves a younger–older dyad—most commonly, child and parent or child and teacher. A basic question is again that of developmental change in how children reason about the issue. Early work by Damon (1977) and Selman (Selman, 1980; Selman & Jaquette, 1977) identified changes that had parallels in these authors' studies of friendship, including a stage-like quality to the developmental progression. Damon, for example, described a movement from an early self-interested perspective (obedience is good because it gets you what you want) to obedience based on the greater power of the authority to eventual obedience grounded in the greater knowledge or competence of the authority figure. Selman tied developmental changes to his general model of perspective taking (Table 7.1), exploring reasoning with respect to both parent and peer authority figures. In both cases children's responses showed a similar movement from an early view of authority as power to an eventual more balanced, voluntary, reciprocal conception of the authority relationship.

More recent research does not deny these early findings but does extend them in a number of ways (Laupa, Turiel, & Cowan, 1995). The most general change is an emphasis on different domains of development, an approach initiated by Elliot Turiel (e.g., Turiel, 1983) and developed further by (among others) Judith Smetana and Marta Laupa. Typically, three general domains are distinguished in this research. The domain of morality has to do with basic questions of right and wrong and the rights and welfare of people. Included are both the production of good behaviors (e.g., helping, sharing) and the avoidance of bad behaviors (e.g., lying, cheating, aggression). The domain of social conventions has to do with the rules that govern the interaction of people within social systems. Examples include forms of address, table manners, and expressions of politeness. Finally, the psychological domain refers to characteristics of people, such as their ideas, attitudes, and feelings. A subset of the domain, labeled personal issues, is often distinguished; examples in this category include choice of friends, style of dress, and taste in music.

Parents and other authority figures do establish and enforce rules within each of these domains. The perceived legitimacy of their doing so, however, shows definite variation across domains. For the most part, children agree that parents are legitimate authorities with regard to both moral and conventional rules. Conflict often occurs, however, when it comes to the psychological domain, especially with respect to personal issues. Not surprisingly, it is in adolescence that such conflict typically peaks (Smetana, 1995). Nevertheless, some ability to distinguish the personal and moral domains, and to judge only the latter as under parental control, is evident as early as age 4 (Lagattuta, Nucci, & Bosacki, 2010).

Even for topics for which parents are admitted to be authorities, exceptions sometimes exist. The social context may be important. Parents' authority clearly holds at home, but may be less certain at a friend's house or at school. A teacher's authority is even more circumscribed—at school certainly, but not necessarily anywhere else. Finally, the nature of the command is also important. In general, parents are regarded as legitimate authorities in the moral domain. Suppose, however, that the parent commands the child to hit a playmate or to steal a peer's lunch money. From middle childhood on, most children indicate that it would be wrong for the parent to issue such a command, and most indicate as well that they would refuse to obey (Laupa et al., 1995).

Children's reasoning about authority has been examined in a number of different cultural settings. Although there are, as we would expect, some variations across cultures, the similarities are perhaps more striking than the differences

(Helweg, 2006; Kim, 1998; Yau, Smetana, & Metzger, 2009). In every culture studied, for example, children have been found to honor the same basic moral–conventional–psychological division. Similarly, although there are certainly changes that come with development, some basic forms of understanding are present very early. In particular, even preschool children have been shown to distinguish between the moral and conventional domains (Smetana, 1981).

Groups

The term *group* has various possible meanings, including the social category within which one falls (e.g., sex, race, ethnicity), the collection of people with whom one interacts (e.g., the crowds and cliques of adolescence), and the state or nation to which one belongs. In this section I address children's understanding of group in the last of these senses. Research under the social-category heading—especially that directed to children's thinking about gender—is too large and too diverse to be reviewed here. A good source on the topic is a book edited by Barrett and Buchanan-Barrow (2005); included among its reviews are chapters devoted to children's conceptions of gender, race, ethnicity, and social class.

As is true of many topics in child psychology, it was Piaget who conducted the first research on children's thinking about nations (Piaget, 1928; Piaget & Weil, 1951). Piaget's studies addressed two sorts of knowledge. One sort was geographical. Do children realize, for example, that Geneva is contained within Switzerland and is therefore smaller than Switzerland? (All of Piaget's participants were Swiss, and most lived in Geneva.) The second kind of knowledge concerned group membership. Do children realize, for example, that they are citizens of both Geneva and Switzerland? In both cases children younger than 6 or 7 showed little understanding, a finding that Piaget interpreted in terms of his general stage model. Just as the preoperational child has difficulty dealing with part–whole relations and multiple classification when thinking about the physical world, so too does the child have difficulty when countries and social groups are the objects of thought.

Later research has been at best only partly supportive of Piaget's claims. Such research (e.g., Jahoda, 1964) verifies that thinking about such issues does improve with age, but also shows that children's response patterns are too variable to fit easily within a Piagetian stage-like progression. The result is that more recent research, with one notable exception, has largely abandoned the Piagetian starting point. The exception comes in two books by Hans Furth (1980, 1996), a long-time proponent and expositor of the Piagetian approach. The first of the books is more relevant to the current concerns. In it, Furth traces children's growing understanding of a variety of aspects of society, including different societal roles (e.g., teacher, doctor, police officer), principles of monetary exchange, and the nature and function of government. The interpretive framework throughout is Piagetian, with developmental changes conceptualized in terms of Piagetian stages and the Piagetian concept of equilibration as the primary explanatory mechanism.

Despite Furth's (1980, 1996) efforts, most researchers remain unconvinced that developments in this domain are best explained by a stage approach—let alone the Piagetian stages. What seems clearer than any qualitative, stage-like changes is that children acquire progressively more and more factual knowledge about nations and states as they develop. The richest source of evidence on this point is a book by Martyn Barrett (2007). Barrett documents advances with respect to a number of different forms of knowledge, including geographical features, history, aspects of government, and national emblems (e.g., flags, anthems). The research encompasses both knowledge about one's own nation and knowledge about other nations; as we would expect, the former typically outstrips the latter. Many of the developments, moreover, show sensible relations to factors that we would expect to be predictive—to schooling, for example, and to IQ, social class, and exposure to relevant material on TV.

The conclusion that much of development in this domain consists of the acquisition of factual knowledge does not mean that such developments are unrelated to other aspects of children's cognitive functioning. One measure of interest in this literature is the development of national stereotypes—that is, beliefs about the characteristics of people who belong to different national groups. When 5- and 6-year-olds provide descriptions of people from different nations the descriptions focus on physical features, appearance, clothing, and typical behavior patterns. When 10- and 11-year-olds provide descriptions such physical characteristics have not disappeared, but the main emphasis is on psychological traits and political and religious beliefs. We see, in other words, the same sort of surface-to-depth progression that characterizes work on person perception, self-perception, and beliefs about friendship and authority.

CONCLUSIONS

This chapter has surveyed a wide range of different approaches devoted to children's understanding of the social and mental worlds, all of which predate the emergence of theory of mind as a distinct area of study. Furthermore, the survey, despite the range of topics covered, was by no means exhaustive. I have already mentioned the omission of work on cognitions about gender. The large literature on moral reasoning is another obvious omission. My excuse for this omission is the same excuse offered by Shantz (1983) and Flavell (1985) for not including moral reasoning in their reviews: This literature is too broad and too multifaceted to be reduced to a subsection within a limited-length overview of social cognition.

Even in its less than complete form, the review provided here makes clear that we knew quite a bit about mentalistic understanding prior to the emergence of theory of mind. And not just prior to theory of mind but apart from it, given that several of the literatures reviewed, in particular metacognition and attribution, are very much ongoing enterprises. What still remains to be considered more fully is an issue touched on at various places throughout the chapter and the book: How do the new and old literatures fit together? How did theory of mind build on and extend what was already known about mentalistic understanding? How, in turn, does the older work enrich the theory-of-mind perspective and suggest directions for further study? And how, in particular, do the two literatures in conjunction speak to the main topic of this book: developments beyond the preschool period? These are the questions to which the final chapter is devoted.

8

Conclusions

This chapter is divided into two sections. The initial section addresses a question that has been touched on at various points throughout the book, most notably in the previous chapter: How does work on theory of mind compare with that under the various earlier research literatures that addressed children's understanding of the social and mental worlds? The goal will be to see how the newer and older literatures fit with and extend each other, identifying both achievements to date and needed future directions. Although I will address developments throughout the lifespan, the emphasis will be on the topic identified in the book's subtitle: developments beyond the preschool period.

The second section of the chapter is in a sense a summary of most of what has gone before. In it I attempt to identify the major changes in theory-of-mind understanding that occur beyond the preschool years.

As I noted in Chapter 1, mine is not the first attempt to draw links between new and old. Among the sources that have addressed this topic in helpful ways are Apperly (2011), Bartsch and Estes (1996), Flavell (2000), Flavell and Miller (1998), Kuhn (2000), and Taylor (1996).

Table 8.1 provides an overview of the contrasts to be discussed.

SOME INITIAL CONTRASTS

I begin with the most obvious contrast, one from which a number of other differences follow. It concerns the age period of interest. As Chapters 3, 4, and 5 indicate—and as I will return to shortly—theory of mind is no longer exclusively a preschool and younger literature. It is still mostly preschool and younger, however. In contrast, most earlier research on social understanding was directed at older children and adults. There was limited work on infancy, and virtually none on the toddler and early preschool periods.

Theory-of-mind research not only tells us more about early development; it also provides a more positive picture of what young children understand and can do than did earlier work. This is not, of course, because today's 4-year-olds are more competent than their counterparts of 30 or 40 years ago; rather, it reflects different

TABLE 8.1 Comparisons Between Theory of Mind and Older Research Literatures

Dimension	Theory of Mind	Older Literatures
Ages studied	Primarily birth to 5	Primarily 5 through adulthood
Characterization of young children	Mixed but many positive developments	Primarily negative
Mental states studied	All	More limited, primarily epistemic
Guiding theories	Theory theory, simulation, modularity	Piagetian, neo-Piagetian, attribution
Stages	No major stage positions	Stage models common
Domain-general or domain-specific	Primarily domain-specific	Primarily domain-general
Executive function and language	Heavy emphasis	Little emphasis
Self–other	Both	Both
Situational or individual	Primarily situational	Both
Existence of individual differences	Limited, primarily differences in rate	Marked across a variety of outcomes
Understanding of individual differences	Limited	An important topic
Understanding of states or traits	Primarily states	Both
Understanding of relationships and groups	Not studied	An important topic
Applications	Limited, primarily clinical syndromes	More general and extensive

methods of study. For one thing, theory-of-mind research has explored a wider range of mental states than did the earlier work, including states (e.g., desire, pretense) that turn out to be relative strengths for young children. In addition, the methods used to study early development are not, as in the older work, simply downward extensions of techniques devised for older populations; rather, they are procedures developed specifically for the study of young children. As such, they are more likely to reveal what young children can do.

The concentration on the early years in theory-of-mind research does, of course, have a downside. At least to date, the approach tells us more about what happens in the first 5 years of life than it does about what happens in the next 70 or so years. In part, however, this relative neglect of later developments is quite defensible. Decades of research had already told us quite a bit about developments beyond age 5, and there was no need for theory-of-mind researchers to duplicate this earlier effort. What was needed was a complementary approach that would fill in what the earlier research was missing. And this, it could be argued, is exactly what the theory-of-mind enterprise has done.

A further positive point (I will get more negative shortly) is that theory-of-mind research no longer stops at age 5. Chapters 3, 4, and 5 discussed a dozen or so research paradigms developed under the theory-of-mind heading for the study of older children (and, in some cases, adults), as well as numerous new findings that have emerged from the application of these approaches. Of course, every theory-of-mind researcher and theorist has always acknowledged that there are changes beyond first-order false belief and other accomplishments of the pre-school period. What the research of the last 25 years has done is to progressively flesh out what these changes are. Furthermore, the developments identified are not simply slight variants of things we already knew about older children's think-ing from thousands of Piagetian studies; rather they include a number of accom-plishments (e.g., second-order false belief, understanding of diversity) not hinted at in earlier work.

The gist of the preceding is that theory of mind has met one goal for a newly emerging research area relative to established fields: add to rather than repeat what was already known. Beyond simply nonredundancy, however, we might hope also for some productive interplay of new and old, some ways in which the new work builds upon what was already there and in turn enhances our understand-ing of the research areas that preceded its emergence. Given the different age periods emphasized by the two literatures, we might expect in particular that research in theory of mind will reveal early forms or precursors of developments that the older research literature identified as achievements of the grade-school and adolescent years.

Several of the commentators who have compared the newer and older lit-eratures have in fact made precisely this point (Bartsch & Estes, 1996; Flavell, 2000; Kuhn, 2000). Kuhn's discussion is the fullest and is based in part on her own research in the domains of scientific reasoning and epistemology. She notes that scientific reasoning depends on the fundamental theory-of-mind realization that the beliefs that constitute theories are separate from evidence and must be evaluated in terms of evidence. Similarly, the starting point for epistemology is the realization—a basic first-order development—that beliefs are simply assertions and not facts, and as such are subject to critical evaluation. Both Bartsch and Estes and Flavell single out a more general across-age link between the two literatures. As they note, the child could hardly develop the metacognitive knowledge of how to regulate mental states without a prior awareness that mental states exist.

Most of the (still limited) attempts to identify relations between developments in the two literatures have been conceptual arguments, a la the examples just cited, rather than empirical tests. Of course, some relations are not really the sort that are subject to empirical test. How could we ever disconfirm the claim that knowledge that mental states exist is a prerequisite for reflecting on and manipulating mental states? Many other possible relations, however, *are* empirical matters, and to date there have been virtually no within-study examinations of theory-of-mind developments and developments from the older research literature (the two metacognitive studies discussed in Chapter 6 being rare exceptions). This neglect extends to the poten-tially most informative form of within-study, within-child examination: longitudinal study of the relations between early developments and later developments. Indeed, even if we limit the scope to theory-of-mind research, longitudinal studies are still fairly rare, and most have concerned relations between infancy and preschool or between early preschool and later preschool—and not, therefore, between early and later developments as defined throughout this book. As I noted in Chapter 3, only three longitudinal studies have looked for possible relations between the two most often used measures in the preschool and grade-school literatures: first-order false belief and second-order false belief. Longitudinal research is always easy to recommend and difficult to do; still, it is a necessary recommendation here.

SOME CONTRASTS IN THEORIES

A further contrast between new and old, one first mentioned in the opening chapter, concerns theories. Not all research under either the newer or the older headings has a clear theoretical focus (indeed, most probably does not). To the extent that theories are important, however, the theories have changed over time. Much of the earlier research had a Piagetian or neo-Piagetian grounding—if not explicitly, then at least in its general assumptions about the nature of children and the nature of development. Most theory-of-mind research of the theoretically grounded sort has its origins in one of three positions: the theory theory approach, simulation theory, or modularity theory. Some would argue that some version of a Vygotskian, socio-cultural position has emerged in recent years as a fourth major theoretical player.

For the most part, however, the theoretical debates in this literature have focused on developments in the first 5 years. Work on higher-order theory of mind has had a remarkably atheoretical quality. In part this fact can be explained by the pragmatic orientation of much of this work, especially the research discussed in Chapter 4. Even for more theoretically loaded topics, however (e.g., second-order false belief), theorizing has been limited. When the major theorists of first-order development have addressed the question of post-preschool developments the discussion has typically been limited to some brief version of a "more of the same" argument (e.g., Leslie, German, & Polizzi, 2005; Perner, 1988; Wellman, 1990). As noted in Chapter 5, Michael Chandler is an exception (e.g., Chandler, 1987); Chandler's work, however, is probably best characterized as a position on certain issues rather than a full-blown theory. It is possible that the Vygotskian socio-cultural approach will prove helpful in explaining later developments; the social constructivist view that is at its core would certainly seem to have a good deal of cross-age applicability. Thus far, however, presentations of the position (Carpendale & Lewis, 2004; Fernyhough, 2008; Symons, 2004) have paid limited attention to older children and advanced forms of theory of mind.

As I discussed in the Conclusions section of Chapter 3, a much debated issue with regard to changes both within and beyond the preschool period is whether development consists at least in part of conceptual change—that is, some qualitative, structural change in the underlying knowledge base. The alternative to conceptual change is one or both of two "nothing but" positions—nothing but improvements in executive function or nothing but improvements in language. That both language and executive function contribute to both first- and second-order developments is, as we have seen, without dispute; debates concern exactly how they contribute and whether they are sufficient or merely necessary or perhaps even just helpful. Note that the question applies not just to developmental change but also to relations between theory of mind and other developments (the issue discussed in Chapter 6)—which is why statistical controls for executive function and language are common in this literature.

One of the most striking differences between the newer and older literatures is the absence of discussions of executive function or language in the latter. The absence of executive function is perhaps not surprising, given that the construct had not yet been identified as a distinct, agreed upon entity for much (although certainly not all) of the history of these literatures. Of course, aspects of what would eventually come to be labeled as executive function *were* studied under other headings, one of which was discussed in Chapter 7: the regulatory aspect of metacognition.

Beyond simply the currency of constructs and measures, this difference between the two literatures may have a deeper theoretical basis. Stage models were common in the older research literatures; Chapter 7 discussed several examples and also mentioned a further prominent example not covered in the chapter: work on moral reasoning. A central element in any stage theory is domain generality: similar reasoning across a wide range of different contents and situations, a similarity that follows from application of the same general cognitive structures to different content areas. Within such a perspective, there was little concern with the possibility that some non-stage-defining element, such as linguistic ability, would make an important contribution to what was being studied. To the extent that linguistic or executive function skills *were* important (assuming they had been studied), a domain-general model would interpret such effects as expressions of, rather than alternatives to, the general stage level.

Work on theory of mind has been much more toward the domain-specific end of the general-specific continuum, a conclusion signaled by (among other characteristics) the absence of stage models in this literature. Indeed, domain specificity is a definitional aspect of both the theory theory and the modularity approaches to theory of mind. Within this perspective, specifying the contribution of executive function and language to the developments being studied is important for two reasons. First and most basically, a claim of domain specificity requires a demonstration that the developments to be explained cannot be accounted for solely by general aspects of the cognitive system such as language or executive function. Such, in fact, is clearly the case; although language and executive function do contribute, such measures never account for all or even most of the variance whatever the outcome being considered: performance on theory-of-mind tasks, developmental changes in performance, relations between theory of mind and other developments. Second, the study of language and executive function provides one way, even within a strongly domain-specific approach, to identify some generality in the cognitive system, some aspects of cognitive functioning that cut across different content areas. Most of us have the intuition that there must be *some* such generality—that not everything can be domain-specific. And the work on language and executive function verifies that this intuition is correct.

Theory of mind is hardly the only topic for which language and executive function have been shown to be important. But for executive function, at least, theory of mind is probably the clearest and most thoroughly studied example. It is a contribution of the theory-of-mind approach—and a contrast with the older research literatures—to have explored the interplay of domain-specific and domain-general factors in children's reasoning about the social and mental worlds. As we saw in earlier chapters, however, this research effort has yet to lead to definitive conclusions; many questions still remain about exactly how language and executive function make their contributions. In addition, the evidential base is a good deal less for higher-order developments than it is at the first-order level. Indeed, it is worth noting that there is essentially no work on either executive function or language with respect to any of the developments discussed in Chapter 5. Clearly, much more remains to be done.

SOME CONTRASTS IN WHAT IS STUDIED

The general topic for both theory of mind and the older research literatures is the same: children's understanding of the social and mental worlds. Under this broad umbrella, however, there are differences both in what is studied and in how particular topics are studied.

Perhaps the most obvious entry in the "what" category is the topic of relationships and groups: important in the older literature, not yet a topic in the theory-of-mind literature. The latter conclusion requires qualification. Children's experience in relationships and groups is certainly studied as an independent variable in theory-of-mind research, that is, as one of the contributors to the developments to be explained. Relationships and groups are also studied as dependent variables in this literature, in the sense that success in various social contexts is one of the outcomes examined in relation to variations in theory-of-mind ability. What have not yet been examined from a theory-of-mind perspective are relationships and groups as explicit targets for children's thinking: How do children think about these topics, and how does their thinking change with development?

Understanding of mental states is a central issue in both the older and newer literatures. As we have seen, however, the specific emphases have changed some over time. Most earlier studies were concerned with mental states of three sorts: epistemic states (knowledge, beliefs, percepts), emotions, and intentions. Theory-of-mind research is more all-encompassing in its scope. On the other hand, there are some respects in which the older literature is the broader one. Such is the case for the topic of belief. It is true that theory-of-mind research has moved beyond the two kinds of beliefs embodied in the typical first-order false belief task: the identity or the location of a hidden object. The beliefs about beliefs that define second-order reasoning are one fundamental expansion, and Chapters 4 and 5 discussed a number of others. Nevertheless, the range still does not equal that found in the older literature. Work on attribution and person perception addresses a topic largely missing in theory-of-mind research: beliefs not just about people in general but about specific people (a contrast to which I will return). The expanded range is probably most obvious, however, in the work on epistemology. This work encompasses beliefs of any sort, including beliefs of great personal significance and beliefs with respect to complex and important real-world issues. Furthermore, the goal of this research is not simply to elicit beliefs of various sorts but to explore thinking about beliefs: Where do they come from? How do they differ? How certainly can they be held? The focus is definitely on beliefs and not (as in most theory-of-mind work) simply a general understanding of belief.

As I noted in the discussion of metacognition, a further contrast is the emphasis in the older literature not simply on mental states per se but on what is done with them—that is, on mental actions. This focus on what children do and not simply on what they know lends itself naturally to application, and applicational efforts of various sorts were in fact more common in the older literature than has been the case, at least to date, for theory of mind. The domain of metacognition is one example, but hardly the only one. Research on children's reasoning about the social world was often the forerunner of programs designed to help children who were having difficulties in the social realm. Reattribution training programs for aggressive children are one example; training of perspective-taking skills for children low in social success is another.

Although contrasts of the what-is-studied sort can be identified, perhaps the more marked contrasts between the older and newer literatures come in how particular topics are addressed. Here I will return to a contrast noted briefly earlier in this section. Work under the older research headings often focused on familiar others as the targets for the child's thinking. Such is the case in most studies of person perception; it is also the case when children describe qualities of their best friend, or, for that matter, qualities of the self. With rare exceptions, research on theory of mind has concerned children's reasoning about generic targets rather than familiar others—thus about how anyone would think, feel, or act in a particular situation. Maxi and John and Mary of false belief fame are examples, as are all the protagonists in the measures reproduced in Chapter 4.

Various points follow from this difference in who is being thought about. Most basic perhaps is the question of generalization: Although it is reasonable to expect consistency, we really do not know whether children would reason in the same way about Mom or younger sibling or best friend as they do about Maxi, John, and Mary. In any case, a point made in Chapter 5 is relevant: The focus not simply on generic but on interchangeable targets means that the standard paradigms tell us only about the situational determinants of beliefs and other mental states, and not about the individual dimension—that is, the contribution of whoever it is who is forming the mental state. There doubtless are cases in which Mom and younger sibling would do quite different things with the same situation, but most theory-of-mind studies do not tell us whether children appreciate this fact.

Because the targets are generic and interchangeable others, most theory-of-mind studies also do not tell us anything about children's knowledge of individual differences among people. This point extends, of course, to whether and when they become able to reason in terms of underlying traits and not only more superficial characteristics. Nor do such studies tell us anything about the evaluative, as opposed to purely epistemic, dimension of social cognition. The examples in Table 7.7 confirm what we all already knew: From early in life, thinking about others is not merely factual; likes and dislikes of various sorts also play an important role.

Note that the points just made apply not just to thoughts about others but also to thoughts about the self. Self-understanding is, of course, a central issue in theory of mind; indeed, in one major position, the simulation approach, understanding of others builds upon understanding of the self. In most theory-of-mind studies, however, the self is as generic a target as Maxi or John and Mary. Thus, children may judge whether they have formed a true or false belief, or whether they now know something given a particular informational input, or whether they can or cannot control a particular line of thinking. There is no way, however, in which the child's distinctive characteristics or beliefs about the self enter into these judgments and thus no reason that the judgments should differ in any way across children.

A point made earlier in the chapter can be raised again here. Decades of research on person perception, self-evaluations, attribution of traits, and other topics in social cognition preceded the emergence of theory of mind, and this research had told us quite a bit about how children think about specific people and about their awareness of individual differences among people. There was no need for theory-of-mind research to redo this earlier effort. Still, it is noteworthy how separate the literatures have remained even when examining the same age period. It would be interesting to know, for example, whether understanding of diversity shows any relation to the increasing knowledge of individual differences that is revealed in the person perception and attribution literatures. Similarly, it would be interesting to know whether reasoning about hypothetical characters in vignettes such as the Strange Stories relates to how children think about their friends or about peers in general. In short, it would be interesting to know more about how person-general and person-specific knowledge fit together.

The point just made was made earlier by Marjorie Taylor (1996), one of the commentators who have addressed the question of how theory of mind (or, as she refers to it, "belief-desire psychology") relates to the research literatures that preceded it. She wrote:

> One of the challenges for the future will be to better understand how children integrate their knowledge about individual differences in behavior based on social category membership, as well as more idiosyncratic variables such as special knowledge about the self or well-known others, with their general explanatory understanding based on belief-desire psychology. (p. 315; copyright 1996 by Academic Press; with permission)

SO WHAT DOES DEVELOP AFTER AGE 5?

I conclude chapter and book with my own list of the major advances in theory-of-mind understanding that succeed the first-order achievements that are in place by age 4 or 5. The entries are drawn from both the newer and the older research literatures (although I place more emphasis on the former). Because there are few instances in which our understanding is complete, I also suggest needed directions for future research. Table 8.2 summarizes the developments to be discussed.

Some developments are primarily absent-to-present transitions—that is, some form of understanding that is absent early in development enters the system and becomes part of the cognitive repertoire. Understanding of second-order false belief falls in this category. It is true that even for a right-answer task such

TABLE 8.2 Developments in Theory-of-Mind Understanding Beyond the Preschool Period

Understanding of second-order false belief

Understanding of interpretive diversity

Understanding of opacity

Understanding of uncertainty

Understanding of a wider range of mental states

Understanding of mental actions, including how to regulate actions

Understanding of differences among different types of beliefs

Further understanding with respect to the origins of beliefs—in particular, better understanding of communication and inference and of the individual determinants of belief formation

For both first-and second order understanding, further developments beyond initial mastery—greater certainty, wider applicability, greater ease and skill in applying

Increased knowledge of memory and other cognitive functions

Decline in egocentrism

Progressively more refined reasoning about both others and the self, including attribution of traits

Increased knowledge of groups and relationships

Expanded consequences of individual differences in theory-of-mind understanding

as second-order belief a simple pass–fail dichotomization is probably an over-simplification; there may well be a transitional period during which children can handle some versions of the problem but not others, or for various reasons only sometimes apply their newfound knowledge. Indeed, the evidence suggests that this is in fact the case (just as evidence indicates that first-order false belief is a gradual rather than abrupt development, and just as earlier research had indicated the same for conservation). As I discuss shortly, there may also be further developmental changes beyond the point of consistent success on the standard tasks. Nevertheless, second-order false belief is the sort of concept for which it makes sense to ask whether children—if not immediately then at least eventually—"have" the knowledge in question. The answer is clear: Younger children do not and older children do.

Although understanding of second-order false belief may sometimes be important in itself, success on the task is also important as an index of more general changes in the cognitive system. Successful response to the task indicates that the child now possesses the fundamental understanding that not only the physical world but also the mental world can serve as the target for beliefs, including beliefs that turn out to be false. Although the standard task addresses beliefs about beliefs, children also come to realize that other mental states can serve as the final link in the A-thinks-that-B… chain. Intentions and emotions are the states that have been studied to date; other possibilities remain for future research to explore. More research is also needed to determine whether B's particular mental state affects the ease with which the child can infer A's belief about B.

Success on the second-order false belief task also stands as the first clear indication of recursive reasoning on the child's part. Or at least the first indication outside the domain of language—as noted, more work is needed to specify the relation, if any, between recursion in the linguistic realm and recursion in reasoning and problem solving. Initially, children are probably limited to the kind of two-loop recursion embodied in the second-order task; eventually they become capable of longer and longer chains (although five links may be the upper limit, and it seems doubtful that many cognitive endeavors require more than three).

A final point about the second-order task was noted in Chapter 6. The need to recognize second-order *true* beliefs is almost certainly more common than the need to infer false beliefs. In most instances this task is probably straightforward, given that the belief corresponds to both reality and the child's own knowledge. Such is also the case for most first-order true beliefs. Recent research indicates, however, that under certain circumstances preschoolers have surprising difficulty in judging first-order true beliefs (Fabricius, Boyer, Weimer, & Carroll, 2010; Riggs & Simpson, 2005). It would be interesting to determine whether a comparable challenge exists at the second-order level.

Understanding of interpretive diversity is a second clear entry on the list. Again, the achievement is of interest as a marker for a broader development. The broader development in this case is one that every theorist of theory of mind agrees is critical: the realization that minds do not merely copy reality but rather impose their own interpretations upon reality. There is no reason to see interpretive diversity as the first step toward this realization; various developments in the preschool period can be argued to take the child beyond a literal copy theory of mind. Interpretive diversity, however, signals a major new advance not seen in preschool: the realization that the same aspect of reality can be interpreted in different ways by different minds.

Like false belief, understanding of diversity is not a one-point-in-time achievement. At least at first, children's success in recognizing diversity almost certainly varies with the context and the salience of the available cues. Children also eventually come to be able to infer not just that two people believe different things but *what* each one believes. And this achievement, in turn, ties in to their growing awareness of where beliefs come from (a topic to which I return).

A further beyond-first-emergence development is suggested by the research by Lagattuta and colleagues discussed in Chapter 5 (Lagattuta et al., 2010). Recall that the Lagattuta et al. study demonstrated that at first children overextend their nascent understanding of diversity, predicting differences in interpretation even when the evidence suggests a common view. It would be interesting to know whether any other higher-level achievements show a similar susceptibility to overextension. The overextension phenomenon did appear in the earlier conservation literature with occasional demonstrations of "overconservation." The clearest and best-known example is, of course, linguistic: children's tendency to apply recently learned grammatical rules too broadly.

A third right-answer sort of development is understanding of opacity. Here, the empirical data are clearer than the explanation for the data. Reasoning about opacity, even with the various simplifications that have been introduced in the task, is more difficult than first-older false belief and other achievements of the preschool period. In one analysis, such reasoning requires second-order, recursive competence—which, assuming the analysis is valid, would account for the task's difficulty. As I have suggested, both this and other accounts await further specification and further testing.

The opacity task is an example of a general point, and that is that often what seem like simple tasks turn out to be more difficult than we might have expected. The findings with respect to reasoning about avoidance are another example. Transforming the standard first-order belief task from an approach to an avoidance paradigm adds considerably to its difficulty. Children (and in some cases adults) also have more difficulty reasoning about an uncertain belief than about a false belief. This difficulty occurs despite the fact that children as young as 4 can make accurate attributions of ignorance when the information is insufficient to support any belief. And, of course, children as young as 4 can attribute false belief. Understanding of uncertainty is a later achievement. Studies of ambiguity are another source of evidence for this conclusion.

As recent research indicates, the more-difficult-than-expected conclusion extends even to what are clearly first-order abilities. Modifications at either the independent or dependent variable end may evoke hitherto unsuspected variation in response to tasks such as first-order false belief. Under some circumstances first-order performance may not be automatic and error-free even in adults. Although any difficulties shown by adults are obviously noteworthy, such research is also a further source of evidence for developmental change. Whatever the challenges faced by adults, the difficulties are almost certainly greater at age 5 or 6. And, in fact, within-study comparisons verify that such is the case.

One of the most pervasive and persistent challenges in reasoning about the mental states of others is a construct first identified in the older research literature—indeed, in the earliest studies that proved to have a lasting influence. It is the Piagetian construct of egocentrism (forms of which have sometimes gone by other names in more recent research—curse of knowledge, hindsight bias, epistemic egocentrism). Whatever the other challenges in mentalistic understanding, overcoming one's own perspective is often a starting point, and this remains a lifelong challenge. Older children are more successful at doing so than are younger children, and adults are more successful than are children—the differences, however, are a matter of degree.

How, apart from declining egocentrism, does the mature cognitive system differ from that of a child who has only recently mastered the knowledge in question? The theory-of-mind literature shares a limitation with the earlier Piagetian literature, and that is that we have limited ways to talk about developments beyond first mastery of a concept. Probably no one believes that a 5-year-old's first-order abilities are fully equivalent to those of an adult, but as long as assessments are limited to pass–fail performance there is no way to specify the differences between the two.

What are the ways a particular form of knowledge might change beyond the point at which the child first "has" the knowledge? Here, briefly, are a few suggestions, based partly on the writings of others, partly on available evidence, and partly on intuition. The knowledge may be applied to an increasingly wide range of relevant contexts. The knowledge may be more readily accessed and skillfully applied when needed. The knowledge may become more integrated with other parts of the cognitive system. The knowledge may become more available as an object of conscious reflection when appropriate. Conversely, the knowledge may become less conscious and more automatic in its expression, thus requiring fewer cognitive resources. Finally, the knowledge may come to be held with greater and greater certainty.

Some of the points just noted are relevant to a comparison between the second-order false belief task and the measures discussed in Chapter 4 (e.g., Strange Stories, Faux Pas). To varying degrees, each of the newer measures is more difficult than the false belief task. One likely basis for the difference in difficulty is the ease-of-application dimension. The belief task is designed to be an optimal, easy-as-possible assessment—something that will elicit the relevant knowledge if the knowledge is present at all. In contrast, Strange Stories and other such measures do not draw out the answer in such a child-friendly way; rather, they require that the child access and apply relevant knowledge in a variety of real-world-like contexts that, like the actual real world, present various obstacles to understanding. Recall, in fact, that creating a more natural, challenging context was one of Happé's (1994) goals in constructing the Strange Stories.

The context is not the only difference between the second-order belief task and measures such as Strange Stories. As I noted in Chapter 4, the latter may sometimes depend on third-order reasoning for their solution. And even when the task remains a second-order one, assessments such as Strange Stories or (even more markedly) Stories from Everyday Life are simply more complex—they require the child to keep track of and to reason about more characters and more mental states than does the second-order belief task. The breadth of mental states with which the child can deal can in fact be singled out as another change that characterizes the post-preschool years. It is true that theory-of-mind research has documented some understanding of a wide range of mental states in preschoolers, and not just states in isolation but often understanding of how they work together (e.g., desire fulfillment as a source of emotion, desire and belief as joint causes of behavior). Nevertheless, with development children become more knowledgeable about how mental states interact with and affect each other, they become aware of mental states that they were not sensitive to as preschoolers, and they become more skilled at using a range of often subtle cues to infer mental states. The Eyes Test is among the sources of evidence for the last two of these conclusions.

With development children also become increasingly knowledgeable about mental activities. We saw in Chapter 5 that theory-of-mind research, which historically has concentrated on mental states, has begun to explore what children know about mental action. Most of what we know about this topic, however, comes from research under the heading of metacognition. Such research documents impressive developments—almost all of which occur after age 5—in both declarative, knowing-that knowledge and procedural, knowing-how knowledge across a wide range of content areas. Both forms of knowledge, moreover, have been shown to contribute to both developmental changes and individual differences in children's cognitive performance, again across a range of content areas.

For the most part, the older research literatures are not sources for discrete developments of the "have or doesn't have" sort. Work on the declarative aspect of metacognition, however, is an exception. Such research has shown that children eventually come to know dozens of facts about memory, attention, language, and other content areas, none of which they knew as preschoolers.

Although understanding of belief is a basic topic in both the old and the new research literatures, the specific emphases differ. Theory-of-mind research has addressed fundamental, starting-point knowledge about beliefs as mental states. The first-order false belief task tests the realization that beliefs are mental representations and not direct reflections of reality, and as such may be false. The second-order task adds the realization that beliefs, including false beliefs, may have other mental representations as their content. Theory-of-mind research also addresses basic questions about the origins of beliefs, including knowledge about different sources for beliefs (perception, communication, inference) and the bases for variations in the accuracy of beliefs (true beliefs, false beliefs, uncertain beliefs, ignorance). Some of this knowledge emerges during the preschool period, but much of it is a later development; in particular, understanding of communication and inference continues to develop throughout much of childhood.

Work under the heading of epistemology also addresses knowledge about belief in general. Central to such work is the question of how beliefs can be justified and whether beliefs are personal, subjective constructions or reflections of an objective reality. A basic epistemological development, however, is the realization that there can be no single in-general answer to such questions; rather, the kind of belief must be taken into account. This work, therefore, requires children—much more than does research on theory of mind—to recognize and to reason about the different types of beliefs that they and others form. And it demonstrates that development in this domain is a long-term, perhaps lifelong process.

Thus far I have said nothing about the material discussed in Chapter 6—that is, the consequences of higher-level understanding. Clearly, though, virtually everything discussed in that chapter falls under the heading of developments beyond age 5. A particular aspect of theory of mind, such as understanding of interpretive diversity, cannot affect other developments if it has not yet developed itself. In general, the variations in theory of mind that might make a difference increase as children grow older, and the possible consequences of those differences also increase.

I conclude with several final developments that come primarily from the older research literatures. They come from the older literatures because they concern a topic virtually unaddressed in theory-of-mind research: How do children think not just about people in general but about particular people, both familiar others and the self?

Thinking about familiar people certainly does not begin at age 5. Infants begin to distinguish between familiar and strange from early in life, and they eventually (at least according to some conceptualizations) form working models of the important people in their lives. The origins of self-understanding also begin soon after birth. Further developments occur across the preschool years, and even preschoolers, as we saw, can eventually make some trait-like attributions for both self and others.

Despite these early achievements, most of the developments in thinking about people come in the years from age 5 onward. As we saw in Chapter 7, these developments show a number of related features. In general, as children grow older, thoughts about people, whether others or the self, become more differentiated, more integrated, more multifaceted, and more accurate. There is a general surface to depth movement, as relatively superficial characteristics give way to deeper, more defining features. The culmination of this development is the ability to characterize both self and other in terms of lasting dispositional traits.

Children's thinking about others extends beyond individuals to conceptions of relationships and groups. In addition to the development of many specific forms of knowledge, thinking about these topics shows the same sort of surface to depth developmental transition that characterizes thinking about individuals.

Children's increasing awareness of differences among people has implications for topics studied under the heading of theory of mind. Realizing that people differ is a necessary basis for inferring that they will interpret an ambiguous stimulus differently, and realizing *how* they differ is a necessary basis for inferring exactly what the difference in interpretation will be. Awareness of differences is also critical for an understanding of how beliefs are formed. Even preschoolers understand many of the basic aspects of belief formation—for example, that someone with adequate perceptual access will know the identity of an object. Most of the developments beyond age 5 concern the effects of individual differences—the realization, for example, that only a sufficiently mature recipient can acquire knowledge from communication or inference.

I will note one final implication of broadening the scope of social understanding beyond forms of knowledge that emerge during the preschool years. It concerns the individual differences that we can identify in children's social understanding. There are two general ways in which the study of older children and higher-order developments extends the study of individual differences beyond what is possible at the first-order level.

The most obvious extension concerns the range of individual differences in quality of performance that can be identified. Most first-order achievements are both dichotomous (the child either possesses the knowledge or does not) and universal (basic forms of knowledge that every typically developing child masters). The only individual differences that can be identified in such a case are either differences in rate of development or deviations from the norm in clinical syndromes. Although some higher-order assessments are also dichotomous, many are not; all of the measures discussed in Chapter 4 offer a range of scores, and the same is true of many measures in the older research literatures. Furthermore, performance on many of these measures is not at ceiling even in adulthood; thus the individual differences they identify are not only of the transient, rate-of-development sort. Compared with the first-order literature, the work on higher-order forms of knowledge thus tells us much more about how people differ in the extent of their mentalistic understanding and about what it means to have a relatively good or relatively poor theory of mind.

The second extension is of a more qualitative sort. Beyond simply more variability in degree of understanding, the measures used in the study of later development have the potential to tell us about the *type* of theory of mind that the child (or adult) possesses. What, for example, is the child's typical attribution pattern, and what sort of theory of intelligence does the child hold, and how does thinking about the self compare with thinking about others? How, moreover, do these various forms of thinking fit together—for example, are epistemological beliefs about the nature of knowledge linked to explanations offered for one's own successes and failures across various domains, or to metacognitive attempts to regulate the relevant cognitive activities? Apart from such variations in content, are there perhaps more general differences in how theory of mind is deployed? Are there differences, for example, in salience or accessibility, such that some people routinely search for mentalistic underpinnings to behavior whereas others require strong prods before moving beyond surface-level explanations? Or as one last possible difference (and to return to the one potential qualitative difference that has been discussed in the literature), is there in fact such a thing as a "nasty" theory of mind, and if so, does the negative element reside in the kinds of cognitions that are formed or simply in the uses to which these cognitions are put?

After 80 or so years of study, it seems doubtful that future research will identify hitherto unsuspected developments in older children's understanding of the social world. What is still needed is work to put together the elements already discovered—in particular, to integrate the person-general knowledge stressed in theory of mind with the person-specific knowledge revealed in earlier research. Such an integrated model would provide a fuller answer to the three questions to which research on theory of mind is directed: What is the nature of children's theory of mind? Where do both the common and distinctive elements come from? And how does theory of mind affect other aspects of the child's development?

References

Abraham, A., Rakoczy, H., Werning, M., von Cramon, D. Y., & Schubotz, R. (2010). Matching mind to world and vice versa: Functional dissociations between belief and desire mental state processing. *Social Neuroscience, 5,* 1–18.

Abu-Akel, A. (2003). A neurobiological mapping of theory of mind. *Brain Research Reviews, 43,* 29–40.

Adrian, J. E., Clemente, R. A., & Villanueva, L. (2007). Mothers' use of cognitive state verbs in picture-book reading and the development of children's understanding of mind: A longitudinal study. *Child Development, 78,* 1052–1067.

Ahmed, F. S., & Miller, L. S. (2011). Executive function mechanisms of theory of mind. *Journal of Autism and Developmental Disorders, 41,* 667–678.

Ahn, S., & Miller, S. A. (in press). Theory of mind and self-concept: A comparison of American and Korean children. *Journal of Cross-Cultural Psychology.*

Amsterlaw, J. (2006). Children's beliefs about everyday reasoning. *Child Development, 77,* 443–464.

Apperly, I. A. (2011). *Mindreaders: The cognitive basis of "theory of mind."* New York, NY: Psychology Press.

Apperly, I. A., Back, E., Samson, D., & France, L. (2008). The cost of thinking about false beliefs: Evidence from adults' performance on a non-inferential theory of mind task. *Cognition, 106,* 1093–1108.

Apperly, I. A., & Butterfill, S. A. (2009). Do humans have two systems to track beliefs and belief-like states? *Psychological Review, 116,* 953–970.

Apperly, I. A., & Robinson, E. J. (1998). Children's mental representation of referential relations. *Cognition, 67,* 287–309.

Apperly, I. A., & Robinson, E. J. (2003). When can children handle referential opacity? Evidence for systematic variation in 5- and 6-year-old children's reasoning about beliefs and belief reports. *Journal of Experimental Child Psychology, 85,* 297–311.

Apperly, I. A., Samson, D., Carroll, N., Hussain, S., & Humphreys, G. (2006). Intact first- and second-order false belief in a patient with severely impaired grammar. *Social Neuroscience, 1,* 334–348.

Apperly, I. A., Samson, D., & Humphreys, G. W. (2009). Studies of adults can inform accounts of theory of mind development. *Developmental Psychology, 45,* 190–201.

Arsenio, W. F., & Lemerise, E. A. (2001). Varieties of childhood bullying: Values, emotion processes, and social competence. *Social Development, 10,* 59–73.

Aschersleben, G., Hofer, T., & Jovanovic, B. (2008). The link between infant attention to goal-directed action and later theory of mind abilities. *Developmental Science, 11,* 862–868.

Astington, J. W. (1993). *The child's discovery of the mind.* Cambridge, MA: MIT Press.

Astington, J. W. (2003). Sometimes necessary, never sufficient: False belief-understanding and social competence. In B. Repacholi & V. Slaughter (Eds.), *Individual differences in theory of mind* (pp. 13–38). New York, NY: Psychology Press.

Astington, J. W. (2005, June). *Beyond false belief: The development of social reasoning beyond the preschool years.* Paper presented at the meeting of the Jean Piaget Society, Vancouver, BC.

Astington, J. W., & Baird, J. A. (Eds.). (2005). *Why language matters for theory of mind.* New York, NY: Oxford.

Astington, J. W., & Jenkins, J. M. (1995). Theory of mind and social understanding. *Cognition and Emotion, 9,* 151–165.

Astington, J. W., Pelletier, J., & Homer, B. (2002). Theory of mind and epistemological development: The relation between children's second-order false belief understanding and their ability to reason about evidence. *New Ideas in Psychology, 20,* 131–144.

Astington, J. W., Pelletier, J., & Jenkins, J. M. (1998, June). *Language and theory of mind development over time: A Vygotskian perspective.* Paper presented at the annual meeting of the Jean Piaget Society, Chicago, IL.

Atance, C. M., Bernstein, D. M., & Meltzoff, A. N. (2010). Thinking about false belief: It's not just what children say, but how long it takes them to say it. *Cognition, 116,* 297–301.

Avis, J., & Harris, P. L. (1991). Belief-desire reasoning among Baka children: Evidence for a universal conception of mind. *Child Development, 62,* 460–467.

Back, E., Ropar, D., & Mitchell, P. (2007). Do the eyes have it? Inferring mental states from animated faces in autism. *Child Development, 78,* 397–411.

Baillargeon, R. (2004). Infants' reasoning about hidden objects: Evidence for event-general and event-specific expectations. *Developmental Science, 7,* 391–424.

Baillargeon, R., Li, J., Ng, W., & Yuan, S. (2009). An account of infants' physical reasoning. In A. Woodward & A. Needham (Eds.), *Learning and the infant mind* (pp. 66–116). New York, NY: Oxford University Press.

Baird, J. A., & Astington, J. W. (2004). The role of mental state understanding in the development of moral cognition and moral action. In J. A. Baird & B. W. Sokol (Eds.), *New directions for child and adolescent development: No. 103. Connections between theory of mind and sociomoral development* (pp. 37–50). San Francisco, CA: Jossey-Bass.

Baird, J. A., & Sokol, B. W. (Eds.). (2004). *New directions for child and adolescent development: No. 103. Connections between theory of mind and sociomoral development.* San Francisco, CA: Jossey-Bass.

Baldwin, D. A., & Moses, L. J. (1996). The ontogeny of social information gathering. *Child Development, 67,* 1915–1939.

Banerjee, M. (1997). Hidden emotions: Pre-schoolers' knowledge of appearance-reality and emotion display rules. *Social Cognition, 15,* 107–132.

Banerjee, R. (2000). The development of an understanding of modesty. *British Journal of Developmental Psychology, 18,* 499–517.

Banerjee, R. (2002). Children's understanding of self-presentational behavior: Links with mental-state reasoning and the attribution of embarrassment. *Merrill-Palmer Quarterly, 48,* 378–404.

Banerjee, R., & Henderson, L. (2001). Social-cognitive factors in childhood social anxiety: A preliminary investigation. *Social Development, 10,* 558–572.

Banerjee, R., & Watling, D. (2005). Children's understanding of faux pas: Associations with peer relations. *Hellenic Journal of Psychology, 2,* 27–45.

Banerjee, R., & Watling, D. (2010). Self-presentational features in social anxiety. *Journal of Anxiety Disorders, 24,* 34–41.

Banerjee, R., Watling, D., & Caputi, M. (2011). Peer relations and the understanding of *faux pas*: Longitudinal evidence for bidirectional associations. *Child Development, 82,* 1887–1095.

Banerjee, R., & Yuill, N. (1999a). Children's explanations for self-presentational behaviour. *European Journal of Social Psychology, 29,* 105–111.

Banerjee, R., & Yuill, N. (1999b). Children's understanding of self-presentational display rules: Associations with mental-state understanding. *British Journal of Developmental Psychology, 17,* 111–124.

Barbaro, J., & Dissanayake, C. (2007). A comparative study of the use and understanding of self-presentational display rules in children with high functioning autism and Asperger's disorder. *Journal of Autism and Developmental Disorders, 37,* 1235–1246.

Barenboim, C. (1978). Development of recursive and nonrecursive thinking about persons. *Developmental Psychology, 14*, 419–420.

Barenboim, C. (1981). The development of person perception in childhood and adolescence: From behavioral comparisons to psychological constructs to psychological comparisons. *Child Development, 52*, 129–144.

Barlow, A., Qualter, P., & Stylianou, M. (2010). Relationships between Machiavellianism, emotional intelligence and theory of mind in children. *Personality and Individual Differences, 48*, 78–82.

Barnes J. L., Lombardo, M. V., Wheelwright, S., & Baron-Cohen, S. (2009). Moral dilemmas film task: A study of spontaneous narratives by individuals with autism spectrum conditions. *Autism Research, 2*, 148–156.

Baron-Cohen, S. (1989). The autistic child's theory of mind: A case of specific developmental delay. *Journal of Child Psychology and Psychiatry, 30*, 285–298.

Baron-Cohen, S. (1994). How to build a baby that can read minds: Cognitive mechanisms in mindreading. *Cahiers de Psychologie Cognitive/Current Psychology of Cognition, 13*, 513–552.

Baron-Cohen, S. (1995). *Mindblindness: An essay on autism and theory of mind.* Cambridge, MA: MIT Press/Bradford Books.

Baron-Cohen, S. (1999). The extreme male-brain theory of autism. In H. Tager-Flusberg (Ed.), *Neurodevelopmental disorders* (pp. 401–429). Cambridge, MA: MIT Press.

Baron-Cohen, S. (2000). Theory of mind and autism: A fifteen year review. In S. Baron-Cohen, H. Tager-Flusberg, & D. J. Cohen (Eds.), *Understanding other minds: Perspectives from developmental cognitive neuroscience* (2nd ed., pp. 3–20). New York, NY: Oxford University Press.

Baron-Cohen, S. (2001). Theory of mind and autism: A review. In L. M. Glidden (Ed.), *International review of research in mental retardation: Vol. 23. Autism* (pp. 169–184). San Diego, CA: Academic Press.

Baron-Cohen, S. (2003). *The essential difference: The truth about male and female brains.* New York, NY: Basic Books.

Baron-Cohen, S. (2010). Autism and the empathizing-systemizing (E-S) theory. In P. D. Zelazo, M. Chandler, & E. Crone (Eds.), *Developmental social cognitive neuroscience* (pp. 125–140). New York, NY: Psychology Press.

Baron-Cohen, S., & Hammer, J. (1997). Parents of children with Asperger syndrome: What is the cognitive phenotype? *Journal of Cognitive Neuroscience, 9*, 548–554.

Baron-Cohen, S., Jolliffe, T., Mortimore, C., & Robertson, M. (1997). Another advanced test of theory of mind: Evidence from very high functioning adults with autism or Asperger syndrome. *Journal of Child Psychology and Psychiatry, 38*, 813–822.

Baron-Cohen, S., Leslie, A. M., & Frith, U. (1985). Does the autistic child have a "theory of mind"? *Cognition, 21*, 37–46.

Baron-Cohen, S., O'Riordan, M., Stone, V., Jones, R., & Plaisted, K. (1999). Recognition of faux pas by normally developing children and children with Asperger syndrome or high-functioning autism. *Journal of Autism and Developmental Disorders, 29*, 407–418.

Baron-Cohen, S., Wheelright, S., Hill, J., Raste, Y., & Plumb, I. (2001). The "Reading the Mind in the Eyes" Test Revised Version: A study with normal adults, and adults with Asperger syndrome or high-functioning autism. *Journal of Child Psychology and Psychiatry, 42*, 241–251.

Baron-Cohen, S., Wheelright, S., Spong, A., Scahill, V., & Lawson, J. (2001). Are intuitive physics and intuitive psychology independent? A test with children with Asperger syndrome. *Journal of Developmental and Learning Disorders, 5*, 47–78.

Barquero, B., Robinson, E. J., & Thomas, G. V. (2003). Children's ability to attribute different interpretations of ambiguous drawings to a naïve vs. a biased observer. *International Journal of Behavioral Development, 27*, 445–456.

Barrett, J. L., Newman, R. M., & Richert, R. (2003). When seeing is not believing: Children's understanding of humans' and non-humans' use of background knowledge in interpreting visual displays. *Journal of Cognition and Culture, 3*, 91–108.

Barrett, J. L., Richert, R. A., & Driesenga, A. (2001). God's beliefs versus mother's: The development of nonhuman agent concepts. *Child Development, 72*, 50–65.

Barrett, M. (2007). *Children's knowledge, beliefs and feelings about nations and national groups*. New York, NY: Psychology Press.

Barrett, M., & Buchanan-Barrow, E. (Eds.). (2005). *Children's understanding of society*. New York, NY: Psychology Press.

Bar-Tal, D., Raviv, A., Raviv, A., & Brosh, M. E. (1991). Perception of epistemic authority and attribution for its choice as a function of knowledge area and age. *European Journal of Social Psychology, 21*, 477–492.

Bartsch, K. (2002). The role of experience in children's developing folk epistemology: Review and analysis from the theory theory perspective. *New Ideas in Psychology, 20*, 145–161.

Bartsch, K., & Estes, D. (1996). Individual differences in children's developing theory of mind and implications for metacognition. *Learning and Individual Differences, 8*, 281–304.

Bartsch, K., & London, K. (2000). Children's use of mental state information in selecting persuasive arguments. *Developmental Psychology, 36*, 352–365.

Bartsch, K., London, K., & Campbell, M. D. (2007). Children's attention to beliefs in interactive persuasion tasks. *Developmental Psychology, 43*, 111–120.

Bartsch, K., & Wellman, H. M. (1989). Young children's attribution of action to beliefs and desires. *Child Development, 60*, 946–964.

Bartsch, K., & Wellman, H. M. (1995). *Children talk about the mind*. New York, NY: Oxford University Press.

Beaumont, R. B., & Sofronoff, K. (2008). A new computerized advanced theory of mind measure for children with Asperger syndrome: The ATOMIC. *Journal of Autism and Developmental Disorders, 38*, 249–260.

Begeer, S., Banerjee, R., Lunenburg, P., Terwogt, M. M., Stegge, H., & Rieffe, C. (2008). Self-presentation of children with autism spectrum disorders. *Journal of Autism and Developmental Disorders, 38*, 1187–1191.

Belenky, M. F., Clinchy, B. M., Goldberger, N. R., & Tarule, J. M. (1986). *Women's ways of knowing: The development of self, voice and mind*. New York, NY: Basic Books.

Bennett, M., & Gillingham, K. (1991). The role of self-focused attention in children's attributions of social emotions to the self. *Journal of Genetic Psychology, 152*, 303–309.

Bennett, M., & Matthews, L. (2000). The role of second-order belief-understanding and social context in children's self-attribution of social emotions. *Social Development, 9*, 126–130.

Bernstein, D. M., Thornton, W. K., & Sommerville, J. A. (2011). Theory of mind through the ages: Older and middle-aged adults exhibit more errors than do younger adults on a continuous false-belief task. *Experimental Aging Research, 37*, 481–502.

Birch, S. A. J. (2005). When knowledge is a curse: Children's and adults' reasoning about mental states. *Current Directions in Psychological Science, 14*, 25–29.

Birch, S. A. J., Akmal, N., & Frampton, K. L. (2010). Two-year-olds are vigilant of others' non-verbal cues to credibility. *Developmental Science, 13*, 363–369.

Birch, S. A. J., & Bloom, P. (2007). The curse of knowledge in reasoning about false beliefs. *Psychological Science, 18*, 382–386.

Birch, S. A. J., Vauthier, S. A., & Bloom, P. (2008). Three- and four-year-olds spontaneously use others' past performance to guide their learning. *Cognition, 107,* 1018–1034.

Bloom, P., & German, T. P. (2000). Two reasons to abandon the false belief task as a test of theory of mind. *Cognition, 77,* B25–B31.

Borke, H. (1975). Piaget's mountains revisited: Changes in the egocentric landscape. *Developmental Psychology, 11,* 240–243.

Bosacki, S. L. (2000). Theory of mind and self-concept in preadolescents: Links with gender and language. *Journal of Educational Psychology, 92,* 709–717.

Bosacki, S. L., & Astington, J. W. (1999). Theory of mind in preadolescence: Relations between social understanding and social competence. *Social Development, 8,* 237–255.

Boseovski, J., & Lee, K. (2008). Seeing the world through rose-colored glasses? Neglect of consensus information in young children's personality judgments. *Social Development, 17,* 399–416.

Botting, N., & Conti-Ramsden, G. (2008). The role of language, social cognition, and social skill in the functional social outcomes of young adolescents with and without a history of SLI. *British Journal of Developmental Psychology, 26,* 281–300.

Bowler, D. M. (1992). Theory of mind in Asperger syndrome. *Journal of Child Psychology and Psychiatry, 33,* 877–895.

Bowler, D. M. (1997). Reaction times to mental state and non-mental state questions in false belief tasks by high-functioning individuals with autism. *European Child and Adolescent Psychiatry, 6,* 160–165.

Bradmetz, J., & Schneider, R. (1999). Is Little Red Riding Hood afraid of her grandmother? Cognitive vs. emotional response to a false belief. *British Journal of Developmental Psychology, 17,* 501–514.

Bradmetz, J., & Schneider, R. (2004). The role of counterfactually satisfied desire in the lag between false-belief and false-emotion attributions in children aged 4–7. *British Journal of Developmental Psychology, 22,* 185–196.

Brent, E., Rios, P., Happé, F., & Charman, T. (2004). Performance of children with autism spectrum disorder on advanced theory of mind tasks. *Autism, 8,* 283–299.

Bretherton, I., & Beeghly, M. (1982). Talking about internal states: The acquisition of an explicit theory of mind. *Developmental Psychology, 18,* 906–921.

Broomfield, K. A., Robinson, E. J., & Robinson, W. P. (2002). Children's understanding about white lies. *British Journal of Developmental Psychology, 20,* 47–65.

Brown, A. L., Palincsar, A. S., & Armbruster, B. B. (1984). Inducing comprehension-fostering activities in interactive learning situations. In H. Mantl, N. L. Stein, & T. Trabasso (Eds.), *Learning and comprehension of text* (pp. 255–286). Hillsdale, NJ: Erlbaum.

Brown, W. T. (2010). Genetics of autism. In A. Chauhan, V. Chauhan, & W. T. Brown (Eds.), *Autism: Oxidative stress, inflammation, and immune system abnormalities* (pp. 61–72). Boca Raton, FL: CRC Press.

Bruell, M., & Woolley, J. D. (1996). Young children's awareness of the origins of their mental representations. *Developmental Psychology, 32,* 335–346.

Burr, J. E., & Hofer, B. K. (2002). Personal epistemology and theory of mind: Deciphering young children's beliefs about knowledge and knowing. *New Ideas in Psychology, 20,* 199–224.

Buttelmann, D., Carpenter, M., & Tomasello, M. (2009). Eighteen-month-old infants show false belief understanding in an active helping paradigm. *Cognition, 112,* 337–342.

Caillies, S., & Le Sourn-Bissaoui, S. (2008). Children's understanding of idioms and theory of mind development. *Developmental Science, 11,* 703–711.

Call, J., & Tomasello, M. (2008). Does the chimpanzee have a theory of mind? 30 years later. *Trends in Cognitive Science, 12,* 187–192.

Caputi, M., Lecce, S., Pagnin, A., & Banerjee, R. (2012). Longitudinal effects of theory of mind on later peer relations: The role of prosocial behaviour. *Developmental Psychology, 48,* 257–270.

Caravita, S. C. S., Di Blasio, P., & Salmivalli, C. (2010). Early adolescents' participation in bullying: Is ToM involved? *Journal of Early Adolescence, 30,* 138–170.

Caron, A. J. (2009). Comprehension of the representational mind in infancy. *Developmental Review, 29,* 69–95.

Carpendale, J., & Chandler, M. J. (1996). On the distinction between false belief understanding and subscribing to an interpretive theory of mind. *Child Development, 67,* 1686–1706.

Carpendale, J., & Lewis, C. (2004). Constructing and understanding of mind: The development of children's social understanding within social interaction. *Behavioral and Brain Sciences, 27,* 79–151.

Carpendale, J., & Lewis, C. (2006). *How children develop social understanding.* Malden, MA: Blackwell Publishing.

Carpendale, J., & Lewis, C. (2010). The development of social understanding: A relational perspective. In W. F. Overton (Ed.), *The handbook of life-span development: Vol. 1. Cognition, biology, and methods* (pp. 584–627). New York, NY: Wiley.

Carr, M. (2010). The importance of metacognition for conceptual change and strategy use in mathematics. In H. S Waters & W. Schneider (Eds.), *Metacognition, strategy use, and instruction* (pp. 176–197). New York, NY: Guilford Press.

Carrington, S. J., & Bailey, A. J. (2009). Are there theory of mind regions in the brain? A review of the neuorimaging literature. *Human Brain Mapping, 30,* 2313–2335.

Carruthers, P., & Smith, P. K. (Eds.). (1996). *Theories of theories of mind.* Cambridge, England: Cambridge University Press.

Casey, B. J., & de Haan, M. (Eds.). (2002). Imaging techniques and their application to developmental science [Special issue]. *Developmental Science, 5*(3).

Cassidy, K. W. (1998). Three- and 4-year-old children's ability to use desire- and belief-based reasoning. *Cognition, 66,* B1–B11.

Castelli, I., Blasi, V., Alberoni, M., Falini, A., Liverta-Sempio, O., Nemni, R., & Marchetti, A. (2010). Effects of aging on mindreading ability through the eyes: An fMRI study. *Neuropsychologia, 48,* 2586–2594.

Chandler, M. J. (1973). Egocentrism and antisocial behavior: The assessment and training of social perspective-taking skills. *Developmental Psychology, 9,* 326–332.

Chandler, M. J. (1987). The Othello effect: Essay on the emergence and eclipse of skeptical doubt. *Human Development, 30,* 137–159.

Chandler, M. J., & Birch, S. A. J. (2010). The development of knowing. In W. F. Overton (Ed.), *The handbook of life-span development: Vol. 1. Cognition, biology, and methods* (pp. 671–719). New York, NY: Wiley.

Chandler, M. J., Boyes, M. C., & Ball, L. (1990). Relativism and stations of epistemic doubt. *Journal of Experimental Child Psychology, 50,* 370–395.

Chandler, M. J., & Carpendale, J. I. M. (1998). Inching toward a mature theory of mind. In M. D. Ferrari & R. J. Sternberg (Eds.), *Self-awareness: Its nature and development* (pp. 148–190). New York, NY: Guilford Press.

Chandler, M. J., Fritz, A. S., & Hala, S. (1989). Small-scale deceit: Deception as a marker of 2-, 3-, and 4-year-olds' early theories of mind. *Child Development, 60,* 1263–1277.

Chandler, M. J., & Hala, S. (1994). The role of personal involvement in the assessment of early false belief skills. In C. Lewis & P. Mitchell (Eds.), *Children's early understanding of mind: Origins and development* (pp. 403–425). Hillsdale, NJ: Erlbaum.

Chandler, M. J., & Sokol, B. W. (1999). Representation once removed: Children's developing conceptions of representational life. In I. E. Sigel (Ed.), *Development of mental representation* (pp. 201–230). Mahwah, NJ: Erlbaum.

Chandler, M. J., Sokol, B. W., & Hallett, D. (2001). Moral responsibility and the interpretive turn: Children's changing conceptions of truth and rightness. In B. F. Malle, L. J. Moses, & D. A. Baldwin (Eds.), *Intentions and intentionality: Foundations of social cognition* (pp. 345–365). Cambridge, MA: MIT Press.

Charlton, R. A., Barrick, T. A., Markus, H. S., & Morris, R. G. (2009). Theory of mind associations with other cognitive functions and brain imaging in normal aging. *Psychology and Aging, 24,* 338–348.

Charman, T., Carroll, F., & Sturge, C. (2001). Theory of mind, executive function and social competence in boys with ADHD. *Emotional and Behavioural Difficulties, 6,* 31–49.

Charman, T., Ruffman, T., & Clements, W. A. (2002). Is there a gender difference in false belief development? *Social Development, 11,* 1–10.

Christie, R., & Geis, F. L. (1970). *Studies in Machiavellianism.* New York, NY: Academic Press.

Clement, F., Koenig, M., & Harris, P. L. (2004). The ontogenesis of trust. *Mind and Language, 19,* 360–379.

Clements, W. A., & Perner, J. (1994). Implicit understanding of belief. *Cognitive Development, 9,* 377–395.

Clements, W. A., Rustin, C. L., & McCallum, S. (2000). Promoting the transition from implicit to explicit understanding: A training study of false belief. *Developmental Science, 3,* 81–92.

Cohen, L. B. (2009). The evolution of infant cognition: A personal account. *Infancy, 14,* 403–413.

Cole, K., & Mitchell, P. (2000). Siblings in the development of executive control and a theory of mind. *British Journal of Developmental Psychology, 18,* 279–295.

Cole, P. (1986). Children's spontaneous control of facial expression. *Child Development, 57,* 1309–1321.

Colonnesi, C., Koops, W., & Terwogt, M. M. (2008). Young children's psychological explanations and their relationship to perception- and intention-understanding. *Infant and Child Development, 17,* 163–179.

Colonnesi, C., Rieffe, C., Koops, W., & Perucchini, P. (2008). Precursors of a theory of mind: A longitudinal study. *British Journal of Developmental Psychology, 26,* 561–577.

Colvert, E., Rutter, M., Kreppner, J., Beckett, C., Castle, J., Groothues, C., … Sonuga-Barke, E. J. S. (2008). Do theory of mind and executive function deficits underlie the adverse outcomes associated with profound early deprivation?: Findings from the English and Romanian adoptees study. *Journal of Abnormal Child Psychology, 36,* 1057–1068.

Comay, J. (March, 2011). *Interpretive understanding and second-order theory of mind: How are they related?* Poster session presented at the biennial meeting of the Society for Research in Child Development, Montreal, Canada.

Comay, J., & Astington, J. W. (2011). *Narrative perspective taking and theory of mind.* Manuscript in preparation.

Corballis, M. (2011). *The recursive mind: The origins of human language, thought, and civilization.* Princeton, NJ: Princeton University Press.

Corriveau, K., Meints, K., & Harris, P. L. (2009). Early tracking of informant accuracy and inaccuracy. *British Journal of Developmental Psychology, 27,* 331–342.

Coull, G. J., Leekam, S. R., & Bennett, M. (2006). Simplifying second-order belief attribution: What facilitates children's performance on measures of conceptual understanding? *Social Development, 15,* 260–275.

Costa, P. T., & McCrae, R. R. (1992). *Manual for Revised NEO Personality Inventory (NEO-PI-R) and Five Factor Inventory (NEO-FFI).* Odessa, FL: Psychological Assessment Resources.

Crick, N. R., & Dodge, K. A. (1994). A review and reformulation of social information-processing mechanisms in children's social adjustment. *Psychological Bulletin, 115,* 74–81.

Crick, N. R., & Dodge, K. A. (1999). 'Superiority' is in the eye of the beholder: A comment on Sutton, Smith, and Swettenham. *Social Development, 8,* 128–131.

Curran, S., & Bolton, P. (2009). Genetics of autism. In Y. Kim (Ed.), *Handbook of behavior genetics* (pp. 397–410). New York, NY: Springer.

Custer, W. (1996). A comparison of young children's understanding of contradictory representations in pretense, memory, and belief. *Child Development, 67,* 678–688.

Cutting, A. L., & Dunn, J. (1999). Theory of mind, emotion understanding, language, and family background: Individual differences and interrelations. *Child Development, 70,* 853–865.

Cutting, A. L., & Dunn, J. (2002). The cost of understanding other people: Social cognition predicts young children's sensitivity to criticism. *Journal of Child Psychology and Psychiatry and Allied Disciplines, 43,* 849–860.

Damon, W. (1977). *The social world of the child.* San Francisco, CA: Jossey-Bass.

Damon, W., & Hart, D. (1982). The development of self-understanding from infancy through adolescence. *Child Development, 53,* 841–864.

Davies, M., & Stone, T. (2003). Synthesis: Psychological understanding and social skills. In B. Repacholi & V. Slaughter (Eds.), *Individual differences in theory of mind* (pp. 305–352). New York, NY: Psychology Press.

Davis, T. L. (2001). Children's understanding of false beliefs in different domains: Affective vs. physical. *British Journal of Developmental Psychology, 19,* 47–58.

Davis-Unger, A. C., & Carlson, S. M. (2008). Development of teaching skills and relations to theory of mind in preschoolers. *Journal of Cognition and Development, 9,* 26–45.

Dennett, D. C. (1978). Beliefs about beliefs. *Behavioral and Brain Sciences, 1,* 568–570.

De Rosnay, M., Pons, F., Harris, P. L., & Morrell, J. M. B. (2004). A lag between understanding false belief and emotion attribution in young children: Relationships with linguistic ability and mothers' mental-state language. *British Journal of Developmental Psychology, 22,* 197–218.

Dickhauser, O., & Meyer, W. (2006). Gender differences in young children's math attributions. *Psychology Science, 48,* 3–16.

Divitto, B., & McArthur, L. Z. (1978). Developmental differences in the use of distinctiveness, consensus, and consistency information for making causal attributions. *Developmental Psychology, 14,* 474–482.

Doan, S. N., & Wang, Q. (2010). Maternal discussions of mental states and behaviors: Relations to emotion situation knowledge in European American and immigrant Chinese children. *Child Development, 81,* 1490–1503.

Dodge, K. A. (1980). Social cognition and children's aggressive behavior. *Child Development, 51,* 162–170.

Dodge, K. A., & Crick, N. R. (1990). Social-information processing bases of aggressive behavior in children. *Personality and Social Psychology Bulletin, 16,* 8–22.

Doherty, M. J. (2009). *Theory of mind.* Philadelphia, PA: Psychology Press.

Dorris, L., Espie, C. A. E., Knott, F., & Salt, J. (2004). Mind-reading difficulties in the siblings of people with Asperger's syndrome: Evidence for a genetic influence in the abnormal development of a specific cognitive domain. *Journal of Child Psychology and Psychiatry, 45,* 412–418.

Dunn, J. (1991). Young children's understanding of other people: Evidence from observations within the family. In D. Frye & C. Moore (Eds.). *Children's theories of mind* (pp. 97–114). Hillsdale, NJ: Erlbaum.

Dunn, J. (1999). Mindreading and social relationships. In M. Bennett (Ed.), *Developmental psychology: Achievements and prospects* (pp. 55–71). New York, NY: Psychology Press.

Dunn, J., Bretheron, I., & Munn, P. (1987). Conversations about feeling states between mothers and their young children. *Developmental Psychology, 23,* 132–139.

Dunn, J., Brown, J., & Beardsall, L. (1991). Family talk about feeling states and children's later understanding of others' emotions. *Developmental Psychology, 27,* 448–455.

Dunn, J., Brown, J., Slomkowski, C., Tesa, C., & Youngblade, L. (1991). Young children's understanding of other people's feelings and beliefs: Individual differences and their antecedents. *Child Development, 62,* 1352–1366.

Dunn, J., Cutting, A. L., & Demetriou, H. (2000). Moral sensibility, understanding others, and children's friendship interactions in the preschool period. *British Journal of Developmental Psychology, 18,* 159–177.

Dunn, J., & Kendrick, C. (1982). The speech of two- and three-year-olds to infant siblings: "Baby talk" and the context of communication. *Journal of Child Language, 9,* 579–595.

Dweck, C. S. (1999). *Self theories: Their role in motivation, personality, and development.* New York, NY: Psychology Press.

Dweck, C. S., & Leggett, E. L. (1988). A social-cognitive approach to motivation and personality. *Psychological Review, 95,* 256–273.

Dyck, M. J., Ferguson, K., & Schochet, I. M. (2001). Do autism spectrum disorders differ from each other and from non-spectrum disorders on emotion recognition tasks? *European Child and Adolescent Psychiatry, 10,* 105–116.

Dyck, M. J., Piek, J. P., Hay, D., Smith, L., & Hallmayer, J. (2006). Are abilities abnormally independent in children with autism? *Journal of Clinical Child and Adolescent Psychology 35,* 20–33.

Dziobek, I., Fleck, S., Kalbe, E., Rogers, K., Hassenstab, J., Brand, M., ... Convit, A. (2006). Introducing MASC: A movie for the assessment of social cognition. *Journal of Autism and Developmental Disorders, 36,* 623–636.

Dziobek, I., Rogers, K., Fleck, S., Hassenstab, J., Gold, S., Wolf, O. T., & Convit, A. (2005). In search of "master mindreaders": Are psychics superior in reading the language of the eyes? *Brain and Cognition, 58,* 240–244.

Eder, R. A. (1989). The emergent personologist: The structure and content of 3 ½-, 5 ½- and 7 ½-year-olds' concepts of themselves and other persons. *Child Development, 60,* 1218–1228.

Eder, R. A. (1990). Uncovering young children's psychological selves: Individual and developmental differences. *Child Development, 61,* 849–863.

Efklides, A., & Misailidi, P. (Eds.). (2010). *Trends and prospects in metacognition research.* New York, NY: Springer.

Eisbach, A. O. (2004). Children's developing awareness of diversity in people's trains of thoughts. *Child Development, 75,* 1694–1707.

Eisenberg, N., Murphy, B. C., & Shepard, S. (1997). The development of empathic accuracy. In W. Ickes (Ed.), *Empathic accuracy* (pp. 73–116). New York, NY: Guilford Press.

Eliot, J., Lovell, K., Dayton, C. M., & McGrady, B. F. (1979). A further investigation of children's understanding of recursive thinking. *Journal of Experimental Child Psychology, 28,* 149–157.

Ellis, B. J., Bjorklund, D. F., & King, A. C. (2011, March). *Surviving the savanna: How reasoning about predators can disrupt theory of mind performance in children.* Paper presented at the biennial meeting of the Society for Research in Child Development, Montreal, Canada.

Epley, N., Morewedge, C., & Keysar, B. (2004). Perspective taking in children and adults: Equivalent egocentrism but different correction. *Journal of Experimental Social Psychology, 40,* 760–768.

Evans, A. D., Xu, F., & Lee, K. (2011). When all signs point to you: Lies told in the face of evidence. *Developmental Psychology, 47,* 39–49.

Fabricius, W. V., Boyer, T. W., Weimer, A. A., & Carroll, K. (2010). True or false: Do 5-year-olds understand belief? *Developmental Psychology, 46,* 1402–1416.

Fabricius, W. V., Schwanenflugel, P. J., Kyllonen, P. C., Barclay, C. R., & Denton, S. M. (1989). Developing theories of the mind: Children's and adults' concepts of mental activities. *Child Development, 60,* 1278–1290.

Farmer, M. (2000). Language and social cognition in children with specific language impairment. *Journal of Child Psychology and Psychiatry and Allied Disciplines, 41,* 627–636.

Feldman, N. S., & Ruble, D. N. (1981). The development of children's perceptions and attributions about their social world. In S. S. Brehm, S. M. Kassin, & F. X. Gibbons (Eds.), *Developmental social psychology: Theory and research* (pp. 191–206). New York, NY: Oxford University Press.

Feldman, N. S., & Ruble, D. N. (1988). The effects of personal relevance on psychological inference: A developmental analysis. *Child Development, 59,* 1339–1352.

Fernyhough, C. (2008). Getting Vygotskian about theory of mind: Mediation, dialogue, and the development of social understanding. *Developmental Review, 28,* 225–262.

Ferrell, J. M., Guttentag, R. M., & Gredlein, J. M. (2009). Children's understanding of counterfactual emotions: Age differences, individual differences, and the effects of counterfactual-information salience. *British Journal of Developmental Psychology, 27,* 569–585.

Filippova, E., & Astington, J. W. (2008). Further development in social reasoning revealed in discourse irony understanding. *Child Development, 79,* 126–138.

Flapan, D. (1968). *Children's understanding of social interaction.* New York, NY: Teachers College Press.

Flavell, J. H. (1963). *The developmental psychology of Jean Piaget.* Princeton, NJ: Van Rostrand.

Flavell, J. H. (1979). Metacognition and cognitive monitoring. *American Psychologist, 34,* 906–911.

Flavell, J. H. (1985). *Cognitive development* (2d ed.). Englewood Cliffs, NJ: Prentice Hall.

Flavell, J. H. (1992). Perspectives on perspective taking. In H. Beilin & P. Pufall (Eds.), *Piaget's theory: Prospects and possibilities* (pp. 107–139). Hillsdale, NJ: Erlbaum.

Flavell, J. H. (2000). Development of children's knowledge about the mental world. *International Journal of Behavioral Development, 24,* 15–23.

Flavell, J. H., Botkin, P. T., Fry, C. L., Wright, J. W., & Jarvis, P. E. (1968). *The development of role-taking and communication skills in children.* New York, NY: Wiley.

Flavell, J. H., Everett, B. A., Croft, K., & Flavell, E. R. (1981). Young children's knowledge about visual perception: Further evidence for the Level 1- Level 2 distinction. *Developmental Psychology, 17,* 99–103.

Flavell, J. H., Flavell, E. R., & Green, F. L. (1983). Development of the appearance-reality distinction. *Cognitive Psychology, 15,* 95–120.

Flavell, J. H., Flavell, E. R., Green, F. L., & Moses, L. J. (1990). Young children's understanding of fact beliefs versus value beliefs. *Child Development, 61,* 915–928.

Flavell, J. H., Friedrichs, A. G., & Hoyt, J. D. (1970). Developmental changes in memorization processes. *Cognitive Psychology, 1,* 324–340.

Flavell, J. H., & Green, F. L. (1999). Development of intuitions about the controllability of different mental states. *Cognitive Development, 14,* 133–136.

Flavell, J. H., Green, F. L., & Flavell, E. R. (1986). Development of knowledge about the appearance-reality distinction. *Monographs of the Society for Research in Child Development, 51* (1, Serial No. 212).

Flavell, J. H., Green, F. L., & Flavell, E. R. (1993). Children's understanding of the stream of consciousness. *Child Development, 64,* 387–398.

Flavell, J. H., Green, F. L., & Flavell, E. R. (1995). Young children's knowledge about thinking. *Monographs of the Society for Research in Child Development, 60* (1, Serial No. 243).

Flavell, J. H., Green, F. L., & Flavell, E. R. (1998). The mind has a mind of its own: Developing knowledge about mental uncontrollability. *Cognitive Development, 13,* 127–138.

Flavell, J. H., Green, F. L., Flavell, E. R., & Lin, N. T. (1999). Development of children's knowledge about unconsciousness. *Child Development, 70,* 396–412.

Flavell, J. H., & Miller, P. H. (1998). Social cognition. In W. Damon (Series Ed.) & D. Kuhn & R. S. Siegler (Vol. Eds.), *Handbook of child psychology: Vol. 2. Cognition, perception, and language* (5th ed., pp. 851–898). New York, NY: Wiley.

Flavell, J. H., Miller, P. H., & Miller, S. A. (2002). *Cognitive development* (4th ed.). Upper Saddle River, NJ: Prentice Hall.

Flavell, J. H., Mumme, D. L., Green, F. L., & Flavell, E. R. (1992). Young children's understanding of different types of beliefs. *Child Development, 63,* 960–977.

Flavell, J. H., Speer, J. R., Green, F. L., & August, D. L. (1981). The development of comprehension monitoring and knowledge about communication. *Monographs of the Society for Research in Child Development, 46* (Serial No. 192).

Flynn, E. (2006). A microgenetic investigation of stability and continuity in theory of mind development. *British Journal of Developmental Psychology, 24,* 631–654.

Flynn, E. (2010). Underpinning collaborative learning. In B. W. Sokol, U. Muller, J. Carpendale, A. R. Young, & G. Iarocci (Eds.), *Self and social regulation: Social interaction and the development of social understanding and executive functions* (pp. 312–336). New York, NY: Oxford University Press.

Foote, R. C., & Holmes-Lonergan, H. A. (2003). Sibling conflict and theory of mind. *British Journal of Developmental Psychology, 21,* 45–58.

Friedman, O., & Leslie, A. M. (2004). Mechanisms of belief-desire reasoning. *Psychological Science, 15,* 547–552.

Friedman, O., & Leslie, A. M. (2005). Processing demands in belief-desire reasoning: Inhibition or general difficulty? *Developmental Science, 8,* 218–225.

Frith, U., & Frith, C. (2003). Development and neurophysiology of mentalizing. *Philosophical Transactions of the Royal Society of London—Series B: Biological Sciences, 258,* 459–473.

Frith, U., Morton, J., & Leslie, A. M. (1991). The cognitive basis of a biological disorder: Autism. *Trends in Neuroscience, 14,* 433–438.

Froese, K. A., Glenwright, M. R., & Eaton, W. O. (2011, March). *Is online data collection a useful approach for studying second-order false beliefs?* Poster session presented at the biennial meeting of the Society for Research in Child Development, Montreal, Canada.

Furth, H. G. (1980). *The world of grown-ups: Children's conceptions of society.* New York, NY: Elsevier.

Furth, H. G. (1996). *Desire for society: Children's knowledge as social imagination.* New York, NY: Plenum Press.

Garner, P., Curenton, S., & Taylor, K. (2005). Predictors of mental state understanding in preschoolers of varying socioeconomic background. *International Journal of Behavioral Development, 29,* 271–281.

Garner, R. (1998). *Metacognition and reading.* Norwood, NJ: Ablex Publishing.

Garnham, W. A., & Perner, J. (2001). Actions really do speaker louder than words—but only implicitly: Young children's understanding of false belief in action. *British Journal of Developmental Psychology, 19,* 413–432.

Garnham, W. A., & Ruffman, T. (2001). Doesn't see, doesn't know: Is anticipatory looking really related to understanding of belief? *Developmental Science, 4,* 94–100.

Gasser, L., & Keller, M. (2009). Are the competent the morally good? Perspective taking and moral motivation of children involved in bullying. *Social Development, 18,* 798–816.

German, T. P., & Hehman, J. A. (2007). Representational and executive selection resources in 'theory of mind': Evidence from compromised belief-desire reasoning in old age. *Cognition, 101,* 129–152.

Gillot, A., Furniss, F., & Walter, A. (2004). Theory of mind ability in children with specific language impairment. *Child Language Teaching and Therapy, 20,* 1–11.

Gini, G. (2006). Social cognition and moral cognition in bullying: What's wrong? *Aggressive Behavior, 32,* 528–539.

Gnepp, J., & Chilamkurti, C. (1988). Children's use of personality attributions to predict other people's behavioral and emotional reactions. *Child Development, 59,* 743–754.

Golan, O., Baron-Cohen, S., & Golan, Y. (2008). The 'Reading the Mind in Films' Task [Child Version]: Complex emotion and mental state recognition in children with and without autism spectrum conditions. *Journal of Autism and Developmental Disorders, 38,* 1534–1541.

Golan, O., Baron-Cohen, S., Hill, J. R., & Rutherford, M. D. (2007). The 'Reading the Mind in the Voice' Test-Revised: A study of complex emotion recognition in adults with and without autism spectrum conditions. *Journal of Autism and Developmental Disorders, 37,* 1096–1106.

Goldberg, W. A., Jarvis, K. L., Osann, K., Laulhere, T. M., Straub, C., Thomas, E., ... Spence, M. A. (2005). Brief report: Early social communication behaviors in the younger siblings of children with autism. *Journal of Autism and Developmental Disorders, 35,* 657–664.

Gonzalez, C. M., Zosuls, K. M., & Ruble, D. N. (2010). Traits as dimensions or categories? Developmental change in the understanding of trait terms. *Developmental Psychology, 46,* 1078–1088.

Gopnik, A., & Astington, J. W. (1988). Children's understanding of representational change and its relation to the understanding of false belief and the appearance-reality distinction. *Child Development, 59,* 26–37.

Gopnik, A., & Rosati, A. (2001). Duck or rabbit? Reversing ambiguous figures and understanding ambiguous representations. *Developmental Science, 4,* 175–183.

Gopnik, A., Slaughter, V., & Meltzoff, A. N. (1994). Changing your views: How understanding visual perception can lead to a new theory of mind. In C. Lewis & P. Mitchell (Eds.), *Children's early understanding of mind: Origins and development* (pp. 157–181). Hillsdale, NJ: Erlbaum.

Gopnik, A., & Wellman, H. M. (1992). Why the child's theory of mind really is a theory. *Mind and Language, 7,* 145–171.

Gopnik, A., & Wellman, H. M. (1994). The theory theory. In L. A. Hirschfeld & S. A. Gelman (Eds.), *Mapping the mind: Domain specificity in cognition and culture* (pp. 257–293). New York, NY: Cambridge University Press.

Gordon, F. R., & Flavell, J. H. (1977). The development of intuitions about cognitive cueing. *Child Development, 48,* 1027–1033.

Gregory, C., Lough, S., Stone, V., Erzinclioglu, S., Martin, L., Baron-Cohen, S., & Hodges, J. R. (2002). Theory of mind in patients with frontal variant frontotemporal dementia and Alzheimer's disease: Theoretical and practical implications. *Brain, 125,* 752–764.

Gross, D., & Harris, P. L. (1988). False beliefs about emotion: Children's understanding of misleading emotional displays. *International Journal of Behavioral Development, 11,* 475–488.

Hacker, D. J., Dunlosky, J., & Graesser, A. C. (Eds.). (2009). *Handbook of metacognition in education.* New York, NY: Routledge.

Hadwin, J., & Perner, J. (1991). Pleased and surprised: Children's cognitive theory of emotion. *British Journal of Developmental Psychology, 9,* 215–234.

Haith, M. M. (1998). Who put the cog in infant cognition? Is rich interpretation too costly? *Infant Behavior and Development, 21,* 167—179.

Hale, C. M., & Tager-Flusberg, H. (2003). The influence of language on theory of mind: A training study. *Developmental Science, 6,* 346–359.

Hansen, M., & Markman, E. M. (2005). Appearance questions can be misleading: A discourse-based account of the appearance-reality problem. *Cognitive Psychology, 50,* 233–263.

Happé, F. (1993). Communicative competence and theory of mind in autism: A test of relevance theory. *Cognition, 48,* 101–119.

Happé, F. (1994). An advanced test of theory of mind: Understanding of story characters' thoughts and feelings by able autistic, mentally handicapped and normal children and adults. *Journal of Autism and Developmental Disorders, 24,* 129–154.

Happé, F. (1995a). The role of age and verbal ability in the theory of mind task performance of subjects with autism. *Child Development, 66,* 843–855.

Happé, F. (1995b). Understanding minds and metaphors—insights from the study of figurative language in autism. *Metaphor and Symbolic Activity, 10,* 275–295.

Happé, F., Winner, E., & Brownell, H. (1998). The getting of wisdom: Theory of mind in old age. *Developmental Psychology, 34,* 358–362.

Harris, J. M., Best, C. S., Moffat, V. J., Spencer, M. D., Phillip, R. C. M., Power, M. J., & Johnstone, E. C. (2008). Autistic traits and cognitive performance in young people with mild intellectual impairment. *Journal of Autism and Developmental Disorders, 38,* 1241–1249.

Harris, K. R., Santangelo, T., & Graham, S. (2010). Metacognition and strategies instruction in writing. In H. S. Waters & W. Schneider (Eds.), *Metacognition, strategy use, and instruction* (pp. 226–256). New York, NY: Guilford Press.

Harris, P. L. (1991). The work of the imagination. In A. Whiten (Ed.), *Natural theories of mind* (pp. 283–304). Oxford: Blackwell.

Harris, P. L. (1992). From simulation to folk psychology: The case for development. *Mind and Language, 7,* 120–144.

Harris, P. L. (2006). Social cognition. In W. Damon & R. M. Lerner (Series Eds.) & D. Kuhn & R. S. Siegler (Vol. Eds.), *Handbook of child psychology: Vol. 2. Cognition, perception, and language* (6th ed., pp. 811–858). New York, NY: Wiley.

Harris, P. L. (2009). Simulation (mostly) rules: A commentary. *British Journal of Developmental Psychology, 27,* 555–559.

Harris, P. L., Johnson, C., Hutton, D., Andrews, G., & Cooke, T. (1989). Young children's theory of mind and emotion. *Cognition and Emotion, 3,* 379–400.

Hart, D., & Damon, W. (1985). Contrasts between understanding self and understanding others. In R. L. Leahy (Ed.), *The development of the self* (pp. 151–178). Orlando, FL: Academic Press.

Harter, S. (2006). The self. In W. Damon & R. M. Lerner (Series Eds.) & N. Eisenberg (Vol. Ed.), *Handbook of child psychology: Vol. 3. Social, emotional, and personality development* (6th ed., pp. 505–570). New York, NY: Wiley.

Harvey, J. H., & Weary, G. (1984). Current issues in attribution theory and research. *Annual Review of Psychology, 35,* 427–459.

Hasselhorn, M., Mahler, C., & Grube, D. (2005). Theory of mind, working memory, and verbal ability in preschool children: The proposal of a relay race model of the developmental dependencies. In W. Schneider, R. Schumann-Hengsteler, & B. Sodian (Eds.), *Young children's cognitive development: Interrelations among executive functioning, working memory, verbal ability, and theory of mind* (pp. 219–237). Mahwah, NJ: Erlbaum.

Hayashi, H. (2007a). Children's moral judgments of commission and omission based on their understanding of second-order mental states. *Japanese Psychological Research, 49,* 261–274.

Hayashi, H. (2007b). Young children's understanding of second-order mental states. *Psychologia, 50,* 15–25.

Hayward, E. O. (2011). *Measurement of advanced theory of mind in school-age children: Investigating the validity of a unified construct.* Unpublished doctoral dissertation, New York University.

Hayward, E. O., & Homer, B. D. (2011, March). *Measurement of advanced theory of mind in school-age children.* Poster session presented at the biennial meeting of the Society for Research in Child Development, Montreal, Canada.

Heerey, E. A., Capps, L. M., Keltner, D., & Kring, A. M. (2005). Understanding teasing: Lessons from children with autism. *Journal of Abnormal Child Psychology, 33,* 55–68.

Heider, F. (1958). *The psychology of interpersonal relations.* New York, NY: Wiley.

Helt, M. S., Eigsti, I., Snyder, P. J., & Fein, D. A. (2010). Contagious yawning in autistic and typical development. *Child Development, 81,* 1620–1631.

Helweg, C. C. (2006). The development of personal autonomy through cultures. *Cognitive Development, 21,* 458–473.

Henderson, H. A., Zahka, N. E., Kojkowski, N. M., Inge, A. P., Schwartz, C. B., Hileman, C. M., … Mundy, P. C. (2009). Self-referenced memory, social cognition, and symptom presentation in autism. *Journal of Child Psychology and Psychiatry, 50,* 853–861.

Heyman, G. (2009). Children's reasoning about traits. In P. J. Bauer (Ed.), *Advances in child development behavior* (Vol. 37, pp. 105–143). London: Elsevier.

Heyman, G. D., & Gelman, S. A. (1999). The use of trait labels in making psychological inferences. *Child Development, 70,* 604–619.

Higgins, E. T. (1981). Role taking and social judgment: Alternative developmental perspectives and processes. In J. H. Flavell & L. Ross (Eds.), *Social cognitive development* (pp. 119–153). Cambridge, England: Cambridge University Press.

Higgins, E. T., & Bryant, S. L. (1982). Consensus information and the fundamental attribution error: The role of in-group versus out-group knowledge. *Journal of Personality and Social Psychology, 43,* 889–900.

Hill, E. L. (2004). Evaluating the theory of executive dysfunction in autism. *Developmental Review, 24,* 189–233.

Hillier, A., & Allinson, L. (2002). Beyond expectations: Autism, understanding embarrassment, and the relationship with theory of mind. *Autism, 6,* 299–314.

Hobson, J., & Bowler, D. (2010). Editorial. *Autism, 14,* 387–389.

Hofer, B. K., & Pintrich, P. R. (1997). The development of epistemological theories: Beliefs about knowledge and knowing and their relation to learning. *Review of Educational Research, 67,* 88–140.

Hofer, B. K., & Pintrich, P. R. (Eds.). (2002). *Personal epistemology: The psychology of beliefs about knowledge and knowing.* Mahwah, NJ: Erlbaum.

Hoglund, W. L. G., Lalonde, C. E., & Leadbeater, B. J. (2008). Social-cognitive competence, peer rejection and neglect, and behavioral and emotional problems in middle childhood. *Social Development, 17,* 528–553.

Hogrefe, G. J., Wimmer, H., & Perner, J. (1986). Ignorance versus false belief: A developmental lag in attribution of epistemic states. *Child Development, 57,* 567–582.

Holmes, H. A., Black, C., & Miller, S. A. (1996). A cross-task comparison of false belief understanding in a Head Start population. *Journal of Experimental Child Psychology, 63,* 263–285.

Homer, B. D., & Astington, J. W. (1995, March). Children's *understanding of second-order beliefs in self and other.* Paper presented at the biennial meeting of the Society for Research in Child Development, Indianapolis, IN.

Homer, B. D., & Astington, J. W. (2001). *Children's representation of second-order beliefs in self and other.* Unpublished manuscript, University of Toronto, Toronto, Canada.

Hughes, C. (1998). Finding your marbles: Does preschoolers' strategic behavior predict later understanding of mind? *Developmental Psychology, 34,* 1326–1339.

Hughes, C. (2011). *Social understanding and social lives.* New York, NY: Psychology Press.

Hughes, C., Adlam, A., Happé, F., Jackson, J., Taylor, A., & Caspi, A. (2000). Good test-retest reliability for standard and advanced false-belief tasks across a wide range of abilities. *Journal of Child Psychology and Child Psychiatry, 41,* 483–490.

Hughes, C., Jaffe, S. R., Happé, F., Taylor, A., Caspi, A., & Moffitt, T. E. (2005). Origins of individual differences in theory of mind: From nature to nurture? *Child Development, 76*, 356–370.

Hughes, C., & Leekam, S. (2004). What are the links between theory of mind and social relations? Review, reflections and new directions for studies of typical and atypical development. *Social Development, 13*, 590–619.

Hulme, S., Mitchell, P., & Wood, D. (2003). Six-year-olds' difficulty handling intensional contexts. *Cognition, 87*, 73–99.

Humfress, H., O'Connor, T. G., Slaughter, J. U., Target, M. U., & Fonagy, P. (2002). General and relationship-specific models of social cognition: Explaining the overlap and discrepancies. *Journal of Child Psychology and Psychiatry, 43*, 873–883.

Hutto, D. D. (2008). *Folk psychological narratives: The sociocultural basis of understanding reasons.* Cambridge, MA: MIT Press.

Iannotti, R. (1978). Effects of role taking experience on role taking, empathy, altruism, and aggression. *Developmental Psychology, 14*, 119–124.

Jahoda, G. (1964). Children's concepts of nationality: A critical study of Piaget's stages. *Child Development, 35*, 1081–1092.

Jahromi, L. B., & Stifter, C. A. (2008). Individual differences in preschoolers' self-regulation and theory of mind. *Merrill-Palmer Quarterly, 54*, 125–150.

James, W. (1890). *The principles of psychology* (Vol. 1). New York, NY: Holt.

Jenkins, J. M., & Astington, J. W. (1996). Cognitive factors and family structure associated with theory of mind development in young children. *Developmental Psychology, 32*, 70–78.

Jingxin, Z., Jiliang, S., & Wenxin, Z. (2006). Second-order false belief attribution and second-order emotion understanding in children. *Psychological Science (China), 29*, 57–60.

Jingxin, Z., Wenxin, Z., & Li, J. (2005). Relationship between children's second-order false belief, prosocial behavior and peer acceptance. *Acta Psychologica Sinica, 37*, 760–766.

Johnson, L., Miles, L., & McKinlay, A. (2008). A critical review of the Eyes Test as a measure of social-cognitive impairment. *Australian Journal of Psychology, 60*, 135–141.

Jones, D. N., & Paulhus, D. L. (2009). Machiavellianism. In M. R. Leary & R. H. Hoyle (Eds.), *Handbook of social behavior* (pp. 93–108). New York, NY: Guilford Press.

Kagan, J. (2008). In defense of qualitative changes in development. *Child Development, 79*, 1606–1624.

Kaland, N., Calleson, K., Moller-Nielsen, A., Mortensen, E. L., & Smith, L. (2008). Performance of children and adolescents with Asperger syndrome or high-functioning autism on advanced theory of mind tasks. *Journal of Autism and Developmental Disorders, 38*, 1112–1123.

Kaland, N., Moller-Nielsen, A., Callsen, K., Mortensen, E. L., Gottlieb, D., & Smith, L. (2002). An 'advanced' test of theory of mind: Evidence from children and adolescents with Asperger syndrome. *Journal of Child Psychology and Psychiatry, 43*, 517–528.

Kaland, N., Smith, L., & Mortensen, E. L. (2007). Response times of children and adolescents with Asperger syndrome on an 'advanced' test of theory of mind. *Journal of Autism and Developmental Disorders, 37*, 197–209.

Kamawar, D., & Olson, D. R. (1999). Children's representational theory of language: The problem of opaque concepts. *Cognitive Development, 14*, 531–548.

Kamawar, D., & Olson, D. R. (2009). Children's understanding of referentially opaque contexts: The role of metarepresentational and metalinguistic ability. *Journal of Cognition and Development, 10*, 285–305.

Kamawar, D., & Olson, D. R. (2011). Thinking about representations: The case of opaque contexts. *Journal of Experimental Child Psychology, 108*, 734–746.

Kamawar, D., Pelletier, J., & Astington, J. W. (1998, April). *"I know where she'll look for it, but I don't know where she'll say it is": The development of children's proficiency with embedded verbs.* Paper presented at the annual meeting of the American Educational Research Association, San Diego, CA.

Kassin, S. M., & Lowe, C. A. (1979). On the development of the augmentation principle: A perceptual approach. *Child Development, 50,* 728–734.

Keenan, T. (2003). Individual differences in theory of mind: The preschool years and beyond. In B. Repacholi & V. Slaughter (Eds.), *Individual differences in theory of mind* (pp. 121–142). New York, NY: Psychology Press.

Keenan, T., & Ellis, B. J. (2003). Children's performance on a false-belief task is impaired by activation of an evolutionary-canalized response system. *Journal of Experimental Child Psychology, 85,* 236–256.

Keenan, T., Ruffman, T., & Olson, D. R. (1994). When do children begin to understand logical inference as a source of knowledge? *Cognitive Development, 9,* 331–353.

Kelley, H. H. (1967). Attribution theory in social psychology. In D. Levine (Ed.), *Nebraska Symposium on Motivation* (Vol. 15, pp. 192–241). Lincoln: University of Nebraska Press.

Kikuno, H., Mitchell, P., & Ziegler, F. (2007). How do young children process beliefs about beliefs? Evidence from response latency. *Mind and Language, 22,* 297–316.

Kim, J. M. (1998). Korean children's concepts of adult and peer authority and moral reasoning. *Developmental Psychology, 34,* 947–955.

Kinderman, P., Dunbar, R. I. M., & Bentall, R. P. (1998). Theory-of-mind deficits and causal attributions. *British Journal of Psychology, 89,* 191–204.

King, P. M., & Kitchener, K. S. (1994). *Developing reflective judgment: Understanding and promoting intellectual growth and critical thinking in adolescents and adults.* San Francisco, CA: Jossey-Bass.

Knight, N. (2008). Yukatek Maya children's attributions of belief to natural and non-natural entities. *Journal of Cognition and Culture, 8,* 235–243.

Kobayashi, C., Glover, G. H., & Temple, E. (2007). Cultural and linguistic effects on neural bases of "Theory of Mind" in American and Japanese children. *Brain Research, 1164,* 95–107.

Kreutzer, M. A., Leonard, C., & Flavell, J. H. (1975). An interview study of children's knowledge about memory. *Monographs of the Society for Research in Child Development, 40* (1, Serial No. 159).

Kuebli, J., Butler, S., & Fivush, R. (1995). Mother-child talk about past emotions: Relations of maternal language and child gender over time. *Cognition and Emotion, 9,* 265–283.

Kuhn, D. (1991). *The skills of argument.* Cambridge, England: Cambridge University Press.

Kuhn, D. (1999). Metacognitive development. In L. Balter & C. S. Tamis-Monda (Eds.), *Child psychology: A handbook of contemporary issues* (pp. 259–286). Philadelphia, PA: Psychology Press.

Kuhn, D. (2000). Theory of mind, metacognition, and reasoning: A life-span perspective. In P. Mitchell (Ed.), *Children's reasoning and the mind* (pp. 301–326). Hove, England: Psychology Press.

Kuhn, D. (2001). Why development does (and does not) occur: Evidence from the domain of inductive reasoning. In J. L. McClelland & R. S. Siegler (Eds.), *Mechanisms of cognitive development* (pp. 221–249). Mahwah, NJ: Erlbaum.

Kuhn, D., Amsel, E., & O'Laughlin, M. (1988). *The development of scientific thinking skills.* Orlando, FL: Academic Press.

Kuhn, D., & Franklin, S. (2006). The second decade: What develops and when? In W. Damon & R. M. Lerner (Series Eds.) & D. Kuhn & R. S. Siegler (Vol. Eds.), *Handbook of child psychology: Vol. 2. Cognition, perception, and language* (6th ed., pp. 953–993). New York, NY: Wiley.

Kuhn, D., Garcia-Mila, M., Zohar, A., & Andersen, C. (1995). Strategies of knowledge acquisition. *Monographs of the Society for Research in Child Development, 60* (Serial No. 245).

Kuhn, D., & Pearson, S. (1998). Relations between metastrategic knowledge and strategic performance. *Cognitive Development, 13,* 227–247.

Kuhn, D., & Pearsall, S. (2000). Developmental origins of scientific thinking. *Journal of Cognition and Development, 1,* 113–129.

Kun, A. (1977). Development of the magnitude-covariation and compensation schemata in ability and effort attributions of performance. *Child Development, 48,* 862–873.

Lagattuta, K. H., Nucci, L., & Bosacki, S. L. (2010). Bridging theory of mind and the personal domain: Children's reasoning about resistance to parental control. *Child Development, 81,* 616–635.

Lagatutta, K. H., Sayfan, L., & Blattman, A. J. (2010). Forgetting common ground: Six- to seven-year-olds have an overinterpretive theory of mind. *Developmental Psychology, 46,* 1417–1432.

Lalonde, C. E., & Chandler, M. J. (2002). Children's understanding of interpretation. *New Ideas in Psychology, 20,* 163–198.

Landry, M. O., & Lyons-Ruth, K. (1980). Recursive structure in cognitive perspective taking. *Child Development, 51,* 386–394.

Langdon, R., Davies, M. & Coltheart, M. (2002) Understanding minds and understanding communicated meanings in schizophrenia. *Mind and Language, 17,* 68–104.

Larkin, S. (2010). *Metacognition in young children.* London, England: Routledge.

Laupa, M., Turiel, E., & Cowan, P. A. (1995). Obedience to authority in children and adults. In M. Killen & D. Hart (Eds.), *Morality in everyday life* (pp. 131–165). New York, NY: Cambridge University Press.

Leahy, R. H. (1979). Development of conceptions of prosocial behavior: Information affecting rewards given for altruism and kindness. *Developmental Psychology, 15,* 34–37.

Leaper, C., Anderson, K. J., & Sanders, P. (1988). Moderators of gender effects on parents' talk to their children: A meta-analysis. *Developmental Psychology, 34,* 3–27.

Lecce, S., & Hughes, C. (2010). The Italian job? Comparing theory of mind performance in British and Italian children. *British Journal of Developmental Psychology, 28,* 747–766.

Lecce, S., Zocchi, S., Pagnin, A., Palladino, P., & Taumoepeau, M. (2010). Reading minds: The relation between children's mental state knowledge and their metaknowledge about reading. *Child Development, 81,* 1876–1893.

Leekam, S. R. (1991). Jokes and lies: Children's understanding of intentional falsehood. In A. Whiten (Ed.), *Natural theories of mind: Evolution, development and simulation of everyday mindreading* (pp. 159–174). Oxford: Basil Blackwell.

Legerstee, M. (2006). *Infants' sense of people: Precursors to a theory of mind.* New York, NY: Cambridge University Press.

Lepper, M. R., Green, D., & Nisbett, R. E. (1973). Undermining children's intrinsic interest with extrinsic rewards: A test of the "overjustification" hypothesis. *Journal of Personality and Social Psychology, 28,* 129–137.

Leslie, A. M. (1994). Pretending and believing: Issues in the theory of ToMM. *Cognition, 50,* 211–238.

Leslie, A. M., German, T. P., & Polizzi, P. (2005). Belief-desire reasoning as a process of selection. *Cognitive Psychology, 50,* 45–85.

LeSourn-Bissaoui, S., Caillies, S., Gierski, F., & Motte, J. (2009). Inference processing in adolescents with Asperger syndrome: Relationship with theory of mind abilities. *Research in Autism Spectrum Disorders, 3,* 797–808.

Leudar, I., & Costall, A. (Eds.). (2009). *Against theory of mind.* New York, NY: Palgrave Macmillan.

Leudar, I., Costall, A., & Francis, D. (2004). Theory of mind: A critical assessment. *Theory and Psychology, 14,* 571–578.

Lewis, C., Freeman, N. H., Kriakidou, C., Maridaki-Kassotaki, K., & Berridge, D. M. (1996). Social influences on false belief access: Specific sibling influences or general apprenticeship? *Child Development, 67,* 2930–2947.

Liddle, B., & Nettle, D. (2006). Higher-order theory of mind and social competence in school-age children. *Journal of Cultural and Evolutionary Psychology, 4,* 231–244.

Lillard, A. S., & Flavell, J. H. (1990). Young children's preference for mental state versus behavioral descriptions of human action. *Child Development, 61,* 731–741.

Lindberg, S.M., Hyde, J. S., Peterson, J. L., & Linn, M. C. (2010). New trends in gender and mathematics research. *Psychological Bulletin, 136,* 1123–1135.

Liu, D., Gelman, S. A., & Wellman, H. M. (2007). Components of young children's trait understanding: Behavior-to-trait inferences and trait-to-behavior predictions. *Child Development, 78,* 1543–1558.

Liu, D., Meltzoff, A. N., & Wellman, H. M. (2009). Neural correlates of belief- and desire- reasoning. *Child Development, 80,* 1163–1171.

Liu, D., Wellman, H. M., Tardif, T., & Sabbagh, M. A. (2008). Theory of mind development in Chinese children: A meta-analysis of false belief understanding across cultures and languages. *Developmental Psychology, 44,* 523–531.

Livesley, W. J., & Bromley, D. B. (1973). *Person perception in childhood and adolescence.* London, England: Wiley.

Liwag, E. C. D. (1999). What do young children think about thinking? Exploring preschoolers' understanding of *Pag-iisip. Philippine Journal of Psychology, 32,* 1–29.

Lockl, K., & Schneider, W. (2007). Knowledge about the mind: Links between theory of mind and later metamemory. *Child Development, 78,* 148–167.

Lohmann, H., & Tomasello, M. (2003). The role of language in the development of false belief understanding: A training study. *Child Development, 74,* 1130–1144.

Lombardo, M. V., Barnes, J. L., Wheelwright, S. J., & Baron-Cohen, S. (2007). Self-referential cognition and empathy in autism. PLoSONE, 9(e883), 1–11.

Loth, E., Gomez, J. C., & Happé, F. (2008). Event schemas in autism spectrum disorders: The role of theory of mind and weak central coherence. *Journal of Autism and Developmental Disorders, 38,* 449–463.

Loth, E., Happé, F., & Gomez, J. C. (2010). Variety is not the spice of life for people with autism spectrum disorders: Frequency ratings of central, variable and inappropriate aspects of common real-life events. *Journal of Autism and Developmental Disorders, 40,* 730–742.

Low, J. (2010). Preschoolers' implicit and explicit false-belief understanding: Relations with complex syntactical mastery. *Child Development, 81,* 597–615.

Maas, F. K. (2008). Children's understanding of promising, lying, and false belief. *Journal of General Psychology, 135,* 301–321.

MacPherson, S. E., Phillips, L. H., & Sala, S. D. (2002). Age, executive function, and social decision making: A dorsolateral prefrontal theory of cognitive aging. *Psychology and Aging, 17,* 598–609.

MacWhinney, B. (2000a). *The CHILDES project: Tools for analyzing talk: Vol. 1. The format and programs* (3rd ed.). Mahwah, NJ: Erlbaum.

MacWhinney, B. (2000b). *The CHILDES project: Tools for analyzing talk: Vol. 2. The database* (3rd ed.). Mahwah, NJ: Erlbaum.

Makris, N., & Pnevmatikos, D. (2007). Children's understanding of human and super-natural mind. *Cognitive Development, 22,* 365–375.

Malti, T., Gasser, L., & Gutzwiller-Helfenfinger, E. (2010). Children's interpretive understanding, moral judgments, and emotion attributions: Relations to social behaviour. *British Journal of Developmental Psychology, 28,* 275–293.

Mansfield, A. F., & Clinchy, B. (2002). Toward the integration of objectivity and subjectivity: Epistemological development from 10 to 16. *New Ideas in Psychology, 20,* 225–262.

Mant, C. M., & Perner, J. (1988). The child's understanding of commitment. *Developmental Psychology, 24,* 343–351.

Markman, E. M. (1979). Realizing that you don't understand: Elementary children's awareness of inconsistencies. *Child Development, 50,* 643–655.

Martin, J., Sokol, B. W., & Elfers, T. (2008). Taking and coordinating perspectives: From prereflective interactivity, through reflective intersubjectivity, to metareflective sociality. *Human Development, 51,* 294–317.

Maylor, E. A., Moulson, J. M., Muncer, A., & Taylor, L. A. (2002). Does performance on theory of mind tasks decline in old age? *British Journal of Psychology, 93,* 465–485.

McAlister, A., & Peterson, C. C. (2007). A longitudinal study of child siblings and theory of mind development. *Cognitive Development, 22,* 258–270.

McGlamery, M. E., Ball, S. E., Henley, T. B., & Besozzi, M. (2007). Theory of mind, attention, and executive function in kindergarten boys. *Emotional and Behavioural Difficulties, 12,* 29–47.

McKeown, M. G., & Beck, I. L. (2009). The role of metacognition in understanding and supporting reading comprehension. In D. J. Hacker, J. Dunlosky, & A. G. Graesser (Eds.), *Handbook of metacognition in education* (pp. 7–25). New York, NY: Routledge.

McKinnon, M. C., & Moscovitch, M. (2007). Domain-general contributions to social reasoning: Theory of mind and deontic reasoning re-explored. *Cognition, 102,* 179–218.

Meins, E., & Fernyhough, C. (1999). Linguistic acquisitional style and mentalising development: The role of maternal mind-mindedness. *Cognitive Development, 14,* 363–380.

Meins, E., Fernyhough, C., Johnson, F., & Lidstone, J. (2006). Mind-mindedness in children: Individual differences in internal-state talk in middle childhood. *British Journal of Developmental Psychology, 24,* 181–196.

Meins, E., Fernyhough, C., Wainwright, R., Clark-Carter, D., Gupta, M. D., Fradley, E., & Tuckey, M. (2003). Pathways to understanding mind: Construct validity and predictive validity of maternal mind-mindedness. *Child Development, 74,* 1194–1211.

Meis, A. P., Call, J., & Tomasello, M. (2010). 36-month-olds conceal auditory and visual information from others. *Developmental Science, 13,* 479–489.

Meltzoff, A. N. (1995). Understanding the intentions of others: Re-enactment of intended acts by 18-month-old children. *Developmental Psychology, 31,* 838–850.

Meltzoff, A. N. (2006). The "like me" framework for recognizing and becoming an intentional agent. *Acta Psychologica, 124,* 26–43.

Meltzoff, A. N. (2007). "Like me": A foundation for social cognition. *Developmental Science, 10,* 126–134.

Meristo, M., Falkman, K. W., Hjelmquist, E., Tedoldi, M., Surian, L., & Siegal, M. (2007). Language access and theory of mind reasoning: Evidence from deaf children in bilingual and oralist environments. *Developmental Psychology, 43,* 1156–1169.

Meristo, M., & Hjelmquist, E. (2009). Executive functions and theory-of-mind among deaf children: Different routes to understanding other minds? *Journal of Cognition and Development, 10,* 67–91.

Miller, P. H. (1985). Children's reasoning about the causes of human behavior. *Journal of Experimental Child Psychology, 39,* 343–362.

Miller, P. H., & Aloise, P. A. (1989). Young children's understanding of the psychological causes of behavior: A review. *Child Development, 60,* 257–285.

Miller, P. H., & Aloise, P. A. (1990). Discounting in children: The role of social knowledge. *Developmental Review, 10,* 266–298.

Miller, P. H., & Bigi, L. (1979). The development of children's understanding of attention. *Merrill-Palmer Quarterly, 25,* 235–250.

Miller, P. H., & Coyle, T. R. (1999). Developmental change: Lessons from microgenesis. In E. K. Scholnick, K. Nelson, S. A. Gelman, & P. H. Miller (Eds.), *Conceptual development: Piaget's legacy* (pp. 209–239). Mahwah, NJ: Erlbaum.

Miller, P. H., Kessel, F., & Flavell, J. H. (1970). Thinking about people thinking about people thinking about…: A study of social cognitive development. *Child Development, 41,* 613–623.

Miller, S. A. (2000). Children's understanding of preexisting differences in knowledge and belief. *Developmental Review, 20,* 227–282.

Miller, S. A. (2009). Children's understanding of second-order mental states. *Psychological Bulletin, 135,* 749–773.

Miller, S. A. (2011). *Children's understanding of second-order false belief: Comparisons of content and method of assessment.* Manuscript submitted for publication.

Miller, S. A., Hardin, C. A., & Montgomery, D. E. (2003). Young children's understanding of the conditions for knowledge acquisition. *Journal of Cognition and Development, 4,* 325–356.

Miller, S. A., Holmes, H. A., Gitten, J., & Danbury, J. (1997). Children's understanding of false beliefs that result from developmental misconceptions. *Cognitive Development, 12,* 21–51.

Milligan, K., Astington, J. W., & Dack, L. A. (2007). Language and theory of mind: A meta-analysis of the relation between language ability and false-belief understanding. *Child Development, 78,* 622–646.

Mills, C. M., & Grant, M. G. (2009). Biased decision-making: Developing an understanding of how positive and negative relationships may skew judgments. *Developmental Science, 12,* 784–797.

Mills, C. M., & Keil, F. C. (2005). The development of cynicism. *Psychological Science, 16,* 385–390.

Mills, C. M., & Keil, F. C. (2008). Children's developing notions of (im)partiality. *Cognition, 107,* 528–551.

Misalidi, P. (2010). Children's metacognition and theory of mind: Bridging the gap. In A. Efklides (Ed.), *Trends and prospects in metacognition research* (pp. 279–291). New York, NY: Springer.

Mitchell, J. P. (2008). Contributions of functional neuroimaging to the study of social cognition. *Current Directions in Psychological Science, 17,* 142–146.

Mitchell, P., Robinson, E. J., Nye, R. M., & Isaacs, J. E. (1997). When speech conflicts with seeing: Young children's understanding of informational priority. *Journal of Experimental Child Psychology, 64,* 276–294.

Mitroff, S. R., Sobel, D. M., & Gopnik, A. (2006). Reversing how to think about ambiguous figure reversals: Spontaneous alternating by uninformed observers. *Perception, 35,* 709–715.

Montgomery, D. E. (1992). Young children's theory of knowing: The development of a folk epistemology. *Developmental Review, 12,* 410–430.

Montgomery, D. E. (1993). Young children's understanding of interpretive diversity between different-aged listeners. *Developmental Psychology, 29,* 337–345.

Montgomery, D. E. (1994). Situational features influencing young children's mentalistic explanations of action. *Cognitive Development, 9,* 425–454.

Moore, C. (2006). *The development of commonsense psychology.* Mahwah, NJ: Erlbaum.

Moore, C., & Corkum, V. (1994). Social understanding at the end of the first year of life. *Developmental Review, 14,* 349–372.

Moore, W. S. (2002). Understanding learning in a postmodern world: Reconsidering the Perry scheme of intellectual and ethical development. In B. K. Hofer & P. R. Pintrich (Eds.), *Personal epistemology: The psychology of beliefs about knowledge and knowing* (pp. 17–36). Mahwah, NJ: Erlbaum.

Mosconi, M. W., Mack, P. B., McCarthy G., & Pelphrey, K. A. (2005). Taking an "intentional stance" on eye-gaze shifts: A functional neuroimaging study of social perception in children. *Neuroimage, 27,* 247–252.

Moses, L. J. (2005). Executive functioning and children's theories of mind. In B. F. Malle & S. D. Hodges (Eds.), *Other minds: How humans bridge the gap between self and others* (pp. 11–25). New York, NY: Guilford Press.

Moses, L. J., Carlson, S. M., & Sabbagh, M. A. (2005). On the specificity of the relation between executive function and children's theories of mind. In W. Schneider, R. Schumann-Hengesteler, & B. Sodian (Eds.), *Young children's cognitive development: Interrelations among executive functioning, working memory, verbal ability, and theory of mind* (pp. 131–145). Mahwah, NJ: Erlbaum.

Myers, L. J., & Liben, L. S. (in press). Graphic symbols as "the mind on paper": Links between children's interpretive theory of mind and symbol understanding. *Child Development.*

Naito, M., & Seki, Y. (2009). The relationship between second-order false belief and display rules reasoning: The integration of cognitive and affective social understanding. *Developmental Science, 12,* 150–164.

Nelson, K. (2007). *Young minds in social worlds: Experience, meaning, and memory.* Cambridge, MA: Harvard University Press.

Nelson-Le Gall, S., & Gumerman, R. (1984). Children's perception of helpers and helper motivation. *Journal of Applied Developmental Psychology, 5,* 1–12.

Nettle, D., & Liddle, B. (2008). Agreeableness is related to social-cognitive, but not social-perceptual, theory of mind. *European Journal of Personality, 22,* 323–335.

Newton, A. M., & de Villiers, J. G. (2007). Thinking while talking: Adults fail nonverbal false-belief reasoning. *Psychological Science, 18,* 574–579.

Newton, P., Reddy, V., & Bull, R. (2000). Children's everyday deception and performance on false-belief tasks. *British Journal of Developmental Psychology, 18,* 297–317.

Nguyen, L., & Frye, D. (1999). Children's theory of mind: Understanding of desire, belief and emotion with social referents. *Social Development, 8,* 70–92.

Nicholls, J. G. (1978). The development of the concepts of effort and ability, perception of academic attainment, and the understanding that difficult tasks require more ability. *Child Development, 49,* 800–814.

Nilsen, E. S., Glenwright, M., & Huyder, V. (2011). Children and adults realize that verbal irony interpretation depends on listener knowledge. *Journal of Cognition and Development, 12,* 374–409.

Norbury, C. F. (2005). The relationship between theory of mind and metaphor: Evidence from children with language impairment and autistic spectrum disorder. *British Journal of Developmental Psychology, 23,* 383–399.

Norbury, C. F., & Bishop, D. V. M. (2002). Inferential processing and story recall in children with communication problems: A comparison of specific language impairment, pragmatic language impairment and high-functioning autism. *International Journal of Language and Communication Disorders, 37,* 227–251.

O'Connor, T. G., & Hirsch, N. (1999). Intraindividual differences and relationship-specificity of mentalizing in early adolescence. *Social Development, 8,* 256–274.

O'Hare, A. E., Bremner, L., Nash, M., Happé, F., & Pettigrew, L. M. (2009). A clinical assessment tool for advanced theory of mind performance in 5 to 12 year olds. *Journal of Autism and Developmental Disorders, 39,* 916–928.

O'Neill, D. K. (1996). Two year-olds' sensitivity to a parent's knowledge state when making requests. *Child Development, 67,* 659–667.

O'Neill, D. K., & Chong, S. C. F. (2001). Preschool children's difficulty understanding the types of information obtained through the five senses. *Child Development, 72,* 803–815.

O'Neill, D. K., & Gopnik, A. (1991). Young children's ability to identify the sources of their beliefs. *Developmental Psychology, 27,* 390–397.

Onishi, K. H., & Baillargeon, R. (2005). Do 15-month-old infants understand false beliefs? *Science, 308,* 255–258.

Ozonoff, S., Pennington, B. F., & Rogers, S. J. (1991). Executive functioning deficits in high-functioning autistic individuals: Relationship to theory of mind. *Journal of Child Psychology and Psychiatry, 32,* 1081–1105.

Ozonoff, S., Rogers, S. J., & Pennington, B. F. (1991). Asperger's syndrome: Evidence of an empirical distinction from high-functioning autism. *Journal of Child Psychology and Psychiatry, 32,* 1107–1122.

Paal, T., & Bereczkie, T. (2007). Adult theory of mind, cooperation, Machiavellianism: The effect of mindreading on social relations. *Personality and Individual Differences, 43,* 541–551.

Palincsar, A. S., & Brown, A. L. (1984). Reciprocal teaching of comprehension-fostering and monitoring activities. *Cognition and Instruction, 1,* 117–175.

Pardini, M., & Nichelli, P. (2009). Age-related decline in mentalizing skills across adult life span. *Experimental Aging Research, 35,* 98–106.

Parker, J. R., MacDonald, C. A., & Miller, S. A. (2007). "John thinks that Mary *feels* …" False belief across the physical and affective domains. *Journal of Genetic Psychology, 168,* 43–62.

Patnaik, B. (2006). Recursive thought in speech acts of children. *Social Science International, 22,* 24–37.

Pears, K. C., & Moses, L. J. (2003). Demographics, parenting, and theory of mind in pre-school children. *Social Development, 12,* 1–19.

Pellicano, E. (2007). Links between theory of mind and executive function in young children with autism: Clues to developmental primacy. *Developmental Psychology, 43,* 974–990.

Pellicano, E. (2010). Individual differences in executive function and central coherence predict developmental changes in theory of mind in autism. *Developmental Psychology, 46,* 530–544.

Pellicano, E., Murray, M., Durkin, K., & Maley, A. (2006). Multiple cognitive capabilities/deficits in children with an autism spectrum disorder: "Weak" central coherence and its relationship to theory of mind and executive control. *Development and Psychopathology, 18,* 77–98.

Perner, J. (1988). Higher-order beliefs and intentions in children's understanding of social interaction. In J. W. Astington, P. L. Harris, & D. R. Olson (Eds.), *Developing theories of mind* (pp. 271–294). Cambridge, England: Cambridge University Press.

Perner, J. (1991). *Understanding the representational mind.* Cambridge, MA: MIT Press.

Perner, J. (1995). The many faces of belief: Reflections on Fodor's and the child's theory of mind. *Cognition, 57,* 241–269.

Perner, J. (1998). The meta-intentional nature of executive functions and theory of mind. In P. Carruthers & J. Boucher (Eds.), *Language and thought* (pp. 270–283). Cambridge, England: Cambridge University Press.

Perner, J. (2000). About + belief + counterfactual. In P. Mitchell & K. J. Riggs (Eds.), *Children's reasoning and the mind* (pp. 367–401). Hove, England: Psychology Press.

Perner, J. (2009). Who took the cog out of cognitive science? Mentalism in an era of anti-cognitivism. In P. A. Frensch & R. Schwarzer *(Eds.), Cognition and neuro-psychology: International perspectives on psychological science* (Vol. 1, pp. 241–261). Hove, England: Psychology Press.

Perner, J., & Davies, G. (1991). Understanding the mind as an active information processor: Do young children have a "copy theory of mind"? *Cognition, 39,* 51–69.

Perner, J., & Howes, D. (1992). "He thinks he knows"; and more developmental evidence against the simulation (role-taking) theory. *Mind and Language, 7,* 72–86.

Perner, J., Kain, W., & Barchfeld, P. (2002). Executive control and higher-order theory of mind in children at risk of ADHD. *Infant and Child Development, 11,* 141–158.

Perner, J., & Lang, B. (2000). Theory of mind and executive function: Is there a developmental relationship? In S. Baron-Cohen, H. Tager-Flusberg, & D. Cohen (Eds.), *Understanding other minds: Perspectives from developmental cognitive neuroscience* (2nd ed., pp. 151–181). London, England: Oxford University Press.

Perner, J., Lang, B., & Kloo, D. (2002). Theory of mind and self-control: More than a common problem of inhibition. *Child Development, 73,* 752–767.

Perner, J., & Ruffman, T. (2005). Infants' insight into the mind: How deep? *Science, 308,* 214–216.

Perner, J., & Wimmer, H. (1985). "John *thinks* that Mary *thinks* that...." Attribution of second-order beliefs by 5- to 10-year-old children. *Journal of Experimental Child Psychology, 39,* 437–471.

Perry, W. G. (1970). *Forms of intellectual and ethical development in the college years.* New York, NY: Holt, Rinehart, and Winston.

Peterson, C. C. (2000). Kindred spirits: Influences on siblings' perspectives on theory of mind. *Cognitive Development, 15,* 435–455.

Peterson, C. C., & Slaughter, V. P. (2003). Opening windows into the mind: Mothers' preferences for mental state explanations and children's theory of mind. *Cognitive Development, 18,* 399–429.

Pexman, P. M., & Glenwright, M. (2007). How do typically-developing children grasp the meaning of verbal irony? *Journal of Neurolinguistics, 20,* 178–196.

Pexman, P. M., Rostad, K. R., McMorris, C. A., Climie, E. A., Stowkowy, J., & Glenwright, M. R. (2011). Processing of ironic language in children with high-functioning autism spectrum disorder. *Journal of Autism and Developmental Disorders, 41,* 1097–1112.

Piaget, J. (1926). *The language and thought of the child.* New York, NY: Harcourt Brace.

Piaget, J. (1928). *Judgment and reasoning in the child.* London, England: Routledge and Kegan Paul.

Piaget, J. (1929). *The child's conception of the world.* London, England: Routledge and Kegan Paul.

Piaget, J. (1932). *The moral judgment of the child.* New York, NY: Free Press.

Piaget, J. (1962). Comments on Vygotsky's critical remarks concerning *The Language and Thought of the Child, and Judgment and Reasoning in the Child.* Addendum to L. S. Vygotsky, *Thought and Language.* Cambridge, MA: MIT Press.

Piaget, J., & Inhelder, B. (1956). *The child's conception of space.* London, England: Routledge & Kegan Paul.

Piaget, J., & Weil, A. M. (1951). The development in children of the idea of the homeland and of relations to other countries. *International Social Science Journal, 3,* 561–578.

Pillow, B. H. (1991). Children's understanding of biased social cognition. *Developmental Psychology, 27,* 539–551.

Pillow, B. H. (1999). Children's understanding of inferential knowledge. *Journal of Genetic Psychology, 160,* 419–428.

Pillow, B. H. (2002). Children's and adults' evaluations of the certainty of deductive inferences, inductive inferences, and guessing. *Child Development, 73,* 779–792.

Pillow, B. H. (2008). Development of children's understanding of cognitive activities. *Journal of Genetic Psychology, 169,* 297–321.

Pillow, B. H., & Heinrichon, A. J. (1996). There's more to the picture than meets the eye: Young children's difficulty in understanding biased interpretation. *Child Development, 67,* 803–819.

Pillow, B. H., Hill, V., Boyce, A., & Stein, C. (2000). Understanding inference as a source of knowledge: Children's ability to evaluate the certainty of deduction, perception, and guessing. *Developmental Psychology, 36,* 169–179.

Pillow, B. H., Pearson, R. M., Hecht, M., & Bremer, A. (2010). Children's and adults' judgments of the certainty of deductive inferences, inductive inferences, and guessing. *Journal of Genetic Psychology, 171*, 203–217.

Pillow, B. H., & Weed, S. T. (1995). Children's understanding of biased interpretation: Generality and limitations. *British Journal of Developmental Psychology, 13*, 347–366.

Platek, S. M., Critton, S. R., Myers, T. E., & Gallup, G. G. (2003). Contagious yawning: The role of self-awareness and mental state attribution. *Cognitive Brain Research, 17*, 223–227.

Polak, A., & Harris, P. L. (1999). Deception by young children following noncompliance. *Developmental Psychology, 35*, 561–568.

Poulin-Dubois, D., Brooker, I., & Chow, V. (2009). The developmental origins of naïve psychology in infancy. In P. J. Bauer (Ed.), *Advances in child development behavior* (Vol. 37, pp. 55–104). London, England: Elsevier.

Povinelli, D. J., & Vonk, J. (2004). We don't need a microscope to explore the chimpanzee's mind. *Mind and Language, 19*, 1–28.

Pratt, P., & Bryant, P. (1990). Young children understand that looking leads to knowing (as long as they are looking in a single barrel). *Child Development, 61*, 973–982.

Premack, D., & Woodruff, G. (1978). Does the chimpanzee have a theory of mind? *Behavioral and Brain Sciences, 1*, 515–526.

Presmanes, A. G., Walden, T. A., Stone, W. L., & Yoder, P. J. (2007). Effects of differential cues on responding to joint attention in younger siblings of children with autism spectrum disorders. *Journal of Autism and Developmental Disorders, 37*, 133–144.

Pressley, M., Borkowski, J. G., & O'Sullivan, J. (1985). Children's metamemory and the teaching of memory strategies. In D. L. Forrest-Pressley, G. E. McKinnon, & T. G. Waller (Eds.), *Metacognition, cognition, and human performance: Vol. 1: Theoretical perspectives* (pp. 111–153). New York, NY: Academic Press.

Qualter, P., Barlow, A., & Stylianou, M. S. (2011). Investigating the relationship between trait and ability emotional intelligence and theory of mind. *British Journal of Developmental Psychology, 29*, 437–454.

Rai, R., & Mitchell, P. (2004). Five-year-old children's difficulty with false belief when the sought entity is a person. *Journal of Experimental Child Psychology, 89*, 112–126.

Rai, R., & Mitchell, P. (2006). Children's ability to impute inferentially based knowledge. *Child Development, 77*, 1081–1093.

Rajendran, G., & Mitchell, P. (2007). Cognitive theories of autism. *Developmental Review, 27*, 224–260.

Randell, A. C., & Peterson, C. C. (2009). Affective qualities of sibling disputes, mothers' conflict attitudes, and children's theory of mind development. *Social Development, 18*, 857–874.

Recchia, H. E., & Howe, N. (2009). Associations between social understanding, sibling relationship quality, and siblings' conflict strategies and outcomes. *Child Development, 80*, 1564–1578.

Reddy, V. (2008). *How infants know minds.* Cambridge, MA: Harvard University Press.

Reddy, V., & Morris, P. (2004). Participants don't need theories: Knowing minds in engagement. *Theory and Psychology, 14*, 647–665.

Repacholi, B. M., & Gopnik, A. (1997). Early reasoning about desires: Evidence from 14- and 18-month-olds. *Developmental Psychology, 33*, 12–21.

Repacholi, B. M., & Slaughter, V. (Eds.). (2003). *Individual differences in theory of mind.* New York, NY: Psychology Press.

Repacholi, B., Slaughter, V., Pritchard, M., & Gibbs, V. (2003). Theory of mind, Machiavellianism, and social functioning in childhood. In B. Repacholi & V. Slaughter (Eds.), *Individual differences in theory of mind* (pp. 67–98). New York, NY: Psychology Press.

Riggs, K. J., & Simpson, A. (2005). Young children have difficulty ascribing true beliefs. *Developmental Science, 8,* F27–F30.

Robinson, E. J., & Apperly. I. A. (2001). Children's difficulties with partial representations in ambiguous messages and referentially opaque contexts. *Cognitive Development, 16,* 595–615.

Robinson, E. J., Haigh, S. N., & Pendle, J. E. C. (2008). Children's working understanding of the knowledge gained from seeing and feeling. *Developmental Science, 11,* 299–305.

Robinson, E. J., & Mitchell, P. (1995). Masking of children's early understanding of the representational mind: Backwards explanation versus prediction. *Child Development, 66,* 1022–1039.

Robinson, E. J., & Nurmsoo, E. (2009). When do children learn from unreliable speakers? *Cognitive Development, 24,* 16–22.

Rochat, P. (2009). *Others in mind: Social origins of self-consciousness.* New York, NY: Cambridge University Press.

Rogers, S. J. (2009). What are infant siblings teaching us about autism in infancy? *Autism Research, 2,* 125–137.

Ronald, A., Viding, E., Happé, F., & Plomin, R. (2006). Individual differences in theory of mind ability in middle childhood and links with verbal ability and autistic traits: A twin study. *Social Neuroscience, 1,* 412–425.

Ross, H. S., Recchia, H. E., & Carpendale, J. (2005). Making sense of divergent interpretations of conflict and developing an interpretive understanding of mind. *Journal of Cognition and Development, 6,* 571–592.

Roth, D., & Leslie, A. M. (1998). Solving belief problems: Toward a task analysis. *Cognition, 66,* 1–31.

Rubin, K. H., Bukowski, W. M., & Parker, J. G. (2006). Peer interactions, relationships, and groups. In W. Damon & R. M. Lerner (Series Eds.) & N. Eisenberg (Vol. Ed.), *Handbook of child psychology: Vol. 3. Social, emotional, and personality development* (6th ed., pp. 571–645). New York, NY: Wiley.

Ruble, D. N., & Rholes, W. S. (1983). The development of children's perceptions and attributions about their social world. In J. H. Harvey, W. Ickes, & R. F. Kidd (Eds.), *New directions in attribution research* (Vol. 3, pp. 3–29). Hillsdale, NJ: Erlbaum.

Ruffman, T., Garnham, W., Import, A., & Connolly, D. (2001). Does eye gaze indicate implicit knowledge of false belief? Charting transitions in knowledge. *Journal of Experimental Child Psychology, 80,* 201–224.

Ruffman, T., Olson, D. R., & Astington, J. W. (1991). Children's understanding of visual ambiguity. *British Journal of Developmental Psychology, 9,* 89–102.

Ruffman, T., & Perner, J. (2005). Do infants really understand false belief? *Trends in Cognitive Science, 9,* 462–463.

Ruffman, T., Perner, J., Naito, M., Parkin, L., & Clements, W. A. (1998). Older (but not younger) siblings facilitate false belief understanding. *Developmental Psychology, 34,* 161–174.

Ruffman, T., Perner, J., & Parkin, L. (1999). How parenting style affects false belief understanding. *Social Development, 8,* 395–411.

Ruffman, T., Slade, L., & Crowe, E. (2002). The relation between children's and mothers' mental state language and theory-of-mind understanding. *Child Development, 73,* 734–751.

Ruffman, T., Slade, L., Rowlandson, K., Rumsey, C., & Garnham, A. (2003). How language relates to belief, desire, and emotion understanding. *Cognitive Development, 18,* 139–158.

Russell, J. (1987). "Can we say…?" *Cognition, 25,* 289–308.

Russell, J. (1992). The theory theory: So good they named it twice? *Cognitive Development, 7,* 485–519.

Rutherford, M. D. (2004). The effect of social role on theory of mind reasoning. *British Journal of Psychology, 95,* 91–103.

Rutter, M., Sonuga-Barke, E. J., Beckett, C., Castle, J., Kreppner, J., Kumsta, R., … Bell, C. A. (2010). Deprivation-specific psychological patterns: Effects of institutional deprivation. *Monographs of the Society for Research in Child Development, 75*(1).

Sabbagh, M. A., & Callanan, M. A. (1998). Metarepresentation in action: 3-, 4-, and 5-year-olds' developing theories of mind in parent-child conversations. *Developmental Psychology, 34,* 491–502.

Sabbagh, M. A., & Seamans, E. L. (2008). Intergenerational transmission of theory-of-mind. *Developmental Science, 11,* 354–360.

Sachs, J., & Devin, J. (1976) Young children's use of age appropriate speech styles in social interaction and role-playing. *Journal of Child Language, 3,* 81–98.

Sapp, F., Lee, K., & Muir, D. (2000). Three-year-olds' difficulty with the appearance-reality distinction: Is it real or is it apparent? *Developmental Psychology, 36,* 547–560.

Saxe, R. (2006). Why and how to study Theory of Mind with fMRI. *Brain Research, 1079,* 57–65.

Saxe, R., Carey, S., & Kanwisher, N. (2004). Understanding other minds: Linking developmental psychology and functional neuroimaging. *Annual Review of Psychology, 55,* 87–124.

Saxe, R., & Pelphrey, K. A. (2009). Introduction to a special section of developmental social cognitive neuroscience. *Child Development, 80,* 946–951.

Saxe, R., & Powell, L. J. (2006). It's the thought that counts: Specific brain regions for one component of theory of mind. *Psychological Science, 17,* 692–699.

Scarlett, H. H., Press, A. N., & Crockett, W. H. (1971). Children's description of peers: A Wernerian developmental analysis. *Child Development, 42,* 439–453.

Scheeren, A. M., Begeer, S., Banerjee, R., Terwogt, M., & Koot, H. M. (2010). Can you tell me something about yourself?: Self-presentation in children and adolescents with high functioning autism spectrum disorder in hypothetical and real life situations. *Autism, 14,* 457–473.

Schmidt, J. Z., & Zachariae, R., (2009). PTSD and impaired eye expression recognition: A preliminary study. *Journal of Loss and Trauma, 14,* 46–56.

Schneider, W. (2010). Metacognition and memory development in childhood and adolescence. In H. S Waters & W. Schneider (Eds.), *Metacognition, strategy use, and instruction* (pp. 54–81). New York, NY: Guilford Press.

Schneider, W., & Pressley, M. (1997). *Memory development between 2 and 20* (2d ed.). Mahwah, NJ: Erlbaum.

Scholl, B. J., & Leslie, A. M. (1999). Modularity, development, and "theory of mind." *Mind and Language, 14,* 131–153.

Schwanenflugel, P. J., Fabricius, W. V., & Alexander, J. (1994). Developing theories of mind: Understanding concepts and relations between mental activities. *Child Development, 65,* 1546–1563.

Schwanenflugel, P. J., Fabricius, W. V., & Noyes, C. R. (1996). Developing organization of mental verbs: Evidence for the development of a constructivist theory of mind in middle childhood. *Cognitive Development, 11,* 265–294.

Schwanenflugel, P. J., Henderson, R. L., & Fabricius, W. V. (1998). Developing organization of mental verbs and theory of mind in middle childhood: Evidence from extensions. *Developmental Psychology, 34,* 512–524.

Scott, R. M., & Baillargeon, R. (2009). Which penguin is this? Attributing false beliefs about object identity at 18 months. *Child Development, 80,* 1172–1196.

Secord, P. F., & Peevers, B. H. (1974). The development and attribution of person concepts. In T. Mischel (Ed.), *Understanding other persons* (pp. 117–142). Totowa, NJ: Rowman & Littlefield.

Selman, R. L. (1976). The development of interpersonal reasoning. In A. D. Pick (Ed.), *Minnesota symposia on child psychology* (Vol. 10, pp. 156–200). Minneapolis: University of Minnesota Press.

Selman, R. L. (1980). *The growth of interpersonal understanding: Developmental and clinical analyses.* New York, NY: Academic Press.

Selman, R. L. (2008). Through thick and thin. *Human Development, 51,* 318–325.

Selman, R. L., & Byrne, D. F. (1974). A structural-developmental analysis of levels of role-taking in middle childhood. *Child Development, 45,* 803–806.

Selman, R. L., & Jaquette, D. (1977). Stability and oscillation in interpersonal awareness: A clinical-developmental analysis. In C. B. Keasey (Ed.), *Nebraska symposium on motivation* (Vol. 25, pp. 261–304). Lincoln: University of Nebraska Press.

Senju, A., Maeda, M., Kichuyi, Y., Hasegawa, T., Tojo, Y. & Osani, H. (2007). Absence of contagious yawning in children with autism spectrum disorder. *Biology Letters, 3,* 706–708.

Senju, A., Southgate, V., White, V., & Frith, U. (2009). Mindblind eyes: An absence of spontaneous theory of mind in Asperger syndrome. *Science, 325,* 883–885.

Shadish, W. R., Cook, T. D., & Campbell, D. T. (2002). *Experimental and quasi-experimental designs for generalized causal inference.* Boston, MA: Houghton Mifflin.

Shaked, M, Gamliel, I., & Yirmiya, N. (2006). Theory of mind abilities in young siblings of children with autism. *Autism, 10,* 173–187.

Shantz, C. U. (1983). Social cognition. In J. H. Flavell & E. M. Markman (Vol. Eds.) & P. H. Mussen (Series Ed.), *Handbook of child psychology: Vol. 2. Cognitive development* (4th ed., pp. 495–555). New York, NY: Wiley.

Shatz, M., Diesendruck, G., Martinez-Beck, I., & Akar, D. (2003). The influence of language and socioeconomic status on children's understanding of false belief. *Developmental Psychology, 39,* 717–729.

Shatz, M., & Gelman, R. (1973). The development of communication skills: Modifications in the speech of young children as a function of listener. *Monographs of the Society for Research in Child Development, 38* (5, Serial No. 152).

Shatz, M., Wellman, H. M., & Silber, S. (1983). The acquisition of mental verbs: A systematic investigation of first references to mental state. *Cognition, 14,* 301–321.

Shaughnessy, M. F., Veenman, M. V. J., & Kleyn-Kennedy, C. (Eds.). (2008). *Meta-cognition: A recent review of research, theory, and perspectives.* New York, NY: Nova Science Publishers.

Shiverick, S. M., & Moore, C. F. (2007). Second-order beliefs about intention and children's attributions of sociomoral judgment. *Journal of Experimental Child Psychology, 97,* 44–60.

Shultz, T. R., Butkowsky, I., Pearce, J. W., & Shanfield, H. (1975). Development of schemes for the attribution of multiple psychological causes. *Developmental Psychology, 11,* 502–510.

Shultz, T. R., & Cloghesy, K. (1981). Development of recursive awareness of intention. *Developmental Psychology, 17,* 465–471.

Siegler, R. S. (1996). *Emerging minds: The process of change in children's thinking.* New York, NY: Oxford University Press.

Slaughter, V. (2011). Early adoption of Machiavellian attitudes: Implications for children's interpersonal relationships. In T. Barry, C. P. Kerig, & K. Stellwagen (Eds.) *Narcissism and Machiavellianism in youth: Implications for the development of adaptive and maladaptive behavior* (pp. 177–192). Washington, DC: APA Books.

Slessor, G., Phillips, L. H., & Bull, R. (2007). Exploring the specificity of age-related differences in theory of mind tasks. *Psychology and Aging, 22,* 639–643.

Smetana, J. G. (1981). Preschool children's conceptions of moral and social rules. *Child Development, 52,* 1333–1336.

Smetana, J. G. (1995). Context, conflict, and constraint in adolescent-parent authority relationships. In M. Killen & D. Hart (Eds.), *Morality in everyday life* (pp. 225–255). New York, NY: Cambridge University Press.

Smith, M. C. (1978). Cognizing the behavior stream: The recognition of intentional action. *Child Development, 49,* 736–743.

Sobel, D. M., Capps, L. M., & Gopnik, A. (2005). Ambiguous figure perception and theory of mind understanding in children with autistic spectrum disorders. *British Journal of Developmental Psychology, 23,* 159–174.

Sodian, B. (1988). Children's attributions of knowledge to the listener in a referential communication task. *Child Development, 59,* 378–395.

Sodian, B. (2011). Theory of mind in infancy. *Child Development Perspectives, 5,* 39–43.

Sodian, B., & Hulsken, C. (2005). The developmental relationship of theory of mind, metacognition and executive functions: A study of advanced theory of mind abilities in children with attention deficit hyperactivity disorder. In W. Schneider, R. Schumann-Hengesteler, & B. Sodian (Eds.), *Young children's cognitive development: Interrelations among executive functioning, working memory, verbal ability, and theory of mind* (pp. 175–187). Mahwah, NJ: Erlbaum.

Sodian, B., Taylor, C., Harris, P. L., & Perner, J. (1991). Early deception and the child's theory of mind: False trails and genuine markers. *Child Development, 62,* 468–483.

Sodian, B., & Wimmer, H. (1987). Children's understanding of inference as a source of knowledge. *Child Development, 58,* 424–433.

Song, H., Onishi, K. H., & Baillargeon, R. (2008). Can an agent's false belief be corrected by an appropriate communication? Psychological reasoning in 18-month-old infants. *Cognition, 109,* 295–315.

Sonnenschein, S. (1988). The development of referential communication: Speaking to different listeners. *Child Development, 59,* 694–702.

Southgate, V., Senju, A., & Csibra, G. (2007). Action anticipation through attribution of false belief by 2-year-olds. *Psychological Science, 18,* 587–592.

Speck, A. A., Scholte, E. M., & Van Berckelaer-Onnes, I. A. (2010). Theory of mind in adults with HFA and Asperger Syndrome. *Journal of Autism and Developmental Disorders, 40,* 280–289.

Spelke, E. S., Breinlinger, K., Macomber, J., & Jacobson, K. (1992). Origins of knowledge. *Psychological Review, 99,* 605–632.

Spelke, E. S., & Kinzler, K. D. (2007). Core knowledge. *Developmental Science, 10,* 89–96.

Sperber, D., & Wilson, D. (1995). *Relevance: Communication and cognition* (2nd ed.). Cambridge, MA: Blackwell Publishers.

Sprung, M. (2008). Unwanted intrusive thoughts and cognitive functioning in kindergarten and young elementary-aged children following Hurricane Katrina. *Journal of Clinical Child and Adolescent Psychology, 37,* 575–587.

Sprung, M. (2010). Clinically relevant measures of children's theory of mind and knowledge about thinking: Non-standard and advanced measures. *Child and Adolescent Mental Health, 15,* 204–216.

Sprung, M., & Harris, P. L. (2010). Intrusive thoughts and young children's knowledge about thinking following a natural disaster. *Journal of Child Psychology and Psychiatry, 51,* 1115–1124.

Sprung, M., Lindner, M., & Thun-Hohenstein, L. (2011, March). *Unwanted intrusive thoughts and knowledge about thinking in maltreated and injured children.* Poster session presented at the biennial meeting of the Society for Research in Child Development, Montreal, Canada.

Sprung, M., Perner, J., & Mitchell, P. (2007). Opacity and discourse referents: Object identity and object properties. *Mind and Language, 22,* 215–245.

Stack, J., & Lewis, C. (2008). Steering toward a developmental account of infant social understanding. *Human Development, 51,* 229–234.

Stiller, J., & Dunbar, R. I. M. (2007). Perspective-taking and memory capacity predict social network size. *Social Networks, 29,* 93–104.

Stipek, D. J., & Daniels, D. H. (1990). Children's use of dispositional attributions in predicting the performance and behavior of classmates. *Journal of Applied Developmental Psychology, 11,* 13–28.

Stipek, D. J., Recchia, S., & McClintic, S. (1992). Self-evaluation in young children. *Monographs of the Society for Research in Child Development, 57*(1, Serial No. 226).

Strauss, S., Ziv, M., & Stein, A. (2002). Teaching as a natural cognition and its relations to preschoolers' developing theory of mind. *Cognitive Development, 17,* 473–487.

Sullivan, K., & Winner, E. (1991). When 3-year-olds understand ignorance, false belief and representational change. *British Journal of Developmental Psychology, 9,* 159–171.

Sullivan, K., Winner, E., & Hopfield, N. (1995). How children tell a lie from a joke: The role of second-order mental state attributions. *British Journal of Developmental Psychology, 13,* 191–204.

Sullivan, K., Zaitchik, D., & Tager-Flusberg, H. (1994). Preschoolers can attribute second-order beliefs. *Developmental Psychology, 30,* 395–402.

Surian, L., Caldi, S., & Sperber, D. (2007). Attribution of beliefs by 13-month-old infants. *Psychological Science, 18,* 580–586.

Sutton, J., Reeves, M., & Keogh, E. (2000). Disruptive behaviour, avoidance of responsibility and theory of mind. *British Journal of Developmental Psychology, 30,* 1–11.

Sutton, J., Smith, P. K., & Swettenham, J. (1999a). Bullying and 'theory of mind': A critique of the 'social skills deficit' view of anti-social behaviour. *Social Development, 8,* 117–134.

Sutton, J., Smith, P. K., & Swettenham, J. (1999b). Social cognition and bullying: Social inadequacy or skilled manipulation? *British Journal of Developmental Psychology, 17,* 435–450.

Symons, D. K. (2004). Mental state discourse, theory of mind, and the internalization of self-other understanding. *Developmental Review, 24,* 159–188.

Symons, D. K., & Clark, S. E. (2000). A longitudinal study of mother-child relationships and theory of mind in the preschool period. *Social Development, 9,* 3–23.

Symons, D. K., McLaughlin, E., Moore, C., & Morine, S. (1997). Integrating relationship constructs and emotional experience into false belief tasks in preschool children. *Journal of Experimental Child Psychology, 67,* 423–447.

Tager-Flusberg, H. (2007). Evaluating the theory-of-mind hypothesis of autism. *Current Directions in Psychological Science, 16,* 311–315.

Tager-Flusberg, H., & Joseph, R. M. (2005). How language facilitates the acquisition of false-belief understanding in children with autism. In J. W. Astington & J. A. Baird (Eds.), *Why language matters for theory of mind* (pp. 298–318). New York, NY: Oxford University Press.

Talwar, V., Gordon, H. M., & Lee, K. (2007). Lying in the elementary school years: Verbal deception and its relation to second-order belief understanding. *Developmental Psychology, 43,* 804–810.

Talwar, V., & Lee, K. (2002). Emergence of white-lie telling in children between 3 and 7 years of age. *Merrill-Palmer Quarterly, 48,* 160–181.

Talwar, V., & Lee, K. (2008). Social and cognitive correlates of children's lying behavior. *Child Development, 79,* 866–881.

Talwar, V., Murphy, H. M., & Lee, K. (2007). White-lie telling in children for politeness purposes. *International Journal of Behavioral Development, 31,* 1–11.

Tarricone, P. (2011). *The taxonomy of metacognition.* New York, NY: Psychology Press.

Taylor, M. (1996). A theory of mind perspective on social cognitive development. In R. Gelman & T. Au (Eds.), E. C. Carterette & M. P. Friedman (General Eds.), *Handbook of perception and cognition: Vol. 13. Perceptual and cognitive development* (pp. 283–329). San Diego, CA: Academic Press.

Taylor, M., Cartwright, B. S., & Bowden, T. (1991). Perspective taking and theory of mind: Do children predict interpretive diversity as a function of differences in observers' knowledge? *Child Development, 62,* 1334–1351.

Taylor, M., Esbensen, B. M., & Bennett, B. T. (1994). Children's understanding of knowledge acquisition: The tendency for children to report that they have always known what they just learned. *Child Development, 65,* 1581–1604.

Tomasello, M. (1999a). Having intentions, understanding intentions, and understanding communicative intentions. In P. D. Zelazo, J. W. Astington, & D. R. Olson (Eds.), *Developing theories of intention* (pp. 63–75). Mahwah, NJ: Erlbaum.

Tomasello, M. (1999b). *The cultural origins of human cognition.* Cambridge, MA: Harvard University Press.

Tomasello, M. (2008). *Origins of human communication.* Cambridge, MA: MIT Press.

Tomasello, M., Kruger, A. C., & Ratner, H. H. (1993). Cultural learning. *Behavioral and Brain Sciences, 16,* 495–552.

Trauble, B., Marinovi, V., & Vesna, S. (2010). Early theory of mind competencies: Do infants understand others' beliefs? *Infancy, 15,* 434–444.

Trillingsgaard, A. (1999). The script model in relation to autism. *European Journal of Child and Adolescent Psychiatry, 8,* 45–49.

Turiel, E. (1983). *The development of social knowledge: Morality and convention.* Cambridge, England: Cambridge University Press.

Turkstra, L. S., Williams, W. H., Tonks, J., & Frampton, I. (2008). Measuring social cognition in adolescents: Implications for students with TBI returning to school. *NeuroRehabilitation, 23,* 501–509.

Underwood, B., & Moore, B. (1982). Perspective-taking and altruism. *Psychological Bulletin, 91,* 143–173.

Van Overwalle, F. (2009). Social cognition and the brain: A meta-analysis. *Human Brain Mapping, 30,* 829–858.

Varouxaki, A., Freeman, N. H., & Peters, D. (1999). Inference neglect and ignorance denial. *British Journal of Developmental Psychology, 17,* 483–499.

Vinden, P. G. (2002). Understanding minds and evidence for belief: A study of Mofu children in Cameroon. *International Journal of Behavioral Development, 26,* 445–452.

Wainryb, C., Shaw, L. A., Langley, M., Cottam, K., & Lewis, R. (2004). Children's thinking about diversity of belief in the early school years: Judgments of relativism, tolerance, and disagreeing persons. *Child Development, 75,* 687–703.

Walker-Andrews, A. S. (1997). Infants' perception of expressive behaviors: Differentiation of multimodal information. *Psychological Bulletin, 123,* 437–456.

Waters, H. S., & Schneider, W. (Eds.). (2010). *Metacognition, strategy use, and instruction.* New York, NY: Guilford Press.

Weiner, B. (1986). *An attributional theory of motivation and emotion.* New York, NY: Springer-Verlag.

Wellman, H. M. (1990). *The child's theory of mind.* Cambridge, MA: MIT Press.

Wellman, H. M. (2010). Developing a theory of mind. In U. Goswami (Ed.), *The Wiley-Blackwell handbook of childhood cognitive development* (2nd ed., pp. 258–284). New York, NY: Wiley.

Wellman, H. M., & Banerjee, M. (1991). Mind and emotion: Children's understanding of the emotional consequences of beliefs and desires. *British Journal of Developmental Psychology, 9,* 191–214.

Wellman, H. M., & Cross, D. (2001). Theory of mind and conceptual change. *Child Development, 72,* 702–707.

Wellman, H. M., Cross, D., & Watson, J. (2001). Meta-analysis of theory-of-mind development: The truth about false belief. *Child Development, 72,* 655–684.

Wellman, H. M., & Hickling, A. K. (1994). The mind's "I": Children's conception of the mind as an active agent. *Child Development, 65,* 1564–1580.

Wellman, H. M., Hollander, M., & Schult, C. A. (1996). Young children's understanding of thought bubbles and of thoughts. *Child Development, 67,* 768–788.

Wellman, H. M., & Liu, D. (2004). Scaling of theory-of-mind tasks. *Child Development, 75,* 523–541.

Wellman, H. M., Lopez-Duran, S., LaBounty, J., & Hamilton, B. (2008). Infant attention to intentional action predicts preschool theory of mind. *Developmental Psychology, 44,* 618–623.

Wellman, H. M., Olson, S., Lagattuta, K., & Liu, D. (2008). Mothers' *and* fathers' use of internal state talk with their young children. *Social Development, 17,* 757–775.

Wellman, H. M., & Woolley, J. (1990). From simple desires to ordinary beliefs: The early development of everyday psychology. *Cognition, 35,* 245–275.

White, B., Frederiksen, J., & Collins, A. (2009). The interplay of scientific inquiry and metacognition: More than a marriage of convenience. In D. J. Hacker, J. Dunlosky, & A. G. Graesser (Eds.), *Handbook of metacognition in education* (pp. 175–205). New York, NY: Routledge.

White, S., Hill, E., Happé, F., & Frith, U. (2009). Revisiting the Strange Stories: Revealing mentalizing impairments in autism. *Child Development, 80,* 1097–1117.

Wimmer, H., Gruber, S., & Perner, J. (1984). Young children's conceptions of lying: Lexical realism-moral subjectivism. *Journal of Experimental Child Psychology, 37,* 1–30.

Wimmer, H., & Mayringer, H. (1998). False belief understanding in young children: Explanations do not develop before predictions. *International Journal of Behavioral Development, 22,* 403–422.

Wimmer, H., & Perner, J. (1983). Beliefs about beliefs: Representation and constraining function of wrong beliefs in young children's understanding of deception. *Cognition, 13,* 103–128.

Wimmer, H., & Weichbold, V. (1994). Children's theory of mind: Fodor's heuristics or understanding informational causation. *Cognition, 53,* 45–57.

Winner, E., Brownell, H., Happé, F., Blum, H., & Pincus, D. (1996). Distinguishing lies from jokes: Theory of mind deficits and discourse interpretation in right hemisphere brain-damaged patients. *Brain and Language, 62,* 89–106.

Winner, E., & Leekam, S. R. (1991). Distinguishing irony from deception: Understanding the speaker's second-order intention. *British Journal of Developmental Psychology, 9,* 257–270.

Woodward, A. L. (2005). The infant origins of intentional understanding. In R. V. Kail (Ed.), *Advances in child development and behavior* (Vol. 33, pp. 229–262). Oxford, UK: Elsevier.

Woodward, A. L. (2009). Infants' grasp of others' intentions. *Current Directions in Psychological Science, 18,* 53–57.

Yau, J., Smetana, J. G., & Metzger, A. (2009). Young Chinese children's authority concepts. *Social Development, 18,* 210–229.

Yirmiya, N., Erel, O., Shaked, M., & Solomonica, D. (1998). Meta-analyses comparing theory of mind abilities of individuals with autism, individuals with mental retardation, and normally developing individuals. *Psychological Bulletin, 124,* 283–307.

Youngstrom, E. A., & Goodman, S. (2001). Children's perceptions of other people: Mentalistic versus behavioristic descriptions of peers and adults. *Developmental Science, 4,* 165–174.

Youniss, J. (1975). Another perspective on social cognition. In A. D. Pick (Ed.), *Minnesota symposia on child psychology* (Vol. 9, pp. 173–193). Minneapolis, MN: University of Minnesota Press.

Youniss, J., & Volpe, J. (1978). A relational analysis of children's friendship. In W. Damon (Ed.), *New directions for child development: No. 1. Social cognition* (pp. 1–22). San Francisco, CA: Jossey-Bass.

Yuill, N. (1997). Children's understanding of traits. In S. Hala (Ed.), *The development of social cognition* (pp. 273–295). Hove, England: Psychology Press.

Yuill, N., & Perner, J. (1987). Exceptions to mutual trust: Children's use of second-order beliefs in responsibility attribution. *International Journal of Behavioral Development, 10,* 207–223.

Zaitchik, D., Walker, C., Miller, S., Laviolette, P., Feczko, E., & Dickerson, B. C. (2010). Mental state attribution and the temporoparietal junction: An fMRI study comparing belief, emotion, and perception. *Neuropsychologia, 48,* 2528–2536.

Zelazo, P. D., Astington, J. W., & Olson, D. R. (Eds.). (1999). *Developing theories of intention.* Mahwah, NJ: Erlbaum.

Zelazo, P. D., Chandler, M. J., & Crone, E. (Eds.). (2010). *Developmental social cognitive neuroscience.* New York, NY: Psychology Press.

Zhang, T., Zheng, X., Zhang, L., Sha, W., Deak, G., & Li, H. (2010). Older children's misunderstanding of uncertain belief after passing the false belief test. *Cognitive Development, 25,* 158–165.

Ziv, M., Solomon, A., & Frye, D. (2008). Young children's recognition of the intentionality of teaching. *Child Development, 79,* 1237–1256.

Author Index

Subject Index